Library of
Davidson College

ENCOUNTER WITH ERIKSON

AMERICAN ACADEMY OF RELIGION
AAR/UC — IRS
Joint Series on Formative Contemporary Thinkers

edited by
M. Gerald Bradford
Charles H. Long
Walter H. Capps

Number 2

ENCOUNTER WITH ERIKSON

Historical Interpretation and
Religious Biography

edited by
Donald Capps
Walter H. Capps
M. Gerald Bradford

SCHOLARS PRESS
Missoula, Montana

ENCOUNTER WITH ERIKSON
Historical Interpretation and
Religious Biography

Edited by

Donald Capps
Walter H. Capps
M. Gerald Bradford

Published by
SCHOLARS PRESS
for
THE AMERICAN ACADEMY OF RELIGION
and
The Institute of Religious Studies
University of California, Santa Barbara, California

Distributed by
SCHOLARS PRESS
University of Montana
Missoula, Montana 59812

ENCOUNTER WITH ERIKSON
Historical Interpretation and Religious Biography

Edited by
Donald Capps
Walter H. Capps
M. Gerald Bradford

922
A15e

Copyright © 1977
by
The American Academy of Religion
and
The Institute of Religious Studies
University of California, Santa Barbara, California

Library of Congress Cataloging in Publication Data

Main entry under title:
Encounter with Erikson.

(Series on formative contemporary thinkers ; no. 2)
Papers presented at a symposium to honor E. H. Erikson on the occasion of his seventieth birthday, held at La Casa de Maria Retreat Center near Santa Barbara, Calif., Feb. 17-19, 1972.
"Erik Homburger Erikson: a bibliography of his books and articles": p.
Includes bibliographical references.
CONTENTS: Introduction.—Luther and Gandhi studies; Lindbeck,.G. A. Erikson's Young man Luther. Bellah, R. N. Young man Luther as Portraiture. Spitz, L. W. Psychohistory and history; the case of Young man Luther. Hay, S. Gandhi's first five years. Geertz, C. Gandhi: non-violence as therapy. Newhall, D. H. Gandhi: the road to holiness. Capps, D. Gandhi's truth as religious biography. [etc.]
1. Religions—Biography—Congresses. 2. Psychohistory—Congresses. 3. Psychology, Religious—Congresses. 4. Erikson, Erik Homburger, 1902- —Congresses. I. Erikson, Erik Homburger, 1902- II. Capps, Donald. III. Capps, Walter H. IV. Bradford, Miles Gerald, 1938- V. American Academy of Religion. VI.California, University, Santa Barbara. Institute of Religious Studies. VII. Series.
BL72.E5   200'.92'2 [B]   76-44434
ISBN 0-89130-090-7

Printed in the United States of America

Printing Department
University of Montana
Missoula Montana 59812

TABLE OF CONTENTS

Introduction vii

SECTION ONE: LUTHER AND GANDHI STUDIES 1

  I. Erikson's *Young Man Luther*: A Historical and Theological Reappraisal
      George A. Lindbeck, Yale University 7

  II. *Young Man Luther* as Portraiture: A Comment
      Robert N. Bellah, University of California, Berkeley 29

  III. Psychohistory and History. The Case of Young Man Luther
      Lewis W. Spitz, Stanford University 33

  IV. Gandhi's First Five Years
      Stephen Hay, University of California, Santa Barbara 67

  V. Gandhi: Non-Violence as Therapy
      Clifford Geertz, Institute for Advanced Studies, Princeton 113

  VI. Gandhi: The Road to Holiness
      David H. Newhall, Portland State University 123

  VII. *Gandhi's Truth* as Religious Biography
      Donald Capps, University of North Carolina Charlotte 141

SECTION TWO: STUDIES OF AMERICAN RELIGIOUS FIGURES 179

  I. Young People of the Great Awakening: The Dynamics of a Social Movement
      Cushing Strout, Cornell University 183

  II. Jonathan Edwards as Great Man: Identity, Conversion, and Leadership in the Great Awakening
      Richard L. Bushman, Boston University 217

  III. The Myth of Father Abraham: Psychosocial Influences in the Formation of Lincoln Biography
      Donald Capps, University of North Carolina Charlotte 253

  IV. Identity and Conversion: Reflections on Nineteenth Century American Religious Experience and Identity
      Robert Michaelsen, University of California, Santa Barbara 281

SECTION THREE: METHODOLOGICAL STUDIES 343

   I.   The Investigator as an Instrument of Investigation: Some Exploratory Observations on the Compleat Researcher
        James E. Dittes, Yale University 347

  II.   Psycho-Biography and the Historian of Religions: Some Methodological Suggestions
        Frank Reynolds, University of Chicago 375

 III.   Acedia: The Decline of Desire as the Ultimate Life Crisis
        Bert Kaplan, University of California, Santa Cruz 389

  IV.   Erikson's Orientation as Process Philosophy
        Walter H. Capps, University of California, Santa Barbara 401

ERIK HOMBURGER ERIKSON: A Bibliography of His Books and Articles 421

INTRODUCTION

The papers included in this anthology were presented in a symposium to honor Erik H. Erikson, noted psychologist, psychiatrist, psycho-historian, and, not least, one of the most significant human beings of our time.

Placed in the idyllic conference setting of La Casa de Maria Retreat Center in the hills of Montecito, above Santa Barbara, California, the symposium brought some thirty-five participants (most of them faculty and graduate students in the University of California) together for a three-day period, February 17-19, 1972. Erik and Joan Erikson were present for the entire time, having been invited "to listen" and, when so inclined, "to respond" to the papers.

Months in planning and delicate in execution, the symposium was scheduled for the year of Erikson's seventieth birthday. Though very conscious of this anniversary, the program was, nevertheless, not designed to encompass Erikson's entire career. Nor are its papers and responses conceived as potential ingredients in an "Erikson festschrift". Instead, attention was concentrated on Erikson's insights and contentions regarding the place of religious factors in society and in human consciousness. This interest came to focus on Erikson's pioneering work in psycho-history, or, as one of the participants in the symposium called it, his creation of a new sort of religious biography. The rationale for approaching the subject this way was straightforward and explicit. Erikson's formal entry into the field of religious studies is usually marked by his monumental and still controversial psycho-historical study of Martin Luther, *Young Man Luther*. The same thrust was sustained, strengthened, and expanded by the sequel to the Luther study, the examination of Gandhi, in *Gandhi's Truth*. Both books have provoked a wide range of energetic responses on the part of those who find theology and/or religious studies to be their identifying *locus operandi*. And in some quarters, Erikson's studies have also stimulated other attempts to come to terms with other religious figures in a like-minded manner. The symposium was designed to identify such psycho-historical ploys, to test their interpretive skills in a number of their potential settings and from a multiplicity of perspectives, and to assess their capacities for advancing historical-religious understanding. But the intention throughout the symposium was to put the several sorts of discussions of various aspects of these issues in touch with each other, and, in bringing all of them up to date together, to update the conception of how Erikson's work ought to be placed and appropriated.

The other reasons for the symposium are less formal and, perhaps, more difficult to state. In fact, were we to admit it, the symposium may have been provoked by a certain embarrassment that not enough has been done yet with or about Erik Erikson. It isn't that his books haven't been noticed. or that he himself hasn't been drawn into current conversations. It isn't as though his work has gone unrecognized or unrewarded; though, too often, it seems, recognition has been too slow and acceptance too grudging. It isn't even that we all need lessons--at least one more--in ways to use the words he has coined for our vocabulary. It is rather that, for some of us, the haunting feeling increases that we have learned only some of the more peripheral lessons. The provocative performance to date entices us into knowing that there is infinitely much more to tap, that the heart of the matter must be reached and then probed much more thoroughly, and that Erik Erikson ought to be able to effect even more for us than he has.

For, ultimately with Erikson, one has something more than the inauguration of a new field of analytical endeavor. The concern is larger than the question whether psychoanalytic insights, which depend ordinarily on face-to-face interviews, have any place in the interpretation of the life-stories of gifted personalities whose location in some earlier time period renders them inaccessible to the usual psychoanalytic techniques. Erikson's achievement stands as something more than the precedent for testing the methodological hypothesis that psychology can add bits of interesting information to historical surveys of areas of particular religious interest. It cannot be reduced to a documentary account of how the fields of history, psychology, and religion illumine and depend upon each other. Nor is that something more made accessible by methodical systematizations of Erikson's contentions, as though systematics and/or programmatics could add anything to the original design.

Finally, with Erikson, one is talking about the makeup of human beings, the makeup of human history, and the coalescence of the two. To this framework reference is made when Erikson observes that *homo religiosus* is one for who ego and ethos have become coordinated. The same setting is implicit in his description of ego integrity as "the accidental coincidence of but one life cycle with but one segment of history." Such concerns are totalizing. Such statements, if accurate, bespeak wisdom. And because they do, they both attract and put off, compel and offend, and separate, often in irreconcilable fashion.

Testifying to the same tenor of response, some reviewers of Robert Coles' biography of Erikson, grateful and dissatisfied simultaneously, have offered the suggestion that someone should attempt to write a book about Erikson like Erikson's books about Luther and Gandhi. The suggestion is a sound one, and yet requires reflexive stances which may be too complicated. Nevertheless, for our culture, and, particularly, for a large group of today's young people, Erik H. Erikson has become the kind of figure whom he also attempts to identify and describe in his psycho-historical studies. Prior to the symposium, there had been no self-conscious attempt to appraise his work and influence with these interests in mind.

Yet we also recognized that such grievances could not be remedied simply by being acknowledged, or by making Erik Erikson the object of prolonged praise. We also knew that the dilemma is not resolved in a single event. And yet we thought that we might be able to do something collectively, if not individually, indirectly, if not directly, and provisionally, if not definitively and programmatically. Our intention was to bring together some of the ingredients necessary for a fuller appraisal. But even in these modest terms, we recognized the elusiveness of the subject and the sensitivities by which it had to be protected.

But there is more to the story about the genesis of the symposium. In addition to wanting to promote clarity and insight regarding Erikson's valuable contributions both to scholarship and to self-consciousness, we were concerned also to draw attention to a significant characteristic of religious studies. We took as starting point the assumption that religious studies is a new field of academic endeavor. We considered the possibility that religious studies possesses no clear operational definition or firmly established ground rules. Then we went on to note that the methodological configuration of the field has not been stabilized; neither has there been a clear demarcation of sub-fields within the larger subject-field. Furthermore, there is as yet no reliable consensus as to whether the subject-field is really generic, parasitical, or manifestly *ad hoc*. But this flexibility, indefiniteness, and lack of fixedness is what one should expect to find given the fact that the scholarly study of religion is a new enterprise. It may well be too that this embryonic period is the enterprise's most exciting period, and that premature closure is the real temptation. In fact, if definiteness is achieved, it may well be a sign, first, that the expectations imposed upon the field have limitations, and, second, that the period of gestation is finished.

We concentrated on but one aspect of the genesis of religious studies, namely, on the role of the significant individual in giving formation to the subject-field. It intrigued us that the

chief contributors to the formation of religious studies
did their primary scholarly work in other fields. One thinks of
figures in the fields of sociology, anthropology, philosophy,
the classics, or in philology, for example, and more specifically
of persons like Ernst Cassirer (who worked with symbolic forms),
Max Weber (who treated social organization), Emile Durkheim (who
concentrated on Australian tribal behavior), J.J. Bachofen (who
examined tombstones), Georges Dumézil (who has been impressed by
the tripartite structure of Indo-European mythology), Claude
Lévi-Strauss (who is primarilly interested in patterns of primitive
kinship), and Geo Widengren (who has concentrated on thr morphology
of kingship in ancient near eastern cultures). But the list goes
on and on. In instance after instance, identifiable individual
contributions of breakthrough proportions have occurred in a
variety of disciplines and fields, and the ramifications have
affected religious understanding and given formation to religious
studies. In all of the ventures it has launched, the Institute
has kept a keen eye on this breakthrough dimension and on its
correlation with individual catalytic contribution. It was for
this reason that a symposium series was established, to direct
concentrated attention to the contributions of significant
living catalytic figures who have influenced religious studies
in this comprehensive formative manner.

    Erikson's work fits the pattern in exemplary fashion.
Though he did not approach religion or religious studies directly,
his work in psychoanalysis and psychohistory have had a catalytic
effect upon religious studies. He has been responsible for
shaping religious understanding and imagination, and has made
aspects of religious consciousness accessible. In its present
and future shape, religious studies is something other than it
would have been had there been no Erik Erikson, and had he not
worked long, persistently, and creatively in the fields of
psychoanalysis and psychohistory. Thus, to recognize this fact,
and to bestow honor where honor is due, the Institute sponsored
a conference in which Erikson was recognized as a scholar whose
work has had a catalytic effect upon religion, religious under-

standing, religious consciousness, religious imagination, and religious studies. He was recognized in this way because of his painstaking research in identifying specific psychological and religious quotients in the human life cycle, and in the way in which he correlated the formation of religious postures with the fusion of ego and ethos in specific individual and historical cases.

This says most of it by way of preamble, but there is an additional wrinkle that must be identified. In trying to find our way into the present scholarly situation in the field of religion, we were also struck by the fact that many of the scholarly ploys used in the field have been trained upon what methodologists sometimes call *patterns of stability*. In both teaching and research in the field, the normative factor has been the core, essence, or otherwise permanent factor; and the methodological scheme has been designed to uncover the primary, fundamental, repeatable, underlying patterns, structures, or morphologies. This is exacting work; it may be productive, and it probably ought to be engaged in, especially if it is undertaken knowingly. But there is another side, the formal counterpart to the pattern of stability: the change factor, the inconstant, spontaneous, irregular, discontinuous, the non-forensic, unlawlike, the once-only. Thus, there is point to trying to capture phenomena in motion, realities in change, entities in process, explosive phenomena, or, to put it more precisely, catalytic and kinetic realities vis-a-vis patterns of stability. Some assistance is found through concentrating on change words: metamorphosis, catalysis, motion, process, transmission, transformation, etc. Additional assistance can be secured through analysis of parallel tendencies toward *kinesis* in the history and theory of art. That is, instead of focusing on "arrested pictures" (as C.J. Bleeker has called them), or moments of stopped action, in the usual phenomenological sense, there is good reason for directing attention toward realities in motion. Initially, this requires the cultivation of multi-dimensional perspectives. But it also lends itself appropriately to forum and symposium formats. As within the kinetic model, this recognizes that comprehension is not restricted to observation, but evokes participation. With kinesis, there are no longer observers, but only participants, and what they see is to a certain extent who they are.

Erikson deserves to be honored for his pioneer work in focusing attention on dynamic realities: behavioral processes, cultural phases, life cycles, processes of history, accidental coincidences, and the like. He is one of a very few scholars who has sought to make "the process of process" self-conscious, that is, to tease out its grammar. This project belonged to his task of describing how it happens that certain gifted individuals bear responsibility for setting new, innovative, cultural, religious, and ideological processes in motion. And, as an unexpected bonus for those whom he has influenced, Erikson's career has become an illustration of the very process he sought to understand. It is in these multiple senses that we refer to him as a catalytic figure.

The title of this volume--"Encounter with Erikson"--can be read in two rather distinct ways; it has both ritualistic and scholarly connotations. On the one hand, there was in fact an "encounter" with Erikson during the symposium. And this encounter, as Erikson intimated in depicting the occasion as a "trial in my honor," had all the earmarks of the ritual engagement he describes in the concluding section of *Gandhi's Truth*. There were the inevitable situational ambiguities involved in occasions of paying homage. There was the close range combat of supporters and loyal opposition. And there were the vulnerabilities which ritual invariably brings out. Indeed, this problem of vulnerability proved an especially important ritual ingredient throughout the symposium. There was, of course, much consideration of our own vulnerability in the face-to-face encounter with "the Professor." But, coupled with this, there was also considerable attention paid to the question of the Professor's own vulnerability. Was Erikson strong enough to stand the sort of trial the encounter quite "unintentionally" became? Some of us almost visibly suffered when colleagues "attacked" the Professor's work, others of us assured ourselves that the Professor and his accomplishments are fully durable enough to withstand any challenge, and still others considered attack the highest form of respect. It is difficult, even in retrospect, to know just how this question resolved itself. Nonetheless, there is this one inescapable fact, that when Erik Erikson is a party of ritual engagement, all participants leave with their dignity intact, even perhaps enhanced. And, as evidence that the "trial" must have given Erikson some pleasure, there was a reconnaissance of sorts in October 1973 when he rejoined many of the original symposium participants at the annual meeting of the Society for the Scientific Study of Religion in San Francisco.

However, "Encounter with Erikson" can be taken in quite another sense. The papers in this volume illustrate some of the various ways that scholars in religious studies, and scholars from other disciplines with special interests in religion, have "encountered" Erikson's *work*. While this collection of essays cannot hope to recreate the original face-to-face encounter, it does provide a representative sample of religion scholars' encounter with Erikson's published work. To be sure, since the conference design focused the face-to-face encounter on the psycho-historical dimensions of Erikson's work, it is undoubtedly the case that the papers do not reflect the extensive range of scholarly encounters with his work. None of the papers addresses Erikson's contribution to the problem of religion and human development. Nor do any of the papers consider in direct fashion Erikson's contribution to the study of religious ethics and therapeutic practice. Indeed, none of the papers directly addresses Erikson's views on religion as these can be collated from his various works. Quite possibly, therefore, a thorough canvassing of the "encounter" with Erikson in religious studies would need to address these and perhaps other topics in more systematic fashion.

On the other hand, the papers collected together in this volume constitute an excellent argument for the centrality of psychohistory in the encounter with Erikson's work. And this for two central reasons. First, the papers demonstrate that *Young Man Luther*, Erikson's first venture into the area of religion, remains a sticking point for many students of religion. As Erikson has said of his various biographical subjects, it has proven difficult for us to "get around" *Young Man Luther* but it has proven equally difficult for us to "get at" it. Of course, this is to put the claim for the centrality of psychohistory in a rather negative way. Thus, secondly, and more positively, the papers seem to indicate that psychohistory is not only a sticking point, but that it is also the channel through which new directions in the study of religious thought and practices may be charted. This is a large claim for psychohistory, and requires documentation--both the brief documentation that we can provide in these introductory comments and the documentation of the essays themselves. In any case, taking both the more negative and the more positive points with equal seriousness, it appears that a volume devoted to psychohistory may not be as limited in scope as the omission of more direct considerations of these other areas may seem, at first glance, to indicate.

Our claim for the centrality of psychohistory to religion scholars' encounter with Erikson's work is based, in part, on the accomplishments of psychohistory to date and on signs of increasing interest in psychohistory in our professional societies. But, more importantly, the claim rests on a seemingly self-defeating observation by Professor Erikson in some informal remarks, the observation that psychohistory as a word should gradually disappear as our current psychological self-consciousness also fades. Now, in religion circles, such expressions of self-effacement-- "He must increase, but I must decrease"--are usually viewed with a skeptical eye. We question the wisdom of a statement which asserts that the profit of the one must necessarily be bought at the expense of the other. However, the apparently self-effacing statement has considerable truth. The psychohistorical studies in this volume, those which "apply" psychohistory to religious figures, move with varying degrees of self-conscious intent into discussions of problems of historical process which psychohistory (as currently defined) cannot reasonably be expected to encompass.

Such problems as the relation of myth and history, the persistence and transformation of personal and social paradigms, the role of religion in the genesis and resolution of social conflict--these are problems which clearly belong within the purview of psychohistory but at the same time require the attention of various disciplines and subdisciplines in religious studies. Psychohistory must be appropriately modest.

But these developments are also a "plus" for psychohistory. For, at the very least, these ventures into the larger problems of historical process indicate that the "religious" dimension of psychohistory is not exhausted by the fact that the biographical subject is a religious man. They suggest, rather, that psychohistory can and does address "religion" in terms of those larger historical and cultural problems that come under its purview.

Psychohistory as a well-defined discipline will undoubtedly decrease in visibility with the increase of creative breakthrought in the study of the religious dimensions of historical processes. At the same time, it will probably be the case that psychohistory will play an increasingly important methodological role in the same creative breakthroughts. The papers in this volume give ample reason for confidence in this respect.

Before allowing the volume to speak for itself, the editors wish to record their thanks to the many who contributed to the success of the symposium, particularly to Carol A. Carrig, Past Director of La Casa de Maria and to her very capable staff. Special thanks are also due to Ernst F. Tonsing, who largely compiled the bibliography, Stanley Sheinbaum, Robert Y. Zachary of University of California Press, to those who prepared and responded to the papers, to Martha S. Oppenheim, Virginia Crockett, and Deborah Sills for typing some of them, and most of all to Erik and Joan Erikson, whose days in Santa Barbara were an encounter and then an Event for those of us who were privileged to be with them.

The Editors

SECTION I

Luther and Gandhi Studies

Most discussions of the psychohistorical work of Erik H. Erikson in theological circles have centered on questions of historical interpretation. Roland H. Bainton has set the dominant tone of such discussions in raising questions concerning Erikson's *modus operandi* as a historian. In his reactions to *Young Man Luther*, Bainton has raised the issue of Erikson's use and abuse of sources, his psychological inferences from insufficient data, his use of apocryphal and other unreliable historical materials, etc. While church historians have been inclined since Bainton's earlier attack to take a somewhat "milder" view of *Young Man Luther*, and while Erikson's stature as an elder statesman in the academic world has somewhat blunted criticisms of *Gandhi's Truth* by historians of religion, the general arguments remain essentially the same. Erikson may be a competent scholar in his own field, but he demonstrates much incompetence when he employs the historian's craft.

But, having said this, it is possible that the appraisals of *Young Man Luther* included in this section of papers dealing with Erikson's psychohistorical work promise a new era in historians' response to the book. While vestiges of the Bainton perspective are to be found in both papers, the strident tone of Bainton's two published critiques of *Young Man Luther* has been eliminated. More important, the absence of such stridency does not simply attest to the fact that the Bainton critique has assumed a muted, irenic tone without fundamental alteration. Of course, neither Professor Lindbeck nor Professor Spitz swallows *Young Man Luther* whole. And both are at times disconcertingly confident of the historical methods and procedures which they employ in critiquing the book. Nonetheless, these papers are clearly differentiated from the Bainton critiques in one extremely important respect, namely, that neither rejects psychoanalytic theory out of hand. Indeed, both are quite able to think psychoanalytically and both recognize the relevance of psychoanalytic insights to the life of Luther. One even suspects that their critiques, in emphasizing the father-son relationship, fix on traditional psychoanalytic categories with greater tenacity than does the psychohistorian himself.

Perhaps this rather easy assimilation of psychoanalytic thought by these historians confirms Jacques Barzun's recent observation that historians tend to employ the psychological notions which have already entered the common idiom, and that psychoanalysis is rather unique among current psychologies in having so entered. It may no longer be possible for the historian to think or express himself in anti-psychoanalytic ways. And if one finally rejects the anticipated psychoanalytic interpretation in given instances (as Erikson himself frequently does), he does so having seriously entertained it. Whatever the case, this openness to psychological modes of thought makes for a considerable difference in the resulting critique of *Young Man Luther*.

This tacit acceptance of psychoanalytic ways of thinking is only one basis for the belief that these papers may presage a new era in historians' critiques of Erikson's psychohistorical work. In addition, the Lindbeck paper especially points to the fact that the psychohistorian is not being recognized simply for his insights into Luther's family history, for filling certain biographical lacunae with plausible, psychologically-informed reconstructions. Rather, Lindbeck, and Spitz to a somewhat lesser extent, finds Erikson making a significant contribution to our understanding of the cultural setting in which Luther played his catalytic role. It would seem that Erikson is being accorded here the same respect that other non-historians (especially sociologists of religion) have commanded as they ventured into the cultural history of peoples and periods for which they could claim no special scholarly expertise. This is not to say that Erikson merely dabbled in Reformation history and from this emerged with a few lucky guesses. Rather, it seems to indicate that his biographical intentions, searching for the unique presence of Luther, proved a valuable instrument for illuminating the larger cultural processes which historians more typically address.

Much of what has been said thus far with regard to the Luther papers is also relevant to the psychohistorical studies of Gandhi (Hay and Newhall) included in this section. If anything, an even more positive attitude toward Erikson's work is evident in these papers. On the other hand, this positive tone is accompanied by a somewhat lesser concern to "get at" Erikson's own study of Gandhi. In addressing themselves primarily to Gandhi's life and only secondarily to *Gandhi's Truth*, the authors of these psychohistorical studies have not addressed the historiographical issues which *Gandhi's Truth* typically evokes, particularly the oft-cited problem of employing a Western psychology to study an Eastern figure.

On the other hand, the focus of these two papers on the life of Gandhi poses a different and potentially illuminating issue for psychohistory. The fact that these papers treat a figure already accorded booklength attention by Erikson must necessarily give us pause. It is true, of course, that these studies do not simply retrace Erikson's steps in *Gandhi's Truth*. But neither do they measureably alter the essential view of Gandhi which Erikson develops. These are not revisionist studies. Rather, they are supplementary, with Professor Hay fleshing out Gandhi's childhood and Professor Newhall shedding additional light on Gandhi's South African period, but both working with essentially the same topic of investigation as Erikson, i.e. Gandhi's "truth." How, then, are we to react to the very existence of these necessarily briefer studies of Gandhi? Given the relative immaturity of psychohistory as a recognizable discipline, it might be argued that this kind of duplication of effort can hardly be afforded. Or, assuming that neither Professor Hay or Professor Newhall could be wrenched away from his chosen biographical subject, it might seem that another issue besides that of Gandhi's "truth" (or the doctrine and instrumentality of Satyagraha) could be broached.

The fact that this adjustment of sights, so typical in other disciplines, did not occur, invites speculation as to whether psychohistory is a typical academic discipline. One senses that those who attended the symposium and listened to the Gandhi papers engaged in some such private speculation. In the judgment of the editors, the very existence of these two psychohistorical studies of Gandhi, and their valuable contribution to the symposium, tells us something about the similarities between psychohistory and religious biography of a more traditional nature. An extremely important characteristic of traditional religious biography or hagiography is the fact that it emerges from what we might call a "biographical milieu." Typically, a number of biographies of a given religious figure appear in written form, each developed by a follower or group of followers of the biographical subject, with no apparent embarassment concerning the fact that their biographical efforts evidence considerable overlap. Like traditional religious biography, psychohistory does not appear to consider overlapping content and repetition of themes an unnecessary luxury. The psychohistorians in this particular instance are involved in illuminating the various facets of the genesis of Gandhi's "truth." Given the rich interpretive possibilities of this fundamental issue, it would scarcely do to observe that this topic was previously and thoroughly addressed in *Gandhi's Truth*. (The duplicative nature of these two studies should not be exaggerated. Both Hay and Newhall draw on historical materials to which Erikson did not have easy access. This is especially true of the paper by Stephen Hay, a specialist in Indian history who works with materials in Gandhi's native tongue as he addresses the matter of Gandhi's extended family relations, a facet of Gandhi's life which Erikson neglected.)

The papers by Geertz and Capps also relate to this hagiographical issue, but in a slightly different way. Less an attempt to supplement Erikson's own work, Geertz's paper concerns itself with Erikson's own effort to penetrate the mystique of Gandhi's religious genius. Geertz shows how Erikson, in his effort to identify the more determinative features of Gandhi's character, stressed Gandhi's ironic, mocking, grating humor as a little noticed but enormously important element in his role as exemplary prophet. This element of the Gandhi character was forged into the political instrument of Satyagraha, its influence on Gandhi's "truth" accounting for much of the moral ambiguity of his prophetic role. Thus, Erikson's work is similar to traditional hagiography in its effort to identify the personal characteristics which lie behind Gandhi's religious genius, but it also differs significantly from these traditional biographical efforts in stressing as absolutely essential to Gandhi's religious genius a personality characteristic which others (supporters and detractors alike) generally overlooked. This, as if to say that even as others have tended to dismiss the importance of the "Event" which Erikson chooses to discuss in *Gandhi's Truth*, so also the personal characteristic most neglected in the traditional biographical literature, becomes the key to Erikson's analysis of Gandhi's religious genius.

The paper by Capps also takes up the hagiographical issue, arguing that critics of Erikson's study of Gandhi impose criteria derived from historical biography on what is essentially a modern hagiographical treatment. In Capps' judgment, *Gandhi's Truth* is religious biography, a particular literary genre whose aesthetic and moral intentions are quite different from that of historical biography. Capps develops this argument by emphasizing the structural features of the book, showing how the narrative fuses traditional religious themes and modern psychological insight. He concludes that, in Erikson's portrait, Gandhi's claim to be an exemplary prophet is similarly related to his success in invigorating traditional convictions with penetrating insights into modern into modern psychohistorical realities. Hence, Erikson's refusal to accept uncritically Gandhi's claim as exemplary prophet (as most forcefully expressed in his famous "personal word" to Gandhi) is based on his judgment that in some areas of Gandhi's life this reconstitution of traditional convictions did not occur.

In short, the four Gandhi papers explore the use of psychohistory in identifying the genesis and function of religious genius.

Newhall and Hay appear to find the psychohistorian's role a congenial one as they scan previously unexplored dimensions of Gandhi's "truth" from their perch atop the giant's shoulders. While Newhall and Hay are viewers, Geertz and Capps are <u>re</u>viewers, scanning *Gandhi's Truth* itself in the attempt to discover its essential meaning as a contemporary cultural product. While equally appreciative of Erikson's work, they appear less inclined to exemplify his psychohistorical labors and more concerned to understand the book's own truth force.

ERIKSON'S *YOUNG MAN LUTHER*:
A HISTORICAL AND THEOLOGICAL REAPPRAISAL

George A. Lindbeck

I

In his book on Erikson, Robert Coles tells us that it is dangerous not to follow Erikson's example of daring to be autobiographical when dealing with the thoughts of others. Heeding this counsel, I shall start by saying something of the history of my own encounters with Erikson's work.

Among those with whom Erikson argues in *Young Man Luther*--professor, priest and psychiatrist--it is, I suppose, the professor, Otto Scheel, whom I must closely resemble. I learned about Luther from men who stood in his tradition. Like him and them, I try to be an historian, a theologian, and also something else which is perhaps not easily compatible with either of these two roles: a Christian who thinks of Luther as one of his fathers in the faith.

There are also, however, points of difference. I am not a professional Luther scholar, for my own areas of specialization are the late middle ages and contemporary Roman Catholic developments, and my own concerns in teaching and writing are perhaps more those of a systematic than of a historical theologian. Further, like many others, I differ from the Luther scholars of an older generation in a way that is perhaps not altogether dissimilar to the fashion in which Erikson himself departs from Freudians of the past. He is more conscious of social and cultural factors than were his predecessors, but this is also true of many contemporary historians and theologians. Erikson is also more positive in his evaluation of at least some forms of religion than were most earlier psychoanalysts. Correspondingly, the religionists and historians of today have inevitably been influenced by psychoanalysis. Their thinking has been molded by it even when their attitudes are negative. Perhaps we did not quite drink Freud with our mother's milk, but I am not altogether untypical in having made the acquaintance of *Totem and Taboo*, *The Future of an Illusion* and *Moses* and *Monotheism* before entering college. (To be sure, I have not looked at these books since. The interest has been casual and personal rather than professional or scholarly.)

As far as *Young Man Luther* is concerned, I heard it discussed when it first came out, but largely in terms of the initial critical reactions of most Luther scholars. As time went on, however, I encountered comments of a rather different character from colleagues whose judgment I respected, but still I did not more than glance at the book. In the meantime, I skimmed *Childhood and Society* and the study of Gandhi; and because of them, as well as innumerable indirect influences, found myself, together with what seems to be a majority of American academicians, talking a great deal about identity. For the last several years I have used Erikson's psychosocial version of this concept when I have had occasion to touch in my classes on the question of why Luther's impact on his age was so enormous.

It is not surprising, then, that when I finally sat down this past year to a thorough reading of Erikson on Luther, I expected to like the psychosocial approach to the causes of the Reformation, but to be skeptical of the psychobiographical elements. Both of these anticipations were fulfilled, but what I had not foreseen was that my over-all response would be so positive. Despite questionable historical details and reservations regarding Erikson's own ideological framework, I found myself feeling in my bones that on one basic level he is fundamentally right about Luther, and that even when he isn't right, he is suggestive. This posed a problem for me: how could so bad a book be so good? The present paper is an attempt to answer this question for myself, and perhaps also for others. I think I have been fairly successful in articulating what is wrong with the book from my perspective, but I have not done justice to what is good about it. In any case, whether successful or unsuccessful, this is intended as a contribution to the clarification in one particular instance of the values and limitations of Erikson's psychoanalytic approach to history.

II

It is best to start with the questionable history which the book contains. I am not so much concerned with the general characterizations of the Middle Ages, the Renaissance and the Reformation. For these, Erikson, like the rest of us, had to rely on the work of others, and this work is now in part inevitably outdated. Defects on this level, even though at times serious for the proper understanding of Luther, are inescapable, and in this sense venial. What I shall concentrate on, therefore, are the biographical errors, i.e., the misinterpretations of the evidence, the texts, with which Erikson deals at first hand.

Before citing examples of the mistakes Erikson makes, it is well to ask why he makes them. In part, once again, the fault is not his, but that of the historians on whom he relies. He was confronted in the fifties when he wrote this book with a much sharper divergence among Luther specialists than exists now, a mere twenty years later. The Catholic reading of the evidence was still generally polemical, and the Protestant, while no longer hagiographical, remained more defensive than it has since become. As Erikson was not committed to either of these groups, he picked and chose among them on the basis of what seemed to him psychologically most plausible. If he were to do the job over again, he would find that a whole set of readings which he sometimes favors now have no scholarly support whatsoever. Contemporary Roman Catholic and Protestant Luther experts are much closer to an ecumenical consensus on previously controverted points. This is not simply a matter of ecumenical good will. A tremendous amount of solid fresh research has been done.

In order to understand this situation, one needs to remember that Luther scholarship is still very much a Catholic-Protestant preserve. Virtually all the really competent scholars who have devoted large parts of their lives to the world of Luther studies have clear confessional attachments.

What then does *Young Man Luther* look like from the viewpoint of current historical scholarship? As far as I can see, Erikson's account of Martin's childhood must be adjudged almost entirely speculative. The treatment of his young manhood, in contrast, is on the whole historically unobjectionable, despite some questionable details. Criticisms of the picture of the older Luther are once again more serious, but this is of minor importance because the focus of the book is on the earlier years.

It is possible here to do no more than sample the reasons for skepticism about the account of Martin's childhood. They are developed at length in articles by Bainton and Bornkamm,[1] and are, I believe, largely, though not entirely, independent of the theological and perhaps also anti-psychoanalytic biases of these historians. A. G. Dickens of King's College in London presents a harsh but on the whole accurate summary of the specialized historians' assessment:

> Dr. Erikson...finds [that]...the adolescent Luther creates a God in the image of his own irascible father, shifts his obedience to this terrible Deity and releases the venom of his defiance against the Pope. Again, Luther is caned for speaking German in school-hours, so he becomes fanatically attached to the German language. Likewise, his resentment against the severity of his mother causes him to dethrone the Virgin Mary.
>
> ...This type of theory seems to base Luther's career upon three or four sentences, selected from the late and unreliable *Table Talk* to the exclusion of much competing or contradictory evidence. When interpreted in the light of contemporary manners, Luther's childhood and adolescence seem strikingly 'normal' and unsensational. By the standards expected in that period, his parents were far from heavy-handed; they were deeply devoted to his welfare and he remained on unusually affectionate terms with them to the end of their long lives. Luther needed no irascible father to provide him with the image of an angry and inscrutable God, for on every side orthodox theologicans and popular beliefs provided such an image. And in the actual event his attack on the Pope brought him no 'release' but only further torment. So far as concerns his alleged complex over the German language, in fact he became just as voluble and prolific in Latin as in German; his Bible-reading and private devotions were carried out in the former. While in his revolt he sought to abolish saint-worship, he did not in actual fact single out the Blessed Virgin, but continued to regard her with heartfelt reverence quite unusual among Protestants.[2]

The statement of Erikson's theses in this quotation is tendentious, and Dickens is overly dogmatic in seeming to imply that historians can prove that Luther's childhood was blessedly free of trauma and that he had no early major problems in his relations with his parents. This exaggerates the case against Erikson. There simply is not enough evidence one way or another.

Still, its specific points are valid. First, the *Table Talk* is often dangerously misleading, as is not surprising when one remembers that it consists of notes on Luther's dinner conversation taken down by student boarders and not reviewed by him nor published in his lifetime. To cite an example Erikson does not use, but where the unreliability can be clearly documented, Luther is reported as saying that Christ committed adultery with, among others, the woman who was a sinner (presumably a prostitute) who washed his feet in tears and wiped them with her hair (Luke 7:37 ff.). But in Luther's sermon on this subject, he adds the crucial words "coram mundo"--i.e., "in the eyes of the world"--and backs up his interpretation by citing the text which says Jesus was regarded by his enemies as a wine bibber, glutton and friend of publicans and sinners (Luke 7:34).[3]

Second, Erikson not only relies too uncritically on unreliable sources, but he sometimes misinterprets what these sources say. For example, Luther describes his father as becoming more genial when he was drinking, rather than angry, as Erikson supposes.[4] Thirdly, it is quite right to point out that Luther's image of an angry God was not so much his own as that of his culture, even if his reactions to it were peculiarly (though by no means uniquely) intense. Fourthly, he was astonishingly eloquent in Latin as in German (as I became very much aware in translating one of his Latin polemical treatises). Fifthly, his affection and respect for the Virgin were indeed superior to that of any other Protestant Reformer.

Finally, Erikson's characterization of Luther's parents is more than questionable. As this point is psychogenetically crucial, it should be enlarged upon, however briefly. He suggests that although Luther's mother was warm and supportive during his infancy "when he was still all hers,"[5] the parents were unusually harsh, and that "the father, behind his disciplined public identity, was possessed by an angry, and often alcoholic, impulsiveness which he loosed against his family (and would dare loose *only* against his family) under the pretence of being a hard taskmaster and righteous judge."[6] "He showed the greatest temper in his attempts to drive temper out of his children. Here, I think, is the origin of Martin's doubt that the father, when he punishes you, is really guided by love and justice rather than by arbitrariness and malice. This early doubt was later projected on the Father in heaven...."[7]

Unfortunately the documentary evidence for this picture of Hans Luder is much weaker than Erikson was or perhaps could have been aware when he wrote his book. There is, to be sure, precious little historical data to appeal to, but on balance it is more unfavorable than favorable to Erikson's speculations about Martin's parents.

There are also historically questionable aspects to Erikson's treatment of the young man Martin. He gives star billing, for example, to the story of Luther's fit in choir[8] which comes to us through a string of Luther's enemies: the bishop of Mansfeld, *via* Nathin, Dungersheim and finally Cochleus. As both Bainton and Bornkamm remark, there is nothing intrinsically implausible about the incident (nor about Erikson's interpretation), but still its use makes one wince. It is rather like citing seriously and discussing extensively a report about Freud whose only source is a succession of Nazi anti-Semites, and which was published by one of them only in its fourth retelling. Similarly, to take a substantively more important illustration, the older Luther is said to have "displayed an extraordinary ability to hate quickly and persistently, justifiably or unjustifiably" and to be possessed of "excessive vindictiveness."[9] This overlooks, however, the extraordinary degree to which Luther's rages, though violent, were concentrated, not on persons, but on whatever it was that endangered the cause, the gospel, for which he fought. He was extraordinarily and apparently quite unaffectedly generous towards enemies once they had lost the ability to harm. Perhaps he can be called vindictive only if Freud is described in the same way because of the character of his fallings-out with a Jung or an Adler. It may be that this is what Erikson had in mind, but if so, most of his readers have probably misunderstood him.

In this connection, I cannot forebear mentioning the treatment of Luther's scatology. Take, for example, a remark reported in the *Table Talk* from when he was old, ailing and presumably feeling rotten: "I'm like ripe shit, and the world a huge ass hole. We'll soon be parted (TR V: 5537).[10] Erikson takes this as a sign of "depressive self-repudiation."[11] Perhaps that is what it would be if said by a patient free-associating on an analyst's couch; but I hear it as a witticism lanced into jovial company and designed to get a laugh. I'm sure it did; and this, I would suppose, makes a difference in its diagnostic import.

It is time now to turn to the other side of the problem. Enough has been said about the defects, but what then is good about this treatment of Luther? What is left if one agrees with the historian's objections and brackets or excises the reconstruction especially of the childhood?

It would seem, oddly enough, that virtually nothing need be changed in the basic outlines of Erikson's portrait of the young man. His feelings towards his father could have been what Erikson describes, and this is true even if the childhood were radically different, even if the parents were not unusually harsh, and even if the relations to Hans Luder were better than those of most Saxon sons to their fathers.

Erikson presumably believes that all youths carry with them a legacy of repressed oedipal rage, and this makes it possible for even the best of childhoods to go awry. Quirks of the family situation may make one child suffer from parents under whom his siblings flourish, and unusual personal or cultural circumstances in later years may create special problems with the father (either as interiorized image or present actuality) which otherwise would not have arisen. To be sure, most young men similar to Erikson's Martin may have fathers similar to Erikson's Hans Luder, but some do not; and this means that Erikson could be right about the psychological factors involved in Luther's entrance into the monastery, his ascetic and moralistic extremism, and his reformatory breakthrough, and still be wrong about his childhood. Thus those who are sympathetic with the psychoanalytic approach will quite legitimately find the picture of the young man persuasive even when they have historically-grounded doubts about the picture of the childhood.

Further, no objections need be raised from the theological side. Luther at least would probably have denied that there is any necessary incompatibility between explanations in terms of divine agency and psychological causation. "Natural" and "supernatural" were not mutually exclusive categories for him in contrast to medieval scholastics or modern fundamentalists. God uses all kinds of profane things to terrorize guilty consciences, why not also displaced fear of one's father? The vehicles of God's grace and inspiration are innumerable, why not also the successful surmounting of an identity crisis? There is no particular reason in principle, as far as I can see, why Luther could not add the whole battery of Freudian psychic mechanisms to his list of the *larvae dei*. From such a theological perspective, Erikson's explanations are no worse, and perhaps better, than the romantic and idealistic interpretive categories which influenced most of the Protestant Luther scholars whom Erikson read in preparation for his book. In any case, theology cannot say whether these explanations are right or wrong. They belong in the second of Luther's two Kingdoms where disputes are adjudicated by reason and its laws rather than by the gospel.

It is, then, only from the viewpoint of reason--of the historical evidence--that Erikson's account of the childhood genesis of Luther's identity crisis is to be criticized. Yet, to repeat, the failure here is not crucial. All that Erikson needs in order to make his portrait of the young man plausible is the undisputed fact that there was a disagreement with the father over the entrance into the monastery, and that this was connected with intra-psychic problems, with guilt and rebelliousness. It makes no difference whether these problems are viewed as basically causes or effects of the decision to become a monk. Perhaps Luther's decision was motivated primarily by social and cultural factors (by the effects of his religious training and the influence of significant models whom he encountered) combined, of course, with the accident of the thunder storm. Perhaps it was his father's *post factum* disapproval which activated infantile conflicts which had been successfully resolved and would otherwise have remained dormant. To my clinically untutored mind, this is just as plausible, even from a psychoanalytic point of view, as the supposition that childhood conflicts are compatible with Erikson's description of the young man. The one which he has proposed may be the psychologically most likely one, particularly from the perspective of his own clinical experience (that is, from the point of view of twentieth century Western developmental patterns), but it is not the only possible one; and so the question of what Luther's parents were like and of the nature of his childhood relation to them can be left cheerfully open without impugning the rest of the psycho-biography.

It is possible that this solution would not be acceptable to Erikson or to psychoanalysts in general, but it makes logical sense in view of the loose character of the causal connections postulated in psychoanalytic explanations; and it makes it possible to embrace one part of the book while remaining highly skeptical of another.

It would take us too far afield to discuss the portrait of the young man himself and of the details of his identity crisis. Emendations are needed at certain points, but its basic outlines are historically unobjectionable. Others are better equipped than I am to assess its psychological persuasiveness, so I shall simply say that, looked at globally, it strikes me as thoroughly plausible within the context of Erikson's insights into adolescent and late adolescent development.

Here again, no objections need be raised from a theological point of view. For the historian of Christian thought, Erikson's view of Luther is largely familiar, even conventional. The Reformer, he says, was first of all a *homo religiosus*, a great man of prayer, who changed the course of history by the power of his insights. His major theological contributions were the doctrines of the Word, the *simil justus et peccator*, a new vision of Christ as the human, crucified and God-forsaken Son who "becomes the core of the Christian's identity,"[12] and the renewal of the *sola gratia* by the *sola fide*. There are other ways of summarizing Luther's breakthrough to a new "ideology" (as Erikson quite non-pejoratively calls it), but this one is well within the range of standard interpretations.

III

It is neither the psycho-biographical nor the theological side of the work, however, which seems to me the most important, but rather the psychosocial dimension.

Stated in general terms, Erikson's thesis is that the development of an effective adult identity involves the acquisition of an ideology--that is, a relatively comprehensive and unified understanding of the nature and meaning of oneself, one's roles and one's world. This ideology need not, of course, be explicitly articulated to any great extent, but it is none the less necessary. One implication of this view is that the range of possible identities is in part dependent on the culturally available ideological options. A second implication is that social changes may produce new psychological-developmental needs which cannot be adequately satisfied by the traditional ideological identifications provided by the society. This can result in a socially generalized identity crisis in which large numbers of people fail for structurally similar reasons to make an effective transition to adulthood. One way in which the difficulty may be solved is for "a great young man" such as Luther to articulate the crisis and its solution for himself in such a way that others recognize their problems in his problem and the possibility of solutions for themselves in his solution. In other words, the new identity and ideology he forges for himself can become culturally paradigmatic.

This provides a highly useful model for understanding the Reformation. In briefly outlining its historical application, I shall, not so much repeat what Erikson says, as develop what his schema suggests as the proper way of organizing what is now known about the period.

In Luther's day, the available answers to what constitutes a Christian identity were becoming increasingly ineffective. This was serious for the whole society because Christian identity in sixteenth century Europe was for most people equivalent to truly human identity. Multitudes suffered from the problem, but it was of course especially acute for those who took their religion with genuine seriousness: who had elected or been elected to embody in themselves the dominant cultural definitions of what a man or woman should be.

The growing crisis had various sources. On the one hand, the concretely available paradigms were increasingly at variance with the traditionally authoritative models rooted in Augustine and, behind him, in the Bible. Growing historical knowledge made this incongruity more and more apparent. Secondly, the current paradigms were becoming psychologically more unsatisfactory in a sense which we shall indicate. Thirdly, the concrete realities of social, economic and political life were making the traditional models unworkable. For example, "The holy beggar was no longer the object of unqualified admiration; partly because experience had shown too high a proportion of frauds, but partly because the moral ideal was beginning to be modified in the presence of social and economic changes."[13]

Now this problem of Christian identity was, not only practical, but also theological (or, if you prefer, ideological or theoretical). The normative options were buttressed with highly articulated, complex and comprehensive systems of interpreting traditional authorities and defining the real, true, good and beautiful. There was also, of course, an institutional problem. Both state and church had vested interests in maintaining certain definitions, and rejecting others, of what constitutes authentic human personhood.

One of the reasons the innumerable reform movements of the late middle ages failed was that they were too limited. They had refurbished outmoded identities rather than creating new ones, or had not shown how their proposals could be grounded in something unquestionably authoritative for the society, such as scripture, or had been simply destructive of institutional arrangements rather than envisaging new and contextually viable patterns.

Now from this point of view, the importance of Luther's identity crisis is not primarily that it was unusual in depth, intensity and personal outcome, but rather that it was structurally similar to what millions of others were experiencing in milder form. Furthermore, it was simultaneously both highly personal and also intellectual or ideological in a publicly definable and generalizable way. Thus in forging a new kind of Christian identity for himself, Luther also forged a new theology; and in solving his own personal problems, he developed a solution of sorts for a major problem of his age. Lastly, he did this in such a way that the established institutional order did not have to be fundamentally subverted in order to make room for Protestant Man, but only reorganized and restructured. It was for these reasons that his identity crisis and identity could become culturally paradigmatic. Without this, there would have been no Reformation. Immense changes would have occurred, but they would have been of a different character and moved in very different (and for us undecipherable) directions.

Whole libraries have been filled with the discussions of this breakthrough, but we must content ourselves with the merest sketch. Luther's age was highly moralistic. Those who took their religion seriously had strong inducements to suppress all awareness of even subjective feelings of anger, despair, pride or concupiscence. They were told that a person must be pure, loving and humble on pain of damnation, and they were trained to test themselves by the introspective techniques fostered by the medieval penitential system reinforced by the individualistic inwardness of Augustinian spirituality. Repressed concupiscence, pride and rage, however, had--and have--a way of venting themselves in cruel self-righteousness and other forms of disguised self-centredness and hostility. This, in turn, added to unacknowledged anxieties. Men sought escape from them by moralistic, ritualistic and monetary methods of buying some degree of assurance of salvation. They were told, however, that the assurance could never be anything except tentative and incomplete. Human beings must always keep trying to do their best (*facere quod in se est*) and can never be sure that they have succeeded.

Thus late medieval Christianity, especially when practised conscientiously by those who aspired to membership in the spiritual elite, was devilishly efficient in stimulating fear and remarkably deficient in means of re-assurance. The morality-enforcing function of religion had hypertrophied and the trust-giving function atrophied to a degree unparalleled in previous Christian history and perhaps in the history of religion in general. What Krister Stendahl has called "the introspective conscience of the West" became an acute and widespread disease. (Nor did it cease to be so as a result of the Reformation, but in Protestantism it took new forms.)

Luther's achievement was that he recognized the problem for what it was: a disastrous imbalance in the ideological system, and not simply a private difficulty. Others failed to achieve this insight even though they suffered from terrorized consciences, seethed with unacknowledged resentment of the Heavenly Father and were secretly obsessed with the question, "Wie krieg' ich ein gnädige Gott?" (How do I get a gracious God?). They yielded to the enormous weight of the religiously sanctioned opinion of their culture that such emotions are signs of damnation, and consequently lapsed into despair or more frequently, escaped into distraction or self-deception. Luther refused these evasions. His inner turmoil made self-deception impossible and, for whatever reasons, he had the strength to resist distraction and despair. He was forced, then, to make his personal difficulties into ideological ones, and somehow he had the courage and creativity to shape a new ideology, forge a new type of identity, which fundamentally altered the balance between terror and trust, between heteronomous law and theonomous confidence.

His solution proved culturally paradigmatic. Multitudes found relief in his insistence that the Christian must, not repress, but frankly confess that anger, anxiety, pride and concupiscence are continually present in even the best of lives (*simul justus et peccator*). They rejoiced at the divine Word of unconditional acceptance by which Luther replaced the doctrine that doing one's best is a pre-condition for forgiveness. (The "optimistically" crypto-Pelagian nominalists were the most threatening, for they said even natural, sinful man can and must do this even apart from the help of grace, but the late medieval *facere quod in sè est* was still dreadful even in its Augustinian and Thomistic forms where it was possible only *sola gratia*.) They delighted in Luther's teaching that it is Christ, not the self, who does good works in and through the believer. Health and salvation are through faith alone, that is, through the *fiducia*, the trust, which clings to God's mercy without any regard for what one is in oneself. Only a little trust is needed: "A tiny faith is faith too. That is why Christ came into the world to accept, bear and show patience to the weak" (WA 17 - I, 458).[14] This is the one thing necessary, not special religious experiences, nor volitional effort, nor love--not even grace--inspired love. To be sure, love and the works of love flow from faith, but they do not save, and without underlying trust they become demonically distorted.

Such words as these were balm in Gilead to myriads of tortured souls. They contributed to the psychic health and maturity of many who were moralistically inhibited. They freed from "works righteousness"--that is, from efforts to save oneself by adherence to ecclesiastically sanctioned false consciousness and false behavior. The kind of identity pictured by Luther in the "Freedom of the Christian Man," and to some extent exemplified in his own person, made possible a new type of adult, a new type of human being.

This, of course, is a very partial account of the Reformation. Its success and direction was dependent on all kinds of political contingencies. According to Weber and Tawney, economic factors played an important role. Guy Swanson has recently argued that there was a close correlation between the spread of the Reformation and certain forms of governmental organization. Nevertheless, the specifically religious breakthrough was clearly an essential, even if not sufficient, condition for the 16th century revolution.

This breakthrough does, I think, become more intelligible when

interpreted in terms of Erikson's psychosocial categories. The
notion of a culturally paradigmatic identity crisis helps explain
how, in contrast to other historically important figures, the intensely private struggles of great ideologists are of such immense
public significance. I feel, even if I cannot prove, that Erikson
has here made a major contribution to historiography.

IV

There is, however, a third dimension of Erikson's work about
which I am much less happy. Erikson has an ideological--or, in
older language, philosophical or theological--preference for explaining cultural phenomena in psychological terms rather than the
reverse. He, of course, is much more aware of cultural factors
than were earlier Freudians, and he acknowledges that cultural and
psychological processes are dialectically related and mutually
condition each other, but he is still enough of a psychoanalyst so
that--perhaps even when he doesn't want to--he sounds reductionist.

This, to be sure, is a function of his approach, not of his
conscious intentions. He repeatedly disavows any claims that concepts of God, for example, are simply projections. Yet he never
says what else they might be. His bias is inevitably towards emphasizing the psychological roots of cultural phenomena, not the
other way around. My disagreement with Erikson at this point is
not, I think, simply an untestable ideological or theological one
(though it is that also), but it is to some extent empirically
assessable. The case for the social construction of human reality,
including psychological reality, is stronger than he seems to realize. Historically viewed, for example, the God of Judaism and
Christianity did not originate as a projected "natural" father figure, but was first conceived in political terms on analogy with the
Near Eastern great king. It was perhaps only after the notions of
what fatherhood should be had been shaped by Hebrew monotheism that
"Father" became an important designation of the deity (indeed, it
became central only with Jesus). This does not mean that one can

simply invert the projective theory and talk about a given concept of the father as an introjected God image. Actually the effect of attributing fatherhood to God within a monotheistic context seems to be to de-absolutize and de-divinize human fathers thereby making them beings which can be "acceptably" rebelled against and hated, (at least this is what is suggested to me by R. Bellah's comparison of the West with a non-monotheistic patriarchal society such as that of China).[15]

Such considerations can be generalized. Perhaps the oedipal conflict as described by Freud is better understood as a function of Moses' monotheism than *vice versa*, and perhaps the fundamental psychological importance which Erikson attributes to trust/mistrust is more the result than the cause of the similar emphasis in the religious-cultural tradition which Luther helped shape.

The same type of question can be raised regarding Erikson's analysis of Luther--although of course, the fact that a culture creates a certain kind of fatherhood does not mean that its *direct* influence on the *individual* is always greater than that of the father. Still maybe Luther's entrance into the monastery is better accounted for by culturally induced fears and longings for saintliness than by repressed oedipal rage. It is possible that he was terrorized more by the religious system (e.g., the arbitrary and demanding God of nominalism) than by childhood problems. Perhaps it was the introspective honesty which this same system commended which made its reassurances inadequate. Lastly, it is conceivable that the emphasis on trust, on the *sola fide*, and the reshaping of the ideological system which followed, was more the function of the objectively compelling evidence of the authoritative texts which Luther studied than of his own psychological and spiritual needs. (They, to be sure, do explain why he studied these texts so intently.)

Perhaps only the last of these points is historically decidable. One can show, I believe, that the reformatory breakthrough was much more like a scientific discovery than an ideological construction unconsciously designed to satisfy psychic needs. Luther was a conscientious and disciplined exegete, thoroughly conversant

with all the interpretive rules of his day. What he discovered
(with the help of St. Augustine and others) was that the Bible was
systematically misread: it not only could, but objectively should
be read in a fundamentally different way. His arguments for this
were thoroughly objective and rational in terms of the canons of
objectivity and rationality which prevailed in the theology of his
day. That is why they proved so widely persuasive to a wide variety of his contemporaries who had all kinds of both psychological
and non-psychological reasons, not only for favoring, but also
sometimes for opposing the Reformation. Luther really meant it
when he repeatedly appealed to scripture as interpreted by reason,
and sharply repudiated the enthusiasts precisely because they argued from personal inspiration and religious experience. He must
be compared, I believe, not perhaps to great pioneers in the physical sciences such as Darwin or Einstein, but to heroes of the
Geisteswissenschaften such as Marx or Freud. What he did was not
only to diagnose a fundamental flaw in a massive ideological system and then recast (not destroy) the system in order to meet the
problem, but he did so in terms of culturally accepted and rationally accessible criteria. His achievement, in other words, is
structurally similar to what Kuhn describes in his book on scientific revolutions.[16] Erikson in part sees this,[17] but not sufficiently.

In fairness it should be admitted that this is not altogether
his fault. He is influenced by the last two centuries of Reformation historiography in which both the theological and non-theological forms of the dominant romantic idealism pictured great historical achievements bursting from the inner depths of inspired geniuses (in a way, oddly enough, not too dissimilar from Erikson's psychoanalytic vision). Furthermore, Protestants and Catholics have
been in violent disagreement over the rationality, the objective
plausibility, of Luther's way of interpreting the Bible, Augustine
and his own theological situation. Now, however, scholarly advances
and ecumenical *rapprochement* have greatly lessened these disputes
so that most specialists describe the Reformation breakthrough
as neither a divine nor demonic intrusion into history, but as a

structured change within the culturally objective and rationally
accessible system of late medieval ideas and practices. This breakthrough had, of course, immense psychological impact on Luther and
others, but this was more effect than cause of what was a rationally persuasive modification of the reigning theology. If it had not
been persuasive in terms of the prevailing theological norms, its
psychological or spiritual appeal would have been insufficient to
carry the day.

It should be observed that Erikson could in principle take account of this "scientific" character of the reformatory discovery.
He would have to change his theory of religion (make it less subjective sounding), but his psychoanalytic and psychosocial approaches could be retained. These approaches, as he himself has noted,
apply also to great scientists.[18]

A society's "religion," contrary to Erikson, is not only an
elaboration "on what feels profoundly true even though it is not
demonstrable."[19] It also defines what is real, valuable, and therefore demonstrable for that society. It is supremely objective in
the sense of having an internal and independent structure and cohesion of its own which determines "feelings" rather than being determined by them[20] (although, as in the case of the deep grammars
of language, this structure may be difficult or impossible to articulate). Psychology and social psychology can help explain why
individuals relate to a religious system as they do--by aversion
or conversion, subversion or support--but not how viable changes
can take place within the system itself. These disciplines can
help explain the *Schwärmer*, perhaps, and the modern crisis of belief, and also why a man like Luther was driven into the path of
theological investigation; but they shed little light on why one
theological or scientific proposal is valid and viable, and another
not, even when both are persuasive or appealing in terms of psychological or psychosocial considerations. What is crucial is the
congruence of the proposal to the inner logic of the system and its
ability to appeal effectively to what the system itself defines as
relevant evidence.

This, of course, corresponds to Luther's own view of the matter. For him it was the external, not the internal, Word which was decisive. The *testimonium internum spiritus sancti* is essential, but only when it is supported by and supports the *verbum externum*. Individuals are created or destroyed by the language systems and corresponding forms of life into which they are inducted, by the cosmic stories in terms of which they live, by the divine or demonic revelations which they internalize. To be sure, psychological and social processes dialectically interact with these ideologies, but the ideologies also have an independent efficacy of their own. That is why Luther insisted that his fundamental quarrel was with his opponents' doctrine, not with their behavior.

In concluding summary, then, Erikson's psychological portrait of Luther is, by and large (with the exception of the characterization of the childhood), historically unobjectionable, but also unprovable. Theologically, it is an *adiophron* which ought to make no difference one way or another in the evaluation of the Reformation. Secondly, Erikson's psychosocial presentation of Luther's achievement as a culturally paradigmatic identity crisis strikes me as historically, and perhaps also theologically, illuminating. Thirdly, the ideological dimension of his work with its bias towards psychological reductionism is empirically questionable from the viewpoint both of historical research and of a sociologically and anthropologically adequate theory of religion. Furthermore, it is opposed to the Lutheran theological perspective which is my own. Although it does not fall into the existentialist extreme--which Erikson himself criticizes--of supposing that meaningful identity and ideology is the free self-creation of the isolated man, still it concedes too much to the subjectivist tendencies of the enthusiasts and their pietistic and romantic successors.

FOOTNOTES

1. Roland H. Bainton, "Psychiatry and History: An Examination of Erikson's *Young Man Luther*," *Religion in Life*, (Winter, 1971), pp. 450-478; Heinrich Bornkamm, "Luther und sein Vater: Bemerkungen zu Erik Erikson, *Young Man Luther*," *Zeitschrift für Theologie und Kirche*, LXVI (1969), pp. 38-61.
2. *Martin Luther and the Reformation* (London, 1967), p. 13.
3. See R. H. Bainton, *Studies on the Reformation* (Boston, 1963), pp. 99-100 for details.
4. Erik H. Erikson, *Young Man Luther* (New York, 1958), p. 66. See also Bainton, "Psychiatry and History," pp. 460-461.
5. *Ibid.*, p. 255.
6. *Ibid.*, p. 66.
7. *Ibid.*, p. 58.
8. *Ibid.*, pp. 23-48.
9. *Ibid* p. 241.
10. Luther, *Tischreden* (Weimarer Ausgabe, rpt. 1967). V:5537.
11. Erikson, *Luther*, p. 206.
12. *Ibid.*, p. 212.
13. Owen Chadwick, *The Reformation* (Baltimore, 1964), p. 18.
14. Luther, *Werke* (Weimarer Ausgabe, rpt. 1969), XVII, Pt. i, p. 458.
15. Robert Bellah, "Father and Son in Christianity and Confucianism," *Personality and Religion*, ed. W. A. Sadler (New York, 1970), pp. 146-147.
16. Thomas Kuhn, *The Structure of Scientific Revolutions*, 2nd. ed. (Chicago, 1970).
17. Erikson, *Luther*, p. 200.
18. e.g. *Ibid.*, p. 177.
19. *Ibid.*, p. 21.
20. To quote the frequently cited recent definition of Clifford Geertz: A religion is "(1) a system of symbols which (2) establish powerful, pervasive and long-lasting moods and motivations in men by (3) formulating conceptions of a general order of existence and (4) clothing these conceptions with such an aura of

factuality that (5) the moods and motivations seem uniquely realistic." "Religion as a Cultural System," in *The Religious Situation*, ed. D. Cutler (Boston, 1968), pp. 639-688.

YOUNG MAN LUTHER AS PORTRAITURE: A COMMENT

Robert Bellah

I would like to make a speech as long as Professor Lindbeck's paper, but I will try to compress what I have to say. I would have liked to go through Professor Lindbeck's paper paragraph by paragraph. I'm not hostile to the paper, because I think it moves at least half-way in the direction that I would argue for. But it smacks of what I think is the chief sin of the historian's profession, namely, idolatry of the letter; although it's a long way from the full-blown form of that which one finds in Bainton.

I could take examples from almost every incident George Lindbeck cites. But, putting it in a nutshell, the essential issue is whether it is possible to get *a* story of Luther or not. A utopianism lies behind the idolatry of the letter in the historian's profession. I would argue that it is not possible to get one final story, no matter how long and how good the research. What Erikson has given us is *an* interpretation of Luther, an interpretation which has been compelling for many students of religion in general and of the Reformation in particular, because of the coherence of the pattern he has discerned. The fact that every detail in the picture is not accurate does not detract from the coherence of the pattern. I would make the same argument about the writings of Max Weber. Weber makes many factual errors; but in some of his greatest works he has given us interpretations which are still unsurpassed; and that, to my mind, is the thing to stress.

In my opinion, the only real critique of Erikson on Luther that will stand up is not one produced by Bainton's method of torpedoing this fact or that fact; but rather by producing another protrait of the same type as Erikson's, a portrait of the cultural development of Luther which is more compelling than the one which Erik has given us. When that comes along, I think we will recognize it. But all the arguments over details, when it does not really impugn the fundamental interpretation, is quite secondary.

A second observation which is only a specification of this general issue. It is not a question, as Professor Lindbeck has it, of the degree to which socio-cultural causes are operating as against psychological causes. There is no solution to such a problem. Rather, psychological conflict is also simultaneously a social conflict. Both types of causes are operating at once in the inextricable pattern of interdependent meanings. Freud would call this the "over-determination of a system of meaning." We can only begin to uncover the layers. We adopt an alien frame of reference, it seems to me, when we talk about the grading of causal factors.

Another issue is the question of Luther's picture of God: did he have such a picture of God because of his harsh father, or because there was a harsh God in the cultural climate? I think all the evidence in the world that the cultural condition portrayed a harsh God does not change the fact that for many people in that culture the psychological impact of that harshness did not have the meaning that it had for Luther. It comes psychologically alive somehow out of his own family context. Nor is it a question of how harsh Luther's father was on some objective spectrum of harshness, because, as we know, in the delicate pattern of the growth of the young child, balances that can hardly be discerned may yield a subjective sense of harshness; whereas in any kind of "objective" measure this particular father is not as harsh as many other fathers. At many points there are delicate questions of interpretation, of hermeneutics, which belie the type of mechanical causal structure that I think lies behind some of the criticisms that have been made of Erikson's book.

Perhaps my comments sound harsher than I feel, because I think that Professor Lindbeck very nearly escaped the particular errors I am criticising. But insofar as he finds a remnant of

psychological reductionism in Erikson's work, I still find a
remnant of idolatry of the letter in him. After all, Erikson is
a psychoanalyst, not a theologican, nor a historian of religions.
A psychological reading phrased the way Erik phrases it is not
psychological reductionism. There are psychological reduction-
ists in the literature by the dozen. We see them; we read them;
we reject them; but a reading which points out the psychological
dimensions and chooses to focus on those rather than on one other
dimensions, which is conscious of the fact that it is not
exhaustive, that it is *a* reading, not *the* reading, is not vulnerable to the charge of psychological reductionism.

PSYCHOHISTORY AND HISTORY: THE CASE OF YOUNG MAN LUTHER

Lewis W. Spitz

Among early twentieth century intellectuals who made a major impact upon the modern mind, Sigmund Freud was the "towering figure of the era."[1] He might well have taken his inspiration from Shakespeare's line in *Measure for Measure*, "Let your reason serve to make the truth appear where it seems hid." For the great achievement of psychoanalysis was a fuller and more systematic examination of the unconscious in mental life. His theories of hysteria and madness, the interpretation of dreams, the psychopathology of everyday living have trickled down into the thought patterns and vocabulary of common men all through western society. Now that the leading psychology departments are disdainful of Freudianism and medical doctors incline more to chemical cures and psychosurgery, historians have discovered the affinity of psychoanalysis to their own discipline in theory and practice, and are making fascinating applications to great men and the masses of time past. The most eminent proponent and practitioner of psychohistory, that paradigm or even discipline emerging in the area of overlay between history and psychoanalysis is Erik Erikson, whose career has spanned the Atlantic and whose exceptional mind has bridged a seemingly even greater intellectual chasm.

Psychohistory and History

Two centuries ago the historian Wegelin (1721-1791) asserted the necessity of understanding the psychology of rulers and the psychological bond with their people, the need to get at their obscure wishes and passions.[2] Historians from Herodotus to the present, in fact, have operated with certain intuited psychological presuppositions about their subjects. Psychoanalysis promises a more coherent pattern of explanations than the casual and amateurish psychological observations ventured by historians. In both history and in the theory and practice of psychoanalysis the "how" and the "why" are inseparable questions. In the search for understanding individuals and groups the deepest inquiry is concerned with motives.[3] Both probe the past, for as Freud stated in his paper *On the History of the Psychoanalytic Movement*, "it appeared that psychoanalysis could explain nothing current without referring back to something past."[4] In both facts are significant only in a context of interpretation.[5] Distrusting surface explanations, both probe the past, the individual or collective memory, and reconstruct in detail the circumstances surrounding an event. Both require sensitivity, imagination, and a feel for the significance of seemingly insignificant detail. They probe the consciousness of the individual person, the springboard for human action in a single life and in history on the collective plane. Case histories are used to arrive at understanding. The aim of both is human self-knowledge and the goal is to understand the past in order to liberate man from the burden of the past and to enable him to gain strength from the experience and understanding of the past with which to shape the future.

Psychohistory appears in two varying modalities. Historical psychology involves a study of the psychology of people who are not great men, the psychology of groups. From the school of Lucien Febvre has emerged one of the finest examples of this approach, Robert Mandrou's *Introduction a la France Moderne (1500-1640). Essai de Psychologie historique*.[6] Psychological history studies the psychology of great men, the event makers, the experiences of unique individuals without whom history might have been markedly different.

In literary, artistic, political, and religious biography and criticism, the value of psychoanalytical insights have been recognized for some time. In *Richard II*, Shakespeare, after all, had probed beneath the surface of the mind:

> My brain I'll prove the female to my soul;
> My soul the father; and these two beget
> A generation of still-breeding thoughts,
> And these same thoughts people this little world.

Psychoanalysis has proved of value in exploring the modes of subjectivity and stream-of-consciousness in the modern novel.[7] Freud with his peculiar Leonardo and pathetic Woodrow Wilson had set a precedent in the artistic and political realms.[8] Freud's *Totem and Taboo* (1913) and *Moses and Monotheism* (1939) were hardly his most substantial pieces, but in daringly arguing that religious phenomena are to be understood on the model of the neurotic symptoms of the individual, he provided a text for a materialistic psychology of religion. Historians struggled long and had to transcend the confines of traditional political and military history to a new history which would include economic, social, and intellectual subjects. But they were slow in coming to the analysis of the psychological dimension either of individuals or of groups, except for the attention paid to the pathological behavior of mobs or the hysterical behavior of sects. The call to the "newest history" was issued by William L. Langer in his 1957 presidential address to the American Historical Association in which he referred "to the urgently needed deepening of our historical understanding through exploitation of the concepts and findings of modern psychology." He was speaking not of classical or academic psychology but of psychoanalysis and its later developments and variations as included in the terms "dynamic" or "depth psychology."[9]

Charles Poore in a review of a Civil War book in the *New York Times* the week after Langer's address reconstructed a conversation which might well become a commonplace among historians and biographers:

> "Have you read the new Freudian biography of Sitting Bull by Pottowatomie Jones of Lewis Nichols University?"
> "No. But I've been helping to read proofs on the Adlerian version by Socrates Robinson, who holds the Kenneth Campbell chair of history at Princeton."
> "That should be interesting."
> "It is, in a measure,"
> "Why the reservation?"

> "Because it's taking an awful lot of time from my own three-volume history of the Black Hawk War, you know. Particularly since I'm following Jung throughout."

He suggested Lytton Strachey's *Queen Victoria* as an appropriate annual prize in the field.[10]

I Psychological Assessments of Luther

In his address Langer spoke of the case of the greatest of the reformers, Martin Luther, who reflected clearly the reaction of the individual to the somber situation of late medieval culture. He spoke of his abnormally strong sense of sin and of the immediacy of death and damnation. He suggested that Luther's trials were typical of his time and argued that it was inconceivable that Luther should have evoked so great a popular response unless he had succeeded in expressing the underlying, unconscious sentiments of large numbers of people and in providing them with an acceptable solution to their religious problem. Luther wore his heart on his sleeve and his volubility has made him a ready object for psychological analysis. The historiography of the problem has already reached formidable dimensions.

In 1837 Joseph Spriszler, a Roman Catholic priest, applied to Luther Aristotle's saying on genius in the words of Seneca: "*Nullum umquam magnum ingenium sine admixtione furiae fuit.*" No doubt Luther was a man of out-sized intellect verging on genius in creativity, brilliance and versatility. He was a heroic type, but notable more for constancy and faith than for the bravado of a Renaissance man. "We know that genius is incomprehensible and unaccountable and it should therefore not be called upon as an explanation until every other solution has failed," wrote Freud. "Everything new must have its roots in what was before. Few tasks are as appealing as inquiry into the laws that govern the psyche of exceptionally endowed individuals."[11] The attempts to understand Luther in terms of genius have indeed added little by way of explanation, inclining either toward extremes of adulation or denigration.[12]

Early in our century polemical Roman Catholic historians, following the lead of Cochlaeus Luther's dedicated defamer, portrayed Luther in unflattering terms. A Dominican, Heinrich Denifle, working in the Vatican archives, proposed what the ecumenical Father Sartory has labelled the pan-sexual interpretation of the Reformation.[13] Denifle defamed Luther as a lust-ridden monk, given to secret vices, driven to oppose celibacy and to break with the church by overpowering sexual urges. Denifle's associate, Albert Marie Weiss, O.P., in a supplementary volume on Luther's psychology revised Denifle's judgments and clarified his argument with less acerbation, and Catholic historians subsequently abandoned the thesis of Luther's moral corruption.[14] But Denifle's text provided many an uncritical Freudian with material for a libidinous interpretation of Luther. If Denifle was over-heated, the Jesuit Hartmann Grisar accorded Luther a cold trial, relating his dogmatic deviation to a pathological manic depressive psychology.[15]

The medical doctors, too, were intrigued by Luther when Søren Kierkegaard had spoken of him in his diary as "a patient of exceeding import for Christendom." In an undistinguished biography of Erasmus, John Joseph Mangan, M.D., introduced a chapter in consideration of Martin Luther in which he assembled evidences of Luther's murderous father, his demonology, sexual drives, physical ills and disturbed psychology.[16] He was sharply refuted by John Alfred Faulkner, M.D., in an article entitled "An American Doctor Looks at Luther."[17] The most exhaustive examination of Luther's physical ailments, however, was that of Wilhelm Ebstein, who noted that Luther was an accurate observer and acute diagnostician of his own ills. Although Luther observed how in his own case worries caused bodily sickness, Ebstein found that in each instance a physical illness precipitated a period of psychological depression, including that of 1527.[18] His depressions lasted two or three days at the most and did not impair his writing or academic work.

The psychologiests and psychoanalysts, too, have been drawn to this unusual man who incorporated a delicate spiritual consti-

tution in a robust physique. Ernst Kretschmer of Marburg and
Hubert Rohracher of Vienna with their peculiar theories correlating personality and body types, have identified Luther with the
cyclothemic temperament and a typical pyknic physique, qualified
by melancholic and schizothymic characteristics.[19] The heretical
Freudian C.G. Jung contrasted Luther's extroverted type with
Zeingli's introverted spiritual type and related the difference
to their position on the sacrament.[20] A great professional historian but very amateurish analysit, Preserved Smith, in 1913
published an article on "Luther's early development in the light
of psychoanalysis."[21] Smith delivered a primer of "Freudian"
observations complete with an alcoholic father, oedipal rage, obsession with the demonic, repressed elementary sexual life, harsh
home discipline, preoccupation with concupiscence, and depressions. He argued that the dogmas of the bondage of the will and
justification by faith were not attained by logical deduction
from Biblical or any other premises, but were merely interpretations of his own subjective life. The horizon began to clear
with his first call to Wittenberg in 1508, due in a measure to
the affection and help given by the Vicar General, Johannes von
Staupitz. He began to sublimate his sexual impulses to professional and intellectual interests. Combining the Catholic jaundice of Spriszler and the Danish dourness of Kierkegaard, the
psychiatrist Paul J. Reiter wrote two massive volumes on the
world about Luther and his character and psychology.[22] In his
analysis of Luther's personality, spiritual life and sicknesses,
Reiter was guided by Alfred Otto S.J., who followed Denifle uncritically in declaring Luther to have been a bad monk and accepted
the worse construction that Grisar had managed to put on things.
When Grisar says that Luther was an epileptic, Reiter concedes
that that is *gar nicht ausgeschlossen*. Otto Pfister of Zurich,
in contrast, turned attention away from Luther's physical or personal problems to the dimension of deep religious fear and his
resolution and the persistence of fear in his theology.[23] And
so the literature grows about the man on whom more has been written than about anyone else in the history of the world with the

exception of Christ.

II Erikson's Luther

Far superior to all previous attempts at a posthumous psychoanalysis of Luther is Erik H. Erikson's *Young Man Luther* (New York, 1958). Erikson presides together with the Princess Royal, Anna Freud, and René Spitz over the "exclusive but still highly creative world of classic psychoanalysis."[24] Erikson has not simply repristinated Freud, but has creatively gone beyond the master to develop on a clinical basis the idea of the life cycle, giving an epigenetic schema which is an elaboration and an extension beyond adolescence over the whole span of an individual's life into old age of Freud's theory of psychosexual stages. He relates the psychological and biological stages of development, each stage of development having crucial tasks to be done. These stages are normative for every individual, having roots in infancy and childhood, and have a strategic priority at special points in the developmental process. The degree of health of the individual depends upon the degree to which these focal tasks or the crises at each stage have been successfully met. The constructive realization of human potential takes place through and by means of the cumulative achievement of a balance of trust over mistrust, autonomy over shame and doubt, initiative over guilt, industry versus inferiority, and so forth.[25] He thus correlates the strengths and weaknesses that can arise at each stage or phase of life. In Luther's case, Erikson explains:

> The characteristics of Luther's theological advance can be compared to certain steps in psychological maturation which every man must take: the internalization of the father-son relationship; the concomitant crystallization of conscience; the safe establishment of an identity as a worker and a man; and the concomitant reaffirmation of basic trust.[26]

Erikson is surely best known popularly as well as in scientific circles for the concepts of identity and identity crisis--there has indeed been a world-wide identity explosion! In psychological terms, Erikson explains, "identity formation employs a process of simultaneous reflection and observation, a process taking place on all levels of mental functioning by which the individual judges himself in the light of what he perceives to be the way in which others judge him in comparison to themselves and to a typology significant to them; while he judges their way of judging him in the light of how he perceives himself in comparison to them and to types that have become relevant to him."[27] This is an unconscious process for the most part except in cases in which inner conditions and outer circumstances combine to aggravate a painful, or elated, "identity consciousness." In Luther's case Erikson finds a prolonged identity crisis and due to the prolongation as well as to a delayed sexual intimacy, intimacy and generativity were fused in his life. Moreover, the integrity cirisis "which comes last in the lives of ordinary men is a lifelong and chronic crisis in a *homo religiosus*. He is always older, or in early years suddenly becomes older, than his playmates or even his parents and teachers, and focuses in a precocious way on what it takes others a lifetime to gain a mere inkling of: the question of how to escape corruption in living and how in death to give meaning to life . . . This short cut between the youthful crisis of identity and the mature one of integrity makes the religionist's problem of individual identity the same as the problem of existential identity.[28]

Moreover, Erikson is concerned with society, social process, culture, and the interpersonal matters of great interest to historians, unlike many psychoanalysts who insist upon keeping their discipline "intrapsychic." Erikson attempts to deal with a process "located" in the core of the individual yet also in the core of his communal culture. In the case of Luther, this means that one cannot separate personal growth and communal change, nor can one separate the identity crisis in Luther's life and contemporary crises in historical development, because the two help to define each other and are truly relative to each other. In fact, Erikson explains, the "whole interplay between the psychological and the social, the developmental and the historical, for which identity formation is of prototypal significance, could be conceptualized only as a kind of psychosocial relativity.[29]

Finally, Erikson sees development and change in both the subject and the observer. The clinical situation, the therapeutic encounter is itself a historical situation. By analogy, this historical study of Luther initially involves the sympathy of the observer and serves as a vehicle for testing and clarifying his statement about identity and related psychological phenomena. "In *Young Man Luther*," he tells us, "I attempted to put the suffering of a great young man into the context of his greatness and his historic position . . . There is often an intrinisic relation between the originality of an individual's gifts and the depth of his personal conflict."[30] The observer is involved in the process and brings to his observations insight and wisdom gleaned from his clinical experience. Erikson's Luther is not the usual applied psychoanalysis nor is it mere biography, the story of a man in action, but it is a notable example of psychohistory. Erikson has suggested that the psychohistorian is an artist who works with "disciplined subjectivity." The distinguished historian Sir Maurice Powicke remarked that what we call the facts of history are really judgments about historical events, judgments which have an experiential base in the life and learning of this historian, and that historical generalizations are judgments about judgments. The historian must, however, reject projections analogous to Freud's "archeological reconstructions" which are mistaken, arbitrary or improbable. There is a common meeting ground between the psychohistorian and the historian, but the good historian is apt to approach that sacred ground with extreme criticality.

Erikson's work is admirable in trimming away the hagiographic mistletoe which from the days of Mathesius on has grown about the Saxon oak, such as the tales of grinding poverty and the rags to riches theme. On the other hand, he rejects the slanderous aspersions of Denifle and is critical of many of Reiter's false diagnoses. He offers valid insights into the aspects of Luther's personality either given scant attention by psychologically less sophisticated biographers or not understood in the total context of his personality and environment. His aim is to elucidate those obscure years in Luther's biography which supposedly saw the resolution of his identity crisis. Erikson pays close attention to Luther's immediate family experience and early life and to three major crises, all three legendary in nature, but intriguing.

III Analysis of the Analysis

The historian's primary objection to the work of the psychohistorian is almost certain to be that the limited source materials available, especially on the young Luther, do not supply sufficient material to sustain a depth-psychological investigation.[31] There are "grave difficulties" to psychoanalyzing the dead. The information available to the historian does not really allow for a dynamic demonstration of unconscious motivation as may be true of a living subject. In Luther's case there are only two basic references which shed direct light upon the disciplinary circumstances of his home and school, both from the somewhat suspect *Tischreden* of 1532 and 1537. The historian must also protest if the psychohistorian's projections wander imaginatively too far away from what the sources indicate or even run contrary to other available evidences. Historians are stuck with the *res particulares* and must accept with good humor charges of being idolators of the letter.

A. Martin's Family Environment. Freud laid Sophocles under contribution for the name Oedipus complex, since he did not only dramatize the myth relating the incest taboo but exposed the suppressed impulse behind it.[32] Erikson sees Luther as the victim of an unhappy home situation in which a severe love/hate relation toward his parents and harsh teachers bred in him a need to rebel. His subconscious hate of his father and drive to disobedience against his father he transferred to the pope and thus became the leader of the schism in Christendom. Here are a few typical statements from the text: P. 58: "This early doubt [whether his father was motivated by love and justice rather than

by caprice and malice] was projected on the Father in heaven with
such violence that Martin's monastic teachers could not help noticing it." P. 65: "I said that Luther could not hate his father openly. This statement presumes that he did hate him underneath. Do we have any proof of this? Only the proof which lies
in action delayed, and delayed so long that the final explosion
hists nonparticipants." Pp. 73-74: "Martin took unto himself
the ideological structure of his parents' consciences: he incorporated his father's suspicious severity, his mother's fear
of sorcery, and their mutual concern about catastrophes to be
avoided and high goals to be met. Later he rebelled: first a-
gainst his father, to join the monaster; then against the Church,
to found his own church--at which point, he succumbed to many of
his father's original values." P. 97: "The conversion was necessary so that Martin could give all his power of obedience to
God, and turn all his venom of defiance against the Pope."

The idea that Luther's father was harsh with him as a regular thing he bases upon one saying in the *Tischreden* of May, 1532,
in which Luther cautions against disciplining children too severely and says that he does not intend to punish his son Hans
too severely for, he recalled *mein vater steupt mich einmal also
sehr, dass ich ihn flohe und ward ihm gram, bis er mich wieder zu
sich gewoehnte.* (My father once whipped me so hard that I fled
from him and [felt ugly toward him; or, became sadly resentful
toward him] until he gradually got me accustomed to him again.)
Erikson criticizes Bainton's translation of *gram* as "I felt ugly"
and argues that "I became sadly resentful" really describes the
feeling of a child toward somebody he loves and that "reaccustom"
could refer only to the purpose of the father of restoring an
intimate daily association. Bainton in a recent article responds
with examples of Luther's use of *gram* as "angry" or "feeling ugly" and denies that it can mean "sadly resentful."[33] But the
historian must insist on a closer look at the best available
text, which in this case is Schlaginhaufen's transcript of the
Tischreden, which reads: . . . *mein vatter steupt mich einmal
also sehr, das ich im floh und das im bang was, bis er mich wider*

zu im gewenet.³⁴ The preferred translation should read: ". . . my father once beat me so severely that I fled from him and he was anxious until he won me to himself again." This interpretation makes the son the hold-out and the father the one who was anxious and concerned because of the unhappy situation. In any case, *bang* can hardly mean "sadly resentful." It is of some interest to note that Luther said *einmal*, once, which does not suggest a customary thing but rather an exceptional situation. *Einmal* can, of course, merely mean "once upon a time" and a psychiatrist could also argue that *once* was enough to induce a lasting trauma. But it should be clear that this passage can hardly be used to create a picture of a tyrannous or cruel father. Father Hans took the initiative in winning Martin back and there is no hint that this was done in a sentimental or unmanly way. Erikson summarizing the father/son relationship writes succinctly in a passage on page 66:

> I have so far mentioned two trends in the relationship between Hans and Martin: 1) the father's driving economic ambition, which was threatened by something (maybe even murder) done in the past, and by a feeling close to murder which he always carried inside; and 2) the concentration of the father's ambition on his oldest son, whom he treated with alternate periods of violent harshness and of habituating the son to himself in a manner which may well have been somewhat sentimental--a deadly combination.
>
> I would add to these trends the father's display of righteousness. Hans seems to have considered himself the very conception, the *Inbegriff*, of justice. After all, he did not spare himself, and fought his own nature as ruthlessly as those of his children. But parents are dangerous who thus take revenge on their child for what circumstances and inner compulsion have done to them; who misuse one of the strongest forces in life--true indignation in the service of vital values--to justify their own small selves. Martin, however, seems to have sensed on more than one occasion that the father, behind his disciplined public identity, was possessed by an angry, and often alcoholic. impulsiveness which he loosed against his family (and would dare loose *only* against his family) under the pretense of being a hard taskmaster and righteous judge.

Such a portrait of Hans, the man who looks out from Lucas

Cranach's drawing with such a plain, honest, workworn face, may well impress the historian who knows the sources as the product of *insufficiently disciplined* subjectivity. The reference to murder, of course, has to do with a story which Georg Witzel told about Luther's father. Witzel had reverted to Catholicism after a brief period as a Lutheran, and Luther once commented that given enough florins he would turn Lutheran again. In actual fact, a younger brother of Hans named Kleinhans was a ne'er-do-well and drunkard who once threatened a shepherd with a dagger. There is no evidence that he killed him, which indeed seems unlikely since in moving from Moehra to Mansfeld he remained in the same legal jurisdiction. Erikson inexplicably transfers this incident to Hans, writing, p. 57 that "the very existence of such a brother whom scandal (maybe even murder) eventually brought to town must have underlined for Big Hans the danger of losing his own hard-won position--and this especially because he himself apparently had a towering temper, and was, in fact, supposed to have killed a shepherd before coming to Mansfeld." Luther occasionally commented that no one could provide better information on his family than the counts of Mansfeld. The scattered archives of the counts of Mansfeld do indeed contain nearly everything that we shall ever know about Hans, including the story of Kleinhans. They were edited by Walter Möllenberg decades ago and should be consulted also by the psychohistorian.[35]

Nor was Luther's father an alcoholic, for the one reference to his drinking suggests a brighter scene. Luther heard that his nephew, Hans Pollner, was drinking to excess and admonished him: "Some when intoxicated are happy and agreeable, like my father, they sing, they joke, but you turn wholly to anger. Such men should abstain from wine like poison."[36] This father was elected to the city council and became one of the Vierherrn in a town to which he immigrated, built up his holdings by hard work and sober management until he owned part of six pits and two smelting operations, and left a considerable estate at the time of his death.

No, Hans Luther was not harsh, drunken, or tyrannous, but rather tender and pious as well as stern and ambitious for himself and his son. Hans was inclined to be tender and deeply moved by suffering. Luther on two different occasions recounts a story which illustrates the point: "My father was asked at Mansfeld by a certain neighbor to come and see him, for he was in mortal agony. Turning on his bed he showed him his posterior and said, 'See, dear Luther, how they beat me!' at which father was so shocked and so shaken by those reflections that he nearly died himself."[37] On one occasion Hans took Martin into a wheat field to show him the grain ripe for harvest and told him how the heavenly Father cares for us. The same man who was merry and humorous when he had belted a few joked with his wife in bed. Luther relates that his sons respect him just as he respected his parents, for his father slept with his mother and joked with her (*mit ihr geschertzt*) just as he did with his wife, and they were nevertheless pious people, just like the patriarchs and prophets.[38]

Hans was a man of genuine piety and an active churchman. He was badly shaken when in 1505 he lost two sons to the plague and reflected that he should perhaps willingly give Martin to the Lord for service as a monk. He had as a very close friend Jonas Cenmerer, a priest, and had priests and teachers as houseguests on occasion. As one of the *Vierherrn* or councilmen he signed endowments for the church and served as a trustee for prebends. In 1497, the year in which Luther went away to Magdeburg to be with the Brethren of the Common Life, Hans, the priest Johann Ledener, and the Mansfeld citizens won a sixty day indulgence from the bishop for all those who attended mass at the two altars of Mansfeld church dedicated to George, Mary, and an assortment of saints. Late in life Luther commented that his father had opposed his entering a monastery "because he knew the rascality of the monks."[39] There is no other evidence that he was opposed to monasticism on those grounds, but it is not improbable given the opposition between secular and regular clergy and the widespread criticism of the lazy and ignorant monks on the popular level as well as among humanists such as Hutten and Erasmus even before 1517.

Hans' work ethic evident in his worldly success and his work-righteous religion dovetailed very smoothly. They did not fall out of phase until he had learned from his son the evangelical way. He died in this faith in 1530. Luther wrote him a letter of consolation and held Christ the Redeemer before him. The priest asked him whether he believed what he had heard and he said, "Of course I believe it. I would be a knave not to."[40] On June 5, 1530, Luther wrote to Melanchthon:

> John Reineck wrote me today that my beloved father, the senior Hans Luther, departed this life at one o'clock on Exaudi Sunday. This death has cast me into deep mourning, not only because of the ties of nature but also because it was through his sweet love to me that my Creator endowed me with all that I am and have. Although it is consoling to me that, as he writes, my father fell asleep softly and strong in his faith in Christ, yet his kindness and the memory of his pleasant conversation have caused so deep a wound in my heart that I have scarcely ever held death in such low esteem . . . . I will not write more about my grief. It is good and godly for me to mourn as a son such a parent by whom the Father of mercy created me and by his sweat made me what I am. I rejoice that he lived in these days so that he could see the light of truth. Blessed be God in all His acts and counsels forever. Amen.[41]

Luther loved his mother much as he did his father, "for they meant well by me." Luther recounts that his mother *once* beat him until the blood flowed for stealing a nut. Such severity, which made him shy and led him into the monastery, he recalled, might be reserved for a worse theft such as a coat or money.[42] Erikson assumes that he must have been deeply disappointed with this mother, for consider what he says about marriage (p. 73). But Luther elsewhere observed how sweetly his mother sang, at 42 he invited her to his wedding, named a daughter after her, and when she was on her deathbed, he wrote her one of the finest letters of love and consolation that can be found in all literature.[43] And as for marriage, no one had for a thousand years preached about and practiced marriage in such a laudable way.[44] The psychohistorian is mistaken in projecting from an alleged disappointment in the mother to Luther's "dethroning of the Virgin Mary." Luther opposed the cult of Mary because as a part of the cult of saints he believed that the idea of Mary interceding for the sinner with her Son made Christ seem forbidding, to be approached only through an intermediary. He denied Mary the extravagant titles such as "queen of heaven" not found in the Scriptures. But he continued to cherish Mary as an ideal of womanhood and honored her as the mother of Christ. He kept an icon of Mary in his study his whole life and wrote a commentary on the *Magnificat*, recently republished by two Catholic publishing houses. Christ himself rebuked Mary though Luther did not. An analyst could perhaps do something positive with Luther's fond allegorizing of the beloved church as a she.

> She is my love, the noble Maid,
> Forget her can I never;
> Whatever honor men have paid,
> My heart she has forever.

Finally, in the same passage which recounts his mother's discipline Erikson recounted how he had once received 15 strokes from the teacher before noon. A *lupus* or spy was appointed to report any child who spoke German instead of Latin on the playground. *Once* Luther had a particularly bad day. Luther criticized such severity as well as the boredom of rote learning in school. Erikson projects with an air of seriousness that because Luther was required to speak Latin and to inhibit German, in later life he became so voluble in German. But as the translators of the new 56 volume American edition of *Luther's Works* know, he was voluble also in Latin. A survey of all the available information suggests that Martin did not have a particularly unhappy childhood so far as parents and school were concerned.[45]

B. Three Major Crises. Erikson analyzes three events and their ramifications in terms of the struggle to achieve identity, a central feature of his psychoanalytic ego psychology. He appreciates the fact that these occurrences may be only legendary, since the information about them is meager and some of the sources suspect.

1. The Fit in the Choir Loft. This incident which supposedly occurred in Luther's early or middle twenties has to do with an occasion when the preacher was reading the story of the youth,

deaf and dumb, possessed of a devil, brought to Christ by his
father (Mark 9:17), Luther is said to have fallen to the floor
of the choir loft and bellowed with a loud voice, *Non sum!* *Non
sum!* Erikson finds the *non sum* to be an expression of an identity crisis. The story, however, is told by Luther's arch-enemy
and dedicated defamer, Johannes Cochlaeus (*Rotzleffel*, Luther
called him) in his commentary on Luther's life and works published three years after Luther;s death, or more than four decades after the event. It is told, moreover, to prove that Luther
had a secret commerce with a demon. Cochlaeus' whole book is so
full of falsehoods that Cardinal Aleander warned against its publication, fearing that the reaction would make it counter-produc-
tive. Cochlaeus seems to have derived the story from Dungersheim,
another foe of Luther, who is purported to have heard it from
Nothin, who was a teacher of Luther, who remained Catholic, who
may have derived it from the Bishop of Mansfeld, in whose church
it might have happened.[46] Given Luther's supercharged medieval
religiosity, preoccupation with the fear of demonic possession
provides an immediate explanation of Luther's alleged reaction
rather than a vocational identity crisis.

    2. The Thunderstorm. During the middle of the spring sem-
ester of Luther's first term in the law school at Erfurt in 1505
he made a trip home, about which we have no further information.
On the way back he was caught in a terrific thunderstorm and a
bolt of lightening struck so close that in terror Luther vowed
to St. Anne that if he were spared he would enter a monastery.[47]
Once before on the way home he had been struck in the leg with
his own dagger and bled so profusely he had called on Mary for
help.[48] But why did he go home on this occasion? Erikson says
that the father may have demanded an accounting about his plan
to leave law for the monastery. This is possible, but Luther recalled that when he entered the father did not know it, and he
became a monk because he was terrified by lightning, feared
death, and took the vow. His father asked, suppose it was a
demon and not God. Near the end of his life Luther recalled that
his father was angry when he wrote him that he had entered the

monastery.[49] When in 1507 Luther celebrated his first mass, his father came with two wagons of twenty friends, brought beer and other gifts, and gave 20 gulden to the monastery. But on that occasion at the banquet Hans spoke and asked whether they had not heard that the fourth commandment enjoins honoring and obeying one's father and mother. In his *De votis monasticis* years later, dedicated to his father, Luther recalled that this thrust of Hans struck home.[50] There was tension then and the strain of going against his father's wishes that he study law, do well in life, and support his parents in their old age. Was there evidence of subconscious hate or was his act motivated by a drive to defy his domineering father? The motive conscious and subconscious seems to have been deeply religious, an expression of fear-motivated piety which Luther had to respond to despite the filial respect and loving concern he felt toward his father who was working so hard to support him in the best schools.

3. The Tower Experience. The *Turmerlebnis* marked Luther's breakthrough to an evangelical understanding of the concept "righteousness of God." In 1545 he related his struggle to understand St. Paul's meaning in Romans 1:17: "In it the righteousness of God is revealed." He had been taught to understand the term righteousness philosophically regarding the "formal or active righteousness" as the righteousness with which God is righteous and punishes the unrighteous sinner. He recalled:

> At last, by the mercy of God, meditating day and night, I gave heed to the context of the words, namely, "In it the righteousness of God is revealed, as it is written, He who through faith is righteous shall live," There I began to understand that the righteousness of God is that by which the righteous lives by a gift of God, namely by faith. And this is the meaning: the righteousness of God is revealed by the Gospel, namely the passive righteousness with which merciful God justifies us by faith, as it is written, "He who through faith is righteous shall live." Here I felt that I was altogether born again and had entered paradise itself through open gates.[51]

There is a massive literature debating the dating of this tower experience ranging from early years such as 1512-1513 to a late date such as 1518-1519. The tendency is now not to ascribe such great importance to this alleged event, in the belief based upon a close study of the exegetical notes from the *Dicata* on the Psalms through the commentaries on Romans, Galatians, and Hebrews, which suggests a gradual clarification in Luther's mind as to the nature of the "passive righteousness" which God bestows upon man by grace alone.

Between June 9 and July 12, 1532, however, in a Table Talk Luther described his struggle to achieve clarity about faith and righteousness and "the Holy Spirit had given him this understanding in this tower." In one of the three rescripts the words *auff diser cloaca* are added.[52] The phrase looms large in the Catholic/Protestant polemic early in this century and has stimulated analysts into a veritable frenzy of speculation about psycho-physiological relationships, oral/anal release, and the Grand Canal controversy. The east tower room on the second floor of the Black Cloister, however, contained the small library reading room with a large Bible where the monks went to read and meditate. It was not a facility. Two explanations of the phrase *auff diser cloaca* seem far more probable than the defecatory hypothesis. As early as 1919 Ernst Kroker, who had edited these passages in the *Tischreden*, in an article in the *Lutherjahrbuch*, argued that the term *cloaca* had to be used in a transferred sense in order to fit the usage of that day. The psychoanalytic explanation is all but untenable in the light of what we know now about the usage of the term by monks and precisely by the Augustinian hermits. In connection with the experience of *accedia*, the *Klosterkrankheit*, the phrase *in cloaca* as well as reference to the *locus*, was used to describe a state of melancholy in a way similar to our colloquial expression "down in the dumps." Thus Luther, troubled in conscience, fearful and anxious suddenly understands that St. Paul is speaking of the righteousness God bestows on man through forgiveness and he is lifted out of the depths into the joy of paradise.

There was a long tradition of theologians who "suddenly" perceived the meaning of a fairly common text, Augustine's confession Thomas Bradwardine, Richard Fitzralph, John Gerson, Andreas Karlstadt, Contarini, Vadian, Calvin. The medieval *stercus-cloaca* tradition of the *Humilitas* theology referred to the humility and low estate of the doer of works, not of good works themselves. Only those who have emptied themselves can come with confidence to the covenant for the forgiveness of sins. At the end of his first lectures on the Psalms Luther says literally that it is the beggars who are *latrina et cloaca, quod est verum*, who come to forgiveness. That is the meaning of the very last words which Luther wrote on a small slip of paper found after his death: "Do not try to fathom this divine *Aeneid*, but humbly worship its footprints. We are beggars. That is true. (*Wir sein Pettler. Hoc est verum.*)[53]

Once again it is evident that the nature of Luther's struggle and resolution was religious and indeed theological in nature. If the late date is to be preferred for the *Turmerlebnis*, which seems to be the growing consensus of scholarly opinion, then it was a mature man of 34 or 35 who came to a new understanding of the all-important text. Luther's time in the monastery was not basically a moratorium for identity crisis resolution but a period of soul-struggle in a religious sense.

There are other rather serious questions to be raised about the psychohistorian's use of evidence and projections. Thus the "turnabout" hypothesis on Luther's rejection of the peasants in 1525 does not hold, for Luther was completely consistent in favoring the peasants and admonishing the nobles before and after the event, but also before, after, and during the peasant revolt he opposed violence, anarchy, murder, rape, theft, and the abuse of the Gospel for worldly ends. The Reformation continued afterwards to spread as a spontaneous people's movement in many new areas of the Empire, for the common men seemed to understand Luther's consistency. Where peasant resistance to evangelical preachers was encountered in back country in subsequent years, it was due to the conservatism of Catholic peasants against evangelical innovators, not opposition to a "turnabout" or to repressors.[54]

Other matters merit discussion but can only be referred to

here. The manner of anality and scatology in the case of Luther, the sweaty realist, as Huxley dubbed the reformers, poses problems. "Love hath built its tent," sings Yeats, "in the place of excrement." The question of singularity and ego development requires further exploration. The critical theological problem of predestination and justification, the nature of Staupitz's theology and influence, the meaning of "meaning it", all deserve detailed study by the historian in dialogue with the psychohistorian. But rather than attempting to crowd a diffuse discussion of many points onto the few remaining pages, more can be gained from suggesting an alternate or at least modified reading of the evidence.

IV The Major Trend

The two most significant recent creations of psychohistory are surely Erikson's *Luther* and his *Gandhi*. In going beyond the biological analysis of some Freudians and polemicists to study Luther's emotional crises in youth and early adulthood in the familial and social setting against a background of his own clinical observation of young men today, Erikson offers a look inside which is more than historical and has the ring of truth. On the methodological problems encountered by the psychohistorian Erikson writes: ". . . a clinician's training permits, and in fact forces him to recognize major trends even where the facts are not all available; at any point in treatment he can and must be able to make meaningful predictions as to what will prove to have happened, and he must be able to sift even questionable sources in such a way that a coherent predictive hypothesis emerges." In psychoanalytic treatment of a living subject the analyst has certain ways of verifying such a hypothesis. "In biography," Erikson observes, "the validity of any relevant theme can only lie in its crucial recurrence in a man's development, and in its relevance to the balance sheet of his victories and defeats."[55] Like the psychohistorian, the historian should be able to establish a major trend which will accommodate the known sources and provide a satisfying interpretation without doing violence to any known or even probable evidences. In a well guarded vault deep beneath the New School is a depository of golden paradigms which serve as the official standard and measurement for behavioral scientists. Whatever facts about any given subject do not fit the paradigm are often trimmed or conveniently forgotten. The great beauty of Erikson's work as a psychohistorian is that he seeks out awkward data and examines them for their heuristic value especially where they create difficulties for theory.

The historian shares the psychohistorian's conviction that Luther was a most unusual young man, brilliant, sensitive, perceptive, tense, articulate, and given from early youth to "ups and downs." A sober psychological assessment suggests that he had a cyclothemic personality varying between hyper- and hypothemic levels in mood. At the same time he enjoyed a sthenic fund of initiative so that no true and lasting synchronized phase of depression and loss of initiative can be shown, not even in the difficult years 1527 and 1528 when he once suffered a depression lasting two or three days. His mood variations created complications for his personal and academic life but left the content of his professional work as a theologian basically unaffected.[56] His productivity remained unimpaired at all times. It is time, the German scholar Hans Preuss has suggested, for a major work on the wholesome Luther, now that his personality complications and existential theological depths have been plumbed.

The historian sees a "trend" in Luther's development that makes his behavior explicable in both psychological and theological terms. Luther's biographer, Otto Scheel, who asserts that there can be no talk of a particularly unhappy childhood for Martin, devotes a full chapter to the religious life in Mansfeld. That religiosity can best be described as a fear-motivated piety, and that is how Luther remembered it--Christ the stern judge. The full picture of Hans Luther reveals a man tender and pious, solicitous of his son's affection, encouraging in his son by his own religiosity and churchmanship a piety of the intense late medieval kind, which the whole environment lived and breathed.

At the same time Hans was ambitious for his own economic improvement and for the success of his eldest son. These conflicting values of an ascetic fearful religiosity and a secular assertive ambition eventually collided in Luther's life, for the course of his life led him to the ever-deepening of the religious dimension to the point where it demanded his total dedication even though it meant abandoning the career planned for by his father and on one level and for a time acquiesced in by the son "Even though" and not "because" it meant going contrary to his father's wishes. The father/son relation so far as the evidence goes was not the kind to produce a need for defiance, Oedipal rage, or an extraordinarily acute hate/love syndrome. The tension with his earthly father from the time of his decision to enter the monastery until he emerged once again resulted from his conscientious need to be earnestly and exclusively about "his heavenly Father's business." He was, in fact, sorry to grieve his father, and ironically it was in good measure his father's own piety that had contributed so much to his predicament.

Luther's mother perhaps even more so with her excessive moralism and strict discipline, however well intended, led him to the monastery, just as Luther said. His teachers, too, ingrained in him a fear-motivated piety so that, as he recalled, he turned pale at the mention of Christ the judge. The devil, too, was portrayed so realistically that he became incorporated into Luther's theology not as a superstitious hangover, but as a central operative factor.[57] The Brethren of the Common Life at Madgeburg, his teachers at Eisenach and the atmosphere at Erfurt, little Rome with its two hundred churches, combined to reinforce the religious impulses of his boyhood.

Given this ideological conditioning, the verifiable events and even the legendary incidents in the life of young man Luther fall into place. In later life Luther recalled that he had suffered depressions from youth on like those that plagued him in old age and those depressions may well have been religious in content. The fit in the choir loft, if it happened at all, can best be understood as Cochlaeus intended it as an evidence of Luther's fear of the demon rather than as a clue to an identity crisis as defined in ego-psychology. Fear of death and divine wrath rather than a subconscious urge to defy his father drove him into the monastery, just as he said. The long search in the monastery for certainty was less a moratorium while searching for identity crisis resolution than it was a struggle to resolve a religious problem acutely felt and critical because he took it and himself so seriously. His resolution was biblical, a product of his exegetical labors, just as other men of that day, Zwingli, Calvin, Vadian, Karlstadt, Müntzer found their basic answers in the Scriptures in ways analogous to but still independently from Luther's resolution.

Luther's religious preoccupation and the nature of its resolution explains the break with the papacy. He was an obedient rebel and a reluctant reformer, for as late as 1520 he "lay prostrate before the pope" and begged for understanding. He did not transfer disobedience against his father to the pope or hate from his earthly to the heavenly Father. He did not, after all break with worldly authorities such as the prince or emperor, and remained the leader of a conservative Reformation. His scrupulosity explains why he trembled when he said his first mass and why he felt struck when his father quoted a divine commandment against him. The intensity of his fear-motivated piety explains his religious rapport with the broad masses of medieval men. The gospel he preached was an answer to the fear-ridden peity which plagued the conscience of a whole generation. From 1512 to 1517 Luther gained confidence as a professor of theology, when he felt the platform firm under his feet and witnessed students taking notes of what he had to say and thousands buying the books of a *doctor in biblia*.[58] But even his new confidence and trust came and went, for in later years he wondered whether he could ever be so bold again as he had been when in 1521 he took his stand.

Seeing Luther in this light calls into question some of the central assertions of *Young Man Luther*. But Erikson's book remains, nevertheless, a great achievement. His explanation of the problem of creative genius, the nature of historical greatness, the relation of an unusual young man to his familial and social environment, and the phenomenology of religious experience constitutes a major achievement. Nor does this revised reading of the evidence subvert completely the assumptions of the psychohistorian about the intimate and delicate relations of father and son, for a father who is a sweet persuader can induce pressures more persistent than one who is overtly gross or hateful. *Young Man Luther* is a marvellous vehicle for relating in a moving parable the way an unusual youth became a great man of history. In fact, historians are in the author's debt for pointing up the great importance for history of a single man and what transpires with the "inner court." For it is, as Veronica Wedgwood observed in her *Velvet Studies*, the great paradox of history that individuals who are like the anonymous waves of the sea, mere grains of sand on the shore of time, infinitesimal dust, nevertheless are the cause of all things.

FOOTNOTES

1. H. Stuart Hughes, *Consciousness and Soceity* (New York, 1958), p. 19. I wish to thank my colleague Dr. Paul Robinson for his critical reading of this paper and many helpful suggestions.
2. Hans W. Gruhle, *Geschichtsschreibung und Psychologie* (Bonn, 1953).
3. H. Stuart Hughes, "History and Psychoanalysis: The Explanation of Motive," *History as Art and as Science* (New York. 1964), p. 42, an excellent statement of the parallels between psychoanalysis and history in aim and method.
4. Sigmund Freud, "On the History of the Psychoanalytic Movement," *Collected Papers, I*, cited in Fritz Schmidl, "Psychoanalysis and History," *Psychoanalytic Quarterly*, XXXI (1962), 532.
5. Hans Meyerhoff, "On Psychoanalysis as History," *Psychoanalysis and the Psychoanalytic Review*, XLIX, 2 (1962). 8.
6. Robert Mandrow, *Introduction a la France Moderne (1500-1640). Essai de Psychologie historique* (Paris, 1961), especially chapter 3, "L'Homme Psychique: Sens, Sensations, Emotions, Passions." Alain Dufour, "Quelques Reflexions sur L'Historiographie du XVIe Siecle," *Histoire Politique et Psychologie Historique* (Geneva, 1966), pp. 9-35, advocates "historical psychology."
7. See Leon Edel, *The Modern Psychological Novel* (New York, 1964); Leon Edel, *Literary Biography* (New York, 1959), pp. 91-122; Leon Edel, *Henry James* (New York, 1953-1972), a case study.
8. Lewis J. Edinger, "Political Science and Political Biography: Reflections on the Study of Leadership (I)," *The Journal of Politics*, XXVI (May, 1964), 423-439, recognizes the need to understand the event-makers in political history. A disciple of Wilhelm Dilthey, the founder of the modern Geisteswissenschaften, George Misch, professor of philosophy at Göttingen University, in his epochal *Geschichte der Autobiographie* (Leipzig and Berlin, 1907) explored the psychological differences of Greeks, Romans and patristic authors as reflected in their auto-biographies. One of the most fascinating psychoanalytic studies of tremendous

political relevance is that of Arnold Künzli, *Karl Marx Eine Psychographie* (Vienna, 1966), opening with the telling lines from *Die Deutsche Ideologie*: "Es zeigt sich, dasz...die Geschchte eines einzelnen Individuums keineswegs von der Geschichte der vorhergegangenen und gleichzeitigen Individuen loszureiszen ist, sondern von ihnen bestimmt wird."

9. William L. Langer, "The Nest Assignment," *The American Historical Review*, LXIII, 2 (January 1958), 283-304. Langer's address is republished in Bruce Mazlish, ed., *Psychoanalysis and History* (Englewood Cliffs, N.J., 1963). Cf. also Langer's forward to *The Psychoanalytic Interpretation of History*, ed. by Benjamin B. Wolman (New York, 1971).

10. Charles Poore, "Books of the Times," *The New York Times* (Thursday, January 2, 1958).

11. David Bakan, *Sigmund Freud and the Jewish Mystical Tradition* (Princeton, 1958), p. vi. On Spriszler, see Heinrich Bornkamm, *Luther im Spiegel der deutschen Geistesgeschichte* (Heidelberg, 1955), pp. 258-261.

12. Hagiographic in nature is Bruno Markgraf, *Der junge Luthers als Genie. Beitrag zur Luther Psychologie* (Leipzig, 1929). Demeaning in nature is Wilhelm Lange-Eichbaum, *The Problem of Genius* (London, 1931), *passim*. Of interest in connection with this general problem is Edward Hitschmann, *Great Men: Psychoanalytic Studies* (New York, 1956).

13. Heinrich Denifle, *Luther und Luthertum in der ersten Entwicklung, quellenmässig dargestellt*, I, 1 and 2 (Mainz, 1904). Adolf Herte, *Das katholische Lutherbild im Bann der Lutherkommentare des Cochläus*, 3 vols. (Münster in Westfalen, 1943) shows how Cochlawus' vitriolic fabrications have poisoned the whole stream of Catholic, and some other, historiography down to the time of the new ecumenical era in church history.

14. Albert Maria Weisz, O.P., *Lutherpsychologie als Schlüssel zur Lutherlegende* (Mainz, 1906), *Ergänzungen zu Denifle's Luther und Lutherthum*. P. 42: "Denifle was a historical researcher of the first rank, but as a historical writer Denifle was no equal to of the researcher." J. Paquier, who translated Denifle into

French, Luther et le Luther-anisme, 4 vols. (Paris, 1910-1916),
in an article in the *Dictionaire de Théologie Catholique*, 15 vols.
(Paris, 1899-1950), vol. 9, 1, col 1168, described Luther as a
"very complex pathological case."
15. Hartmann Grisar, *Luther Werden*, 3 vols. (1911-1912), English
tr., *Luther* (London, 1913-1917); and *Martin Luthers Leben und sein
Werk*, 2nd ed. (Freiburg i. Br., 1927). The pioneer ecumenical
Catholic history of the Reformation rehabilitating Luther as a
person and as a sincere character was Joseph Lortz, *Die Reformation in Deutschland*, 2 vols. (Freiburg i. Br., 1939-1940; 4th ed.,
1962). Lortz had predecessors in this rehabilitation but they
were less influenctial than he, such as F.X. Kiefel, "Martin Luthers religiöse Psyche. Zum 400-jährigen Reformationsjugiläum,"
Hochland, XV, 1 (1917/17), 7-28; S. Merkle, "Gutes an Luther und
übles an seinen Tadlern," *Luther in okumenischen Sicht*, ed. by
Alfred von Martin (Stuttgart, 1929), pp. 9-19.
16. John Joseph Mangan, *Life, Character, and Influence of Desiderius Erasmus of Rotterdam*, 2 vols. (New York, 1927).
17. John Alfred Faulkner, "An American Doctor Looks at Luther,"
Princeton Theological Review, 26 (1928), 248-264.
18. Wilhelm Ebstein, *Dr. Martin Luthers Krankheiten und deren
Einflusz auf seinen Körperlichen und geistigen Zustand* (Stuttgart,
1908). A recent retrospective diagnosis confirms Ebstein's analysis, Annemarie Halder, *Das Harnsteinleiden Martin Luthers* (Trier,
1969), on his stones in the bladder and urinary tract, 1537-1546.
Luther's observation on psychosomatic illness is in WA TR, V,
6024, p. 445: Ubi animus est aeger, ibi sequitur corpus languidum.
19. Ernst Kretschmer, *Physique and Character. An Investigation
of the Nature of Constitution and of the Theory of Temperament*
New York, 1936), pp. 225, 227, 239, 250, 256· *The Psychology of
Men of Genius* (London, 1931), pp. 155-156, "attacking the father
image in the form of the Pope." Rohracher lectures on *Characterkunde* at Vienna in basic agreement with Kretschmer. See also Jean
Delumeau, *Naissance et Affirmation de la Réforme* (Paris, 1968),
pp. 289-295: La These Psychoanalyste a propos de Luther.
20. C.G. Jung, "Der Abendmahlstreit zwischen Luther und Zwingli.

Das Typenproblem in der Geistesgeschichte," *Gesammelte Werke*, VI (Zurich and Stuttgart, 1960), 67-69.

21. Preserved Smith, "Luther's Early Development in the Light of Psychoanalysis," *American Journal of Psychology*, XXIV (1913), 360-377.

22. Paul J. Reiter, *Martin Luthers Umwelt, Charakter und Psychose*, 2 vols. (Copenhagen, 1937-1941).

23. Oscar Pfister, *Christianity and Fear. A Study in History and in the Psychology and Hygiene of Religion* (London, 1948). Pfister much earlier published a book on *The Psychoanalytic Method* (New York, 1917), with an introduction by Sigmund Freud. Pfister was a correspondent of Freud's and the only religionist for whom he had much use. Pfister was also the first clergyman to use psychoanalytic ideas and methods in his pastoral work. To be taken considerably less seriously is Norman O. Brown, *Life Against Death. The Psychoanalytic Meaning of History* (Middletown, Conn., 1959), whose 14th chapter, "The Protestant Era," is a fabric of questionable value based on a distressing amount of historical misinformation. For an intelligent critique of Brown in comparison with Marcuse, see Paul A. Robinson, *The Freudian Left* (New York, 1969), pp. 223-233.

24. Donald M. Kaplan, "Since Freud," *Harper's Magazine*, CCXXXVII, 1419 (August, 1968), 55-60. The very moving biography of Robert Coles, *Erik H. Erikson. The Growth of His Work* (Boston, 1970), is a great human document. Chapter VII, pp. 205-254, gives the *Entstehungsgeschichte* and a running resume of *Young Man Luther*. Psychiatrist Coles was himself the subject of a cover story of *Time* (February 14, 1972), 36-42. See also Henry W. Maier, *Three Theories of Child Development. The Contributions of Erik H. Erikson, Jean Piaget, and Robert R. Sears, and their Applications* (New York, 1965), pp. 12-74.

25. Perry Lefevre, "Erikson's *Young Man Luther*: A Contribution to the Scientific Study of Religion," *Journal for the Scientific Study of Religion*, II, 2 (April, 1963), 248-252, 250; the other two statements in this "Bibliographical Focus" are also worth consulting, Paul W. Pruyser, "Erikson's *Young Man Luther*: A New

Chapter in the Psychology of Religion," pp. 238-242, and Philip Woollcott, "Erikson's Luther: A Psychiatrist's View," pp. 243-248. The *textus receptus* is, of course, Erikson's *Childhood and Society* (New York, 1950), especially chapter 7, "Eight Ages of Man."
26. Erikson, *Young Man Luther*, p. 213.
27. Erik H. Erikson, *Identity, Youth and Crisis* (New York, 1968), p. 22. Richard I. Evans, *Dialogue with Erik Erikson* (New York, 1967), pp. 35-36: Identity means an integration of all previous identifications and self-images including the negative ones.
28. Erikson, *Young Man Luther*, pp. 260-261. The problem of delay in the achieving of identity, related to the need for achieving a moratorium in the monastery. This delay is especially problematical in view of the possibility that the epigenetic cycle may not have been so constant in times past as presently observed in the clinical situation. The Duth psychologist Jan Hendrik van den Berg, *Metabletica über die Wandlung des Menschen. Grundlinien einen historischen Psychologie* (Göttingen, 1960), has a lengthy discussion in chapter 2 showing that during the 16th and 17th centuries children were assimilated rapidly and prematurely into adulthood. The "cases of stupefying precocity are legion."
29. Erikson, *Identity, Youth and Crisis*, p. 23.
30. *Ibid.*, p. 249.
31. It is interesting to note that although the book received much attention from psychologists and religionists, few historians other than Greenslade, Donald Meyer, and Bainton have reviewed it. Roland Bainton has given it repeated attention, "Luther: A Psychiatric Portrait," *The Yale Review* (Spring, 1959), pp. 405-410 republished in Roland H. Bainton, *Studies on the Reformation* (Boston, 1963), pp. 86-92; "Psychiatry and History. An Examination of Erikson's *Young Man Luther*." *Religion in Life*, XL, 4 (Winter, 1971), 450-478. Of interest also are Bainton's articles "Interpretations of the Reformation," *The American Historical Review*, LXVI (1960), 74-84; and "Luther's Struggle for Faith," *Church History*, XVLL (1948), 193-206, both republished in Lewis W. Spitz, ed., *The Reformation--Material or Spiritual?* (Boston,

1962), pp. 1-7, 92-99.

32. See the sprightly essay of Edmund Wilson. "Philodetes: the Wound and the Bow," *The Wound and the Bow* (Cambridge, Mass., 1941), p. 290. Wilson relates genius and disease, superior strength and crippling disability.

33. Erikson, *Luther*, pp. 64-65; Bainton, "Psychiatry and History," *Religion in Life*, XL, 4 (Winter, 1971), 461. Both take their reading from Otto Scheel, *Martin Luther. Vom Katholizimus zur Reformation*, I (Tubingen, 1921), p. 11, which is to be found in Aurifaber's parallel text, WA TR, II, 1559, p. 134. Whoever edited Fb. 4. 76 obviously preferred to make Luther angry or sadly resentful, but this was misleading. If the word gram is taken as a noun the sentence would read: "I fled from him and was a grief to him, until he again won me over to him."

34. WA TR, II, 1559, p. 134, lines 5-7. Heinrich Fausel, *D. Martin Luther. Der Reformator in Kampf um Evangelien und Kirche. Sein Werden und Wirken im Spiegel eigener Zeugnisse* (Stuttgart, 1955), p. 4, no. 4 gives this reading: ...Mein Vater stäupte mich einmal so sehr, dasz ich vor ihm floh und dasz ihm bange war, bis er mich viwder zu sich gewöhnt hatte.

35. Walter Möllenberg, "Hans Luther, Dr. Martin Luthers Vater, ein mansfeldischer Bergmann und Huttenmeister," *Zeitschrift des Harz-Vereins für Geschichte und Altertumskunds*, CIII (1906), 169-193. For a favorable account of Witzel, see Winifried Trusen, *Um die Reform und Einheit der Kirche. Zum Leben und Werk Georg Witzels* (Munster i.w., 1956).

36. WA TR, IV- 5050, p. 636.

37. WA TR, II, 2370, p. 436; *ibid.*, 1308, p. 36.

38. WA TR, III, 3181b, p. 213; WA TR, II, 1659, pp. 166-167.

39. WA TR, III, 3556 A, pp. 410-411.

40. WA TR, I, 933, p. 470; WA TR, II, 1388, p. 81. See also Otto Scheel, *Martin Luther*, I, pp. 8-11, 14-15.

41. WA TR, V, 1584.

42. WA TR, III, 3556A and 3556B, pp. 415-417.

43. WA TR, VI, 1820.

44. See Olavi Lahteenmaki, *Sexus und Ehe bei Luther* (Turku, 1955).

45. *Commentaria Ioannis Cochlaei, de Actis et Scriptis Martini Lutheri Saxonis* (Mainz, 1549), pp. 1-2. Cochleaus, Luther's slanderous enemy, relates the incident in a few lines to illustrate *Commercium Lutheri occultum cum Demonio*.'
46. Bainton, "Psychiatry and History," p. 466.
47. WA TR, I, 881, pp. 439-440. Related in the first half of the 1530's. "Cum Martinus Lutherus *inscio patre suo* monesterium ingressus esset territus fulmine, aegerrime hoc tulit ac rescripsit: Wie, wens ein gespenst were?" Cf. Carl Stange, *Luthers Gedanken über die Todesfurcht* (Berlin, 1932).
48. WA TR, I, 119, p. 46.
49. WA TR, V, 5373, p. 99.
50. WA TR, II, 1558, pp. 133-134.
51. This account is known as *Luthers groszes Seibst-Zeugnis* and is found translated as "Preface to the Complete Edition of Luther's Latin Writing, Wittenberg, 1545," *Luther's Works*, 34 (Philadelphia, 1960), 327-338; reprinted in Lewis W. Spitz, ed., *The Reformation—Material or Spiritual?* (Boston, 1962), pp. 74-79: "Luther's Road to Reformation."
52 WA TR, III, 3232a, b, c, p. 228. No. 3232b reads: *Dise khunst hat mir der Heiig Geist auff diser cloaca auff dem thorm gegeben.*
53. Heiko A. Oberman, "Wir sein pettler. Hoc est verum. Bund und Gnade in der Theologie des Mittelalters und der Reformation," *Zeitschrift für Kirchengeschichte*, 78 (1967), 232-252.
54. See Franz Lau, "Der Bauernkrieg und das angebliche Ende der lutherischen Reformation als spontaner Volksbewegung," *Lutherjahrbuch*, 26 (1959), 109-134. Vadian's famous tract of 1521 entitled *Karsthans* shows how widely understood it was that Luther opposed "fighting and killing and consistently held to the principle that only constituted authority had the power of the sword." Cf. Lewis W. Spitz, *The Renaissance and Reformation Movements* (Chicago, 1971), pp. 346-347.
55. Fritz Schmidl, "Psychoanalysis and History," pp. 537-538.
56. This is the sensible diagnosis of Eberhard Grossmann, M.D., Th.D., *Beiträge zur Psychologischen Analyse der Reformatoren*

Luther und Calvin (Basel, 1958). Grossmann rejects the analysis of Reiter that Luther suffered from an organic endogenous cyclophrenia even in a mild form. On Calvin Grossmann simply concludes that there are a number of personality traits which contribute to the understanding of the uniqueness of Calvin but which cannot be grasped by the mere use of the notions of any constitutional typology. Horst Beintker, *Die Uberwindug der Anfechtung bei Luther* (Berlin, 1954), pp. 70-77, discusses the shortcomings of a psychological explanation of Luther's *Anfechtung* or soul-struggle.

57. See Hans Martin Barth, *Der Teufel und Jesus Christus in der Theologie Martin Luthers* (Göttingen, 1967).

58. See the precocious essay of Peter G. Sandstom, *Luther's Sense of Himself as an Interpreter of the Word to the World* (Amherst, 1961). German Luther research has not produced a full-length biography since Julius Kostlin's which was first published in 1875. Heinrich Bornkamm, who is presently engaged in writing such a work, has taken cognizance of the need fro the biographer to take the psychological dimension seriously. "Probleme der Lutherbiographie," *Lutherforschung Heute* (Berlin, 1958), pp. 20-21.

GANDHI'S FIRST FIVE YEARS

Stephen Hay

When Erik Erikson turned his attention from Luther to Gandhi, he was frawn to concentrate, not on "young man Gandhi," but on the "Middle-Aged Mahatma." One reason for doing so was that his 1962 visit to Ahmedabad had brought him in touch with persons who had worked both with and against Gandhi there when, at the age of 48, he assumed the leadership of a textile workers' strike. "Here I had witnesses," Erikson writes, candidly rejoicing in the fact that he could interview them, and thus employ his skill as an experienced clinical psychologist to enrich his and our understanding of a great historical figure. But he was also motivated by the feeling that "it was time for me to write about the responsibilities of middle age." Perhaps his deepest reason for turning away from the study of Gandhi's early years (a task I urged him to undertake when we first met in 1964) was that he "sensed an affinity between Gandhi's truth and the insights of modern psychology." Only by studying Gandhi in action as a mature leader and exponent of the "healing power" of "truth force" could Erikson hope to discover and demonstrate that affinity. Accordingly, the structure of his widely-acclaimed *Gandhi's Truth* reflects this attention to Gandhi's middle years.[1]

In this essay I take the road Erikson chose not to travel by, the road leading back to Gandhi's earliest experiences. If Erikson, a specialist in child psychology, focuses on Gandhi the mature maker of history, may not I, a practising historian, attempt to discover what Gandhi was like as a child--how he felt and thought, and how he was influenced by the behavior and ideas of those closest to him? Indeed, I have felt compelled to undertake this study of Gandhi's earliest environments and experiences by my difficulties in understanding his later actions and statements.

Some ten years ago I began an inquiry into Gandhi's role in the 1928 political crises that paved the way for the 1947 partition of India and Pakistan. Gradually I realized that before I could unravel that tangled story I needed a clearer picture of Gandhi's basic system of ideas and practices--a problem that had puzzled me ever since my first visit to India in 1948-49. On my third and fourth visits in 1959-60 and 1970-71 I visited his two home towns--Porbandar, where he was born in 1869, and Rajkot, where he lived from 1876 to 1888, when he left to study law in England. These visits gave me some awareness of his physical surroundings in his early years, and an opportunity to interview one of his younger cousins. About five years ago I began to piece together some of the evidence for Gandhi's intellectual development in his late teens and early twenties.[2] When Walter Capps invited me to present a paper on young Gandhi at the Erikson symposium, I felt I should probe more deeply into the origins of his ethical and religious ideas. But after spanning Gandhi's first eighteen years in that paper, I found I had bitten off more than I could chew, much less digest. Hence my present concentration on his first five years--a period relatively brief in time, yet more important for his emotional and motivational growth than any other in his life.[3]

For there seems to be universal agreement that the earliest months and years in a child's life are the most critical for his or her psychological development--that the basic structure and functioning of an individual's personality, psyche, or character come into being at this time. Gandhi put it this way: "The child never learns in after life what it does in its first five years. The education of the child begins with conception. . . . Then during the period of pregnancy it continues to be affected by the mother's moods, desires and temperament, as also by her ways of life. After birth the child imitates the parents, and for a considerable number of years entirely depends on them for its growth."[4] In trying to reconstruct what Gandhi experienced and did as a child, we are hoping to discover the first traces of those basic patterns of feeling and acting, learned unconsciously, by which he was moved and guided throughout his life.

Problems of Evidence and Interpretation

It follows that the more we are able to learn about a person's earliest years, the better we should be able to understand and interpret his or her actions and statements at various points in latter life. The paradox, however, is that these decisive years are precisely the ones it is most idfficult to get reliable information on. This is probably why most biographers (Ernest Jones, for example, in his *Life and Work of Sigmund Freud*) devote only a few pages to their subjects' childhoods passing quickly on to the mature years where documentation of the life and times is abundant.

In the case of Gandhi, however, the historian is fortunate to have a good deal of material relating both to his early experiences and activities, and to those of other members of his immediate (nuclear) and extended (joint) families. Two features of this evidence make it advisable to treat his first five years as a unit of study. For one thing, our most important source, the recollections of his elder sister (as told to three different interviewers) seem to refer to this period only, as she was married when Gandhi was about six and left to live with her husband's family. Then, too, soon after his seventh birthday, young Mohandas moved with his parents and brothers from his native town of Porbandar to the distant town of Rajkot, and in this new environment his experiences and activities, and his memories of them, were to change considerably.

After his sister's recollections of his childhood, Gandhi's own are our most important source of information. More reliable as evidence of how he felt, they are less detailed about his first five years, and the attitudes and experiences he recalled are less easily dated. Where Gandhi did remember an incident, I find him a truthful witness (and what man has labored more earnestly to be truthful in all respects?). He sometimes erred, however, when he tried to date an event from memory.[5]

Other kinds of evidence can help us reconstruct the various contexts or environments--geophysical, economic, military, political, social, and cultural--within which Gandhi lived as an infant and child from 1869 to 1876. Government-compiled reports in the 1870's, both in published gazetteer and census volumes and in unpublished letters and memoranda give us a wealth of data on the kingdom of Porbandar and the surrounding region. Some of this material has been effectively used by Pyarelal, Chandran Devanesen, and J.M. Upadhyaya, three scholars whose work on Gandhi's early years has been of great value to me.[6] Sociologists, anthropologists, and psychologists have published in recent decades studies of the social and cultural practices and beliefs of families to some extent similar to the Gandhi family as it functioned a century ago.[7] One living member of this family, Prabhudas Gandhi, has been most helpful in interviewing persons with some knowledge of Gandhi's childhood environment and experiences.

The main task in dealing with such a disparate body of evidence and possible interpretations is to construct, by repeated intuitive leaps of the mind, those more general patterns or structures within which all the available, reliable data can be seen as resting without being "forced" or distorted. For, to quote Albert Einstein, my favorite writer on scientific research, "we are looking for the simplest possible system of thought which will bind together the observed facts," recognizing at the same time that "there is no logical path" to the discovery of valid generalizations correlating all the evidence, for "only intuition, resting on sympathetic understanding of experience, can reach them." That we must combine both evidence and interpretation is well expressed by Lewis Namier's epigram: "What matters in history is the great outline and the significant detail." What matters even more, in my view of the historian as scientific rediscoverer of past human actions, feelings, and thoughts, and how they were interrelated, is that each detail fit harmoniously into the outline. If it fails to--if one tiny note of hard evidence jars with a great symphony of interpretation--them the interpretation must be modified until it harmonizes with all the reliable evidence that is relevant to it. As Einstein declared, "in practice the world of phenomena uniquely determines the theoretical system."8

The Gandhis of Porbandar

Two features leap to our attention when we first look at the family into which the infant they were to call Moniya was born: its large size and its high status in the community. Following the traditional joint or extended family pattern, the household was organized around the brothers of a common father. In the smaller, sunnier wing of the three-story limestone house lived one or two of the sons of the father's first wife, along with their wives, sons, and one or more grandchildren. (A third brother had moved to a distant town, and the fourth had died in an accident.) The larger wing was inhabited by the widowed second wife, her two sons (the elder being Karamchand, or Kaba Gandhi, father of Moniya), their wives and children. And somewhere there was room for a servant or two. The old house may have held between twenty and twenty-five people.9

The Gandhi family owed their high social status to the fact that their head, Kaba Gandhi, held the topmost administrative and judicial post in the port city (1872 population 14,563), and surrounding kingdom (population 72,077) of Porbandar. Other men in the family held lesser offices in the administration. Ultimate power in the city-state rested in the hands of the martial Rajput caste whose senior member, the proud and stubborn king, was addressed by his faithful Hindu subjects as "pure and sacred as the waters of the Ganges, the protector of the cow and Brahmin."10 Occupying 608 square miles of the coastal region on the Kathiawar peninsula of western India, Porbandar was so remote from the main centers of India's population and commerce that the British were content to leave it under local rule but subject to their ultimate control.

The Gandhi house was a few doors down the principal street from the king's palace, and the men of the family had been in his service for at least six generations by the time Moniya was born. Moniya's grandfather, by his astute and devoted service, had risen to the high post of dewan: chief minister or administrator of the kingdom (rather like the vizier of Islamic sultans). The King of Porbandar was so impressed by his dewan that he promised him that successive generations of Gandhi men would be given appointments in the state's administration. It appears that four out of five of Moniya's uncles were so employed, and his father, Karamchand or Kaba Gandhi, succeeded *his* father as dewan in 1845. The patriarchal grandfather, in recommending the fifth of his six sons to take his place, may have decided that the ablest, not the eldest son, should inherit the coveted chief ministership.11 (Kaba Gandhi, when his turn came to hand over the reins to the next generation, was to choose his youngest son, Moniya as his successor.)

Kaba Gandhi seems to have married three times in all. His first wife gave him two daughters but no son; this wife died young. His second wife, being sickly, bore no children at all. As time passed, he was reminded by his elders that he needed sons to perform the funeral ceremonies that would prevent his soul from wandering on earth as a disembodied spirit after his death. He was about thirty-five when he took his third wife.12 Her name, Putaliba, means "doll," or "beautiful woman," and implies that she had been an attractive baby, and would be a comely bride.

Gandhi's Mother

Considering how important Putaliba was in shaping the character and conscience of her youngest child, it is unfortunate that almost no research has been undertaken concerning her life and ideas. We are not even sure when she was born. Prabhudas Gandhi, the family historian and grandson of Gandhi's first cousin Khushalchand, recorded an elder relative's statement that Putaliba and Kaba Gandhi were married in 1857.13 Marriage ceremonies among Hindus of their caste group in those days were customarily performed when the girl was seven, nine, or eleven years old, the bride then remaining with her parents until she reached puberty.14 Putaliba was perhaps the normal age of eleven when they were married, some twenty-four years younger than her husband.

The development of Putaliba's character as a child was presumably shaped by her mother, father, siblings, and other relatives, about whom we know very little. In search of information about her family, Prabhudas Gandhi and I made a brief visit in 1971 to her native village of Dantrana, fifty-five miles inland from Porbandar. The setting is entirely rural. Her father, we were told, was a farmer who also kept a store on one side of the family house, located in the center of the village where the dirt roads come together to form a small plaza. That he was striving to move up in the world is suggested by his ability to arrange for his daughter's marriage to the dewan of a neighboring state.

That Putaliba, like her father, was ambitious for her offspring is attented by that son, for he was once reminded of a time she had been most anxious for him and his brothers to join a wedding party that would receive handsome gifts. Gandhi commented: "She had a fascination for money and for fame also," and added: "But fame is a woman [$k\bar{i}rti$ in Gujarati being a noun of feminine gender] and how can she marry a woman? All the same she had a craze for fame also."[15] At a time when his own ambition for worldly success was at its height, Gandhi at eighteen was able to win his mother's approval for his danger-fraught plan to study law in England "by showing the exaggerated advantages" of the project, which were that her sons "might thereby maintain the status of our father more or less, be well off and enjoy the good things of life." Asked later by an English friend why he had made the difficult journey to England, Gandhi gave but one reason: "In a word, ambition."[16]

Putaliba's relations with the other women in the Gandhi household when she joined them at the age of twelve or so may have been such as to put her on her mettle and to quicken the development of those qualities her famous son later recollected: her "strong common sense" and her "saintliness."[17] Imagine her situation: she was a junior wife, and the senior wife (who lived until c. 1862) no matter how considerate she tried to be, would have felt some resentment at the girl who was taking her place in her husband's life. The fact that Putaliba was a village girl, not used to city life, probably caused her some tension as she learned the more intricate rules of behavior in her new surroundings. Her village upbringing, on the other hand, may have made her physically and emotionally well-prepared to assume the strenuous domestic duties she was to grow into as the dewan's chief wife. Notice this comment by a member of the same sub-caste as the Gandhis, in a city near Porbandar, made to an inquiring sociologist in the 1960s: "I got him [my son] married to a girl from a village. She won't grumble about hard work and will pay respect to elders."[18]

A major source of anxiety for the new bride could have been her mother-in-law, Kaba Gandhi's widowed mother Lakshmima. We have no direct evidence of how they got along with one another, but we do know that it was Lakshmima's opposition to the unjust treatment of a minor official by the ruling Rajput princess in the early 1840's that had led to the princess's cannonading of the Gandhi house, the intervention of the British to stop the siege, and the retirement of Gandhi's grandfather from his position as dewan.[19] We may assume that Lakshmima was a woman of strong character, and of principle. It was customary for the mother-in-law to take her young daughter-in-law in hand and train her in the ways of the family. Although a Gujarati proverb has it that "the animosity between a mother-in-law and a daughter-in-law is as natural as that between the grinding mill and wheat,"[20] the relationship between Lakshmima and Putaliba may have been a relatively warm one. For one thing, Lakshmima was considerably older than she had been when her elder son's first and second wives entered the household. Rather than feeling the jealousy that the first wife was likely to arouse by taking away her son's love,[21] Lakshmima was probably longing for her son's third wife to give him male heirs and thus ensure his soul's safe passage into the other world. It may have been Lakshmima's insistence, in fact, that prompted Kaba Gandhi to marry again while his second wife was still living. Her sense of justice, evident in the 1840s conflict with the ruling princess, would have induced her to protect young Putaliba against any unfair treatment by the second wife or the other daughters-in-law of the family.

Still another source of domestic tension may have motivated Putaliba to try harder to win the acceptance of her husband's family--the unusual religious sect in which she was raised as a child. Gandhi once told his private secretary after meeting some weavers belonging to this sect:

> My mother was the fourth wife of my father. It was not easy even for [a king's] state minister to get a fourth wife. The search discovered her in some village near Junagadh. She belonged to this 'Pranami' sect....how could my father have any idea then....of what the Pranami *dharma* [ethical-religious duties] meant? But I came to know afterwards that in that sect there is some admixtures of Islam also.[22]

Gandhi also recalled that Putaliba's family was considered socially inferior to Kaba Gandhi's,[23] and this is corroborated by the remark on Gujarat religious sects in the Bombay gazatteer: "Of the minor sects Bijmārgis and Parnāmis have a large following among the lower classes chiefly in north Gujarāt and Kāthiāvād."[24]

The Gandhi family belonged to the dominant group of Hindu castes in Gujarat, the Vanias (elsewhere known as Baniyas), and accordingly were followers of the Vallabhacharya sect, which used the image of Krishna in its temple and domestic worship. Like any child bride, on joining her husband's family Putaliba made their religious practices her own, and her son remembered her repeating quietly the Vallabhacharya sect's prayer, "*Shri Krishna sharaṇam mama*"--"the Lord Krishna is my refuge."[25] She made offerings at least twice daily at the temple immediately adjoining the Gandhi house.[26] Worship at different Hindu temples was not mutually exclusive, and on certain festival days the Vania women would tour the various Vaishnava temples of the city, including the Pranami temple situated about a hundred yards down the lane that passed the Gandhi house, and then a few yards along another lane to the right.

Whatever her anxieties on first entering the Porbandar Gandhi household, Putaliba proved herself worthy of her husband's family by giving birth to their first son, Lakshmidas, sometime between 1860 and 1863. In view of the importance to her of this event, and consistent with the beliefs of her time, she probably repeated innumerable prayers, made frequent offerings at the temple, gave alms daily to religious mendicants and the poor, and kept fasts on certain days of the lunar month--all in order to gain the favorable result the family had hoped for so long to achieve. For the birth of a son was not just a lucky event; it was thought to be the "fruit" of good *karma*: good actions, good words, and good thoughts, and of the favorable intervention of the gods or goddesses to whom prayers, gifts, and promises were made. So also the survival of an infant at a time when infant mortality was high. And a good wife had to fast and pray for her husband's health and longevity as well. A nearly contemporary source tells us that on certain days of the year, "some high caste married women, to lengthen their husband's lives, fast during the whole day;" or, "to ensure male offspring... worship the sun on Sundays, sometimes for twelve years."[27]

The extraordinary piety that her youngest son later observed in Putaliba must have had its roots in her childhood training in a village community where religious beliefs were firmly held, but it was undoubtedly stimulated and further developed by her experiences as a successful bearer and nourisher of male children in a highly-placed family that desperately needed them. She and the rest of the family probably perceived her religious practices as a vital factor in producing the much-prized first son. Then the birth of a girl as her second child was followed by the much preferred arrival of a second boy, Karsandas, in 1866 or 1867. With each subsequent son, her standing in the family rose, as did her physical and emotional capacity to look after, not only her own little ones, but also other family members (her aging mother-in-law, most importantly), and her husband's many guests. By the time she was heavy with her fourth child, she must have felt a sense of security in the family and a confidence in her own powers as a mother she could not have known when she first arrived in Porbandar. Presumably, being herself both more loved and more practised in loving than before, she was able to give each successive child an increasing measure of devotion. At the age of about twenty-three, her body also had reached its optimum ability to nourish the growing embryo in her womb, and to sustain it with rich milk after its birth.

The Infant Moniya

In addition to being definitely a "wanted" child, the baby boy born on October 2, 1869 seems to have been genetically endowed with an unusual amount of physical and nervous energy. An aunt recollected how attractive he was as a child: "He had a wide shining brow, a well-shaped nose and bright eyes."[28] These qualities may have been noted by the Brahman astrologer who was called in to cast the baby's horoscope; in any case, he produced a very auspicious one and predicted that the child would become a learned man and a fine dewan like his father.[29] It is of course sheer speculation, but it seems to me possible that these favorable signs may have caused Putaliba to wonder is she had just become the mother of the savior, the *avatār* promised in the final chapter of her parent's Pranami sacred book, the chosen one who would be at once the awaited Christ of the Christians, the Imam or Mahdi or the Muslims, and the Kalki avatar of the Hindus, whose coming would bring to an end the present degenerate age and the religious divisions that have grown up in it.[30] The imagination of the rest of the women in the Gandhi household might not have soared so high; at most they would have seen in the charming baby the Balakrishna, (Krishna in the form of the divine, playful child) whose worship was common in both their Vallabhacharya sect and in the Pranami sect.

Custom decreed that each babe would be named by the father's sister as soon as the astrologer decided what its first initial had to be. Kaba Gandhi's sister Mulibehn picked the name Mohandas, "slave of delusion," perhaps poking fun at her forty-seven year-old brother for having a fourth child so late in life, for Mohan also refers to the infatuation produced by an arrow of the god of love, the Hindu cupid. His parents, however, called him by the more affectionate pet name of Moniya, or little Mohan.

The emotional advantages to Moniya of his being the youngest child strike us particularly when we consider how long a time his mother may have nursed him before weaning him. There is no way to establish just when this important change in his relations with his mother took place, but several observers of child-rearing practices in Gujarat and adjoining regions inform us that late weaning has been a common practice in Hindu families. The closest of these observers to Gandhi's time and location, a Gujarati-speaking Christain missionary and brilliant student of Rajkot Brahman, Untouchable, and Jain customs, reported: "...the mother goes on nursing the child, sometimes up to five years if no other child be born in the interval, though nowadays [1920] it is considered wiser only to nurse a child till it is about two years of age. The mother feeds the child quite irregularly, any time night or day when it cries...."[31] This pattern of feeding on demand was confirmed by a study in the Central Provinces (now Madhya Pradesh), which also found weaning to be a very gradual process, thus giving the infant minimal emotional stress: "Breast-feeding is irregular but frequent, depending on when the child cries. Weaning is deferred as long as possible, and a child may continue to suck intermittently after weaning, frequently for several months, sometimes for more than a year." A more recent study in Rajastan, by an Indian-born British psychiatrist, agreed in general with the Central Provinces study and noted that the age of weaning in upper caste Hindu families was customarily between one and a half and two, but that "the youngest child of a family may have a prolonged suckling period. The mother of one of my informants...[of the Vania caste grouping, like the Gandhis] told me that he still occasionally took the breast when he was six years old."[32]

The chances are that Moniya, being the youngest, was weaned late, and gradually. Not so his next elder brother Karsandas, however, for Putaliba became pregnant before he was one and a half, and "it is thought injurious to the foetus for a mother to continue suckling while she is pregnant."[33] The contrasting, and clashing, characters of the two boys (a point I shall soon take up) tend to bear out this contrast in their experiences. So also does Gandhi's reproachful reference to his own mother (in connection with her avoidance of Untouchables), which could be based on an actual memory of her:

> Were she alive and did the same thing, I would first bow down to her [taking the dust from her feet and putting it on his head, the proper way to show reverence to a parent or teacher] and then protest, 'What's this you are doing.' I would tell her, 'This is certainly anything but the religion I sucked from your breast.'[34]

But even before his weaning was over, how much of his mother's attention could little Moniya have monopolized during his first few

years in the world? Not only had she three older children to look
after, but as the wife of the head of the large joint family with
numerous kinfolk in the city she had to see that food was prepared
for many people daily. Naturally she had servants, and by this
time the help also of her elder brother's daughter, who had joined
the family as the bride of Kaba Gandhi's orphaned half-nephew and
adopted son, Khushalchand. This niece told her grandson Prabhudas
that an average of twenty people sat down to the main meal every
day at about noon and that Putaliba

> ...would never eat until everyone else had eaten, including the small children, and never used to get angry or be rude to anyone. [This suggests there were others in the family who were less good tempered.] Even though there were many servants, daughters, and daughters-in-law, she was never idle. From morning to midnight she used to work in the house and kitchen. She was very simple in eating. She would eat from whatever was left over, and would see that nobody in the family ate less than they needed.35

How Moniya was affected by his mother's alternating between
loving care for him and her duties to the rest of the family is
suggested in Erikson's hypothesis about Indian family life as he
observed if (largely, it appears, in Gujarat):

> The deep nostalgia for usion is reborn, it seems, from generation to generation out of the diffusion of the mother in the joint family, in which she must respond to each and, at the same time, to all.... For the child wants his mother to himself, while she must spread her love.36

Compensating for this diffusion of the mother's attention, however,
is "the unbelievably intense importance in Indian life of aunts
and uncles and of brothers and sisters"--and, in Moniya's case most
especially, of his first and second cousins. "The wider family,
therefore, permits a closeness, often expressed physically and
affectively in true 'togetherness'...."37 This picture of physical and emotional closeness among the members of joint families
fits neatly what our best informant on this period, Putaliba's
niece, had to say about the Gandhi family during Moniya's first
four years. She recalled that her aunt, "having to look after a
large family...seldom had any leisure for him [Moniya]. It was
left to the younger women in the house to play with him."38 My
wife and I have observed in India that in families with *ayahs* (the

word means "nurse," but "second mother" comes closer to the actual role performed) a child is never left to cry, but is picked up and soothed immediately. The Gandhi womenfolk, in this same spirit of complete care, probably never allowed little Moniya to be hungry, dirty, or sleepy for very long. And we should bear in mind that theirs was a society where being a mother was the highest privilege a woman could aspire to (and a clear proof of good *karma*). It is easy to see why the grown-up Gandhi was so fond of jokes and teasing, and so aware of those around him, when we imagine him (justifiably, I think) as the typical one year-old described by two veteran students of child behavior:

> The year-old child likes an audience. This is one reason why he is so often the very center of the household group. As such he shows a Thespian tendency to repeat performances laughed at. He enjoys applause.[39]

Under His Sister's Care

As soon as he was able to move about on his own two legs, that is, by the age of a year or fifteen months, Moniya began coming into closer contact with his brothers, sisters, and cousins. The closest of them for the next two years was his sister, for she was given the task of taking care of him throughout the day, as elder sisters all over the world often are. From four to six years his senior, she was also growing through the years when girls may take real pleasure in "mothering" a smaller sibling.[40] Her budding maternal instincts were undoubtedly encouraged by her mother, who knew it would not be long before her daughter would herself become a bride and then a mother. Raliatbehn, or Goki as she was known in the family, recalled in her old age how lively a child her younger brother was, and how closely she had held him (probably planted securely on her hip, in the usual South Asian fashion):

> Moniya could be said to have grown up on my lap. I used to carry him in my arms when I went out for a walk or for recreation. Mother used to be worried lest I should drop him or lose sight of him. Moniya was restless as mercury, could not sit still even for a little while. He must be either playing or roaming about. I used to take him out with me to show him the familiar sights in the street--cows, buffaloes and horses, cats and dogs. He was full of curiosity. At the first opportunity, he would go up

to the animals and try to make friends with them. One of his favourite pastimes was twisting dogs' ears.[41]

Growing up with a sister a few years older seems to be one of those little-noticed but important features of the childhood of some public men with unusual self-confidence and ambition; Abraham Lincoln, Karl Marx and George McGovern are among those who enjoyed this advantage. Moniya was perhaps even more fortunate than they in that his sister was old enough to act as a mini-parent, and it may have been her constant teaching of the rules of proper behavior, the "do's" and "don'ts" that two and three year olds must be patiently trained to obey, that laid the foundations for his extemely sensitive conscience. Likewise his immense verbal facility as an adult could well have owed much to his sister's day-by-day lessons in correct speech (in Gujarati, of course) during his third and fourth years. She would also have protected him both from harming himself (a distinct possibility, given his curiosity and, in Erikson's apt phrase, his "locomotor restlessness and energy"[42]), and from the blows of other children.

A Sibling Quadrangle

Those blows probably came most often from his brother Karsandas, who was about five when Moniya was three. This was the brother who, when they were in their mid-teens, led Mohan into painful conflict with his parents' mores by urging him to eat meat and to pick some gold out of his armlet to pay for their secret feasts. If we follow Erikson's suggestion that the saintly man needs in his youth a "counterplayer"[43] whose bad example he uses as a stimulus, reacting against which strengthens his own striving to be good, then the better candidate for this role would be, not Karsandas' friend Sheikh Mehtab, who entered his life only in his adolescent meat-eating period, but Karsandas himself. That they differed in temperament was attested by Gandhi's reminiscence on the day he learned of his brother's death:

> Karasandas and I were very fond of each other. Being about the same age we were together most of the time. He was of a very different temperament. He would be very upset if I did not join him in the things I did not like. Still he was very affectionate to me. Not

> to fit in with your own brother's wishes is something
> to be regretted. Unfortunately, I had to feel that
> regret all the time, for not agreeing with his ideas,
> I could not help hurting him.[44]

In their early years, it was more often Karsandas who hurt Moniya than the other way around.[45] Once--it may have been when they were six and four respectively--Karsandas struck Moniya, who ran to his mother. When she suggested he hit back, he reproached her, saying it was her duty to restrain Karsandas rather than urge him to fight.[46] This is the first recorded instance when Gandhi refused to return blow for blow, and it is probable that the knowledge that he could not win that way against his bigger brother was an important factor inducing him to adopt the policy of non-violence at this early age. He sometimes used this pragmatic argument in his mature life, telling his followers both in South Africa and in India that they simply could not win by force of arms because the British (and the Boers) had all the weapons. Karsandas evidently had different views on the role of force in human affairs: when he grew up he joined the police department in Porbandar.

Moniya's relations with his sister and brothers may be seen as prototypical of his later relations with females and males. Though physically weaker than most men as an adult, he persevered in his line of action when threatened by them, but without retaliating. Often he received valuable support from women, and he prized such support highly. Ultimately he prevailed over his male opponents without using force, but in almost every case the non-violent struggle was long drawn-out. These same patterns may also be said to have characterized his relations with his two older brothers in the nine years from the family's move to Rajkot from Porbandar to his father's death in 1885, shortly after the sixteenth birthday of the son he then called Manu. To the extent that there existed a sense of rivalry among the three sons, the youngest one ultimately "won out," and received his father's portentous deathbed blessing: "Manu here will keep up my reputation. He will increase the fame of our lineage."[47]

To understand the feelings of those involved in this sibling quadrangle let us imagine how Karsandas and Goki might have felt about their younger brother. For Goki he was a new baby to play with, more tractable than his predecessor, Karsandas, because younger and smaller. Presumably she had been given, or assumed, a protective role over Karsandas when he was a toddler, and this experience would have made her both more confident and more competent in looking after Moniya. Karsandas, however, had good reason to resent Moniya's arrival in the family after he, Karsandas, had enjoyed for two years the special treatment accorded him as the youngest, and as a male child. As a suckling infant, Moniya first absorbed his mother's attention, and then, after a year or so, he monopolized his sister's playtime hours as well. Karsandas could well have regarded Moniya as a double usurper, and felt justified in hitting him every now and then just to work off his hostility. Karsandas' relations with his elder brother Lakshmidas might also have been frustrating at times, and a blow from him could have set off a chain reaction, resulting in Karsandas's inflicting blows on Moniya, who then ran to his mother for more effective protection than his sister could provide. As for Lakshmidas' role in the childhood life of his younger brother we have no anecdotes to serve as clues, but he appears from his photograph a mild-mannered person, and Gandhi wrote of him, "My brother's love for me was boundless, and my devotion to him was in proportion to it."[48] Lakshmidas may therefore have at times protected Moniya against Karsandas, thereby only increasing the latter's feeling (not unusual for the middle one of three sons[49]) of being frustratingly "boxed in."

    Meanwhile, down at thr bottom of this fraternal pecking order, Moniya was becoming aware of his cousins as well. His presumed feelings of physical weakness would have increased as he came in contact with his three boy cousins, the sons of his father's younger (and only full) brother, all of them older than he. Another half-cousin was two years older, and two younger boy cousins more distantly related were born when he was two or three and five or six. And there were probably girl cousins in the household also. The contant presence of so many children, most of them older, and the customary joint family rule that except in sleeping arrange-

ments all the children were to be treated equally regardless of
who their parents were must have been both stimulating and sometimes frustrating to little Moniya. It was not a coincidence, I
think, that he surrounded himself with similar groups of people
in his later years, recreating the joint family pattern of communal living in one ashram after another: Phoenix Settlement and
Tolstoy Farm in South Africa, the two Satyagraha Ashrams at Kochrab and Sabarmati (Ahmedabad), and his final one at Sevagram in
Madhya Pradesh.[50]

The Ethos of the Elders

Overarching the world of the small children of this large
family, shaping their developing characters by providing models
of behavior and administering rewards and punishments, was the
world of the grownups--"the elders," as Gandhi calls them in his
autobiography. Although as a child his comprehension of why they
acted and disciplined him as they did was necessarily vague, as
an adult he adopted and actively propagated the rationale by which
their conduct had been guided. The linchpin holding their system
of ideas together was the assumption (so congenial to the thinking
of the small child, keenly interested in animals) that in every
living creature's body (and even in stones) dwells a soul (the
$\bar{a}tma$, $j\bar{\imath}va$, or $j\bar{\imath}v\bar{a}tma$). Why then did some souls inhabit the
bodies of humans, others the bodies of animals? Wasn't this unfair, especially when some humans were well-born and respected,
and others poor and despised, even touching them being thought defiling to one's own soul? The accepted answer rested on two further assumptions: that each soul was reborn countless times in a
succession of different bodies ($sams\bar{a}ra$); and that the worldly
status of the body it entered in each birth was determined by the
innate properties ($bh\bar{a}va$) acquired as the result of all its previous activities ($karma$). It followed from these assumptions that
the members of the Gandhi family, because they occupied highly respected positions in society, must be the vehicles for very advanced souls--souls whose good actions in previous bodies had
caused them to be born in a family whose prescribed social duties

(*dharma*) were more difficult to perform than the average, more laden with responsibilities requiring special purity and effort to carry out successfully. Proper performance of these difficult duties, however, was thought to speed the soul in its progress towards eventual release (*moksha*) from the painful necessity of being incarnated again and again.

There were numerous consequences of these universally held beliefs for the Gandhi family. One was a profound inner certainty about who they were and what they were to do in this life, a certainty evident in their famous son from at least the age of eighteen onward (and visible in his face in the photograph taken at that time). Another was a strong sense of duty, corresponding in part to the European idea of *noblesse oblige*, and conducing to the development of habits of constant self-scrutiny and obedience to the voice of conscience--"the inner voice," Gandhi called it. Along with inner certainty and fidelity to duty went an extremely strong social conservatism. It was axiomatic that the son must follow his father's calling in life: it was for that precise purpose that his soul was incarnated in that particular family and no other. As a leading cultural historian of Gujarat has explained:

> The castes were not allowed to compete with one another. A man born in a particular group was trained to its manner, and he found it extremely hard to adjust himself to a new way. Each man was said to have his own specific nature (*sva-bhāva*) fitting him for his own specific function (*sva-dharma*) and changes of Dharma or function were not encouraged....51

Yet another consequence was a reverence for parents approaching the intensity of religious worship in the *bhakti* or devotional tradition. Gandhi's filial piety is well expressed in his autobiography and in his comments to his private secretary, as we shall see later in this essay, but the depth of his feeling of self-suffering love cannot be grasped except in the context of this theory of the soul and its progress towards *moksha* through the faithful performance of its special duties--in this case those binding a son to obey and serve his parents.

No doubt Moniya at the age of two or three had only the faintest glimmer of this theory, but its application by his elders to the minutiae of their daily tasks created around him from the day of his birth a life-style and an emotional atmosphere--an ethos and an accompanying pathos--that gradually built itself into his own neuroendocrine system. We might characterize this life-style as one of minute self-regulation, each member of the family performing her or his alotted duties, primarily for the good of her or his soul, and secondarily for the good of the family and clan. What those duties were in each case was laid down by tradition, and changed only as a person aged and passed from one stage of life to the next. The children were all trained to assume the duties of the elders of their sex: The girls to become wives and mothers in the households of whatever husbands their parents chose for them, the sons to carry on the work of their father, and to remain under the father's roof after he had provided them with brides of their own. To a child growing up in such a family tradition, there was only one choice to be made: to do as it was told either carelessly or conscientiously, for to rebel was hardly thinkable, let alone possible. Unlike attitudes toward parental authority in the contemporary American family, however, blind obedience to elders and to the training they imparted was in Hindu families considered a blessing productive of both worldly and trans-worldly rewards. "Wealth is fickle when one does not get the chance of serving one's elders," remarked a Brahman respondent to a sociologist studying family life in a Gujarat town similar to Porbandar in the 1960's; and a respondent there (from the same Modh subcaste as the Gandhis) observed: "In [the] joint family we learn to live for others. We have responsibility for our parents, brothers, sons and other relatives."[52]

The Nonviolent Father

Such was the ideal the Gandhi family strove to live up to, and Kaba Gandhi, the head of the family, was described by his wife's niece as exemplifying it:

> [He] gave up his sleep and his leisure to see to the

> happiness of the people under his protection. Even
> though earning more than any of his relatives, he
> spent almost nothing on himself, and saw that his
> remaining money went to buy food and clothing for
> those in the Gandhi clan earning the least; he was
> constantly looking for ways to help them get ahead
> in life.[53]

His youngest son remembered him slightly differently, and summed up his character with these five attributes: "a lover of his clan, truthful, brave and generous, but short-tempered."[54] As to the temper, he recalled:

> He was a very strict disciplinarian. "No; you will
> do this, not that." "This has got to be done." "What's
> this nonsense?" "Who did it this way?" came out from
> his lips with irresistible finality. He insisted on
> having his way always.[55]

Evidently Kaba Gandhi "ran a taut ship." So did his son Mohandas when he assumed the functions of a dewan--not in Kathiawar, but first as *de facto* leader of the Indian community in South Africa from 1894 to 1914, subsequently in India as chief executive of the nationalist movement between 1920 and 1946, in both roles emulating his father's skill in solving "the most intricate questions and in managing hundreds of men."[56]

To his three year-old son, the fifty year-old father must have seemed a godlike figure--dignified, kindly, and protective, but at times erupting in wrath. Moniya would have observed him at home as the patriarch surrounded by relatives and visitors, or seated in the position of honor on the wooden platform at the entrance to the nearby temple to Rama. As the men talked, the dewan would peel and slice vegetables for his wife to cook, and those sitting near him would join in the work. From where he sat, Kaba Gandhi had a good view of the main street connecting his house with the square in front of the king's palace, the square where his sons and nephews loved to play games.[57] Once when one of Moniya's younger playmates slapped him, Moniya did not hit back, but quietly led the boy to his father, who warned him not to do it again. This playmate, in his old age, recalled that the dewan's son was called by the neighbors Mohanbhai (brother Mohan, a respectful form of address) "since he belonged to a well-to-do house," and that "nobody tried to be familiar with him or to tease him."[58]

Putting this incident alongside the one of his appealing to his mother to stop his brother from fighting with him, we get the picture of a boy who look to his parents to protect him and to discipline those who threatened him. In his refusal to hit back at his brother I have suggested an element of expedience, but in the case of his later refusal to retaliate against a younger boy his non-violence seems to have been based on principle. Perhaps Moniya was modeling his behavior on his father's, for he could not recall Kaba Gandhi ever using corporal punishment on his sons.[59] But the father did resort to the more agonizing punishment of making those in his care feel guilty by hitting himself on the forehead, loudly, several times to dramatize his grief over their lapses--a method the grown-up son was also to employ.[60] The use of bodily force was also inconsistent with the father's public demeanor as a judge and revenue administrator: under the old Mughal Empire system, which the Rajput states generally adopted, the dewan and his officials were charged with civil and revenue work, while military and police duties were performed by the governor and his subordinates. In this way the king could use each "to keep a strict and jealous watch" over the other, a check and balance system that made his own position more secure. The dewan thus could not punish, except by such non-violent means as withholding pay or refusing promotions or appointments to desirable offices.[61]

Kaba Gandhi's observance of non-violence probably had its roots in the soul theory already outlined and in the social divisions it sanctioned. For physical force, and even worse, the passion of anger which accompanies it, were believed to mislead the soul into identifying itself with its gross and temporary vehicle, the physical body. Observance of *ahimsā*, or non-injury to the bodies housing other souls, was therefore an essential requirement for advanced souls if they were to progress toward full consciousness of the separateness of the soul from all passions, and from the succession of bodies those passions tied them to. The same reasoning imposed a ban on eating meat or taking intoxicating beverages or drugs, all of which aroused the bondage-making

passions. These restrictions on what went into the body gave the
Gandhis and the other Vania families of Gujarat the conviction
that they were morally superior to the meat-eating and liquor-and
opium-taking Rajput clans of their region, even though the latter
exercised military and political power over them. This did not
seem to bother the Rajputs, who were happy to employ Vanias, as
well as Brahmans, to administer their states. Not only their sober habits, but also their customary thrift made Vanias good officials, and their aversion to violence virtually guaranteed the
ruler that they would never attempt to seize his power. A Vania
dewan could defy his Rajput employer, as both Kaba Gandhi and his
father Ota Gandhi did on occasion, but his defiance would take
the form of a fast or a refusal to obey a command he considered
unjust. It is not difficult to find in this Rajput-Vania symbi-
osis a foreshadowing of two aspects of the grown-up Gandhi's relationship to his military-minded British rulers: cooperativeness
on the whole, but non-violent non-cooperative when necessary.

The right to bear arms and to use them to enforce the laws
and the commands of the ruler was not exclusively the right of
Rajputs in old Porbandar, for both the king and his dewan employed
Arab Muslim mercenaries as personal bodyguards. The Gandhi family
admired the loyalty and courage of the leader of the Arab guard
who had died defending their house against an attack in Ota Gandhi's time, and had a plaque inscribed to his memory in the temple
adjacent to the house.[62] We can picture the three or four year-
old Moniya making friends with one of his father's Arab guards
(their knowledge of Gujarati may not have been much greater than
his), and feeling the thrill a little boy does at watching a
strong, armed man who has sworn to protect him with his very life
if necessary. Such a picture is consistent with Gandhi's great
admiration in his mid-teens for the stronger and more courageous
Muslim boy, Sheikh Mehtab, and with his lifelong respect for the
physical courage of India's Muslims.[63] And the alert little Moniya probably joined the other boys of Porbandar in watching the
troops of the Bombay Army disembark at the port on the other side
of the town, stand or parade in formation, and march off to the

interior.

Troop movements were common in the years of Moniya's childhood, for the Bombay Government had grown impatient with the unsettled state of the western part of Kathiawar, and it set up a special police force with headquarters at Porbandar to suppress the roving bands of outlaws that had long been pillaging villages in the region. By April 1874 the Porbandar Commission had killed or captured 140 outlaws, thus giving "warning that the pleasures of outlawry will now be brief and its punishment swift."[64]

Considering these troubled conditions, we can imagine the anxiety of the Gandhi family when Moniya disappeared one festival day when he was three years and nine months old, an age at which an active child tends to resist being directed and often goes "out of bounds."[65] His sister had taken him with her on the Goyro or Molakat holiday in July (when unmarried girls went around to all the temples making offerings to the gods and asking for the boon of a good husband) and he had slipped away from her in the crowd. After the family had searched the city for him in vain, he was brought back at nightfall by one of the group of girls he had followed to the lonely Bajeshwar temple outside the city's medieval walls.[66] His parents must have given him a good scolding for his escapade to make him feel the dangers of getting lost again.

Apparently prompted by this scare, Kaba Gandhi decided that new security arrangements were needed to keep his youngest son from harm. He had just grown too big and active for his elder sister to keep up with. And so Rambha, a widow of good family (a Vania like the Gandhis) who lived nearby was engaged to take complete charge of him, and was instructed to keep him in her sight at all times.[67] Childless herself, she took readily to her new assignment, becoming physically even closer than his mother to Moniya, feeding him his meals and sleeping alongside him.[68] She became very fond of him, and he in turn grew very attached to her, without however giving up his practice of roaming the neighborhood. Her protecting watch over him, in fact, gave him greater liberty than before to move about without danger.

Still more evidence might be added to fill out this sketch

of the life of the Gandhi family during Moniya's first four years, but the main outlines are fairly clear. It was a family of extremely high social status; its adult members had a strong sense of duty and active service, both towards other members of the family and towards the wider society around them. It was also a large family, made up of several brothers, their wives, children, and some grandchildren. Male dominance was the rule, the women serving the men. Moniya, one of the littlest members of the group, was well cared for by the womenfolk, and especially by his sister. From an early age he was probably made aware that great things were expected of him. There were times when he was hit by other children, but for the most part his earliest years were ones of great physical and emotional security. A psychic core was established during his first four years, a complex system of neural pathways, that was from then on to give him a strong inner sense of his own worth, and of harmony between his inner self and the world around him.

Possible Effects of His Father's Absence

Most of these basic patterns continued into his next year, but one fundamental change came about that stimulated a particular kind of socioemotional growth at about the end of his fourth year. In the next year--his fifth--he probably drew closer to his mother than he had been at any time since his first year, and in so doing he came even more strongly under the influence of her daily conduct and the system of values by which she regulated it.

The critical event that ushered in this new pattern was his father's departure late in 1873 for Rajkot, a five days journey inland, to take up an appointment as a judge on the newly-created Rajasthanik Court. Rajkot was a city-state in the center of the Kathiawad Peninsula where the British were developing a complex of political and educational institutions in order to "reform" the semi-independent Rajput principalities of Western India. Even though Kaba Gandhi knew no English, British officials had visited Porbandar numerous times and reported back to Rajkot favorably on his knowledge of customary law, his ability as an administrator, and his general integrity.[69] Hence he was regarded as a good nominee when the Rajasthanik Court was set up to adjudicate the many disputes over boundaries and revenue rights between the Rajput rulers and their subordinate landholders.[70] Apparently Kaba Gandhi liked his new surroundings, for in November 1874 he accepted an appointment as dewan to the young ruler of Rajkot State; the British, who had the power to veto such appointments, quickly sanctioned it, on the condition that he resign his dewanship in Porbandar. Kaba Gandhi returned to Porbandar to do this and to have his eldest son Lakshmidas married. He then took Lakshmidas and his bride, as well as his orphaned nephew Khushalchand and his wife, to Rajkot, where he put the young men in the British-supervised school and let their wives take care of the household. According to Prabhudas Gandhi, Kaba Gandhi left Putaliba in Porbandar to take care of his aged mother Lakshmima.[71] Perhaps, however, he was just being cautious, not wanting to move the whole family until he was sure his new job would work out satisfactorily. Two years later when the Rajkot prince came of age and was given full powers by the British, he confirmed Kaba Gandhi as his dewan.[72] Only then did Kaba Gandhi bring his wife and two younger sons to Rajkot, putting the boys in primary school there.

Kaba Gandhi's absence from his family for most of the three years from late 1873 to late 1876 must have affected Moniya's emotional development in several ways. He probably sensed a loss of protecting care from elder males in the family—not only from his father but from his cousin Khushalchand and his eldest brother as well. Moniya's uncle Tulsidas succeeded to the dewanship of Porbandar, and apparently became the *de facto* head of the Gandhi household there as well. From Gandhi's references to this uncle in his autobiography, the feelings between them do not seem to have been very warm.[73] The opinions of British officials on Tulsidas (or Chackan) Gandhi were not favorable, quite in contrast to their reports on Kaba Gandhi.[74]

This loss of emotional (and potentially of physical) support from three elder males came at a time when it is natural for a child to experience a period of fearfulness.[75] One ingredient in the fears of a four and five year-old may be the fear of death, especially so if a death occurs in the family and makes the child vividly aware that he or she will some day surely die. Such a death had come when Moniya was two or three to his aunt Mulibehn's husband--a tragic death, as this uncle was still in his early thirties. Moniya may also have been upset by the death of a baby girl, an event frequent enough in those days of high infant mortality and probable enough considering the small proportion of females recorded in the Gandhi family tree.[76] And it is possible that, despite all explanations to the contrary, the boy may have interpreted his father's continuing absence as another death in the family.

Another way his father's absence may have affected Moniya's emotional evolution can be inferred from the change it probably produced in his mother's life-style. Her husband being no longer the city-state's chief minister, she no longer had to do the work she used to of preparing food for him and his many guests. Probably her sister-in-law, Tulsidas Gandhi's wife, took over from her the direction of the kitchen and the household servants, and Putaliba would then have had more time to look after her daughter and two younger sons. She might well have felt anxious for the health and safety of her distant husband--and for herself and the children, since he was no longer there to watch over them. Possibly she experienced a revival of the anxieties I suggested she felt earlier as a junior wife from an inferior branch of the caste, trained as well in a different religious sect from the other women. Whether or not she experienced greater anxiety, the mere fact of having more free time coincided with Moniya's greater need of her attention because of the departure of his father, senior elder brother, and favorite male cousin.

Early Spiritual and Religious Education

At four and five, a child becomes interested in religious ideas and activities especially if his or her parents are religious, and accepts with few questions their beliefs and practices.[77]

Moniya seems to have followed this pattern, except that the absence of his father and his consequent closeness to his mother appear to have encouraged him to identify completely with her ways, more than with his, and to accept her beliefs insofar as he could understand them. We find evidence that he did this in at least five ways: by fasting, telling the truth, praying, believing in God, and finding joy in helping and serving others.

Moniya seems to have been especially impressed by his mother's frequent fasts, for he imitated her example and understood her motivation. "At a very early age I began fasting for self-purification," he once wrote. Her longing for purity became his, as did her second motive for fasting. "Our mother used to pray and fast for us," he reminisced during the last of his many prison terms. "It was her love for us that made her fast."[78] A Hindu mother in New Delhi made clear to me this second purpose. When she was worried about her talented son's lack of seriousness in his studies, she vowed to go without food every Tuesday. Perceiving her concern for him, he soon mended his ways and became a very good student. She continued to observe her vow, however, as it had not been taken to coerce him, but was a promise made by her to her God. Gandhi's non-public fasts were similarly motivated, his main aim being self-purification; he did hope, nevertheless, that his example would help others to try to lead purer lives.

In later life, Gandhi made it clear that his ideal of inner, spiritual purity was derived from his mother's practices and beliefs. "My mother was a lovely lady of extraordinary purity. She was a treasury of virtues. If I look stainless and bright before you, it is due to her."[79] "If you notice any purity in me," he told his personal secretary, "I have inherited it from my mother, and not from my father....I have been a witness of her behaviour in the flower of youth, but never did I see in her any frivolity, any recourse to beauty aids or interest in the pleasures of life. The only impression she ever left on my mind is that of saintliness."[80] Asked by a South African woman for the origins of his concept of God, he replied: "From my childhood, remembering my mother's constant visits to the temple. Sometimes these were as many as four or five a day, and never less than two. Also my nurse used to tell me I must repeat the name of God if I felt afraid."[81]

His mother's influence on his moral and religious development was supplemented in several ways by his nurse's example and instruction. Asked by Vincent Sheean for the origin of his practice of imposing on himself self-restraining vows (such as fasting, days of silence, eating before sunset, etc.), he paid tribute to both women: "I owe them [the vows he had taken] first of all to my saintly mother and to my good nurse. These were noble women. They taught me to tell the truth and not to fear."[82] Their teaching, that truthfulness and fearlessness go together, seems to me the point of origin for the mature Gandhi's faith in the almost magical power that comes to one who is completely truthful.

Gandhi credits his nurse Rambha with teaching him another way to calm his fears: calling on God in the form of His incarnation Rama. Recalling Rambha's affection for him, he writes: "I had more faith in her than in her remedy, and so at a tender age I began repeating Ramanama [the name Rama] to cure my fear of ghosts and spirits. This was of course short-lived, but the good seed sown in childhood was not sown in vain."[83] Like the mustard seed, the prayer later grew to startling proportions: "What I learnt in my childhood has become a huge thing in my mental firmament. It is the sun that has brightened my darkest hour."[84] Revived in middle age, Gandhi's use of the prayer to Rama increased as he grew older, and was on his lips in his last conscious moment.

Even during his absence, Moniya's father also played a role in nourishing the seed of faith. Both Kaba Gandhi and his father before him were devotees of Rama, and Kaba Gandhi used to hold court every day in the entrance hall to the temple to Rama and Rama's grandfather, Raghunathji. Seated on a raised wooden platform, he would hear complaints and pleas and give his decision on behalf of the ruling king, who considered them final.85 Whether with his nurse, his grandmother, or his mother, Moniya went frequently to the temple where his father used to sit: "My memory revives the scenes of my childhood when I used daily to visit the

Ramji Mandir adjacent to my ancestral home. My *Rama* then resided there. He saved me from many fears and sins. It was no superstition for me....Temple worship supplies the felt spiritual want of the human race."[86] Worshipping his father's God seems to have been a way of re-experiencing his father's protective presence, and of gaining the courage he needed to rid himself of fear and the temptation to be "bad."

Kaba Gandhi's widowed mother Lakshmima, than in her last years, may also have influenced her grandson Moniya's spiritual and religious growth in ways he did not write or speak of, or even recall. A Hindu widow in Kathiawar was expected to live on an abstemious diet, keep her hair close-cropped and her clothing undecorated, and to spend her remaining days in penitence for the sins of her previous lives--for only her bad *karma* could explain why her husband had died before she did.[87] A local historian in Porbandar says that, according to oral tradition, Moniya as a toddler used to be seen holding onto his grandmother's finger as she took him along to the temple for worship. This was probably in the afternoon, when the ladies of the Modh Vania families used to gather in the temple to hear religious stories recited and to chant popular hymns.[88] Lakshmima's piety may have exceeded and stimulated her daughter-in-law's, and the religiosity of these two women, along with that of the widowed Rambha, would have made an indelible impression on the young mind of the child whose care thay all had a share in.

But of the three, Gandhi preserved most vividly the memory of his mother. This was natural, as he spent his life up to the age of eighteen under her influence, whereas Lakshmima died when he was about six, and Rambha appears to have been left behind when the family moved, shortly afterward, from Porbandar to Rajkot. How deeply he had experienced his mother's love, and how selfless and spiritual he had felt that love to be, is suggested in his attempt many years later to describe his experience of God's presence:

> Seeing God face to face is to feel that He is enthroned in our hearts even as a child feels a mother's affection without needing any demonstration. Does a child reason

out the existence of a mother's love? Can he prove it to others? He triumphantly declares: "It is." So must it be with the existence of God. He defies reason. But He is experienced.[89]

The Beginnings of His Joy in Selfless Service

Gandhi's love for his mother--his response to her love for him--can similarly be seen as the first stage in the gradual development of his desire to imitate her example of selflessly serving others. Here is how he recalled her when he was thirty-eight (his words being summarized by an interviewer):

> When Mr. Gandhi speaks of his parents, those who listen realise that they are on holy ground....But above all, it was the mother who won the boy's unreserved devotion. His voice softens when he speaks of her, and the light of love is in his eyes. She must have been a beautiful character....She was severely religious. Folk whispered that they had known her to fast for seven days at a time, and life was all religion with her; she made it the atmosphere of the home. She believed in stern discipline, yet withal, this mother bore such a strain of tenderness and sympathy in her heart, that the children clung to her with boundless affection. If there were sickness in the home, she would sit up night after night discharging the duties of nurse. If any one nearby was in need, Brahmin or Shudra [next to lowest of the five main caste groupings], she was the one to render help as soon as possible. Every morning the old gate was besieged by twenty or thirty poverty-stricken people, who came to receive the alms or the cup of whey which was never refused....It was her influence, more than any other, that formed the character of her boy.[90]

All these traits--severe religiosity, strenuous fasting, stern discipline, tenderness and sympathy, patient nursing, and readiness to help those in need--can be documented many times over in the later life of her youngest son.

Seeing every day his mother's example of selfless service-- and his nurse's--Moniya began to find a special kind of pleasure in imitating her by being of help whenever he could. In this respect he was like the American youngsters observed at the Yale Clinic of Child Development in the 1930s. "FIVE enjoys helping his mother and running errands. He likes to please, to do things in the right, accepted way....FIVE is 'good' because he loves his mother and wants to please her."[91] But Moniya seems to have worked unusually hard at being helpful--certainly in later life he demonstrated this trait most sedulously and successfully--and his own memory of this period suggests why:

> I was my mother's pet child, first because I was the smallest of her children, but also because there was nothing dearer to my heart than her service. My brothers were fond of play and frolic. I found not much in common with them. I had no close bond with my sister either. Play had absolutely no fascination for me in preference to my mother's service. Whenever she wanted me for anything, I ran to her.[92]

Embedded in this reminiscence is, I feel, a sense of triumph at having discovered the way to secure his mother's affection--and not only her affection, but also her greater attention to him than to his elder brother Karsandas. The fact that he felt loved by his mother with special intensity appears to have brought to an end his earlier anxiety about his brother's hostility, and thus completed the foundations of a strong sense of his own worth as a person. Freud, who had experienced as a child both the frustrations of a Karsandas and the triumph of a Moniya, ascribed to Goethe also the feelings of victory that follow such puny wars: "He who has been the undisputed darling of the mother retains throughout life that victorious feeling, that confidence in ultimate success which not seldom brings actual success with it."[93]

Gandhi gives two reasons for his mother's special fondness for him. One was merely an accident of his birth: the fact that he was her last, and therefore her smallest child. His aunt, Putaliba's niece, confirmed this part of his recollection: "Being the youngest in the family, he was his mother Putaliba's pet."[94] Had a fifth child appeared after him, he or she (but especially a he) would have displaced Moniya as the apple of his mother's eye. In smallness, therefore, lay an inherent souce of importance: in weakness there was strength. Here, possibly, was one of the roots of Gandhi's later genius for identifying himself with the underdog, the outcaste, the poor, and the sick. Here also was an experience consonant with his mature conviction that genuine humility was a source of great strength in dealing with other persons.

The second reason Gandhi gives for his mother's partiality toward him refers to an acquired rather than an accidental trait: his delight in being of service to her. He must have felt her attention to him varying during his first four years, from his first years, when she fed him at her breast, to the next years, when he was placed in his sister's care. Now that his mother was closer to him again, with no husband and fewer household duties to distract her, he may have reasoned that special efforts on his part were needed to secure her attention and keep it constant in the future. On her part, Putaliba was probably pleased by his willingness to help her. In addition to having him run errands she could not do herself because of purdah restrictions, she may have had him cut and peel vegetables for her, as her absent husband used to do. For Moniya such demands appeared as signs of special favor, indications that he had moved up in the world, leaving behind the infantile stage of always being helped, and entering the higher stage of helping others--as his mother, nurse, and others in the family, both male and female, were doing.

A chance remark by Gandhi in 1940 on the subject of protecting cows suggests the possibility of a third causative influence for Moniya's delight in serving his mother. "Our mother gives us milk for a couple of years and then expects us to serve her when we grow up."[95] Did Putaliba continue to nurse her youngest child at her breast as a reward for his helping her in her household duties? Such a deliberate policy on her part could have stimulated his pleasure in serving her, a pleasure noticeably greater than that of his older siblings, who had long since been weaned.

Some Later Continuities

By the age of five, the evidence suggests, Moniya had already taken his first steps along the path of selfless service he was to pursue with increasing effectiveness for the rest of his long life. As he moved along, his actions were rewarded with the approval of his elders, for he was demonstrating his obedience to the ethos on which their high social status depended--a status they expected him to help maintain when he grew to manhood. His earliest training in service came from his mother, and this prepared him to respond with equal eagerness to the demands of his father during the next ten years from the time they joined him in Rajkot in 1876 until Kaba Gandhi's death in 1885. Notice in the following reminiscences of this period how young Mohandas felt that love from parents to child was expressed in demands for his services, while the performance of those services had the effect of increasing the parents' love:

> Nobody in the world, perhaps, has tasted the joys of parental love [*mabapno prem*, the parent's love for him] as much as I. My claim in that matter is very high. If I am told that so-and-so loves his father or mother more than I, I would say, "All right, bring him to me; let me test him first." My parents had surrendered themselves to my love. My father would never ask any of the servants to do anything for him, but he would insist on my doing it. If it was water that he wanted, or a shampoo of his legs, or any other personal service, small or big, there was sure to be a call for me. He simply doted on me. It is hard to find a father so loving as he.
>
> Haven't I told you that I have gained everything from *pitribhakti* [literally devotion to father, but in this passage implying devotion to mother as well] and *pitriseva* [service to father and mother]?...[Here Gandhi related the incident of his seeing the pictures and reading the story of the boy Shravana carrying his aged parents on their pilgrimage, and his dying on the way.] It struck me, "May I not serve my parents with the same devotion? And I have actually done it. Mother insisted that I and none else was to press [massage] her legs, and Father would never accept any service whatever from anybody else. I would go on pressing his legs at night, till he would cosily fall asleep. That happened till the last day of his life.[96]

Erikson has dealt sensitively with the "double shame" Gandhi felt the night his father died--one shame being that he so desired his pregnant wife that he was absent at the moment of his father's passing, the other being that the child his wife was carrying was born prematurely soon afterward, and died a few days later. Gandhi's main regret was that he had lost the "privilege" and "honour" of serving his father in his last moments.[97]

Two years later, at eighteen, the whole point of making the long, expensive, and (in the eyes of his caste) defiling voyage to study law in England was to live up to his father's expectation that he was the son most capable of carrying on the duties of a chief minister. At first his mother withheld her permission, fearing he would be corrupted by the immoral customs of the British. But, he explained later, "fortunately I was the pet of my mother. She had much faith in me, and so I succeeded in getting [her] over her superstition...."[98] Recalling his homesickness during his first weeks in London, Gandhi wrote, "I would continually think of my home and country. My mother's love always haunted me. At night the tears would stream down my cheeks and home memories of all sorts made sleep out of the question."[99] Throughout his three-year study of the law in London, he seems to have pictured himself as serving his mother on his return.[100] On landing in Bombay in 1891, his eldest brother informed him that she had died only a few weeks before. (It was quite possibly her fasting on his behalf which brought on the stomach ailment that caused her death in her mid-forties.[101]) Young Gandhi retired to a bathroom and wept for about an hour. When he emerged, dry-eyed, he announced: "Now that the real mother is no more, I shall serve India as my mother."[102]

Fifty-six years later, then in the last year of his life, Gandhi was closely studied by a sympathetic yet independent-minded professor of anthropology who served as his interpreter and secretary in Bengal, Nirmal Kumar Bose. Bose concluded (perhaps underrating somewhat the importance of Gandhi's father's influence):

> The love for saintliness, for hard vows and an unflinching adherence to them even in the midst of severe trials, in other words, a heroic devotion to high ideals, were all apparently imbibed by Gandhiji from the example of his mother's life. For these very traits in his mother's character had evoked the deepest admiration within his soul while he was yet very young....This mother-cult of Gandhi's boyhood days remained throughout his life a very strong element in his philosophy, and he tried to enlist men and women in private as well as in public life to his cult of purity, love and self-suffering. This mission of civilization, which was Gandhi's greatest contribution to modern life, was thus, in the last analysis, an external projection on the larger canvas of the world's life of the saintliness which was embodied in that noble woman who shone like a pole star over her son's great

life.[103]

A Summary and a Methodological Reflection

Many other continuities between Gandhi's boyhood and his adult attitudes, motivations, and aspirations might be adduced, but I must postpone that work until I have completed the detailed description and analysis of his middle childhood years, his adolesence, and his young adulthood that will fill the book I am now writing. Let me therefore conclude with a summary of the main patterns or hypotheses, that seem to me supported by the evidence available to me:

1. Moniya was a *gifted child*, genetically endowed with an unusual amount of energy, and probably more intelligent than his two elder brothers. (His later success in the high school at Rajkot, compared with their failures at the progressively more difficult examinations there, tend to bear this out.[104])

2. In his earliest years, as later, the development of his social skills were *stimulated by a high level of interpersonal interaction* with the many adults and children in the joint family household.

3. Throughout his first five years both his physical and his emotional needs were *constantly cared for by the women and girls of the family*, especially by his mother (who possibly weaned him late), his sister, his grandmother, and his nurse.

4. There are grounds for believing that during his fourth and fifth years he *developed some anxiety over the absence of his father*, as well as *conflict with his next elder brother*.

5. As part of his natural maturation in his fifth year, and motivated to allay this anxiety and overcome this conflict, he developed an *intense devotion to his mother and to her way of selfless service to others*.

6. Partly in response to his devotion and services to her, *his mother was especially affectionate to him*, more than to his two elder brothers. Her attachment to him thus reinforced his to her, and strengthened both that deep self-confidence and that practice of humble and loving service Gandhi displayed at so many

critical points in his mature life.

7. Through a combination of these factors, and perhaps of others I have overlooked, Moniya the boy began to feel what Bose calls "a heroic devotion to [the] high ideals" of his elders, and consequently to their religious beliefs and spiritual practices--a devotion that was to grow ever stronger throughout his adult years, once he had, as he put it, "crossed the Sahara of atheism" in mid-adolescence.[105]

Our present understanding of the totality of the experiences and activities of individual human beings, may be compared to the degree of understanding of the physical world achieved by the ancient Greeks. We have made remarkable progress in understanding the physical realm in the past twenty-five hundred years, but remarkably little in understanding ourselves. Progress in the natural sciences has even created mental obstacles to progress in the human sciences, for our fascination with the qualities and movements of objects has persuaded us that all understanding must be objective--an impossibility when our attention is focused on subjective experience itself. The time has come for a larger view of the nature of scientific understanding, a view that can do justice to the complexity, variety, affective quality, and other characteristics of the unique-yet-comparable, ever-changing-yet-often-similar subjective experiences of individual persons.[106]

As one contribution to this emerging scientific understanding of personal experiences, I offer the foregoing preliminary study of Gandhi's childhood experiences. Others may compare it with their inquiries into the basic patterns of feeling, acting, and thinking of any individual person at any point or points in his or her life. As the natural scientist does, I have tried to gather as much evidence as I could, providing it was both as reliable and as relevant to the inquiry as possible. I have also designed as many hypotheses as seemed necessary to correlate this evidence in the most complete and fair manner possible, providing these hypotheses passed as many tests of consistency with the evidence and with each other as I could think of. For the most ingenious hypothesis without a shred of evidence to support it is as empty of real meaning as are mountains of evidence without hypothesis-like interpretations to bring out their interconnections. My ideal has been to see each fragment of evidence as a significant part of one or more larger wholes. For, as Einstein noted, the aim of scientific thought is "to bring together...the perceptible phenomena of this world into as thorough-going an association as possible. To put it boldly," he added in words the historian of childhood should find encouraging, "it [science] is the attempt at the posterior reconstruction of existence [and is not human experience a vital part of existence?] by the process of conceptualization."[107]

While scientific work involves striving for the utmost accuracy, what Aristotle had to say about the study of politics is true for work in the human sciences generally: "It is a mark of the educated man and a proof of his culture that in every subject he looks for only so much precision as its nature permits."[108] In trying to reconstruct what Gandhi experienced and did as a child, I have had to make use of diverse kinds of evidence, some of it more reliable, some less, and the sum total of it very incomplete. My intuitively constructed hypotheses[109] connecting these fragmentary clues to how a particular child felt, acted, and thought are therefore necessarily imperfect and incomplete. They represent this particular inquirer's "tentative but persistent groping for more reliable generalizations about the real world that is the heart and soul of scientific work."[110] They therefore await, and invite, whatever corrections and improvements other, better-informed, and more insightful scholars can provide--and I hope especially that among those scholars will be some whose childhoods have been spent in Gujarat families somewhat similar to Gandhi's in their cultural and social practices, beliefs, and aspirations.[111]

FOOTNOTES

1. Erik H. Erikson, *Gandhi's Truth: On the Origins of Militant Nonviolence* (New York: W. W. Norton & Company, 1969), pp. 52, 440, 247, 410 ff.
2. "Between Two Worlds: Gandhi's First Impressions of British Culture," *Modern Asian Studies* 3.4 (1969), 305-19; "Jain Influences on Gandhi's Early Thought," in *Gandhi, India, and the World: An International Symposium*, ed. Sibnarayan Ray (Philadelphia: Temple University Press, 1970), pp. 29-38.
3. Also since the conference I have decided to write my next book on Gandhi's formative experiences from birth to the age of twenty-five, when (at the end of his first year in South Africa) he resolved both an inner crisis of religious belief and an outer one of worldly vocation.
4. M. K. Gandhi, *An Autobiography: Or, The Story of My Experiments with Truth* (Boston: Beacon Press, 1957), p. 204; also in *Collected Works of Mahatma Gandhi* (New Delhi: Ministry of Information and Broadcasting, 1958-), 39:165.
5. For example, Gandhi writes in his autobiography that he was thirteen at the time of his marriage (*Works*, 39:11), whereas a photograph in the Gandhi Smriti (Museum), Rajkot, of the Rajkot State Treasury register shows that the Rajkot ruler's wedding gift was disbursed on April 14, 1881, when Gandhi was eleven. See also J. M. Upadhayaya [Upadhyaya], *Mahatma Gandhi--A Teacher's Discovery* (Vallabh Vidyanagar, Gujarat: Sardar Patel University, c. 1969), pp. 43-44.
6. Pyarelal, *Mahatma Gandhi. Volume I: The Early Phase* (Ahmedabad: Navajivan Publishing House, 1965); Chandran Devanesen, *The Making of the Mahatma* (New Delhi: Orient Longmans, 1969); for Upadhyaya's two books, see n. 5 above and n. 104 below.
7. See notes 1, 18, 20, 31, and 32.
8. Albert Einstein, *Essays in Science* (New York: Philosophical Library, [c. 1950?]), p. 113; Albert Einstein, *Ideas and Opinions* (New York: Crown Publishers, 1954), p. 226; L.B. Namier, *Avenues of History* (London: Hamish Hamilton, 1962), p. 8; Einstein, *Ideas*,

p. 226.
9. Conversation with Prabhudas Gandhi in the Gandhi house, Porbandar, 7 Mar. 1971. See also nn. 11, 12 below.
10. *Census of the Bombay Presidency, 1872. Part III* (Bombay: Printed at the Government Central Press, 1875), pp. 709, 424; National Archives of India, Kathiawar Political Agency (hereafter NAI, KPA), 1881, vol. 32, comp. 115, p. 445.
11. See the genealogical tables in Pyarelal, *Mahatma Gandhi, Volume I, The Early Phase* (Ahmedabad: Navajivan, 1965), p. 184 b-c, and Prabhudās Chhaganlāl Gāndhī, comp., *Otābāpāno vaḍlo* [Ota Gandhi's family tree (in Gujarati)] (Amadāvād: Navajīvan Prakāshan Mandir, 1972), part 2, p. i, and appendix 1, p. 1.
12. Prabhudas Gandhi, *My Childhood with Gandhiji* (Ahmedabad: Navajivan Publishing House, 1948), pp. 18-19.
13. *Ibid.*, p. 19.
14. *Gazetteer of the Bombay Presidency. Volume IX, Part 1. Gujarat Population: Hindus* (Bombay: Printed at the Government Central Press, 1901), p. 90; R.B. Govindbhai H. Desai, *Hindu Families in Gujarat* (Baroda, 1932), p. 275.
15. Mahadev H. Desai, *Day-to-day with Gandhi. Secretary's Diary*, tr. Hemantkumar Nilkanth (Varanasi: Sarva Seva Sangh Prakashen, 1970), 5:297 (entry for 15 Feb., 1925).
16. Gandhi, *Works*, 1 (2nd rev. ed., 1969), p. 44, 6:432, 1:42.
17. Gandhi, *Autobiography*, pp. 4, 5, in *Works* 39:8, 9.
18. I.P. Desai, *Some Aspects of Family in Mahuva* (New York: Asia Publishing House, 1965), p. 186.
19. Pyarelal, *Gandhi, Early Phase*, pp. 176-78.
20. A.D. Shah, *Gujarātī kahevatasamgraha* [A collection of Gujarati proverbs], p. 175, as quoted in G.S. Ghurye, *Family and Kin in Indo-European Culture*, 2nd ed. (Bombay: Popular Book Depot, 1962), p. 312.
21. See Ghurye, *Family*, pp. 311-14, for examples of such jealousy in folk literature.
22. M. Desai, *Day-to-day*, 5:118-19; H. Desai, *Hindu Families*, p. 280.
23. Pyarelal, *Gandhi, Early Phase*, p. 186.
24. *Gazetteer of Bombay*, 9.1:530.
25. Pyarelal, *Gandhi, Early Phase*, p. 201.

26. F. Mary Barr, *Bapu, Conversations & Correspondence with Mahatma Gandhi* (Bombay: International Book House, 1949), pp. 116-17.
27. *Gazetteer of Bombay*, 9.1:400, 394.
28. P. Gandhi, *My Childhood*, p. 25.
29. Narrated to me by Prabhudas Gandhi, 4 March 1971, who heard this from his grandfather, and from his grandmother, who was Putaliba's niece.
30. F. S. Growse, "The Sect of the Prān-nāthis," *Journal of the Royal Asiatic Society of Bengal*, (1879) 48.1:171-80. See also Pyarelal, *Gandhi, Early Phase*, p. 214.
31. Mrs. Sinclair [Margaret] Stevenson, *The Rites of the Twice-born* (London: Humphrey Milford, Oxford University Press, 1920), p. 20.
32. William Stephens Taylor, "Basic Personality in Orthodox Hindu Culture Patterns," *Journal of Abnormal and Social Psychology*, (1948) 43.1:10; G. Morris Carstairs, *The Twice-born: A Study of a Community of High-Caste Hindus* (London: Hogarth Press, 1957), pp. 150, 64.
33. *Ibid.*, p. 64.
34. M. Desai, *Day-to-day*, 6:18.
35. Prabhudās Gāndhī, *Jīvannum parodh* [At the dawn of life] (Amadāvād: Navajīvan, 1948), p. 18. This and other Gujarati passages in this article were co-translated by Indira Shah and myself.
36. Erikson, *Gandhi's Truth*, p. 42.
37. *Ibid.*, p. 32.
38. P. Gandhi, *My Childhood*, p. 25.
39. Arnold Gesell and Frances L. Ilg, *Child Development. An Introduction to the Study of Human Growth*, 2 vols. in one (New York: Harper, 1949), 1:125.
40. "Seven....is a time when girls in particular may manifest an intense desire to simply hold a baby, and to have a baby in the family." Gesell and Ilg, 2:315.
41. Pyarelal, *Gandhi, Early Phase*, p. 194.
42. Erikson, *Gandhi's Truth*, p. 108.
43. *Ibid.*, pp. 134-40.
44. P. Gandhi, *My Childhood*, pp. 122-23.
45. "Six may be bossy with a young sibling. He argues, teases,

bullies, frightens, torments, makes him cry, hits him, gets angry with him, and may on occasion fight terrifically." Gessel and Ilg, 2:120.

46. Pyarelal, *Gandhi, Early Phase*, p. 195.
47. P. Gandhi, *Jīvannum paroḍh*, p. 23.
48. Gandhi, *Autobiography*, p. 115 in *Works*, 39:76-77.
49. Conversation with William Altus, Dept. of Psychology, UCSB, November, 1966; Theodore Lidz, *The Person: His Development Throughout the Life Cycle* (New York: Basic Books, 1968), p. 222.
50. "All had their meals in a common kitchen and strove to live as one family," he wrote of the first Ahmedabad ashram at Kochrab. *Autobiography*, p. 396, in *Works*, 39:315. See also his *Ashram Observances in Action* (Ahmedabad: Navajivan Publishing House, 1955), p. 3: "I feel that an ashram was a necessary of life to me."
51. M.R. Majumdar, *Cultural History of Gujarat (From Early Times to Pre-British Period)* (Bombay: Popular Prakashan, 1965), p. 191.
52. I.P. Desai, *Some Aspects of Family*, pp. 169, 186.
53. P. Gāndhī, *Jīvannum paroḍh*, p. 18.
54. Gandhi, *Autobiography*, p. 3, in *Works*, 39:7.
55. M. Desai, *Day-to-day*, 1:61.
56. Gandhi, *Autobiography*, p. 4, in *Works*, 39:8.
57. P. Gandhi, *My Childhood*, p. 17; conversation with Prabhudas Gandhi at Porbandar, 8 Mar. 1971.
58. P. Gandhi, *My Childhood*, p. 29.
59. Gandhi, *Autobiography*, p. 27, in *Works*, 39:27.
60. Gandhi, *Autobiography*, p. 28, in *Works*, 39:28; M. Desai, *Day-to-day*, 1:61; P. Gandhi, *My Childhood*, p. 116; Nirmal Kumar Bose, *My Days with Gandhi* (Calcutta: Nishana, 1953), pp. 116, 120.
61. Jadunath Sarkar, *Mughal Administration*, 4th ed. (Calcutta: M.C. Sarkar & Sons, 1952), p. 53; see also pp. 6-7.
62. P. Gandhi, *My Childhood*, p. 13.
63. See for example, Gandhi, *Works*, 14:510: "Total disregard for death in a Mahomedan lad is a wonderful possession."
64. NAI, KPA, 1875, vol. 1, comp. 3, "The Kattywar Administration Report, 1874-75," p. 3. The movements through Porbandar of four contingents of the Bombay Army between 10 November 1873 and 29

April 1874 are documented in NAI, KPA, 1874, comp. 79, pp. 13-17.
65. Gesell and Ilg, *Child Development*, 1:224, 2:413.
66. P. Gandhi, *My Childhood*, p. 26· Pyarelal, *Gandhi, Early Phase*, p. 194.
67. *Ibid.*
68. Conversation with Maneklal Gandhi at Porbandar, 4 Apr. 1960.
69. NAI, KPA, 1867, vol. 4, comp. 31, "Porebander Affairs," pp. 287a-299a.
70. NAI, KPA, 1873, vol. 27, comp. 89, "Rajasthanik Court," p. 339. Pyarelal, pp. 180-81 and 733-34, reproduces British orders of 1867, 1870, and 1873 summoning Kaba Gandhi to Rajkot.
71. *Gāndhī--Kathanāmrita* (Porbandar: Mahātmā Gāndhī Kīrti Mandir, n.d.), p. 3. Prabhudas Gandhi, in a letter to me of 7 June 1974, stated that he wrote this pamphlet at an early stage in his research.
72. Pyarelal, *Gandhi, Early Phase*, pp. 735-36.
73. See *Autobiography*, pp. 25, 30, 37-38, in Gandhi, *Works*, 39:26, 29-30, 36.
74. For example, on 20 Nov. 1876, Tulsidas was denounced as having "neither the intelligence, rectitude [n]or energy fitting him for the post" of dewan. NAI, KPA, 1877, vol. 24, p. 423a.
75. L. Joseph Stone and Joseph Church, *Childhood and Adolescence: A Psychology of the Growing Person*, 2nd ed. (New York: Random House, 1968), pp. 304-05.
76. P. Gāndhī, *Otābāpāno vadlo*, appendix 1, p. 1, and *passim*. Note, however, that the genealogies of the Gandhi family published prior to this one, in P. Gandhi, *Jīvannum parodh*, p. xviii, and Pyarelal, *Gandhi, Early Phase*, pp. 184a-b, mention no women at all, so strong was the tradition that only male ancestors were important.
77. Gesell and Ilg, *Child Development*, 2:450.
78. *Harijan*, 11 Mar. 1939, quoted in *To the Princes and Their People*, ed. Anand T. Hingorani (Karachi: Anand T. Hingorani, 1942), p. 128; Pyarelal, *Gandhi, Early Phase*, p. 202.
79. M. Desai, *Day-to-day*, 6:19. I have corrected the translator's "white" for *ūjlo* to "stainless and bright," after consulting *The Modern Gujarati-English Dictionary*, comp. Bhanusukhram N. Mehta

and Bharatram B. Mehta, 2 vols. (Baroda: M. C. Kothari, 1925). For the original Gujarati passage, see *Mahādevbhāinī dāyarī* (Amadāvād: Sābarmati Āshram Suraksha ane Smārak Trast, 1965), 7:186.

80. *The Diary of Mahadev Desai. Volume I* (no more published), tr. Valji Govindji Desai (Ahmedabad: Navajivan Publishing House, 1953), p. 52.

81. Barr, *Bapu*, pp. 116-17.

82. Vincent Sheean, *Lead, Kindly Light* (New York: Random House, 1949), p. 200.

83. Gandhi, *Autobiography*, p. 32, in *Works*, 39:31. Her teaching of the prayer seems to have been repeated when he returned to Porbandar at eleven. See *ibid.*, 19:570.

84. Gandhi, *Ramanama*, 2nd ed. (Ahmedabad: Navajivan Trust, 1949), p. 13.

85. P. Gandhi, *My Childhood*, p. 17.

86. *Harijan*, 18 Mar. 1933, in Gandhi, *None High: None Low*, ed. Anand T. Hingorani (Bombay: Bharatiya Vidya Bhavan, 1965), p. 99.

87. Stevenson, *Rites*, pp. 202-08.

88. Conversation with Manilal P. Vora, Porbandar, 8 Mar. 1971.

89. Gandhi, *Works*, 27:347.

90. Joseph J. Doke, *M. K. Gandhi: An Indian Patriot in South Africa* (Varanasi: Akhil Bharat Sarva Seva Sangh Prakashan, 1956 [1st ed. 1909]), pp. 25-26.

91. Gesell and Ilg, *Child Development*, 2:85-86.

92. Pyarelal, *Gandhi, Early Phase*, p. 201.

93. Sigmund Freud, "A Childhood Recollection from Dichtung und Wahrheit," in *The Standard Edition of the Complete Psychological Works of Sigmund Freud*, 23 vols. (London: The Hogarth Press and the Institute of Psychoanalysis, 1955), 17:156. See also Ernest Jones, *The Life and Work of Sigmund Freud*, ed. Lionel Trilling and Steven Marcus (Garden City: Doubleday & Co., 1963), pp. 6-13.

94. P. Gandhi, *My Childhood*, p. 25.

95. *Harijan*, 15 Sept. 1940, in Gandhi, *India of My Dreams*, comp. R. K. Prabhu, rev. ed. (Ahmedabad: Navajivan Publishing House, 1959), p. 127.

96. M. Desai, *Day-to-day*, 1:60-61; *Mahādevbhāinī ḍayarī* [Mahadevbhai's dairy], ed. Narhari Dvā. Parīkh (Amadāvād: Navajīvan Prakāshan Mandir, 1950), 4:52; M. Desai, *Day-to-day*, 6:48.
97. Erikson, *Gandhi's Truth*, 128-30; Gandhi, *Autobiography*, pp. 28-31, in *Works*, 39:28-30.
98. Gandhi, *Works*, 1 (2nd rev. ed.), p. 44.
99. Gandhi, *Autobiography*, pp. 44-45, in *Works*, 39:42.
100. See Gandhi, *Autobiography*, p. 87, in *Works*, 39:74, where he writes "Most of my cherished hopes were shattered" when he learned of his mother's death.
101. Conversation with Mathurabehn Modi, daughter of Putaliba's neighbor in Rajkot, 5 Mar. 1971, as translated by Prabhudas Gandhi.
102. Conversation with Prabhudas Gandhi, 6 Mar. 1971.
103. Nirmal Kumar Bose, *My Days with Gandhi* (Calcutta: Nishana, 1953), pp. 192, 206.
104. See J. M. Upadhyaya, *Mahatma Gandhi as a Student* (New Delhi: Ministry of Information and Broadcasting, 1965), and his *Mahatma Gandhi - A Teacher's Discovery*, mentioned in n. 5 above.
105. Gandhi, *Autobiography*, p. 69, in *Works*, 39:62.
106. See Roger Poole, *Towards Deep Subjectivity* (New York: Harper & Row, 1972) for some recent thoughts on these problems. Abraham H. Maslow, *The Psychology of Science: A Reconaissance* (New York: Harper & Row, 1966), also deals with the prospects for a more inclusive view of science. For earlier works in this vein, see Michael Polanyi, *The Study of Man* (London: Routledge & Kegan Paul, 1959), and J. Bronowski, *Science and Human Values*, rev. ed. (New York: Harper & Row, 1965).
107. Einstein, *Ideas*, p. 44.
108. J. A. K. Thomson, *The Ethics of Aristotle: The Nicomachean Ethics Translated* (Harmondsworth, Middlesex: Penguin Books, 1953), p. 28 (Book I, chapter 3).
109. On the crucial role of intuition in scientific discovery, see P. B. Medawar, "Hypothesis and Imagination," in his *The Art of the Soluble: Creativity and Originality in Science* (Harmondsworth, Middlesex: Penguin Books, 1969), and the same author's *In-*

duction in Scientific Thought (London: Methuen & Co., 1969).

110. Stephen N. Hay, *Asian Ideas of East and West: Tagore and His Critics in Japan, China, and India* (Cambridge, Mass.: Harvard University Press, 1970), p. viii.

111. I would like to express here my gratitude to Nirmal Bose, recently deceased, and to many others who have helped me in my research and writing: to Pyarelal and Prabhudas Gandhi, for answering many questions, and to Prabhudas Gandhi especially for his kindness in accompanying me to the scenes of Gandhi's childhood, and of Gandhi's mother's and father's childhoods; to S. K. De of the Gandhi Smarak Sangrahalaya, New Delhi, and Arvind Desai of Ahmedabad, for help at critical points in the research; to the staffs of the National Archives of India, the Nehru Memorial Museum and Library, and the Gandhi Smarak Sangrahalaya, New Delhi, and of the India Office Library, London; and to these critical and encouraging readers of various drafts of this article: Lloyd deMause, Doris Hay, Eloise Hay, Zoë Hersov, Robert McLean, Katherine Myers, and Ann Watt.

GANDHI: NON-VIOLENCE AS THERAPY[1]
Clifford Geertz

"Whence, however," the *Mahabharata* asks, "does Hope arise?" For twenty years, since his *Childhood and Society* announced the Freudian vocation to be the empowerment of the ego, Erik Erikson has been asking the same question. His whole career has proceeded from a settled determination to turn psychoanalysis away from fascination with weakness toward detection of strength, to dissolve its hospital odor and connect it up with the public aspirations of men. In modern India, where despair is more than an emotion--a quality of the landscape, a dimension of the weather-- hope arose most eloquently with Gandhi. In addressing himself to the question of whence, in the convolutions of the Mahatma's life, that hope came, what it consisted in, and why, at least for a while, it caught most of India in its grasp, Erikson has found a most appropriate subject. But he has found as well a most refractory case.

A man who claims to be a saint, as Gandhi did, if not in so many words, certainly in almost every action he took after his return from South Africa in 1915 (he arrived at the banquet, with which Bombay high society greeted him, in peasant dress and announced that he would rather have been received by indentured servants), demands, above all, a moral response. Rather like the little girl who did not know whether she wished to see the dinosaur in the museum until she found out whether it was good or bad, we have to decide how to feel about him before we really understand him, and coming to understand him does not actually help very much in deciding how to feel about him.

Indeed, when it is a dinosaur like Gandhi one is going to see, coming to understand him only makes the problem worse. The deeper the labyrinth of his personality is penetrated the higher rises the tension between admiration and outrage, awe and disgust, trust and suspicion, until the encounter with him

---
[1] This article originally appeared in *New York Review of Books*, November 20, 1969. It is reprinted here by permission.

becomes as painful and disaccommodating as he wished to make it. It is the triumph of Erikson's book that in uncovering the inner source of Gandhi's power it does not dissolve but deepens his inherent moral ambiguity, and in so doing extends the intent of his career: to make of himself an exemplary prophet, a man who recommends his character to the world as a saving revelation.

The more prominent features of Gandhi's character are only too well known. His sexual and dietary asceticism, his hatred of filth, his shyness, his restlessness, his penchant for self-inflicted suffering, his moralism, his romanticism, his vanity, have all been described over and over again in what is by now a fairly sizeable hagiographic and anti-hagiographic literature both inside India and out. Erikson inspects these familiar traits and traces their roots in Gandhi's childhood and adolescence. But it is to a less noticed aspect of Gandhi's character that he turns as the psychological axis of his religious genius--his ironic, mocking, grating humor.

Erikson's Gandhi is an obsessive tease, a man with an extraordinary capacity to make others feel furious and foolish at the same time. At Benares, the arch symbol of Hindu humility, he dressed up as a pauper and offers a penny to the Well of Knowledge and is duly rewarded by having a custodian of orthodoxy (and, apparently, of the Well) inform him that he will land in hell for his stinginess. In South Africa, he organizes a boycott against the Black Act and then escorts Indians who wish to break it through the picket lines of his own followers. At a meeting with the Viceroy arranged to end his disobedience campaign against the salt tax he draws a packet of salt from his shawl and pours it ceremoniously into his tea. He praises anarchy to lawyers, patience to students, manual labor to civil servants, poverty to economists, simplicity to maharajas, Hindu to college professors, and violence to Annie Besant.

He is always taunting, testing limits, playing up to some finely calculated point, with others' emotions. The essence of his spiritual gift is an edged gaiety, an Indic variety of kidding on the level, which keeps everyone--intimates, followers, rivals, officials, wisdom seekers from the West--psychologically off balance, unable to find their moral feet with him. Forged into a political instrument this becomes the famous *Satyagraha*, which literally means "truth force" or "perseverance in truth," is usually translated as "passive resistance" or (somewhat better) "militant non-violence," but which could perhaps be most informatively rendered as "mass taunting" or "collective needling." What in the end Gandhi did to colonial India was drive it to distraction.

Erikson centers his investigation of this intricate art around an incident--he calls it "The Event"--which, occurring at the very beginning of Gandhi's Indian career (though, as he was nearly fifty, well along in his life), demonstrates its workings in a parochial, highly personal, mocro-context--a small intense circle of intimates. Working into this "Event," the Ahmedabad textile strike of 1918, from Gandhi's youth and young manhood (Gujerat, London, South Africa), on the far side, and outward from it to the days of his Mahatmaship, when "all India would hold its breath while (he) fasted," on the near, he uses it, like a true clinician, to uncover the psychological materials out of which *Satyagraha* was made.

What made the Ahmedabad strike such a natural for Gandhi was the ingrown character of it all. The workers, many of whom were women, were led by the feminist sister of the main mill owner, one of the earliest of Gandhi's long string of devoted female disciples. Management was led by her less visionary brother, whose wife was also a Gandhi partisan, and who, for all his defensive bluffness, had himself been Gandhi's first important financial backer in India. Together with a few other early adherents--an energetic Bombay social worker, a mousy male secretary, one of Gandhi's squad of attendant nephews--this little group formed a mock family, thick with oblique affections and equivocal motives, which the intrusion of the strike threw into precisely the kind of psychological disarray in which an inspired tease with a passion for toying with others' emotions could effectively maneuver. "I am handling a most dangerous situation here," he wrote exultantly to one of his sons as irresistible sister and immovable brother set out on a collision course, "and preparing to go on to a still more dangerous."

After such promising beginning, however, the affair turned out, on the surface at least, to be a bit of a fizzle. Seated beneath a bulbul tree Gandhi lectured to thousands of people each afternoon on the principles of *Satyagraha*. He extracted, almost without quite realizing it, a sacred pledge from the workers neither to resume work nor to cause any disturbance until their demands had been met. And, when their resolution began to fail, he launched the first of his seventeen famous "fasts to the death." In the end, despairing of the moral fiber of the workers ("After twernty years' experience I have come to the conclusion that I am qualified to take a pledge," he told them with headmaster rudeness." "I see you are not yet so qualified.") he negotiated a settlement between the sibling antagonists which saved the workers' pride, the owners' pocketbook, and his own reputation.

It seemed to Gandhi a rather sordid end to what was to have been a moral revolution. ("My co-workers and I," he wrote later in his *Autobiography*, "had built many castles in the air, but they all vanished for the time being.") But for Erikson it is the point at which Gandhi set definitely off down the road to sainthood, the point at which the philosophy of militant nonviolence freed itself from his personal biography to become part of the collective consciousness of modern India:

> ...Casting Ahmedabadis against one another (The Event) was largely a local show, like a rehearsal before a provincial audience. This (becomes) especially clear when we look back on Ahmedabad from the first nationwide Satyagraha exactly one year later.... Ten hundreds of thousands of Indians of all regions and religions would be the principal counter-player, and world opinion the awed onlooker. But at least Ahmedabad (was) a real, a cratsmanlike rehearsal, in spite of a

few devastating shortcomings such as earnest rehearsals bring to life.

At Ahmedabad, teasing was finally raised to a philosophical plane, taunting exalted into a religious act. To an extent this had already occurred in the agitations in South Africa. But there it had all been rather pragmatic, ad hoc, a day-to-day experimentation with styles and devices, immediate reactions to immediate injustices. At Ahmedabad, where the personal, social, ethical, and practical flowed into one another in such a way as virtually to dissolve the line between private emotions and public acts, such ideological innocence could no longer be maintained. The inner connection between Satyagraha as individual experience - what Gandhi taxed the workers with not having - and as collective action - what he taxed himself for not controlling - was openly exposed, and with it the fact that shaming men into virtue was a complex and treacherous business, both less selfish and less pacific than it looked.

The violence that non-violence contains, has, of course, often been noted; since Nietzsche, it has been a commonplace. But what Gandhi came, after Ahmedabad, to believe - and in so doing plunged himself into a forest of puzzles - was that this contained violence was precisely what gave non-violence its moral grandeur. As a weapon of the weak, Satyagraha is reduced to cowardice, it is what the defenseless must do to survive; as a weapon of the strong, it is the highest form of courage, the willingness to suffer evil rather than commit it. From someone powerless to strike back, turning the other cheek is a token of submission, a victim mollifying his tormentor by dissembling his rage. From someone competent to strike back, and even to kill, it is a provocation, an assertion of moral superiority which an aggressor, whether with renewed brutality or crushed repentance, must necessarily acknowledge. The road to true non-violence passes then through the attainment of power, that is of the means of violence, a doctrine which, when stated in the context of India fifty years ago, breathes the same chill of desperate logic as it does in that of the contemporary United States:

> What am I to advise a man to do who wants to kill but is unable owing to his being maimed? Before I can make him feel the virtue of not killing, I must restore to him the arm he has lost....A nation that is unfit to fight cannot from experience prove the virtue of not fighting. I do not infer from this that India must fight. But I do say that India must know how to fight.
>
> I have come to see, what I did not see so clearly before, that there is non-violence in violence. This is the big change which has come about. I had not fully realized the duty of restraining a drunkard from doing evil, of killing a dog in agony or one infected with rabies. In all these instances violence is in fact non-violence. Today I find that everybody is desirous of killing, but most are afraid of doing so or powerless to do so. Whatever is to be the result I feel certain that the power must be restored to India. The result may be carnage. Then India must go through it.

Whether one hears Malcolm X or Dean Rusk in these quotations - and it is part of the now-you-see-it-now-you-don't quality of Gandhi's Truth that one can hear something of both - this is clearly dangerous doctrine; the carnage after all did come, martyring Gandhi with it, and, as I write, Ahmedabad, of all places, is the scene of the bloodiest communal riots since Partition. The moral doubletalk to which it can lead is apparent, not only in Gandhi ("...Our offspring must be strong in physique," he said, urging Indians into the British Army. "If they cannot completely renounce the ruge to violence, we may permit them to commit violence, to use their strength to fight and thus make them non-violent"), but, on occasion, in Erikson as well:

> In view of the values which the Jews of the diaspora have come to stand for, the belated proof that Jews could fight a national war, may impress many as an historical anachronism. And, indeed, the triumph of Israeli soldiery is markedly subdued, balanced by a certain sadness over the necessity to re-enter historical actuality by way of military methods not invented by Jews, and yet superbly used by them. I would go further: it is not possible that such historical proof of a military potential will make peace-loving Jews better potential Satyagrahis?

Yet, however one may prefer the bleak candor of *Realpolitik* to images of a saddened soldiery fighting to advance the cause of pacifism (as Burkhardt said, there is enough hypocrisy in the world already), the argument that a sacred pledge to abstain from the use of force can have moral reality only with respect to people who have a genuine possibility of effectively using force is surely correct. And, as Gandhi himself recognized ("...This new aspect of non-violence which has revealed itself to me has enmeshed me in no end of problems....I have not found one masterkey for all the riddles....My powers of thinking fail me...") the acceptance of this hard truth introduces a paradox into the very heart of Gandhian doctrine. As ideological slogans, "Peace Through Strength" and "Strength Through Peace" do not sit altogether comfortably together.

Not, at least, in thought. In action, Erikson argues, this contradiction was transcended by the sheer force of Gandhi's commitment, his readiness when faced with the immediate possibility, a possibility he had had usually himself specifically created, to get hurt rather than to hurt. Like Luther and like St. Francis, the two other men with a subversive sense of humor, Gandhi was "a religious actualist," a man for whom truth resides neither in tradition nor in doctrine, but in "that which feels effectively true in action." In the carefully staged politico-moral dramas which he calls his "experiments with truth" - Ahmedabad, the salt campaign, Hydari Mansion - Gandhi made his argument that the active decision not to do harm was the basic law of life come alive both to himself and to large masses of Indians. Stymied by the paradox that non-violence is the reciprocal of strength, power the prerequisite of self-command, his "philosophy" dissolved into a collection of colliding homilies and Indic eccentricities. Fired by the same paradox, his "method" focussed into a rising series of studied provocations designed to expose at once the pretensions of colonial society and the impotence of political brutality.

In attempting to clarify the anatomy of this exercies in collective truth-finding, Erikson follows a famous remark of Nehru's to the effect that what Gandhi accomplished for India was "a psychological change, almost as if some expert in psychoanalytic methods had probed deep into the patient's past, found out the origins of his complexes, exposed them to view, and thus rid him of that burden." Erikson constructs an extended parallel between the technique developed by Freud for renewing growth in neurotic individuals and that developed by Gandhi to restore hope to a crippled people. Both relied on engagement at close range between the agent and the subject of change; both attempted to give the subject courage to change by confronting him as a full and equal human being with a latent capacity to trust and love, rather than as a lunatic, an inferior and enemy, or a savage; both eschewed any form of coercion, even moral coercion; both regarded as critical the agent's openness to change as well as the subject's, and saw the process of "cure" as involving a deepening of insight and consequent self-transformation, on both sides. And so on. *Satyagraha* is Analysis writ large; Analysis *Satyagraha* writ small. Politics and therapy coincide.

Perhaps one should not expect an analyst, even an heterodox one, to come to any other conclusions. ("When I began this book, I did not expect to rediscover psychoanalysis in terms of truth, self-suffering and non-violence," be concludes somewhat ingenuously. "But now that I have done so I see better what I hope the reader has come to see with me, namely, that I felt attracted to the Ahmedabad Event...because I sensed an affinity between Gandhi's truth and the insights of modern psychology.") But there is in this analogy a rather serious defect: in a clinical encounter ultimate interests merge, in the political one they do not. It is the deliberate exclusion of extrinsic concerns from the therapeutic situation, the stripping away of everything but a common concentration on emotional exploration that gives it, when this in fact occurs, its enormous force. With politics it is just the reverse: the wider the range of divergent concerns with which it can manage to cope the deeper it cuts. As models for each other, the consulting room and the textile strike seem peculiarly likely to mislead.

Yet, even if the therapeutic image of political process, like the therapeutic images of art, law, or education, fails at a general level to do justice to its object, and even distorts

it, with respect to Gandhi that image was, as Erikson clearly
demonstrates, centrally relevant. And this in turn reveals why,
even when brought down to the solid outlines of a polished method,
Gandhi's teachings remain, like the man himself, ambiguous and
only half-convincing.

Gandhi *was*, as Erikson is, powerfully attracted by a therapeutic view of politics - one which abstracts from the realities of group solidarity, divergent interest, social hierarchy, and cultural difference (and this is India!) in order to concentrate on exploiting the imotional involvements of individuals in one another's lives. At Ahmedabad, he had a situation in which such exploitation was possible, and though, characteristically, the strike failed, the therapy worked. "I have never come across the like to it," he said in his final speech to the workers. "I had the experience of many such conflicts or heard of them but have not known any in which there was so little ill will or bitterness as in this." And a few days later he wrote to the *Bombay Chronicle* to justify his own role which the paper had questioned as wasting large talents on parochial issues. "I have not known a struggle fought with so little bitterness and such courtesy on either side. This happy result is principally due to the connections with it of Mr. Ambalal Sarabhai (the mill-owner brother) and Anasuyaben (the labor-leader sister)."

Removed from this intimate context, he would never know it again. And in attempting again and again to re-enact this family drama on the national stage his career revealed both the intrinsic power of attraction that a view of politics as a process of inward change possesses - its ability to move men - and its radical inability, having moved them, to deal with the issues - whether workers' wages or the threat of Partition - thereby raised.

The contrast which appeared already at Ahmedabad between Gandhi's extraordinary ability to shape the personal lives of those immediately around him and his inability to control the direction of the strike as a collective act grew greater and greater as he extended himself across India and into larger and larger mass settings, and became, as violence followed violence to the climax of Partition and his own assassination, the distinguishing feature of his career. Nehru was wrong. Gandhi did not psychoanalyze India, he (though of course not alone) politicized it; and having politicized it, could not - a fact our own "religious actualists," taunting power, toying with social passions, and finding truth "in that which feels effectively true in action" might well ponder - in the end control it.

"Who listens to me today," he wrote just six months before his death,

> ...I am being told to retire to the Himalayas. Everybody is eager to garland my photos and statues. Nobody really wants to follow my advice....Neither the people nor those in power have any use for me.

Today, when his centenary is being celebrated by men for whom he is neither a personal presence nor a moral force but a marketable national treasure, like the Taj Mahal, this is even more true. Erikson's penetrating book, more convincing in describing the dinosaur than in judging him, deepens our understanding not only of the inward sources of personal greatness but those, as well, of its self-defeat.

GANDHI: THE ROAD TO HOLINESS

David H. Newhall

This paper adds some details to the story of Gandhi's life by describing a few events in which he participated between 1906 and 1908. This was an important period in Gandhi's life. It was during this time, for example, that he achieved personal focus and was able to maintain his singleness of purpose in face of interests and pressures that might have spread him too thin and torn him to pieces. It was during the same period of time that he developed Satyagraha (that is, the method of nonviolent passive resistance as a means of achieving social and political reform), and learned to practice it with success. As Erik Erikson notes in more detail in his book, *Gandhi's Truth*, there are strong and direct linkages between ego and ethos in Gandhi which are manifested in his personal identification with creative social action. Thus the events of 1906 to 1908 reveal something of Gandhi's character at a time of severe testing and challenge.

My primary source of information is *Indian Opinion*. Gandhi commenced publication of *Indian Opinion* in 1903.[1] A useful feature for my purposes was the inclusion of a considerable amount of material, mostly hostile, from several other South African papers. This was an effective reminder of the pressure constantly exerted against the Indian community by the powerful and prejudiced white community. Here, for example, is an explicit statement of the widespread, conscious, and deliberate intent to humiliate:

> It was the servility involved which they (the Indians) would not submit to. And that is exactly what they *must* submit to . . . . Any Indian who expects to establish better footing here than our own natives enjoy is doomed to disappointment and he may as well know it first as last.[2]

Indian Opinion was published weekly with unfailing regularity from 1903 to 1914, at which time Gandhi left South Africa. The quality of journalism was excellent. Publication continued for another decade.

Remember that Gandhi is thirty-six years old. He has lived in England for three years. He has lived in South Africa for the immediately preceding thirteen years.[3] He has become the acknowledged leader of the Indians in South Africa. He is known by everybody. His competence as a lawyer has been established beyond a doubt. He has encounted violence directed against himself. Satyagraha is as yet unknown. He has not entered into any program of civil disobedience. He has not yet been thrown into jail for any reason. The Indians are voiceless and voteless in the legislative assemblies of South Africa with their "petitions flung in the wastebasket."[4]

Rightly fearful of anti-Asiatic legislation about to be passed by the all-white government of the Transvaal, approximately three thousand Indians meet in the Empire Theatre and resolve never to submit to a special registration required by the proposed law. *Indian Opinion* refers to this meeting as a "unique and magnificient spectacle."[5] A newspaper normally hostile reports:

> The United protest of the British Indian community against the Draft Asiatic Ordinance constituted one of the most remarkable gatherings Johannesburg has seen. The size of the meeting, the enthusiasm of the audience--practically the entire Indian population ceased work for the day--and the depth of feeling displayed, formed striking testimony to the indignation which the proposed legislation aroused.....[6]

The crux of this meeting is the transformation of a political resolution to be passed by majority vote into a personal commitment binding upon each person who supports it. What is Gandhi's role in this?

The resolution (the fourth of five presented at the meeting) had been carefully prepared. Gandhi was not only aware of what it said but had without a doubt bee centrally invovled in writing it. It is strongly worded:

> ..... this mass meeting of British Indians here assembled solemnly and regretfully resolves that, rather than submit to the galling, tyrannous, and un-British requirements

laid in the above Draft Ordinance, every British Indian in the Transvaal shall submit himself to imprisonment and shall continue to do so until it shall please his Most Gracious Majesty the King-Emperor, to grant relief.[7]

This resolution is moved by Hajee Habib who has come over from Pretoria for the occasion. It is seconded and supported by eight men several of whom are soon to become heroes of the movement. Gandhi's mane appears as one of the eight. Events unfold with several speeches. *Indian Opinion* reports:

> Hajee Habib..... solemnly declared that if the Ordinance ever became law he would not submit to it and he asked the audience to make similar declaration. (Here the vast audience rose as one man and said, "We will go to gaol").[8]

Another speaker, H.O. Ally, soon to go with Gandhi to plead the Indian cause in London, quotes some nice remarks from King Edward VII about the rights of British subjects and concluded a long speech saying that if the Ordinance became law on that very day he would wrap himself up in the Union Jack and would present himself at the police station and tell the sergeant to arrest him, for he declined to register himself, and he hoped that all the rest would go too.[9]

Gandhi is the *twelfth* and last speaker. The resolution is put to a vote. It carries by acclamation, "the whole audience rising and cheering wildly." This sequence does not suggest that Gandhi "immediately ask(ed) for the rostrum," as Erikson has it.[10] Rather, he remained silent for a considerable lenght of time. He had indeed helped to "create an expectancy from which he would take his cues,"[11] but he does not rush to speak. He seems to want to be sure that he is hearing the cues correctly. Ten speeches come between that of Hajee Habib and his own. *Indian Opinion*'s report of his speech is brief,[12] far briefer than one would expect on the basis of space normally given to Gandhi's speeches. That is to say, it falls short of Gandhi's reconstruction of his speech in *Satyagraha in South Africa*, written about eighteen years later.

There is no doubt that Gandhi supported what was going on, but it seems clear that it was not he who transformed the situation from a political resolution to be forwarded through channels into a personal commitment entered into by three thousand Indians. That was done before he took the floor. His role, I think, was to prepare the resolution, to listen attentively to what happened when it was presented, and to reinforce the decisive turn of events. This was the birth of Satyagraha. It was a *communal* birth, and it is much to Gandhi's credit that he permitted it to be so. This restrained performance fits with his later remark that Satyagraha is a policy of "communal suffering."[13] The weekly record of these years makes it abundantly clear that Gandhi knew the importance of solidarity among the Indians if they were not to be further humiliated and ultimately driven from South Africa.

His contribution, then, was not to steer the Johannesburg meeting. Lut us put it more positively: his contribution was to let that meeting be a genuinely communal experience, to let it take its dramatic course without his direct leadership. It was his *restraint* that was vital. His follow up was magnificent. In the months and years to come he was anything but reluctant to remind the Indians of whay they had done. He told them on countless occasions that they were honor-bound, and they had a sacred duty to resist the Registration Law. This performance was especially important because the Indians were not required to commence civil disobedience until July 1907, nearly ten months later because the law did not become operative until then. Few persons would have been surprised if they had forgotten the whole thing. But not with Gandhi there to remind them! He was still talking about this commitment of 1906 as late as September of 1913 when the third phase of the long drawn out struggle was about to begin.[14]

As to partial discrepancies between the current report of *Indian Opinion* about the Johannesburg meeting and the much later account in *Satyagraha in South Africa*, we need not be too much concerned. To me, it seems likely that Gandhi's retrospective account telescopes with accuracy the ideas he kept repeating to the Indians over a period of at least several months about the nature of their action on that very special occasion.[15] What we cannot doubt is his sensitivity to the occasion, his personal restraint for the sake of communal solidarity, and his tremendous follow-through.

<u>September 1906. The Punia Case</u>: The record of this case is interesting because it displays Gandhi, his finger in many pies, about to depart for England, moving smoothly at several levels to handle this case and make the most of it on behalf of the British Indians of South Africa.

Three days after the mass meeting in Johannesburg, and Indian woman named Punia was arrested while traveling with her husband from Durban to Johannesburg. Her husband had the required permit and registration certificate for residence in the Transvaal. These papers made mention of his wife, but she had no permit in her name, this not yet being a legal requirement. After a night in jail, Punia was tried. The presiding magistrate ordered her to leave the Colong. At Gandhi's advice she proceeded toward Johannesburg and was again arrested.

At the point of Punia's second arrest, Gandhi publishes the facts in *Indian Opinion* and *three other* newspapers. His story includes the following statement:

> May the Government in the name of the people of the Transvaal, thus set up a rign of terror for British Indian women and children? It was admitted at the trial that this was not an isolated case.[16]

The arresting office, a Constable McGregor, had testified:

> My instructions are to arrest all Indians entering this Colong without permits--no matter whether male or female--minors or adults. There is no age limit. These instructions apply even when women and young children accompany their husbands and parents. It is of no account for the registration permit to mention a wife.[17]

Gandhi writes:

> Remember that, according to the authorized and printed permit regulations, wives and children under sixteen years accompanying their husbands or parents are not required to take out permits. Are Indian women now to go to the Permit Office, and after exhausting and exasperating examination, to take out their permits? Infants hardly able to crawl have been detained.....[18]

Gandhi's information produces considerable discussion. Subsequent accounts reveal that Punia had been made to give her finger-prints, all ten of them, in both places of her arrest. Finger-prints are a sore subject to the Indians. Ostensibly required for identification, they carry unfavorable connotations of crime. They are felt to be unnecessary. A jovial Indian announces to a judge that *one* fingerprint is alright, *ten* are against his religion. Harrassment via fingerprints is a long stroy, not to be pursued here.

Defending Punia's arrest, an immigration official now announces that the reason for tightened procedure is that Indian men are bringing women of "indifferent character" into the Transvaal under the pretence that they are their wives. Gandhi responds with a two column article which says in part:

> There never has been any reproach against Indian womanhood in South Africa except now, for the first time, in the sinful imagination of an anonymous immigration official. But even if a few miserable specimens of Indian humanity were to introduce into the Colong women of indifferent character, will that be any justification for submitting wives of hundreds of honest Indian settlers in Johannesburg to the painful porcesses required to be undergond by the Permit Office.[19]

The Permit Office is a miserable operation, specializing in procrastination, duplication, and demands for repeated appearances on the part of persons seeking permits. Gandhi continues to spread letters around in several papers.

> I can only use one expression to fit the wicked libel on Indian womanhood--namely that it is an infamous lie. You should publish the name of the immigration official who is said to have given this precious reason. I challenge him to publish the name of one such woman.[20]

There is quite a hullabaloo. Finally, the Registrar of Asiatics, in answer to a telegraphic demand from Gandhi, reports:

> No such statement as that alluded to in your message was made by any officer in the service of this department.[21]

This exchange is made public, but Gandhi is not yet finished. He now demands that the reporter who wrote the story that refers to the immigration official whose existence is denied by the Registrar of Asiatics say who this official is! Here the coverage in *Indian Opinion* fizzles out because Gandhi left for London. What happened to Punia? We learn elsewhere[22] that the case is satisfactorily settled.

There is no great drama here, but the Punia case is a solid reminder of Gandhi's capacity for work. Think of him in this situation, hammering away at the following levels of action. He conducts an on-going legal defense. He arouses public interest in the case. He responds in detail to conflicting stories. He comments on editorial comment in several papers. He offers his own interpretation. The entire incident is a minor but typical example of his characteristic "militancy *ad hominem*," as Erikson puts it.[23]

August 1907, Gandhi as Public Relations Man: The Asiatic Regristration Act became law in May, 1907. Civil disobedience became mandatory for the Indians as the law began to be implemented in July. At this time Gandhi is extremely active. In the space of a few days in August, 1907, he is involved in the following series of written exchanges:[24]

- a) A reminder of the "solemn declaration at Johannesburg in September 1906.
- b) A proposal for *voluntary* registration that would meet the legitimate needs of the government and also be acceptable to the Indians.
- c) An expression of hope that the humanity of the white colonists will win out over their prejudices and that the suffering of the Indians will result in recognition of the justice of their cause.
- d) A letter to General Smuts, the Colonial Secretary, denying charges that he (Gandhi) has inflamed the Indians. Gandhi takes responsibility for explaining objectionable law to them and voicing their sentiments. He includes some draft legislation that he holds would serve the purposes of both sides of this dispute.
- e) There is a negative response from General Smuts.
- f) Gandhi replies to this, arguing that his proposal would work. He requests permission to publish the correspondence between General Smuts and himself. One sided excerpts had already found their way into hostile newspapers. This request is granted, and the correspondence is published in full in several newspapers.
- g) These newspapers comment editorially, urging Gandhi to give up.

h) Gandhi responds, pointing out the several unacceptable features of the Asiatic Registration Law. He makes clear the relevance of Indian honor and the Johannesburg Oath to the present civil disobedience.

i) In response to this, there is renewed editorial criticism.

j) To this criticism Gandhi replies at some length; you don't really grasp the issue.

The Punia incident indicates and this series of letters, articles, and editorials *confirms* the idea that Gandhi would have made an outstanding public relations man. In fact, he *was*. Later, in a context only slightly different, he refers to

> having had the position of a publicist practically forced upon my by circumstances.... [25]

Considering his several publication ventures, it would be more accurate to say that he gobbled up this role. It was natural for him and essential to his cause.

There is no lack of passion in the material to which I have referred. The point to be stressed, however, is Gandhi's concern for truth in the familiar sense of accuracy with respect to fact. He communicates with Indians, South Africans, and ultimately the world about the issues. He is indefatigable and meticulous. His follow through is tremendous. He initiates proposals and explanations. He responds to responses. He attempts to correct errors. He even responds to responses to his previous responses. *Indian Opinion* frequently follows a topic for more rounds of correspondence and discussion than one would expect. A reader gets the impression of sharpness of mind, fluency in speaking and writing, no great literary style, but a tremendous zest for the tasks.

July, 1908, A Courtroom Scene: Gandhi has served his first prison term. A second and a third are to come within a year. The Indians have registered voluntarily on the basis of the Settlement of February 1908. This Settlement has broken down because the Registration Law of 1907 was not repealed. The second phase of civil disobedience is underway. Feelings are running high. It will be nearly three years before this phase of civil disobedience comes to an end. Here is a glimpse of Gandhi at work in a courtroom in Johannesburg.

Several Indians have been arrested for hawking without licenses, that is, for selling fruit and vegetables from a basket or cart in the street. They have refused bail, spent a night in jail, and are brought into court the following morning. One of them is Mr. Iman Abdool Cader Bawazeer, the dignified, well-known, respected Chariman of the Hamidia Islamic Society and Assistant Priest of the Indian Mosque. He has lately taken to hawking. Gandhi, defense lawyer, asks Mr. Bawazeer to explain why. The report in *Indian Opinion* proceeds as follows:[26]

> Because there was a compromise between General Smuts and some of the Indian leaders.....
>
> The Crown Prosecutor intervened and asked if the witness knew this of his own knowledge.
>
> The Magistrate inquired: Has he got permission from the Colonial Secretary to hawk without a license?
>
> Mr. Gandhi: no... The Court has a right to know why a gentleman occupying the position of the accused had taken to hawking.
>
> The Magistrate said it was not a matter which concerned the Court.

You can see Gandhi rising to this retort. He says:

> If it was not a matter of interest, it was a question of justice.

Gandhi must have had his way at this point because Mr Bawazeer proceeds to explain why he has taken to hawking. Then an unexpected question comes up quite suddenly:

> The Magistrate asked was he one of the fourteen people exempted.

This is a startling development:

> Mr. Gandhi said he did not know of any exemptions...
>
> The Crown Prosecutor said there was a certain number of exemptions, and the witness would probably know it if he were exempt.

Gandhi calls the Chief Inspector of Licenses who says that he received a list of exempted persons the day before but he does not know now if any of the persons on trial today are on the list.

Then Gandhi makes a speech:

> He asked the Court to take note of the arbitrary proceedings on the part of the Government. He had absolutely no

> knowledge that there were any exemptions, but he wished
> to point out that in the Asiatic Act there was absolutely
> no authority given to the Government to grant exemptions,
> and was the Court going to countenance an arbitrary ad-
> ministration of the Act.

Mr. Bawazeer was judged by the Magistrate to have admitted the charge. He was sentenced to pay a fine of ten shillings or four days imprisonment. Seven other men were similarly sentenced after brief trials. All chose imprisonment rather than pay the fine.

> The Indians about the Court were afterwards addressed by
> Mr. Gandhi.

He was always doing this. When Indians were gathered in a group, Gandhi was likely to be present making a speech.

Notice some interesting features of this typical situation. A distinguished member of the Indian community is involved. This man is a Moslem, not a Hindu. Gandhi is totally unconcerned about these religious differences. The Court claims no interest in his reasons for breaking the law, but Gandhi thrusts them upon the Court. Following the court session Handhi takes time to talk with the Indians who are gathered there, probably several score, possibly more.

During the same week there is a protest meeting of fifteen hundred Indians at the Hamidia Mosque. Gandhi attends and makes a speech.[27] His themes are simple: the solidarity of the Indian community, a review of the current situation, his own role in the movement, maintainence of non-violence, the abuse suffered by the Indians, perseverance with dignity, and assurance of final victory.

Another meeting is planned to greet prisoners upon completion of their short sentences. Gandhi speaks again at this celebration.

<u>August 1908, Some Harsh Judgements</u>: During this period of intense involvement and strong emotional currents, Gandhi allowed himself to express some harsh personal judements, understandable in terms of his unsuppresible moralism and the need for clear, simple issues; not so understandable in terms of his ideal of reconciliation. They are foreshadowed in 1906 when be began to write about the Asiatic Registration Act. One editorial is headed

"Abominable" and refers to the Registration Act and its advocates as follows:

> It sets at nought the British principle of justice and fairplay, and it tramples upon the ordinary ideas of right and wrong as they are known to mankind for ages past... The most pitiable part of it consists in the fact that what the Boer Government did in ignorance of facts and without meaning to do much harm and in respect of persons not its own subjects, the British Government is doing with the fullest knowledge of the facts with the deliberate intention of injuring the Indian community and in respect of British subjects.[28]

One week later the editorial heading is "Criminal," and Gandhi writes:

> The only apparent reason for this Ordinance is to cover hopeless incompetence in the administration of the present laws... In Russia, when it suits the authorities, they do not hesitate to murder people openly and directly [Gandhi had recently been reading Tolstoi], in the Transvaal, because the authorities wish to do away with the Indians, but cannot do so openly and honestly, instead of resorting to the direct method of murdering them or banishing them from the Colony, they intend to kill them by inches.[29]

One year later, it so happened that the first man to be imprisoned for violating the Registration Act fled the country upon his release from a short prison term. He had been glorified as a hero. Now he is read out of the community in a manner reminiscent of excommunications, such as Spinoza's from the Synagogue:

> As far as the community is concerned, Ram Sundar is dead as from today. He lives to no purpose. He has poisoned himself by his own hand. Physical death is to be preferred to such a social death.[30]

Another recipient of Gandhi's blasts is Mr. Chamney, Registrar of Asiatics. Mr. Chamney is a familiar figure. He was present at the Mass Meeting of September 1906 where he was ceremoniously treated. He responded properly, if not sympathetically, on that occasion. Coming now to August 1908, relations between the Indians and Mr. Chamney's office are severely strained, to say the least. There is a public meeting at which there is a demand not accepted to include Mr. Chamney's removal among the several terms essential to a settlement of the Indian problem and cessation of civil disobedience. Gandhi communicated with General

Smuts by letter saying this about Mr. Chamney:

> I cannot help recording my opinion that Mr. Chamney is ignorant and hopelessly incompetent. This I say in the interests of the Colong at large. I have personally nothing against him. I have always received courtesy from him....

This combination of courtesy and incompetence may have been particularly infuriating to Gandhi. He goes on:

> I am sure he never knows from one hour to another what his decision should be... In my opinion, what is required is a man of judicial talent and wide sympathies. If this suggestion is not accepted, I fear that there will always be irritation and consequent difficulty in the administration of any Act however well devised.[31]

Gandhi's letter was lengthy and discussed a variety of topics. Parts of it were published without his consent. The entire letter was then published in *Indian Opinion* with his consent.

In a speech on the occasion of the burning of no-longer acceptable registration cards, Gandhi gets onto the subject of Mr. Chamney. It sounds a little like Mark Antony talking about Brutus:

> Mr. Chamney is an estimable man.... He is above suspicion but that is not all that is required in the head of a Department...

The tirade continues and concludes with:

> Mr. Chamney has been tried and found wanting, and no matter how much attached General Smuts may be to Mr. Chamney.... there will be no peace.[32]

The circumstance that riled Gandhi is Chamney's belated support of General Smuts in the latter's claim that in reaching the Settlement of February, 1907, which temporarily brought civil disobedience to an end, he (Smuts) never agreed to repeal the Asiatic Registration Act. Of this specifically, Gandhi speaks as follows:

> Mr. Chamney has been less than a man in putting his signature before a Justice of the Peace to an affidavit that was made on oath to the effect that he was present on the interview on the 3rd day of February and General Smuts never promised repeal of the Act. I say that the affidavit is untrue.

How much closer could Gandhi come to calling a man an out-and-out liar without actually doing so? Gandhi continues:

> He [Mr. Chamney] not only listened to the promise made by General Smuts as to the repeal of the Act, but he repeated that promise to me; he mentioned that promise to me, if once, twelve times, and each time he said that General Smuts was going to play the game, that he was going to repeal the Act.[33]

It may be true that in later life, Gandhi no longer permitted himself explosive utterances of this kind. But there they are at the age of thirty-eight. They provide support for Erikson's surmise that "a man like Gandhi... early knew that he had to contain a superior energy of destructive, as well as benevolent, forces...."[34] They also show that the discipline required is difficult, and Gandhi was not always successful in exercising the necessary control. It is impossible to believe that he was "putting on for an audience." To some extent he was fighting for his own credibility with both Indians and whites. He had by now coined the term "Truth force," and no doubt he felt full of it.

We understand him best between 1906 and 1908 as a hard-driving lawyer and political leader totally dedicated to the welfare of his people.

1908 to 1914: Gandhi remained in South Africa for six more years. The files of *Indian Opinion* provide tales of unsung heroes, organization, and staying power that deserve telling in detail. The second phase of civil disobedience came to an end in 1911 on the basis of correspondence between Gandhi and General Smuts, but the troubles of the Indians did not. For three successive years the South African Government failed to meet its obligations under this agreement (this time, it seems, through no lack of effort on the part of General Smuts).

A single incident illustrates the extremities to which the South Africans were willing to go in dealing with the Indians. Late in March, 1913, Justice Searless of the Supreme Court of South Africa handed down a decision that invalidated all non-Christian marriages.[35] The fact of this decision is bad enough. It turns wives into concubines, children into bastards, invalidates inheritance laws for Indian families, and raises additional problems of residence and travel. The key concept involved in the decision is incredible. Justice Searless invented, so far as I know of, *monogamous polygamy*. The adjective serves to acknowledge the fact that ninety nine per cent of Indian marriages in South Africa involve only one woman. The noun declares these marriages polygamous on the grounds that the *system* under which they were solemnized permits additional wives, so that the man is not properly bound to the woman; and the marriage is no marriage. Editorial comment in *Indian Opinion* declares this to be a fitting subject for satirical treatment were it not so painfully serious to so many persons.[36]

It was at this point that Kasturbai decided that the time had come for her to go to jail, which she did shrotly thereafter, with Gandhi's consent. Reaction to this marriage incident certainly added numbers and incentive to the third phase of civil disobedience. This phase began in September, 1913 and ended in January, 1914. The settlement this time confirmed in legislation that was passed in June 1914. The Asiatic Registration Act of 1907 was finally repealed, and other adjustments were made. The Indians felt that they had achieved a victory. Viewed in terms of outward achievements, they had mainly prevented a bad situation from getting very much worse. They had not made substantial progress toward social justice.[37] Many had indeed fallen by the wayside as indicated by a population decrease of Indians in the Transvaal of approximately 5,000 persons. The achievement has to be assessed in different terms. It is a long way from that movement in Johannesburg in 1893 when an Indian told Gandhi, "This country is not for men like you. For making money we do not mind pocketing insults, and here we are," to the moment thirteen years later in the same city when three thousand Indians committed themselves to civil disobedience because they would no longer pocket those insults. And it is a long way from that moment to the Settlement of 1914 which left the Indians unimproved materially but with a radically altered consciousness of themselves and what is possible in this world.

Lesser men than Gandhi might well have stayed home to enjoy the glory. Not so Gandhi. His departure is prompt and without hesitation, like an athlete ready and willing to move from the minor leagues into the majors.

Conclusion: Unmentioned explicitly so far but perhaps as significant as any single point is the nearly perfect record achieved by the Indians in remaining non-violent through this strenuous period. Gandhi's personal commitment might have been contagious and his leadership miraculously effective in this regard. I have not found a single suggestion that a turn to violence might be desirable. Just the opposite, there are frequent reiterations of the idea that violence is mistaken in principle. Violence was not a live option for the Indians, not because it would have been suicidal but because they were committed to non-violence.

The material presented here serves to throw a slightly different light on Gandhi's role at the Johannesburg Mass Meeting; it reinforces his well-deserved reputation as a capable lawyer; it stressed his energy and skill in public relations; and it verifies a capacity for harshness in him that was not fully under control. His own assessment is worth remembering. He is reported to have said that he was at this time "a politician trying my hardest to be a saint."[38] Gokhale, in 1912, commented on Gandhi's capacity "to turn ordinary men around him into heroes and martyrs."[39] He was a man totally involved.

Perhaps he was no saint, but he superbly exemplifies Dag Hammarskjold's assertion that "in our era, the road to holiness necessarily passes through the world of action."[40]

FOOTNOTES

1. Hammarskjold is quoted by W.H. Auden in the latter's Foreword to Day Hammarskjold, *Markings* (New York, 1965), p. xxi.
2. The first issue of *Indian Opinion* is dated June 4, 1903, published in Durban, South Africa, later in Phoenix. Early issues were published in English, Gujarati, Tamil, and Hindi. The Tamil and Hindi pages were subsequently dropped. *Indian Opinion* will be referred to hereafter as *IO*.
3. Quoted in *IO*, February 8, 1908 from an editorial in the *Heidelberg News*.
4. During this period Gandhi made two trips to India, the first in 1896 and the second in 1901-2 (from which he returned only at the request of the South African Indians).
5. Gandhi's phrase in a speech, *IO*, August 10, 1907.
6. *IO*, September 15, 1906.
7. Quoted in *IO*, September 22, 1906 from the *Rand Daily Mail*.
8. *IO*, September 15, 1906.
9. *IO*, September 22, 1906.
10. *IO*, September 22, 1906.
11. Erik H. Erikson, *Gandhi's Truth* (New York- 1969), p. 199. Hereafter *Gandhi's Truth* will be referred to as *GT*.
12. *GT*, p. 199.
13. *IO*, September 22, 1906.
14. *IO*, July 6, 1907.
15. *IO*, September 20, 1913.
16. "The meeting was heroic and sacramental," writes Geoffrey Ashe in *Gandhi* (New York, 1968), p. 99.
17. *IO*, September 22, 1906.
18. *IO*, September 22, 1906.
19. *IO*, September 22, 1906.
20. *IO*, September 29, 1906.
21. *IO*, September 29, 1906.
22. *IO*, September 29, 1906.
23. *The Collected Works of Mahatma Gandhi* (Ahmedabad, 1961), VI,

p. 119. Testifying in London on November 8, 1906 before Lord Elgin, Gandhi refers to this case and says that "relief was granted in the end, as the matter was taken up in time." The reference hereafter to these volumes will be *CWMG*.
24. *GT*, p. 444.
25. See the August issues of *IO*, especially August 24, 1907.
26. *IO*, May 21, 1910. Gandhi had recently written *Hind Swaraj* (Madras, 1921).
27. References here are either direct quotations or slightly edited quotations from *IO*, July 25, 1908.
28. *IO*, August 1, 1908.
29. *IO*, September 1, 1906.
30. *IO*, September 8, 1906.
31. *CWMG*, VII, p. 4.
32. *IO*, August 29, 1908.
33. *IO*, August 22, 1908.
34. *IO*, August 22, 1908.
35. *GT*, p. 101.
36. *IO*, April 5, 1913. See also Ashe, *op. cit.*, p. 122.
37. *IO*, October 8, 1913.
38. *GT*, p. 216.
39. Louis Fishcer, *The Life of Mahatma Gandhi* (New York, 1950), p. 143.
40. Hammarskjold is quoted by W. H. Auden in the latter's Foreword to Dag Hammarskjold, *Markings* (New York, 1965), p. xxi.

THEME AND EVENT:
GANDHI'S TRUTH AS RELIGIOUS BIOGRAPHY

Donald Capps

Most discussions of the psychohistorical work of Erik H. Erikson in theological circles have centered on questions of historical interpretation. Roland H. Bainton has set the dominant tone of such discussions in raising questions concerning Erikson's *modus operandi* as a historian.[1] In his reactions to *Young Man Luther*, Bainton has raised the issue of Erikson's use and abuse of sources, his psychological inferences from insufficient data, his use of apocryphal materials, etc., etc. There is nothing especially new in this type of response to psychobiographical studies. William E. Barton, a noted Lincoln scholar and minister of the First Congregational Church in Oak Park, Illinois in the 1920s, reacted in a similar way to a psychological biography of Abraham Lincoln by L. Pierce Clark, a psychoanalyst. Barton observes that Clark's "method of study appears to exhibit certain marked defects." The major such defect "is a very meager and incomplete and quite inaccurate gathering of the material for his induction." Barton is ready to presume "that Dr. Clark is a competent scholar in his own field" and to accept the fact "that much of the blame for his inconclusiveness should be laid at the door of the authors whom he trusted." Nonetheless, "a psychologist must be a master of inductive logic, and he cannot afford to take chances such as Dr. Clark has taken."[2]

Hence, responses to psychobiography by historians, including historians with strong ecclesiastical ties, have not changed very much over the years. While church historians have been inclined since Bainton's earlier attack to take a somewhat "milder" view of *Young Man Luther*, and while Erikson's stature as an elder statesman in the academic world has somewhat blunted criticisms of *Gandhi's Truth* by historians of religion, the general arguments remain essentially the same. Erikson may be a competent scholar in his own field, but he demonstrates much incompetence when he employs the historian's craft.

My concern in this paper is to locate the psychohistorical work of Erik Erikson within a rather different kind of discussion in religious studies. By centering attention on *Gandhi's Truth*, I want to develop this new sort of inquiry with the suggestion that Erikson's psychohistorical studies are essentially religious biography. In making this suggestion, I mean to point to the fact that Erikson's psychobiographical work has affinities to a tradition in ecclesiastical historiography which is no longer honored by church historians of religion. I would further argue that this affinity may have more to do with negative reactions to his work than does his psychoanalytic persuasion.

When I use the term "religious biography" I do not simply mean that *Gandhi's Truth* is about a religious man. Erikson's chapter entitled "Homo religiosus" clearly indicates that he understood Gandhi to be a religious man. Rather, I am making a different point, namely, that *Gandhi's Truth*--the book--is a religious biography. I would use the more traditional term, hagiography, but this term conjures up in our minds thoughts about medieval Christian saints. I want us to think about religious biography in a rather different way; or, at least, as being a literary genre which is larger and more diffuse than medieval lives of the saints. For the same reason, I will not use the term "sacred biography" which has come to mean, in the history of religions, biographies written by intimate contemporaries of the subject. In a broad sense, Erikson qualifies as Gandhi's contemporary; but the term "sacred biography" usually implies a closer relationship between biographer and subject than Erikson can claim (e.g.

that of follower to leader). So I will use the term "religious biography" as being less clearly defined than hagiography and sacred biography but at the same time distinguishable from biography written from a historical-critical perspective.

Before I move into this discussion, it is reasonable for the reader to want to ask: Why should one want to argue that *Gandhi's Truth* is a religious biography? What is at stake in this kind of argument? By way of answer, I would like to draw more explicit attention to historians' criticisms of Erikson's psycho-biographical writings, especially *Gandhi's Truth*. One of the most eloquent critiques of *Gandhi's Truth* is that of David Donald, the noted Civil War historian who used psychological concepts himself in his celebrated biography of Charles Sumner. Donald's criticisms of Erikson were made in an address to the American Psychiatric Association in Dallas in May, 1972.[3] In this address, Donald saw himself as playing the role of family counselor, advising those who are engaged in this strange marriage of psychology and history how they might salvage the affair short of outright divorce. Given this assumed role, Donald's mood is grimly serious. I want to quote his criticisms at some length so that the general tone of the critique is preserved. Donald writes: "So great is Erikson's vogue today that his work is not merely read but imitated. Characteristically, his disciples often lack his strengths but exaggerate his weaknesses in their own books. Since Erikson's biographical studies have not hitherto been subjected to critical scrutiny by historians, it may be well to warn would-be psychographers of some difficulties posed by his method.

"The first of these stems from the fact that Erikson has never been willing to train himself as a historian. Like so many other psychoanalysts, he appears to believe that wide reading and a little common sense are substitutes for the historical method. Unfortunately, however, Erikson's unfamilarity with historians' tools has impaired the usefulness of his work. Lacking an acquaintance with the historical methods for testing evidence, he, as has already been mentioned, rested a crucial chapter of his Luther biography upon words that nobody is sure young Martin ever uttered. Lacking the historian's determination to get as close to his original source as possible, Erikson made no effort to master Gandhi's native Gujarati language but relied upon English translations --at the same time rather unkindly ridiculing the efforts of the translator. Lacking an understanding of how a historian sifts and measures belated and contradictory accounts of an event, Erikson interviewed the surviving witnesses to Gandhi's hunger strike at Ahmedabad but was unable or unwilling to make use of the material he gathered in retelling the story of Gandhi's life.

Second, Erikson has failed to master what J.H. Hexter has called the 'rhetoric of history.' There is not, of course, one distinctive style in which all history must be written, but there are common elements in all good historical writing. One of these is the recapturing of a sense of the past, the recreating of a feeling of immediacy, so that a reader will not merely understand what happened but in a vicarious sense participate in the event. Erikson's literary purposes are entirely different. '...I can do no better by my readers than to consider them participants or auditors in a seminar in which a first batch of material has been presented' he explains in his *Luther*; 'I shall try to formulate, on the basis of my experience, what the material suggests we should be watching for in our search for further material.' Following this method, Erikson devotes an extraordinarily small portion of his books to the straightforward telling of his story or even to the presentation of his own analysis of the evidence. Most of the books consist of descriptions of the psychoanalytic techniques he has employed and of explanations of the difficulties he has encountered. However usual in psychiatric literature, such discussions have about the same place in a work of historical biography as an account of the difficulties an author has had in filling his notes or in securing permission to photocopy manuscripts in the British Museum.

"A third, closely related weakness in Erikson's books results from the exaggeration of one of their notable strengths. 'Since any *reviewer* of a bit of history makes it his own by the mere circumstance of his selective attention,' he writes, 'a reviewer trained in clinical observation must account--at least to himself--for his own initial involvement much more systematically than has been the rule in most writing of history.' Consequently he keeps constantly in mind his own relationship to his subject, asking why he selected this biographical topic and why he is interested in that aspect of his hero's life. In proposing this admirable objective, however, Erikson has tended to forget his phrase, 'at least to himself,' and has increasingly devoted more and more space to the eluciadation of his own mental processes. In *Young Man Luther* the presence of the clinician was noticable but not obtrusive; in *Gandhi's Truth* it is so conspicuous as to make that work virtually a double biography of Gandhi and Erikson. Indeed, by the middle of the book the psychoanalyst takes over the stage completely, interrupting the narrative with a twenty-five page 'letter,' addressed to the Mahatma, expounding not Gandhi's opinions but Erikson's.

"These criticisms are not at all intended to question the importance of Erikson's work. Even if the author is careless in handling historical method, if he indulges in clinical rhetoric, and if he lapses frequently into autobiography, his books will continue to attract readers because Erikson himself is as interesting a man as Luther or Gandhi. Unless future psychobiographers are prepared to make the same claim, they had better borrow insight from Erikson's books but avoid them as models."

In short, Donald argues that Erikson exhibits grave weaknesses in his historical method, in his historical narrative and in his tendency to intrude himself into that narrative. I think one could only conclude from this assessment that a book like *Gandhi's Truth* has been judged to be "bad" history. The mitigating element in Erikson's own case is that he is so good at doing "bad" history that he necessarily evokes our admiration. As Professor George Lindbeck asked concerning *Young Man Luther*, "How can such a bad book be so good?"

Now, how might an Eriksonian respond to this assessment of his psychobiographical writings? One could respond to specific points and attempt to refute them one by one. One could say, for example, that Erikson himself was intrigued by the fact that historians who doubted the authenticity of the event to which Donald alludes in the Luther biography--the so-called "fit in the choir"--that these same historians found themselves almost compelled to incorporate the event into their own narratives even though they doubted its authenticity. It must have been such a singularly powerful event to these historians that they would violate their own historical canons and treat it as if it were true. Can we blame Erikson, therefore, for also treating the story as if it were true; especially if he (like some other historians) considered it appropriate to introduce apocryphal materials if these are consistent with what he perceived to be generally true about his subject's personality?

We could take up each of Donald's points in this fashion, trying to refute them by reference to the texts themselves. But I suspect that the problem runs deeper than this. Donald might well respond to the effect that, if these examples are not enough to persuade us that Erikson's psychobiographies are "bad" history, then other examples could be cited. Indeed, I can imagine that he might finally show us two books--one of Erikson's psychobiographies and a book such as Lacey Baldwin Smith's *Henry VIII: The Mask of Royalty*, a book which has been acclaimed for its penetrating psychological perception into the personality of Henry VIII.[4] Donald would ask us to compare the two books in terms of historical method, historical narrative and the problem of the author's intrusion into his narrative. On every point, Smith's book will pass muster and Erikson's will not. On the basis of this comparative analysis, we might be led, as Donald was, to make a few gratuitous comments with regard to Erikson's work--i.e. that Erikson can allow himself to intrude in the narrative because his life is as interesting as Gandhi's. But, on the matter of historical method, narrative and the problem of the historian failing to allow his materials to speak for themselves--on each of these points, Erikson's work will appear the inferior of the two books.

So what does the Eriksonian do? He can say: "Well, it may be bad history but I like it anyway; Professor Donald and his ilk have no right to tell me what I should or should not like." Obviously, though, this kind of obscurantism will not do.[5] I would propose, therefore, that we address the problem as an issue of *genre*. Perhaps Erikson's psychobiographies are a peculiar kind of biography. Supposing they belong not in the genre of *historical* biographies, but in another genre which we may call *religious* biography. If this is so, then we might say that Donald's points are not so much mistaken as beside the point. Criticisms appropriate to the novel may be entirely inappropriate when applied to poetry. However, in the case of Erikson's books on Luther and Gandhi, one would have to acknowledge that there is some basis for this employment of inappropriate cannons. Historical and religious biography are both forms of biography, and it is frequently difficult to distinguish the two. The distinction between poetry and novel is usually not difficult to make. Usually the difference is apparent to the naked eye; a page of poetry and a page of a novel simply do not look the same. With historical and religious biography, the difference may not be as easy to detect. Yet, as I now want to argue, I think we can distinguish them and precisely on the basis of their form or formal structure.

In developing this argument, I want to center attention on three critical formal issues. The first concerns the relation of theme and event. The second concerns the use in religious biography of the biographical pattern. The third concerns the relation of myth and ritual. As I discuss these three issues, I will allude to my own psychobiographical studies for illustrative purposes when appropriate. I will also, of course, relate what I have to say to *Gandhi's Truth*. However, I am assuming that my readers are quite familiar with the book, so I will not engage in a great deal of documentation.

The Relation of Theme and Event:

Much discussion of Erikson's *Gandhi's Truth* has centered around his choice of the Ahmedabad event.[6] Why did Erikson select this event as the origin of militant nonviolence? Were there not more obvious choices he may have made? Now, Erikson's choice of the Ahmedabad event can probably be defended on historical grounds. However, the whole discussion of his choice of this event has diverted attention from the really important question--namely, what is an "event"? My answer to this question takes the following form: First, it is evident that in Erikson's biographical studies, the narrative is structured around "the event." This is evident in *Young Man Luther*, as Erikson devotes each chapter to a single critical event in Luther's life. This is also evident in *Gandhi's Truth*, where the whole book is structured around the Ahmedabad event. In Erikson's view, events are those occurrences which assume an importance which distinguishes them from ordinary episodes. The debate about his choice of the Ahmedabad experience centers around this distinction. Was it truly an "event" or was it merely an episode? And, as I have indicated, this issue has been primarily considered a historical issue. However, as we focus more directly on the question, "What is an event?" we begin to recognize that it is more than a historical issue. It is at least a literary issue (relating to the structure of the narrative). But, even further, it is a matter which invites considerations of a religious nature.

An important clue as to how Erikson understands an "event" appears in his chapter "A Seminar in Ahmedabad" in the section "Echoes of an Event." In this chapter, Erikson reports on two of his own experiences while visiting in Ahmedabad. The first was a seminar in which his life cycle theory was compared to the Hindu life stages. The second was his observation of school children engaged in play construction. I want to comment on the second experience first. As you will recall, the children were asked to invent scenes from an imaginary moving picture, using the toys placed in front of them. The observers' task was then to view these scenes as a kind of pictorial narrative which yields a dominant theme. The scene is a spatial event and this spatical event lends itself to thematization. I might note, parenthetically, that this procedure was developed under the tutelege of Henry Murray, the Harvard psychologist with whom

Erikson worked after coming to the United States in the 30s. Murray is known for his development of the Thematic Apperception Test (or TAT) in which there is a similar procedure of isolating themes from the examinees' stories or narratives in response to given pictures.[7] More recently, Murray applied this same procedure to the interpretation of myths. Viewing myths as "represented events," Murray interpreted these represented events according to their "basic thema." Within the basic thema, he would distinguish between simple and complex thema. For example, taking the Garden of Eden myth, he suggested that its simple thema could be described as "prohibition-transgression-punishment." The complex thema would then specify that the prohibition was from God, the transgression was eating the fruit, two persons were the transgressors, and punishment was expulsion from an idyllic environment.[8]

Interestingly enough, Erikson employs a rather similar distinction between themes in his essay on the nature of clinical evidence.[9] Here he suggests that the therapist is attentive to "recurrent themes" which reappear in the course of therapy; as these "recurrent themes" begin to form a pattern, the therapist then hazards an interpretation which attempts to integrate these recurrent themes, and Erikson calls this the "unitary thema." This unitary thema, like the "simple thema" in Murray's interpretation of myths, is brief, conceptual and usually imageless and undramatic.

Returning to the Indian children's play constructions: Erikson, as observer, notices that the Indian children attempted to use all the toys at their disposal, creating a play universe filled to the periphery with blocks, people and animals, but with little differentiation between outdoors and indoors, jungle and city, or, indeed, one scene from another. And, as Erikson notes, if one asks the children what or where is "the exciting scene," one finds it imbedded somewhere where nobody could have discerned it as an individual event and certainly not as a central one. (This obscuring of the real "event" in a mass of detail is illustrative of Freud's notion of displacement, an interpretive principle used in dream interpretation; displacement occurs when the dream narrative hides the important image in the dream by giving undue prominence to relatively minor and incidental dream elements.) In any case, the task for the observer when confronted with this particular form of play construction is to formulate a simple or unitary thema. And Erikson says that, in the case of the Indian children's scenes, the thema is, in a word, *fusion*. This fusion is evident in the difficulty the observer has in distinguishing an "event" from the flux of episodes, a fact out of the stream of feelings, a circumscribed relationship from multiple encounters. Now, of course, this theme of fusion becomes an argument in favor of the Ahmedabad event; in India, one should not be surprised to find an important event obscured within a mass of unimportant episodes. However, I am less interested in this apologetic for the Ahmedabad event than in the basic proposal that an event has a theme. And the theme which Erikson proposes for the Ahmedabad event is *fusion*.[10]

Before moving on to the second issue before us, I would like to digress somewhat and illustrate this theme-event relationship with an example from Western materials. This illustration provides a useful comparison to the theme-event relationship in *Gandhi's Truth*. I have been engaged for a number of years with a psychobiographical study of John Henry Newman, the 19th Century English ecclesiastical leader who, in mid-career, left the Church of England and converted to Catholicism. Shortly after his conversion, he wrote an autobiographical novel entitled *Loss and Gain: The Story of a*

Convert.[11] Newman developed the notion in the novel that the conversion event was a mixture of loss and gain. Now, it occurred to me that Newman came to understand every significant event in his life in terms of this loss-gain theme. Events are dual, not singular. If they appear on the surface to be mere loss (e.g. his examination failure as an Oxford undergraduate), one should be attentive to the element of gain which lies beneath the surface. Or, if they are ostensibly events of gain (e.g. his winning a coveted Oxford University fellowship), he cautioned himself that he should be attentive to the potential loss implicit in this ostensible gain.

Newman viewed his own personal life in terms of this loss-gain theme. But, in addition, he viewed the whole course of ecclesiastical history in this light as well. Once, in commenting on ecclesiastical controversies, he asked: "What is ecclesiastical history but a record of the ever-doubtful fortune of the battle.... Scarcely are we in peace, when we are in persecution; scarcely have we gained a triumph, when we are visited by a scandal. Nay, we make progress by means of reverses; our griefs are our consolations; *we lose Stephen to gain Paul*."[12] Hence, historical events are also dual; when we think we are losing, we are gaining; when we think we are gaining, we are also losing. Events have a built-in ambivalence. They are "ever-doubtful."

I should like to discuss a single event in Newman's life which dramatizes this loss-gain theme. I choose this event because it bears remarkable parallels to Gandhi's Ahmedabad event. Three years before Newman became engaged in the Oxford Movement, he was involved in a very curious affair which many of his friends were quite embarassed about. They were ashamed that he would involve himself in such a trivial dispute and that he would have employed such underhanded methods in the affair.

The event involved his activity in the local Oxford chapter of the Church Missionary Society in the Church of England. (Years later, his brother reminded his readers in his short biographical study of John Henry Newman that it involved the local Oxford chapter of the Society; by this time, many had come to believe that the event involved the national Society.) Newman was the secretary of the chapter at Oxford and had been secretary for nearly five years before the dispute in 1829. The Society was largely controlled by the Evangelical faction within the Church of England, a faction which had proven itself more zealous than moderate Anglicans with regard to missionary work. In 1829, Newman's own Evangelical leanings were beginning to wear thin. The clergyman who had been responsible for converting him to the Evangelical cause had died the previous year, and this death probably evoked in Newman some feeling that he was now free to dissociate himself from the Evangelicals. However, it was the vehemence with which he dissociated himself from the missionary society which distrubed many of his friends. I would argue, without taking time to support this argument, that some of his vehemence was due to the fact that his Evangelicalism had been the ostensible basis for his estrangement from his father a few years earlier. Now, his father was dead and he could not restore the relationship; but perhaps he could demonstrate his profound regrets for the rift in their relationship.

In any case, it occurred to him in 1829 that control of the Church Missionary Society could be wrested from the Evangelicals and placed under the direct control of the Bishops. His plan was simple. As secretary of the local chapter in Oxford, he would send out a pamphlet which set forth the principles according to which non-Evangelical clergymen could in good conscience join a society established by these dissenters. If enough new churchmen joined, the

Evangelicals would lose control of the group. It would appear that Newman himself doubted that the plan would actually succeed. However, as Erikson says of Gandhi in the Ahmedabad event, Newman was looking farther ahead and saw this event as the initial stage of an extended conflict. Thus, he acknowledged in a letter to his sister that he was exposing himself publicly: "Now, if it be a silly thing, why, I am exposing myself and doing what is unsafe; but one must run risks to do good, and fortune favors the bold; so I must hug myself, if no one else will hug me." As he expected, the scheme failed to gain the support of non-Evangelicals and, at the March, 1830 meeting of the local chapter, he was turned out of his secretaryship on the grounds of insubordination and in response he withdrew his membership in the society.

There were at least three eye-witness responses to Newman's actions in this event. One friend, when he heard of the scheme, refused to believe it. When the evidence was incontrovertible, he commented that the plan was "really mean" of Newman. Newman's brother Francis had this to say about it: "Yet no sooner do events begin to open favorably, than he will not allow his seed to ripen; but, as if a momentary success had intoxicated him, he at once flares into a hostility, which looks like treachery." However, another close friend and future loyal supporter in the Oxford Movement took the far-sighted view that Newman also took: "Very few approve of this plan, or think it practicable; but Newman is not a man to be deterred by temporary failures. He is, indeed, better calculated than any man I know...to release the Church of England from her present and curtailed condition." In short, Newman's friends and relatives viewed this event in different ways: some saw it as nothing more than a loss for Newman (the failure of his political objectives, the loss of esteem). But others, including Newman himself, considered the gain that lay beneath the apparent loss. Temporary failure, but ultimate success. However, because his biographers also consider the whole event demeaning to Newman, they also "play it down" (as Gandhi's biographers have "played down" the Ahmedabad event) and give considerably greater prominence to his involvement in parliamentary elections that year.

In this illustration, we see how it is possible to give a thematic rendering to the structure of an event. This example parallels Erikson's thematization of the Ahmedabad event, though it plays on the notion of duality and contradiction rather than an undifferentiated fusion. On the other hand (and this leads us to the second issue I want to discuss --the matter of biographical pattern), Erikson also makes clear that there is a basic duality inherent in the fusion. In a word, at issue in this theme of fusion is the intimacy vs. isolation conflict. As Erikson describes this duality: "But fusion and isolation are polar themes.... The fusion enforced and, no doubt, often enjoyed in the joint family and in crowed life (in India) in general results in a polarity. There is, no doubt, a deep recurring need to escape the multitude, and there is a remarkable capacity for being alone in the middle of a crowd. I have, in fact, never seen so many individuals in a catatonic-like isolation in the middle of a chattering crowd. But aloneness, too, is often dominated by a deep nostalgia for fusing with another, and this in an exclusive and lasting fashion, be that 'Other' a mentor or a god, the Universe--or the innermost Self." Here, then, Erikson's articulation of the fusion theme is derived from the intimacy-isolation polarity--i.e. his sixth stage of the life cycle. (Incidentally, I would argue that Newman's loss-gain thema concerns autonomy vs. shame and self-doubt conflicts. According to Erikson's life-cycle theory, the task of "holding on" and thus of acquisition was introduced in the earliest stage of the life cycle. The dilemma faced in the second or autonomy vs. shame and self-doubt stage has to do with determining when and under what circumstances one can relinquish the support and sustenance of those around him and rely on his own capacities and strengths. To "let go" or relinquish under such conditions is to experience a kind of "loss" but at the same time a necessary "gain." Thus, this very experience of "letting go"--and running the risk of self-determination--is fraught with ambiguity. It is not that loss simply turns into gain eventually but that one experiences loss and gain simultaneously. "Gain" is predicted on the capacity to "lose." In short, the second stage of the lifecycle captures the "ever-doubtful" quality of human events.) We come, then, to my second point, the use of the biographical pattern in religious biography.

The Biographical Pattern in Religious Biography:

I would now like to return to the other experience which Erikson recounts in his chapter entitled "A Seminar in Ahmedabad." This was the seminar in which discussion focused on the attempt to relate the Hindu life stages to Erikson's life cycle. Erikson indicates that he did not resist these correlations, recognizing that his life-stages, for all their seemingly scientific aura, harbored a "mythological trend" of their own. Hence, he acknowledges that his own life-cycle schema was as suspect to the modern sceptic in the seminar as was the Hindu schema. He writes" "A group of otherwise well-trained individuals when confronted with religious world-images never quite knows whether to consider the existence of such remnants of magic thinking the result of meaningless habituation or an irrational systematization. And yet, a pragmatic world-view which shuns all concepts of the cycle of generations can cause widespread disorientation. In such a dilemma, one cannot help admiring the ideational and ceremonial consistency of the older world-images."[13] Erikson here does not claim that his life-cycle schema qualifies as a "religious world-image." But he does recognize that it articulates similar religious meanings. And this recognition is especially evident in his use of both life-stage schemas--the Hindu dharmic structure and his own life-cycle theory--to provide the *pattern* which structures the biography as a whole. While the Hindu stages are especially prominent in chapter headings --that is, at the formal structural level--the Eriksonian life-cycle stages operate more prominently at the level of biographical narrative. Nonetheless, the point is that there is a structural fusion of the Hindu and the Eriksonian life-cycle schemas. And it is this fusion that enables Erikson to claim that he brings to the traditional interpretation of the events in Gandhi's life "a new awareness."[14] In short, we have moved from event to theme and now to pattern. Let us look more closely at this matter of pattern--biographical pattern.

In discussions of Erikson's psychobiographical studies, it is customary to say that he employs psychoanalytic concepts.[15] I believe this is generally true, even though he frequently surprises the reader by refusing to advance the anticipated psychoanalytic interpretation of an episode (e.g. Gandhi's dizzy spell immediately preceding his trip to England[16]). However, while granting that psychoanalysis is especially important to psychobiography, most discussions of this influence have centered on dynamic considerations-- i.e. on the psychobiographer's use of Freud's dynamic theories of personality. There is, however, another more structural emphasis in psychoanalytic thought, and this bears especially on the matter of biographical pattern. I should like to sketch the basic contours of this structural emphasis.

The psychoanalytic interest in biography has roots in the early psychoanalytic theorists' immersion in mythology.

Their interest in myth provided the basis for a derivative interest in biography. The common element in these excursions into mythology and biography was their central interest in the figure of the hero. Undergirding this interest, in turn, were their efforts to discover the "biographical pattern" behind myths, legends and folklore.[17] If mythology manifests a biographical pattern to which all mythical heroes conform, and if this pattern could be shown to be universal in its scope, then this pattern or aspects of the pattern might appear in historical lives as well. In *The Myth of the Birth of the Hero*, Otto Rank believes that he has isolated such a pattern. It includes such events as (1) the hero is born of distinguished parents; (2) his origin is preceded by difficulties, such as the continence or prolonged barrenness of the parents; (3) during or before the pregnancy, there is a prophecy cautioning against his birth and usually threatening danger to the father or father-surrogate; (4) once born, he is surrendered to the water, then saved by animals or lowly people and suckled by a female animal or a humble owman; (5) after he grows up, he finds his parents, takes his revenge but is acknowledged as their rightful heir; (6) he finally achieves rank and honors. Now, I am not so much interested in the specific pattern which Rank develops; the pattern has been considerably expanded and refined since Rank addressed the problem.[18] But what does attract our attention is the fact that Rank's biographical pattern is structured in terms of a limited number of critical events in the life of the hero. More recently, within psychological circles, Joseph Campbell has carried forward Rank's interest in the universal biographical pattern in his book *The Hero with a Thousand Faces*.[19] Campbell observes that, with the increasing importance of individuality in the West, the biographical pattern has become internalized, with the hero understood as on an internal journey. The problem, for Campbell, becomes how do we restore the objectivity of the pattern? Nonetheless, Campbell's account of the biographical pattern also employs critical events in the pilgrimage of the hero as its fundamental structuring device.

However, the psychoanalytic theorist who has worked most closely with the biographical pattern is the art historian, Ernst Kris. Kris is important in two very critical ways: (1) First, in an important chapter in his book *Psychoanalytic Explorations in Art*,[20] Kris moves the discussion of biographical pattern from myths to actual biographies; in this case, medieval and Renaissance biographies of artists. (2) Second, he makes a strong case for the evolutionary quality of the biographical pattern. Campbell recognizes the evolutionary quality of the pattern inasmuch as he notes its increasing internalization. But Kris is concerned with the fact that biographical patterns may themselves undergo change. Hence, he wants to recognize the "social function" of the biographical pattern of life-events. This social function, which he calls "enacted biography," is based on the fact that once the biographical pattern becomes known or assimilated into the culture, individuals begin quite self-consciously to pattern their lives according to the biographical pattern. Thus, the pattern becomes constitutive of human life and not merely its consequence. However, as the pattern becomes constitutive, it also undergoes changes. In some cases, the pattern assumes new depth as new life-events are added and old ones reinterpreted or discarded. In other cases, the pattern is trivialized with melodramatic events being substituted for genuinely dramatic "events" in the original pattern. (One such melodramatic event in later forms of the biographical pattern of artists' lives is the suicide of the artist because he discovers he has omitted the horseshoes from an equestrian statue.) However, the basic point is that biographical patterns, being of evolutionary quality, are not static but dynamic. They can, as Erikson himself suggests, incorporate "new awarenesses."

Supposing, then, that we consider Erikson's own life-cycle theory to be a biographical pattern; one intended, in Kris' words, to "realize the old ideals of biographers in a new form." This would be another way of saying that the life-cycle schema has continuities with traditional biographical formulae. But, at the same time, insofar as his life-cycle theory articulates an evolution in the traditional biographical patterns, it may simultaneously realize the old ideals of biographers and also express new awarenesses. Indeed, the life-cycle concept has become constitutive of the lives of many of Erikson's readers; while the life cycle theory was originally offered as a descriptive theory, it has now become constitutive--we expect to have identity crises, intimacy conflicts, generativity problems, and all in this chronological order. In fact, even Erikson himself is not immune from this effect. He recently mentioned that a woman asked him how he, in the eighth stage of life, was developing the art of equanimity in his own life. His reply, let me have my despair first.

But the crux of the matter is, simply, the capacity of the life-cycle schema to articulate new awarenesses as these emerge out of older traditional patterns. Take, for example, Gandhi's first appearance as a lawyer in the section which Erikson entitles, "Arjuna in the Court of Small Claims." On the one hand, Gandhi's experience here is reminiscent of the event recounted in the Bhagavad-Gita when Arjuna shrinks from engaging in battle. (This event would seem to fit within the apprentice of *Antevasin* stage in the Hindu life cycle and within the identity stage in Erikson's cycle.) It is quite interesting to note that Arjuna's reluctance to fight was not simply due to fright, but to the fact that he would be involved in fighting against members of his own family. We seem to have a parallel here to Gandhi's decision to begin his work in India in his own home town. But the basic issue which the Arjuna event poses is that Gandhi seems vaguely aware that the incident in the court of small claims--his inability to plead the case--fits the Arjuna event. Erikson points out, for example, that Gandhi used language taken from this Bhagavad-Gita when describing a similar experience in England. So, on the one hand, we have Gandhi reflecting a traditional biographical pattern in this event in the court of small claims. But, on the other hand, Erikson wants to infuse this traditional event with new awarenesses--the awarenesses which he senses Gandhi has brought to this event and has thereby transformed it. Hence, Erikson notes that Gandhi was smitten in the drabness of a court of "small claims"--as if to suggest that his future style of leadership would involve seeking out "the smallest and most local situations as a great soul's proper battleground." He would stake his leadership on "small claims" which had much larger moral and legal implications. Perhaps this is the way that the modern lawyer transforms the ancient warrior's critical life-events.

In the foregoing example, the event in the biographical pattern remains essentially unchanged; it simply assumes new meaning as Gandhi infuses it with new awarenesses. However, there is another element in the process of the evolution of biographical patterns that also requires mention. At times, there is not simply the transformation of traditional events but the inclusion of new ones into existing patterns. I am not sufficiently familiar with Indian biographical patterns to know whether certain unique events in Gandhi's life might be incorporated into certain traditional Hindu patterns. However, given Erikson's dedication of his book to Martin Luther King, it is interesting to note that many autobiographies written by American blacks in recent years incorporate into the Western biographical pattern (as reflected in the autobiographical mode) events similar to Gandhi's incident in the train in South Africa. Invariably, the black autobiographer will give an account of an episode in which he was slighted by a white individual--frequently with no words being spoken--and he will suggest that this episode changed his life. Now, Erikson says, in response to queries, that the train episode in South Africa would best qualify as marking Gandhi's identity crisis. In similar fashion, black autobiobraphers clearly want their readers to understand that similar events in their lives were "identity" events. So perhaps we see here some infusion of new events--explicitly identity related--into more traditional biographical patterns. And perhaps the fact that Gandhi's life-events have been preserved in mural form in the Birla house in Delhi (a memorial shrine to Gandhi) would indicate that some fusion of his life with more traditional patterns is inevitable.[21]

But, finally, any adequate consideration of the use of biographical patterns in *Gandhi's Truth* would need to recognize Erikson's own accomplishment, namely, the fusion of his life cycle schema with the more traditional Hindu model. He appears to seek this kind of fusion of biographical patterns because he recognizes that Gandhi himself represented the infusion of traditional life-structures with "modern" understandings. Erikson and Gandhi, the one in his psychological work and the other in his political activity, share this common understanding of their life tasks. This is perhaps most dramatically evident in Erikson's famous letter to Gandhi. This letter, which does not simply appear willy-nilly in the middle of the book, but instead concludes the householder or intimacy-isolation stage of the narrative, seems to want to tell Gandhi that it was in matters of intimacy that he failed to infuse the traditional Hindu pattern with "new awarenesses." On the other hand, this letter also suggests that Erikson is acknowledging his difficulty with his own intimacy-isolation responses to Gandhi. He wonders whether he should address Gandhi with "a personal word." But then we ask, is this not precisely the dilemma which the writer of *religious* biography has to face at some point in his narrative? He needs to ask himself and at the same time inform his reader as to whether the subject of his biography is to be taken as exemplary. Is his subject's life worthy of being emulated, as the basis for future biographical enactments? If Erikson finally concludes that Gandhi's *personal* standards are at once too high and too low (Erikson is very conscious of the importance of middle-range dignity[22]), nonetheless, as *religious* biographer, this kind of intrusion is not only acceptable, but expected. The historian's neutrality is not appropriate to religious biography. The religious biographer must take a position with respect to his subject as an *exemplary model*.[23]

The Relation of Myth and Ritual:

In the foregoing discussions we have moved from event to theme to pattern. In this third and final section I want to discuss briefly the myth-ritual configuration which seems to encompass Erikson's employment of the biographical pattern. We might put the issue in this way: Erikson, like most proponents of the myth-ritual school, recognizes that ritual is in some sense primordial, i.e. ritual gives rise to myth. It is quite evident that his *Gandhi's Truth* plays heavily on ritual. He views the strategy of Satyagraha as a new ritual strategy; and his account of the Ahmedabad conflict plays to a great extent on its public ritual aspects. Then, of course, in the concluding section of the book, he discusses the place of ritual in the containment of violence.

On the other hand, Erikson does not say a great deal about the fruit of these ritual encounters, namely, the myths which they engender. I believe this is because, for

Erikson, Gandhi *is* the myth and *Gandhi's Truth* itself is in some sense an effort to capture that myth. There are certain parallels here to some work I have been doing with Abraham Lincoln, especially with the myth of martyrdom which developed spontaneously after Lincoln's death. I would like to comment on some of these parallels as they center on this problem of myth and ritual. Then, in conclusion, I will try to indicate how this problem is especially critical for *religious* biography.

Many of the interesting parallels between Lincoln and Gandhi are in terms of the intimacy-isolation conflict. In his early life in southern Illinois, Lincoln had difficulty establishing relationships with women. He had a series of courtships which did not work out (including but not primarily centering around his ill-fated relationship with Ann Rutledge); and his marriage to Mary Todd was preceded by a broken engagement then reconciliation. There are two early stories, possibly apocryphal, which biographers take to be illuminative of his relationship to Mary Todd. The two stories are of particular interest here because they bear remarkable similarities to the famous "chamber pot" episode in Gandhi's South African period (before he, too, rose to national prominence). It is said that Lincoln and his wife Mary burst out of their house in Springfield on one occasion, with Lincoln shouting, "You make the house intolerable, damn you, get out of it." On another occasion, Sunday morning churchgoers were startled to see Mary threatening her husband with a kitchen knife, and he attempting to push her back into the house with remonstrances about their making an awful scene in front of their church-bound neighbors. In another paper, I have developed the implications for Lincoln's future leadership of the fact that the neighborhood in frontier towns was beginning to threaten familial solidarity. These stories in some sense exemplify this conflict and play heavily on the intimacy-isolation motif.24

Lincoln's intimacy-isolation conflicts were also evident in his relationship to his father and here, too, we find this relationship prefiguring his future leadership role. While Gandhi rued the fact that he had not attended his father's deathbed, Lincoln was informed that his father was dying but refused to travel the necessary seventy-odd miles to see his dying father. The fact that he gave as his excuse his wife's "baby sickness" may suggest that, underneath it all, concern for his own householder responsibilities took precedence over filial piety. In this, there is a fairly direct parallel to Gandhi's decision to be with his wife on the night of his father's death. Nonetheless, Lincoln's deliberate refusal to visit his father stands in marked contrast to Gandhi's explanation of his behavior as the effect of impulse and lust. This fundamental difference in their responses to their father's deaths may relate to Erikson's suggestions concerning the family dynamics which undergirded their respective intimacy-isolation conflicts. In the Gandhi study, Erikson makes much of the problem of the diffusion of the mother; she has various needs to take care of and connot attend to the requirements of any single child. In contrast, in his discussion of frontier America in *Childhood and Society*, Erikson points to the diffusion of the father.

Given the importance of this diffusion of the father for Lincoln's own perception of his leadership role, I should like to quote Erikson's comments on this point in full. Erikson suggests that we have in America "an ingenious arrangement...which diffuses the father ideal." He goes on: "The boy's male ideal is rarely attached to his father, as lived with in daily life. It is usually an uncle or friend of the family, if not his grandfather, as presented to him (often unconsciously) by his mother. The grandfather, a powerful and powerfully-driven man--according to a once widely prevailing American pattern, another composite of fact and myth--sought new and challenging engineering tasks in widely separate regions.... His sons could not keep pace with him and were left as respectable settlers by the wayside; only his daughter was and looked like him. Her very masculine identification, however, did not permit her to take a husband as strong as her powerful father. She married what seemed, in comparison, a weak but safe man and settled down. In many ways, however, she talks like the grandfather. She does not know how she persistently belittles the sedentary father and decries the family's lack of mobility, geographic and social. Thus she establishes in the boy a conflict between the sedentary habits which she insists on, and the reckless habits she dares him to develop.... It is as if these boys were balancing on a tightrope. Only if they are stonger than or different from the real father will they live up to their secret ideals, or indeed, to their mother's expectations; but only if they somehow demonstrat that they are weaker than the omnipotent father (or grandfather) image of their childhood will they be free from anxiety."[25] On the basis of this account of the diffusion of the father ideal in frontier America, we can understand Lincoln's refusal to pay his last respects to his well-intentioned but uninspiring father. But, beyond his personal life, we can see the effects of this diffusion of the father ideal in his leadership role. For large numbers of his fellow countrymen, Lincoln as President symbolized the restoration of the father ideal. Less reckless than the powerful grandfather but stronger than the sedentary father, he was the strong but faithful "father Abraham"--in much the same way that Gandhi came to personify the personally-attentive "mother India."

In speaking of what these two national leaders came to personify in the hearts and minds of their fellow countrymen, we are already verging on the problem of myth. But let us press the issue further, again with the intimacy-isolation conflict in mind, as we consider the mythical effects of martyrdom. What especially interests me here is the fusion--the link between these intimacy-isolation concerns and biographical patterns--which was effected through Lincoln's martyrdom. Immediately after his death, there were numerous biographies written, both from the literary East and from the frontier West, which centered on different aspects of Lincoln's life-history. In his essay "The Folklore Lincoln," David Donald contrasts these two traditions, the Eastern tradition based on the biographical pattern of the "representative man" (following George Washington and Christ) and the Western tradition based on the biographical pattern of the folk hero.[26] Now, as Roy P. Basler points out in his study of the Lincoln legend, these two biographical patterns soon became fused. In a very short time, it became difficult to distinguish biographies in terms of Eastern and Western biographical patterns.[27] Hence, the myth of Lincoln--especially as crystallized through his martyrdom--effected a new synthesis of existing biographical patterns of the American hero. Further, we might say that, while the "ritual" engagement between North and South in the Civil War exemplified the country's diffusive of isolationist tendency, the myth of martyrdom centered in Eastern and Western biographical traditions affirmed its fusion, or intimacy tendency. The martyred Lincoln becomes a man of intimacy, a man who cannot endure the isolation of the grave. As Vachel Lindsay has it, "He cannot sleep upon his hillside now. He is among us, as in times before." Hence, the ritual of the Civil War manifested the nation's inherent tendency toward isolation, while the myth of the martyred President recalled it to its pledge of intimacy.

I have no competence to argue that a similar fusion occurred in the myth of Gandhi's martyrdom. However, the two experiences which Erikson recounts in his chapter "A Seminar in Ahmedabad" imply Erikson's own sense that, in *his* search for Gandhi, he would find this wiry little man in the fusion of elite and folk, wise and simple. The first of these experiences centers on the seminar in which Hindu theology was discussed. The second centers on his asking small children to create a folk play. Perhaps some kind of fusion of elite and folk elements in Indian society is implicit in these two experiences. In any case, it seems to be the function of such hero myths to represent the unification of the body politic. It is almost as if to say that, if the ritual enactments of the leader are only partially successful and do not finally succeed in containing violence, then perhaps the myth of their martyrdom will so succeed. But to sustain this myth, there is a need for biographers. Religious biographers who perceive their task not as the accurate recording of recent history, but as contributing to the restoration of the social order.

Let me conclude with one final reference to Henry Murray's discussion of myth. In this discussion, Murray calls for what he terms the "metabiography of the individual." Presumably, this metabiography would focus not on the everyday events of the individual life, but on the mythic understanding of the life--on events which represent what has been, will be, or continues to be of crucial importance. I think *Gandhi's Truth* falls into this general category of "metabiography." I do not think that this type of biography could or should corner the market. But, in the long tradition of historical scholarship, religious biography will continue to have its place. The problem in our own era is that religious biography is not easy to identify as such.

FOOTNOTES

1. Bainton's first response to Erikson's *Young Man Luther* was a review entitled "Luther: A Psychiatric Portrait" *Yale Review*, vol. 48, no. 3 (1959) pp. 406-10. A more recent full-length article by Bainton entitled "Psychiatry and History: An Examination of Erikson's *Young Man Luther*" appears in *Religion in Life*, Winter, 1971, pp. 450-78.

2. Barton's comments occur in a letter intended for publication in *The Psychoanalytic Review* in response to Clark's "Unconscious Motivations Underlying the Personalities of Great Statesmen and Their Relation to Epoch-Making Events (I. A Psychologic Study of Abraham Lincoln)" *The Psychoanalytic Review*, vol. 8, no. 1 (January 1921) pp. 1-21. Barton's letter was rejected by the editor on the grounds that it might prompt an "endless" discussion. This correspondence is inserted in Barton's copy of the Clark paper in his private collection, The Regenstein Library, University of Chicago. Clark later published a full-length study of Lincoln entitled *Lincoln: A Psycho-biography*, New York: Charles Scribner's Sons, 1933.

3. David Herbert Donald "Between History and Psychology: Reflections on Psychobiography," Benjamin Rush Lecture (American Psychiatric Association, Dallas, Texas, May 3, 1972). I am indebted to James Anderson, graduate student in the department of psychology, University of Chicago,

for drawing my attention to this lecture.

4. Lacy Baldwin Smith *Henry VIII: The Mask of Royalty*, Boston: Houghton Mifflin Company, 1971.

5. There is the tendency among psychohistorians to reject *in toto* such critiques of psychobiography. See, for example, Frederick Harling's response to Jacques Barzun's "History: The Muse and Her Doctors," *The American Historical Review*, vol. 77, no. 1 (1972), pp. 36-64. The response appears in *Newslatter of the Group for the Use of Psychology in History*, vol. 2, no. 2 (August 1973), pp. 3-4.

6. Susanne H. Rudolph has most effectively addressed this issue. See her review of *Gandhi's Truth* in *Contemporary Psychology*, vol. 15, no. 8, pp. 484-86.

7. Henry A. Murray ed. *Explorations in Personality*, New York: Oxford, 1938.

8. Henry A. Murray "The Possible Nature of a 'Mythology' to Come," in Henry A. Murray, ed. *Myth and Myth-Making: A Symposium of Mythology in Religion, Literature, Psychology, Politics, and Other Aspects of Society*, Boston: Beacon Press, 1968, pp. 300-53.

9. Erik H. Erikson "The Nature of Clinical Evidence," *Insight and Responsibility*, New York: W.W. Norton and Company, Inc., 1964, pp. 49-80. An earlier discussion of the use of themes in play construction by Erikson appears in Murray, *Explorations in Personality, op. cit.*, pp. 552-82.

10. Erik H. Erikson *Gandhi's Truth: On the Origins of Militant Nonviolence*, New York: W.W. Norton and Company, Inc., 1969, pp. 39-41.

11. John Henry Newman *Loss and Gain: The Story of a Convert*, London: Burns and Oates, 1886 (first published 1848).

12. John Henry Newman *Essays Critical and Historical*, London: Longmans, Green and Company, 1995, vol. 3, p. 3 My italics.

13. *Gandhi's Truth*, p. 38.

14. This phrase occurs in the following context: "I see better what I hope the reader has come to see with me, namely, that I felt attracted to the Ahmedabad Event not only because I had learned to know the scene and not only because it was time for me to write about the responsibilities of middle age, but also because I sensed an affinity between Gandhi's truth and the insights of modern psychology. That truth, and these insights, are the legacy of the first part of this century to its remainder. A concrete event has served to illustrate their origins in all the complexity of historical actuality. I did not undertake to do and could not do more than that. But as we historicize more consciously, we also assume some of the burden of tradition. Even one past event, seen in the light of a new awareness, must make it apparent that man denies and abandons the visions and the disciplines he has already acquired only at the risk of historical and personal regression. pp. 439-40.

15. Jacques Barzun contends that "in order to be of use to

the historian or biographer, psychological or other technical terms must have fallen into the common domain." In his view, this accounts for the use of specifically psychoanalytic terminology in modern psychological biography and for the neglect of classical and "academic" psychological terminologies (e.g. Gestalt, behaviorist). *op.cit.*

16. *Gandhi's Truth*, pp. 137-38. Here Erikson resists the interpretation that the dizziness was a latent homosexual reaction to Gandhi's leaving his best friend. Erikson prefers the view that the dizziness signified an acute identity conflict. pp. 137-38.

17. Archer Taylor uses this term in his essay "The Biographical Pattern in Traditional Narrative," *Journal of the Folklore Institute*, Vol. 1 (1964), pp. 114-29

18. Otto Rank *The Myth of the Birth of the Hero*, ed. Philip Freund, New York: Vintage Books, 1959, p. 65. For an important expansion of the biographical pattern to include some 22 events, see Lord Raglan's *The Hero: A Study in Tradition, Myth, and Drama*, New York: Vintage Books, 1956, pp. 173-85. A briefer argument in behalf of the myth-ritual school appears in Lord Raglan's "Myth and Ritual" in Thomas A. Sebeok, ed. *Myth: A Symposium*, Bloomington: Indiana University Press, 1958, pp. 76-83. Raglan's recognition of the relation between ritual and the biographical pattern prompts aspects of my discussion in the third section of this paper.

19. Joseph Campbell *The Hero with a Thousand Faces*, Princeton: Princeton University Press (Bollingen Series XVII), *2nd. ed.*, 1968, pp. 36-37. Discussion of the

internalization of the pattern is on pp. 381-91.

20. Ernst Kris *Psychoanalytic Explorations in Art*, New York: Schocken Books, 1952, ch. 2. See also Ernst Kris and Otto Kurz, *Die Legende Vom Kunstler*, Wien: Krystallverlag, 1934.

21. Joanne Punzo Waghorne has pointed out to me that Ambedkar, one of Gandhi's rivals, structured his autobiography so as to demonstrate parallels between his life and popular lives of Buddha. I have observed a similar self-conscious identification with a traditional biographical pattern in John Henry Newman's lives of early Christian saints. Cf. my "John Henry Newman: The Reformer as Biographer" in Frank E. Reynolds and Donald Capps, eds. *The Biographical Process*, Utrecht: The Mouton Press, 1975 (forthcoming).

22. See, for example, his account of ritual engagements which allow the participants to disengage with their sense of dignity intact. *Gandhi's Truth*, pp. 434-35.

23. It is interesting to note that Clark's psychoanalytic study of Lincoln contains numerous intrusions on the part of the author, many of which involve observations concerning Lincoln's exemplary status. For example, Clark tells us that "Lincoln through the years goes his way, voicing his own creed with gentleness and humility, trusting that the people will follow, understand what his lofty moral purpose is and what it portends. It is a manifestation of the deepest 'meaning of his meaning' when he says that those who will can understand just what his purpose is, and those who are disinclined to do so--well, they 'do not matter,'" *Lincoln: A*

Psychobiography, op. cit., pp. 496-97. It is relatively easy to show that Clark's study had a "religious" intent, inasmuch as he wanted to demonstrate to victims of the Depression how lincoln used "temporary setbacks" to effect significant movements forward. This "myth" of Lincoln contrasted greatly with the biographies wirtten by Lincoln's contemporaries who saw Lincoln's "steady rise to greatness."

24. Donald Capps "Intimacy and Isolation: A Psychological motif in the Life and Myth of Abraham Lincoln." Unpublished paper presented at the annual meeting of the Society for the Scientific Study of Religion, 1973.

25. Erik H. Erikson *Childhood and Society*, rev. ed., New York: W.W. Norton and Company, 1963, pp. 312-13. An earlier version of Erikson's analysis of the American frontier and the diffusion of the father appears in his "Childhood and Tradition in Two American Indian Tribes with some Reflections of the Contemporary American Scene" in Clyde Kluckhohn and Henry A. Murray, eds. *Personality in Nature, Society, and Culture*, New York: Alfred A. Knopf, 1948, pp. 176-203.

26. David Donald "The Folklore Lincoln" in *Lincoln Reconsidered: Essays on the Civil War Era*, New York: Vintage Books, 1961, pp. 144-66.

27. Roy P. Basler *The Lincoln Legend: A Study on Changing Conceptions*, New York: Octagon Books, 1969, chs. 1-2. Basler points out that in the fusion of the two traditions, the New England "high culture" view tended to dominate: "Thus the wilderness hero has remained somewhat a local legend confined to the Lincoln country.

The drinking, cock-fighting, rough-and-tumble hero,
'the big buck of the lick' who dared anyone to 'come on
and whet his horns,' the lover of broad humor--such a
hero was worthy idolatry on the frontier, perhaps, but
not in New England. Hence New England made its own
Lincoln which it was able to a certain extent to foist
upon the Lincoln country. And as the spiritual picture
grew, the reminiscences became more and more in keeping
with it. What there is of the frontier hero in the
great Lincoln of poetry and fiction, is spiritualized
and hallowed by the simple process of omission, emphasis,
and invention, *which has so largely biased even the biographical accounts*." p. 147. My italics. Arthur F.
Wright discusses a similar fusion of biographical traditions in an wholly different cultural setting in his
essay "Sui Yang-Ti: Personality and Stereotype,"
Arthur F. Wright, ed., *Confuciansim and Chinese Civilization*, New York: Atheneum, 1965, pp. 158-87.

SECTION II

Studies of American Religious Figures

This section of papers on American religious figures bears a somewhat anomalous relationship to the volume as a whole. We say this for a number of reasons. First, Erikson himself has not written a full study of an American figure. His published efforts in this direction, such as his psychohistorical comments on William James, were not intended as discussions of representative American figures. The James discussion is not meant to illuminate the American experience, but to point to those dimensions of American psychology which anticipate Erikson's own notion of identity. Erikson does not treat William James, as Professor Michaelson does, as a representative American, much less a religious genius. Second, the symposium itself was not intended to provide a forum for "applied" psychohistory. While applications of Erikson's work to other religious figures were not discouraged, the intention of the symposium was to encourage "encounters" with Erikson's own work. Applied psychohistory may be one way of encountering Erikson, but the papers included in this section tend to use Erikson as a point of departure. At first glance at least these papers give the impression of being exercises in "getting around" instead of "getting at" Erikson's own work.

How, then, to explain this set of papers on American figures? The answer is relatively simple. The importance of this section of the volume is directly related to the fact that, for all his attention to reformations in 16th Century Europe and 20th Century India, the central locus of Erikson's psychohistorical work is America. For example, the Luther book grew out of clinical reflections on the difficulties of American youth with the problem of identity. Similarly, the Gandhi book reflects a concern with American social conflict in the 60s. In short, in Erikson's psychohistorical work the themes which inform the biography are fundamental to the American experience.

In one sense, this is simply to assert the obvious. We are reminded that all historians write from their own experience; subjective influence simply cannot be expunged from historical reconstruction. And for Erikson personally, probably the most momentous event in his own life was his immigration to America. Significantly, he prefaced his informal lecture at the symposium with reference both to the *fact* of his being an immigrant and to his *sense* of no longer being one. But there is also an important truth imbedded in this obvious assertion. For, in his whole corpus of writings, Erikson has been continually engaged in probing the American experience. Preceding the Luther study, there were his early reflections on the American identity in *Childhood and Society*. And subsequent to the Gandhi book, he has offered further reflections on the American identity in his Jefferson Lectures for the National Endowment for the Humanities.[1] Throughout this probing into the American identity, he has continued to pose and refine the same larger questions of historical and cultural process which are evident in the studies in this section. Within the general framework of the American identity, Erikson has addressed such problems as the relation of myth to history, the role of religion in the genesis and resolution of social conflicts, etc.

But most significantly, his latest treatment of American identity, the Jefferson Lectures, goes furthest in making explicit the *religious* dimensions of these various themes. From his *Childhood and Society* discussion of the coalman John Henry (working in the depths of the earth) to his Jefferson Lectures' treatment of the surveyor Thomas Jefferson (working from his perspective on the mount of Monticello), Erikson has addressed with increasing directness and immediacy issues of a religious nature. Thus, in the Jefferson Lectures he introduces religious themes as he considers Jefferson's vision of the American as a new type of man, a man whose own self-image incorporates the transcendence of tribal, national, credal and professional commitments. As Erikson outlines his then forthcoming lectures: "The lecturer will use a compendium produced in Jefferson's old age to show the relation

---

1 *Dimensions of a New Identity*. New York: W.W. Norton, 1974.

in the mind between the new American Identity and that religious part of any identity which deals with the awareness of death. There are two roads to a sense of immortal identity: "one via one's earthly identity with a special species of man led by 'immortal' leaders; and the other via the transcendence of that identity as exemplified (in our civilization) in the life and death of Jesus." Thus religion, even to the cultivated and enlightened Jefferson, is the basis for a new American identity founded on a "transcendent" self-image. On the other hand, the promise of this new identity underscores the failure of the Jefferson vision from the mount of Monticello, a failure evidenced in the continued glorification of class, nation, race, creed and occupation which comprises the darker side of the American experience. Thus, identity is a peculiarly hard problem for the American. His *sense* of self-transcendence, the self stripped of mundane legitimations, is continually threatened by the *fact* of "pseudo-speciation," the persistence of claims to ethnic, occupational, class and credal superiority.

In short, Erikson's psychohistorical interests are firmly established on American soil. In spite of the fact that his biographical subjects have not been American, this American thrust should not be surprising. As a method, psychohistory itself has firm roots in American scholarship. While the method itself can be traced to the psychoanalytic community in Europe, it has always thrived better in America. From L. Pierce Clark's study of Abraham Lincoln, published in 1933, to Erikson's study of Gandhi, published in 1969, America has seen a steady procession of psychobiographical studies. This favorable climate for psychohistory is attributable, in large part, to the continuing interest in American academic psychology in the "idiographic" mode of psychological research. However, more recently, psychohistory has also gained stature among professional historians. In 1957 William Langer delivered his Presidential address before the American Historical Association calling on historians to work toward the "deepening of our historical understanding through exploitation of the concepts and findings of modern psychology."[2] Hence, historians are not

---

[2] "The Next Assignment," *The American Historical Review*, LXIII, 2 (Jan. 1958), 285-304.

longer interested spectators; if anything, they form the largest group of active psychohistorians in America today. Given this favorable climate for the flowering of psychohistory, it is altogether fitting that psychohistorians should begin paying attention to the religious prophets in their own midst.

YOUNG PEOPLE OF THE GREAT AWAKENING: THE DYNAMICS OF A
               SOCIAL MOVEMENT

Cushing Strout

"I have been a good deal interested in the 'Great Awakening' and its results...In America, as in France, the old religious conceptions were in a sense being transformed into a kind of civil religion, and in this change is to be found much that helps explain the revolution--so I think at present."
Carl L. Becker to William E. Dodd,
March, 1914

    Historians are especially concerned with the understanding and explanation of social movements because they represent the agencies of significant changes. As they seek to get closer to the process of change, historians become interested not only in deeds but in the intentions, values, and orientations that sponsor them. This interest may guide them to the leaders and sometimes they may find themselves faced with the evidence of inner turmoil in a growth process that calls for the sensitive instruments of the psychoanalytically oriented student of personal development. Under the influence of the psycho-biographic method of Erik H. Erikson, this work has recently produced studies in political and intellectual history that have demonstrated their power to illuminate without the crudity, dogmatism, or the speculation that for so long dogged the early efforts to apply the resources of the Freudian tradition to the tasks of humanistic historiography.[1]

    Sometimes such work has been met by the charge that biography is not history, begging the question of by whom and just how history is actually made. But even if psycho-biographers can do much to satisfy in the new way the old nineteenth-century historical concern for the relationship of "the life" to "the times," the historian must often deal not with the lives of great men but with the collective experiences of their followers and and lesser leaders. How can depth psychology be relevant to this process? Surely it is too much limited to case histories of patients and leaders? Yet suppose the movement is itself involved with the psychology of "the sick soul" on a mass basis. Less dramatically, what of the collective formations of new commitments, whether in religion or politics or in some strange amalgamation of both? In such cases many individuals experience similar conversions in resonance with their peers and in relation to public issues. The movement then invites a psychological analysis because deep feelings seem to be at work in the reorientation of people who are not essentially mobs or hordes, randomly grouped for the moment. These feelings appear to link up intrapsychic conflict with social issues in a way that justifies the hyphen in "Psycho-history."[2]

Many collective movements yield their secrets to familiar considerations of political or economic interest, of ethnic loyalties, or explications of ideology, or of the sociology of prestige in a stratified society. But the deeper the process of conversion cuts into the inner life of the converted, the more difficulty the historian will have in fully understanding the evidence according to these familiar signposts. In such an emergency it is necessary to ask if the resources of the tradition of dynamic psychology can be called on to help understanding and explanation.

I wish to present such a case, which has attracted much recent interest among American scholars, in the modest spirit of the historian who is fascinated with the particularities of some puzzling piece of human affairs and therefore is in the market for limited context-bound explanations that fall short of the sweep and power of grand theory. I shall, in Isaiah Berlin's image, be in the position of the fox, who knows many things, rather than in that of the hedgehog, who knows one big thing. Nevertheless, I shall argue that the hedgehogs can be useful to the foxes in dealing with the dynamics of a social, religious, and psychological movement, so long as theory is tested pragmatically.

The religious revivals of the Great Awakening in mid-eighteenth century colonial America pose the problem in classic form of explicating the meaning and explaining the dynamics of a social movement. Every historian who has dealt with the Awakening has assumed its importance for a sequence of events that eventually led to the Revolution. It has seemed to be one of those cases, like the Puritan revolution in England, in which historians can show important connections between religion and politics. Yet in practise the scholarly record of interpretation is remarkably confusing, for all the agreement on the nature of the ideological differences between the friends of the revivals and their enemies. Only as the argument has moved closer to psychological insight has the fog lifted.

Historians have wavered between seeing the Awakening as a manifestation of "the spiritual hungers of the lower classes" against the "upper or educated classes," and, on the contrary, seeing it as a movement so general "that it knew no boundaries, social or geographic."[3] There is, however, a strong tendency for historians to believe that the Awakening was of great historical consequence for the rise of democracy. The first historian of the Awakening in the Middle Colonies saw it as "a democratic religious movement" that "prepared the way for the American Revolution" and created "a common American spirit."[4] The historian of the Awakening in Virginia believed that it "gradually welded the common people into a democracy which in the end was to change inevitably the temper, if not the form, of government."[5] Evangelical groups were intrinsically democratic because "each emphasized the worth and equality of the individual."[6] The revivalist agonies and ecstasies he accounted for by the observation that "this type of religious propaganda was particularly adapted to the South, because of the isolation of rural life and the small amount of education which was accessible to the small farmers and plain folks."[7]

More recent historians are skeptical of the relevance of class categories. A thesis on the MIddle Colonies finds the soil of the Awakening not in any social or political motives but in the inability of many Americans "to relate their traditional religious beliefs to the conditions of their new home."[8] C.C.

Goen's valuable study, *Revivalism and Separatism in New England, 1740-1800*, concludes that even the radical separated churches of the revival represented "a fair cross-section of the culture in which they existed."[9] Alan Heimert, a student of Perry Miller, makes in *Religion and the American Mind* the most ambitious claims for the Awakening, finding in the evangelical clergy the birth of the American tradition of Populists, Jacksonians, and Jeffersonians. Heimert at the same time, however, denies the relevance of "the categories of Marx and Beard," finding instead the ultimate meaning of the division over the Awakening in terms of "taste," a judgment its more sniffish enemies might have made.[10] Yet he claims also that evangelical religion in the 18th century "embodied a radical and even democratic challenge to the standing order of colonial America" and asserts that its sermons represented American counterparts to the social theory of Rousseau.[11] He concedes, however, that the immediate effect of the revivals was to temper "the fierce social, economic and political antagonism that had racked the colonies since the beginning of the century."[12] Heimert blithely leaves his sweeping assertions hanging by denying that it is his purpose "in any case to trace institutional changes and developments" or to demonstrate "how any event or activity was a consequence of the Awakening or of any idea espoused by either Calvinists or Liberals."[13] But he also thinks that "the evidence cries out for some connecting of the political behavior of Americans with the ideas of one or another of its variant brand of religion." To this plea he admits to offering "a few surmises," but they soon become major underlying assumptions which are simply taken for granted in the structuring and interpreting of his narrative. For him the Awakening becomes *equivalent*, eventually, to "liberty, equality, and fraternity."[14]

Heimert's mentor Perry Miller powerfully subverted the Manichaean dialectic of Vernon Louis Parrington with its depreciation of Edwards and Calvinism as reactionary victims of the march of liberal Progress; Heimert himself has inverted Parrington on his head in a similar Manichaean style, accusing rationalist liberals with being "nearly to a man, if not outright

Tories," then preaching Locke as "a justification of the *status quo*" while "deploring and seeking to subdue the revolutionary enthusiasm that was, despite their hopes and efforts, arising in the American populace."[15] This argument unconsciously reflects the penchant of Whig historians for finding spiritual ancestors because it sees the evangelical past as "an evident anticipation of what, by the early nineteenth century, emerged clearly as the more vital of American democratic traditions."[16] All this despite the admitted fact of "the disengagement of the evangelical ministry and populace from the usual institutions and processes of government and politics" and the remarkable concession of the fact that "in the thirty years before the Revolution" Calvinists had argued for political restraint of sinful men.[17]

Richard Bushman, in *From Puritan to Yankee*, has dealt in a much more credible and impartial way with the paradoxes entangled in these same issues. He believes that in Connecticut the Awakening "affected people of all classes" and though "probably more intense in the east than in the west and on the coast and large rivers than inland, no area was immune to the contagion."[18] Bushman shows that New Divinity men were "among the most avid proponents of rigid sumptuary legislation" and quite capable of supporting purges for orthodoxy at Yale.[19] Instead of standing Parrington on his head, as Hiemert had done, Bushman found the rationalists "still more daring" than the evangelicals because with the former "freedom of impulse was not restricted to those who laid some claim to grace." Therefore "the posthumous judgment" that rationalists "paved the way to larger liberty was essentially correct."[20]

Bushman modifies these observations by eventually linking New Lights to class and sectional alignments, seeing them as enterprising merchants, small traders, and small farmers in the eastern section, in contrast to Old Lights, linked with large landholders and conservative merchants of the western section.[21] The New Lights were a "heterogenous amalgamation" of New Divinity heirs of Edwards, of Yale Orthodoxy bent on stamping out heresy,

and of the eastern wing that was concerned more with toleration and
economic issues. By the eve of the Revolution, however, New Lights
were the "acknowledged champions of popular liberties after the
Stamp Act crisis."[22] How had this process come about? Was it
implicit in the ideology of Calvinist evangelism or a function
of its social position? Or due to some other reason?

Bushman couches his explanations in terms of a subtle mixture
of contingent, ideological, and characterological elements. He
has clarified the movement precisely because of his willingness to
venture psychological readings of the turmoil. The evangelicals
were important because they had weakened Puritan faith in the legalized authoritative social order: "In view of the makeup of the
Puritan personality, the courage ot contend openly with the fathers
of society had to have a religious source. Only when faith in the
divinity of earthly law and authority had been weakened, could a
party wholeheartedly seek the downfall of its rulers. After the
civil government's hostility to the revival disillusioned the New
Lights, conscience urged on rather than limited political activity.
The New Lights consequently had the power to transform the character of politics."[23] This explanation points to circumstances,
but it is supplemented by the argument that ideological emphasis
on live not law made voluntarism and "a free society" seem superior
to one based on "law and authority."[24] The Awakening itself,
furthermore, had provided a psychological mechanism for releasing
the conflict "between ambition and traditional authority." Guilty
men admitted their culpability and called upon Him to save them.
"But the God to whom they surrendered was not He whose authority
invested social institutions. Newborn men relied wholly on the
God they had discovered in a personal experience. Far from instilling submission to the old authority, the revival planted the
conviction that God's power was given to individuals, clearing
the way for men to resist in good conscience when the occasion
arose."[25] Already in the 1730's, according to Bushman, "the
conflict between order and piety defined a fissure along which
the religious quakes accompanying the Great Awakening split Connecticut society wide open." The Awakening as a "Psychological

and of the eastern wing that was concerned more with toleration and economic issues. By the eve of the Revolution, however, New Lights were the "acknowledged champions of popular liberties after the Stamp Act crisis."[22] How had this process come about? Was it implicit in the ideology of Calvinist evangelism or a function of its social position? Or due to some other reason?

Bushman couches his explanations in terms of a subtle mixture of contingent, ideological, and characterological elements. He has clarified the movement precisely because of his willingness to venture psychological readings of the turmoil. The evangelicals were important because they had weakened Puritan faith in the legalized authoritative social order: "In view of the makeup of the Puritan personality, the courage to contend openly with the fathers of society had to have a religious source. Only when faith in the divinity of earthly law and authority had been weakened, could a party wholeheartedly seek the downfall of its rulers. After the civil government's hostility to the revival disillusioned the New Lights, conscience urged on rather than limited political activity. The New Lights consequently had the power to transform the character of politics."[23] This explanation points to circumstances, but it is supplemented by the argument that ideological emphasis on love not law made voluntarism and "a free society" seem superior to one based on "law and authority."[24] The Awakening itself, furthermore, had provided a psychological mechanism for releasing the conflict "between ambition and traditional authority." Guilty men admitted their culpability and called upon Him to save them. "But the God to whom they surrendered was not He whose authority invested social institutions. Newborn men relied wholly on the God they had discovered in a personal experience. Far from instilling submission to the old authority, the revival planted the conviction that God's power was given to individuals, clearing the way for men to resist in good conscience when the occasion arose."[25] Already in the 1730's, according to Bushman, "the conflict between order and piety defined a fissure along which the religious quakes accompanying the Greak Awakening split Connecticut society wide open." The Awakening as a "psychological earthquake reshaped the human landscape."26

This account, much the best that we have, seems lacking only in its power to reconcile some of the author's own insights by looking even deeper into the dynamics of the process. Bushman shows that church government was a major issue in the years before the Awakening and that the minister's position in keeping order in the midst of community contention was becoming more and more difficult, despite legislative attempts by the Assembly to shore him up. One of the sources of trouble afflicted both Jonathan Edwards and his father. Timothy Edwards refused communion to his church for several years because it protested against his disciplining a young man for marrying without the permission of the girl's eminent father. Roger Wolcutt, a magistrate who later was lieutenant governor during the Awakening, wrote a pamphlet condemning the power of clergymen who, in his view, needed the check of ordinary laymen, experienced in secular life, and Wolcutt led a party in a dispute involving the daughter of another town leader in East Windsor.27 Timothy's son Jonathan would be challenged by his parish because of a similar disciplinary issue involving youths sniggering over a mid-wives' manual.

In such cases the issues cannot be framed in terms of piety *against* order for the clergy stood for both. Edwards and Nathaniel Whitaker, leading New Lights, were deposed from their parishes because they sought to deny the sacrament of communion except to visible saints, a return to earlier Puritanism and a tightening of discipline. Bushman says that New Lights "escaped the power of the social order in the Awakening and immediately put their trust in God."28 The evidence for their "escape" is that their own experience of conversion was held to be fundamental in the Awakening. Yet the older authoritarian Puritans had also insisted on the necessity of a personal witness to "a saving experience" and it sealed one's obedience to the social order, as it also granted political power. By the 1740's church membership had not been a prerequisite to exercising citizenship rights for several decades, even though legal establishment survived.

In what sense was conversion an escape?

Bushman shows that New Lights acquired political power in the lower House and by the 1760's were affiliated with popular economic issues, which only then came to the fore.[29] But the Awakening had raged over twenty years earlier. Can the "worldly ambitions" and "resistance to social authority" evident in later New Light political activity be read back as the "two main causes" of the Awakening itself?[30] Certainly it is true that as our explanations get better, we tend to redescribe what we previously understood to be the facts requiring explanation. But there is always the danger that we shall be turning intensions into results, becoming victims of the irony of history rather than its interpreters.

Bushman solves the problem by seeing a mutation from the Puritan to the Yankee character, and he sometimes implies that it is the Yankee that is at work in the resistance of the New Lights to social authority. He cites the example of a vigilante mob that forced the resignation of Jared Ingersoll as collector of the hated Stamp Act tax. "The testy independence of these protestants," he comments, "was akin to a quality later manifested in Thoreau, a quality more characteristic of Yankees than Puritans." Actually, it is Ingersoll, displaying unusual poise and conviction in confronting the mob, who seems more akin to Thoreau's belief that a majority is always likely to be wrong and a minority of one likely to be right, but the more important point is that Bushman concludes that by 1765 "the Yankee spirit had replaced the Puritan" in many ways. "Puritan resistance characteristically turned inward and produced guilt," he acutely observes; "Yankee resistance more often turned outward and produced conflict."[31] Presumably the Awakening occupied a midpoint on this spectrum, partaking of both characters.

This subtle solution leaves us, however, with a Puritan-Yankee split character that yokes guilt and resistance. But this pairing was always implicit in the Calvinist idea of order. Sinful men, in obedience to a God whom they had been elected to serve in total commitment, worked out their sainthood in both church and

In what sense was conversion an escape?

Bushman shows that New Lights acquired political power in the lower House and by the 1760's were affiliated with popular economic issues, which only then came to the fore.29 But the Awakening had raged over twenty years earlier. Can the "worldly ambitions" and "resistance to social authority" evident in later New Light political activity be read back as the "two main causes" of the Awakening itself?30 Certainly it is true that as our explanations get better, we tend to redescribe what we previously understood to be the facts requiring explanation. But there is always the danger that we shall be turning intentions into results, becoming victims of the irony of history rather than its interpreters.

Bushman solves the problem by seeing a mutation from the Puritan to the Yankee character, and he sometimes implies that it is the Yankee that is at work in the resistance of the New Lights to social authority. He cites the example of a vigilante mob that forced the resignation of Jared Ingersoll as collector of the hated Stamp Act tax. "The testy independence of these protestants," he comments, "was akin to a quality later manifested in Thoreau, a quality more characteristic of Yankees than Puritans." Actually, it is Ingersoll, displaying unusual poise and conviction in confronting the mob, who seems more akin to Thoreau's belief that a majority is always likely to be wrong and a minority of one likely to be right, but the more important point is that Bushman concludes that by 1765 "the Yankee spirit had replaced the Puritan" in many ways. "Puritan resistance characteristically turned inward and produced guilt," he acutely observes: "Yankee resistance more often turned outward and produced conflict."31 Presumably the Awakening occupied a midpoint on this spectrum, partaking of both characters.

This subtle solution leaves us, however, with a Puritan-Yankee split character that yokes guilt and resistance. But this pairing was always implicit in the Calvinist idea of order. Sinful men, in obedience to a God whom they had been elected to serve in total commitment, worked out their sainthood in both church and state. When governments failed to reflect Calvinist norms, they could not expect to command the loyalty of the saints. The saints had always been activists, resolving their guilt in the communal public life of Puritan institutions. It is necessary to look more closely at the believers themselves in the search for clues to an explanation of this large-scale making of new men, who felt capable both of guilty self-condemnation and unusual independence. Where were they located in the life-cycle of psycho-social development?

A systematic concept for placing any social movement in generational terms had been outlined by the philosopher Ortega. As a preliminary move, it is worth testing his theory against the evidence. He finds at any historical date the co-presence of four generations: the survivors of an earlier period, "without full historical parts to play anymore" the generation in power, "whose aims correspond in general to the prevailing world style"; the opposing generation that "struggles against the ruling generation and tries to replace it in authority so as to be able to bring about the changes it feels called upon to champion"; and the youthful generation that is being educated. These demarcations correspond to four social stages in the life cycle of individuals, bounded by the ages fifteen, thirty, forty-five, and sixty. Ortega's method is to take a date marking the thirtieth year of a representative man of an important new orientation, made by a creative minority, and then to treat it as the center of a fifteen-year "generation."[32] This procedure would make the year 1733 the center of Jonathan Edwards's "generation." In that year he gave his sermon *A Divine and Supernatural Light, Immediately Imparted to the Soul by the Spirit of God, Shown to be Both a Scriptural and a Rational Doctrine*, taken by his parishioners (and some of his commentators) as the most eloquent brief exposition of New Light Calvinism. It was also the threshold of the Edwards-led Northampton revival, a model for all later revivals. In Ortega's terms the years in a man's life approximately from thirty to forty-five represent a "struggle" to impose a certain world structure," the previous fifteen years having been occupied with preparation state. When governments failed to reflect Calvinist norms, they could not expect ot command the loyalty of the saints. The saints had always been activists, resolving their guilt in the communal public life of Puritan institutions. It is necessary to look more closely at the believers themselves in the search for clues to an explanation of this large-scale making of new men, who felt capable both of guilty self-condemnation and unusual independence. Where were they located in the life-cycle of psycho-social development?

    A systematic concept for placing any social movement in generational terms has been outlined by the philosopher Ortega. As a preliminary move, it is worth testing his theory against the evidence. He finds at any historical date the co-presence of four generations: the survivors of an earlier period, "without full historical parts to play anymore" the generation in power, "whose aims correspond in general to the prevailing world style"; the opposing generation that "struggles against the ruling generation and tries to replace it in authority so as to be able to bring about the changes it feels called upon to champion"; and the youthful generation that is being educated. These demarcations correspond to four social stages in the life cycle of individuals, bounded by the ages fifteen, thirty, forty-five, and sixty. Ortega's method is to take a date marking the thirtieth year of a representative man of an important new orientation, made by a creative minority, and then to treat it as the center of a fifteen-year "generation."[32] This procedure would make the year 1733 the center of Jonathan Edwards's "generation." In that year he gave his sermon *A Divine and Supernatural Light, Immediately Imparted to the Soul by the Spirit of God, Shown to be Both a Scriptural and a Rational Doctrine*, taken by his parishioners (and some of his commentators) as the most eloquent brief exposition of New Light Calvinism. It was also the threshold of the Edwards-led Northampton revival, a model for all later revivals. In Ortega's terms the years in a man's life approximately from thirty to forty-five represent a "struggle" to impose a certain world structure," the previous fifteen years having been occupied with preparation for his action.[33] The Great Awakening, then, was for Edwards his master effort to make pietistic Calvinism the ruling style of American religion.

Edwards and Gilbert Tennent, the major evangelist in the Middle Colonies, were both thirty-eight at the time of the 1741 revival. George Whitefield, the catalytic itinerant from England, was twenty-seven. The oldest revival leader, Theodorus Frelinghuysen, and the youngest, James Davenport, were separated from Edwards by only about a dozen years, and in tendency they did represent, respectively, a relatively conservative and radical version of his own pietism, consistent with their distance from him in age, as if they occupied different slopes of the same generational ridge, a metaphor implicit in Ortega's scheme. Ninety ministers met in Boston in July, 1743, to testify to the great work of the revival. Most were from New England, which is estimated to have had four hundred clergy.[34] Sixty-eight signed a document of moderate support and forty-six who were absent sent their blessings later, making 114 in all. Ninety-six of these had taken their degrees in American colleges at least ten years ago; fifty-six of these had taken them (as Edwards had) at least twenty years ago, and twenty-six of these had earned them over thirty years ago. The group of ministers who had graduated with Edwards or at a later time totalled fifty-eight, or 50% of the attestors.[35] The moderate supporters were evenly divided in terms of "predominance" and "dominance" people, while among five representative leaders of the Separates, the radical left-wing of the movement, only one was in the period of "dominance" during the revival.[36]

The anti-revivalist leaders were not necessarily aging spokesmen for an entrenched position. They could see themselves as rational Calvinists fighting obscurantist fanatics. Historians speak about "Old Lights" in tones which suggest they were old men. Yet, Charles Chauncy, the leading opponent of Jonathan Edwards, was two years younger than he was; Jonathan Mayhew, who was even more "Arminian" in tendency, was four years younger than James Davenport, the most radical New Light of the Awakening. Famous later critics of the revivals, like Lemuel Briant and Samuel Webster, were nineteen and twenty-two, respectively, at the time of the Awakening in 1741. The revivalists and some of their most articulate opponents were both in the age brackets coming before the period that Ortega allots to the group in power, which exercises "dominance" and defense "against innovations proposed by the younger generation."[37] The struggle was among Calvinists who were fighting for control of the future, and they were joined by a common concern for the saliency of the same issues.

A public conflict offers satisfactions as well as frustrations, and every polemicist leans on his opponent to clarify and bolster his own role, like actors in a play. Seen in this way, the Old Light opposition was necessary to the success of the pietists. Before the Awakening there had been much bitter contention in the churches between ministers and their congregations, on whom they were usually dependent for meager economic support. The revivals, with their attacks on the spiritual danger of an unconverted ministry, provided a vent for religious anti-clericalism. In a new rugged country, subject to continual influxes of believers from different countries and faiths, the clergy's prestige could not borrow from a dominating central source of religious authority, and (except for the Anglicans) they had to train their own ministers, always in short supply, on their own territory.[38] Yet as a result of the Awakening the New Light ministers gained prestige and authority. How did this happen? Revivalists did not flatter their constituents' spiritual condition; on the contrary they at first condemned it. But they were the instrument of offering them a final solution through the experience of crisis in the twice-born soul, and the itinerants' huge audiences provided a setting in which the process could be suffered collectively and relatively quickly. By this means they also redirected popular hostility towards the clergy in general against the Old Lights in particular who found the revivalists injudicious, immoderate, and subversive of order. In sociological terms the revivals were functional for the clergy in displacing hostility and gaining new prestige, as well as in satisfying their missionary obligations.

Venting hostility was, of course, a dangerous process for revivalists to encourgae. When radicals pushed the pietist position closer to the "antinomian" conclusion that inner certainty of grace and future freedom from sin were entirely possible, sensible New Lights eventually drew back from attacks on other ministers to define a more moderate Calvinism. James Davenport was persuaded, with the excuse of suffering "the cankry Humor," to confess his errors: attacking ungodly clergy in public prayers, encouraging lay preaching, singing in the streets, and leading a mob in New London, bent on burning books and worldly clothing.[39] Antinomian conclusions threatened to make New Light ministers superfluous or vulnerable. They held the line according to the position of Edwards--only habitual lifelong practice could prove the true glory of the saints, not the subjective **certainities of an** emotional crisis, even though twice-born agonies were necessary.

This pragmatic position was reaffirmed in the twentieth century by William James, whose *The Varieties of Religious Experience* focused on the conversion experience of "the sick soul." James wrote not only out of the example of his dramatically disturbed and converted father, but from his own experience of suicidal depression. It was his point that in such crises the "subliminal self" below the level of ordinary consciousness is a double key that opens doors to inhibitions, hallucinations, convulsions, paralyses and delusions, on the one hand, and to spiritual conversion, saintly obsession, and "a wider world" of spiritual meaning, on the other.[40] Religion, in this view, is deeply engaged with the dynamics of the unconscious that Freud was concurrently analyzing in a systematic theory and therapy.

Certainly there was evidence in the revivals of responses which resemble the hysteria that Freud located on the clinical map. Jonathan Edwards, for example, celebrated the piety of Abigail Hutchinson, a young woman "infirm of body" who was inspired (he tells us) by "a spirit of envy" towards the conversion of another young woman "to do her utmost to obtain the same blessing." Known for her dutifulness as a daughter, Abigail became agonized with doubts precisely on this point. Edwards also reports her to be full of an overwhelming "flow of affection to those whom she thought godly" and also of a morbid longing to die, expressed in pleasure at the idea of worms feeding on her body.[41] One is not surprised to learn that she suffered terribly from an inability to swallow food and eventually died of famine. This pitiful story vividly enough illustrates James's point that "morbid-mindedness" in the "neurotic temperament" may furnish "the chief condition of the requisite receptivity" to "inspiration from a higher realm."[42] It cannot convince most of us, however, that such morbidity was widespread enough, even in Northampton, to provide the historical key to the Awakening, nor are we likely to share his belief that the subliminal self connects with a supernatural order, divine or diabolic.

James provides a primary historical clue when he notes that "conversion is in its essence a normal adolescent phenomenon, incidental to the passage from the child's small universe to the wider intellectual and spiritual life of maturity." James also notes that commonplace conversions are "kept true to a pre-appointed type by instruction, appeal and example. The particular form which they affect is the result of suggestion and imitation."[43] The late teens and early twenties, as Erikson has said in commenting on the age of the converts discussed in James's *The Varieties of Religious Experience*, is a time "painfully aware of the need for decisions, most driven to choose new devotions and to discard old ones, and most susceptible to the propaganda of ideological systems which promise a new world-perspective at the price of total and cruel repudiation of an old one."[44] It is in keeping with this observation that such later influential New Light preachers as Isaac Backus, David Brainerd, Samuel Langdon, Joseph Bellamy, Samuel Davies, John Cleaveland, Jacob Green, and Samuel Hopkins should all have been between seventeen and twenty-three in the year of the Awakening. They were essentially products of the movement itself.

But of course, emphasis on the identity-crisis stage does not explain why any particular ideology is adopted, rather than another. Yet the gospel of the twice-born sick soul, as James characterized it, must have a particular appeal to young people, because it accentuates and interprets the crises of growth, and it has not been sufficiently noticed in the historical literature that documents produced by the revivals themselves point to the importance of young converts. Edwards noted that his grandfather, Solomon Stoddard, in each of his five "harvests" of souls, stressed that "the greater part of the young people in the town seemed to be mainly concerned for their eternal salvation."[45] The grandson specifically pointed to the death of a young man and the pious death of a young married woman as being very influential in arousing concern among other young people, and his own revival efforts were first directed in 1734 at the young people whom he organized into "private companies" for the practice of "social religion" after the usual evening lectures. This process was greatly facilitated by the conversion of another young woman, known to be "one of the greatest company-keepers in the whole town."[46] whom many thereafter went to see. The most commonly repeated theme in the various contemporary accounts of the origins of revivals is the lament by ministers that the young people in town are much engaged in "frolicing," tavern-going," "company-keeping," "night-walking," and other signs of the decay of "family government." Revivalists were worried about the loose living of the younger generation, a perennial American and evangelical theme.

They were also justifiably worried about the failures of the clergy in America, who were often uninspired and uninspiring examples. But beyond these realities the Awakening also drew on a process of imitative contagion observable in youth culture today. Edwards candidly spoke in 1736 of the power of emulation in the conversion process: "There is no one thing that I know of which God has made such a means of promoting his work amongst us, as the news of others' conversion."[47] Just as Abigail Hutchinson envied the distinction of a celebrated converted young woman and thought her eminence unmerited, so whole towns could be stimulated by the news of mass conversions elsewhere into a competitive rivalry in witnessing to the true faith, just as every liberal campus in the late 1960's felt ashamed if it did not have its own "Berkeley rebellion" as proof of an awakened social consciousness. Edwards again made the point clearly:

> As what other towns heard of, and found in this, was a great means of awakening them; so our hearing of such a swift and extraordinary propagation, and extent of this work, did doubtless for a time serve to uphold the work amongst us. The continual news kept alive the talk of religion, and did greatly quicken and rejoice the hearts of God's people, and much awakened those who looked on themselves as still left behind, and made them the more earnest that they also might share in the great blessings that others had obtained.[48]

Historians of the Awakening have treated the event as if they were talking about people engaged in adult activities and responsibilities, but the literary evidence of the preachers' accounts, and their own description of the particular sins that the revivals are supposed to illuminate and regulate, clearly point in a different direction. This oversight is probably related to an unconscious effort by historians to dignify the revivals and their leaders by connecting them with substantial adult issues regarding economics and politics, matters of familiar conventional historical interest. Richard Bushman, in a provocative article on Jonathan Edwards, has suggested that Calvinists were "bound to select from the legacy of childhood the patterns surrounding the Oedipal crisis and give them standing in the adult world,"[49] but even he does not see in his book that the revivals themselves were closely linked to moral and emotional issues characteristic of young people on the border country between childhood and adulthood, persons old enough to be treated as subject to ecclesiastical and legal discipline, but not yet old enough to be married property-holders with civic power.

A central document for the Awakening is *The Christian History*, a journal published to celebrate the Awakening in a series of ministerial reports from the colonies, Scotland, and Wales. Whenever ministers speak here of the sociology of their converts, whether in New England or in some Pennsylvania and New Jersey towns, they point out that it is "young people" who are especially affected.50 Statistically minded modern historians have recently provided hard evidence, at least for the Massachusetts towns they have studied. In Norton "a disproportionately large number of young people were coming of age" in 1740, and the males joining in the Awakening were "significantly younger, less established, and less successful" than earlier converts.51 In Middleborough, an ardent revival town, 72.6% of the new male converts in 1740-43 were under thirty-one years of age.52 In Andover almost 60% of all revival converts were in the group aged 15-24.53 In Longmeadow, Suffield, Northampton, Deerfield, and Springfield the mean age of 1,183 known ages of converts in 1741-42 was 21.7, a drop of about ten years from the pre-revival period.54 Consistent with these findings, the preacher Samuel Allis of Somers highlighted "the rising generation" as having experienced the "outpouring" in "a more general and remarkable manner."55 Probably the average truth about the process was formulated in the report from the town of Harvard: "This visible Reformation among the *young People* was (under God) a Means of stirring up many *middle-aged* and *elder* Persons to think more seriously about their Souls, and what they should do to be saved."56

Edwards, in his letter to *The Christian History*, noted that the work of the revival was "almost wholly upon a new Generation: those that were not come to Years of Discretion in that wonderful Season nine years ago, *Children*, or those that were *then Children*: Others that had enjoyed that former glorious Opportunity without any Appearance of favoring Benefit, seem'd now to be almost wholly passed over and let alone."57 He had himself precipitated matters in his town of Northampton by calling together in 1741 a group of people between the ages of fifteen and twenty-six, years that overlap with the stage that Erikson has identified as the "identity crisis." In March, 1741, Edwards led a ceremony of public renewal of covenant with all those Christians above fourteen, pledging them to "Honesty, Justice, and Uprightness" in dealing with their neighbors. Collectively they promised to pay their debts, avoid "backbiting," revere the common good, and repress those "Freedoms and Familiarities in Company" which tended to "stir up or gratify a Lust of Lasciviousness." A glimpse of the non-political tenor of the revival is evidenced by Edwards's view that the main influence of the revival on public affairs was to diminish party division in the town over the problem of the "Common Lands," an issue for fifteen years "above any other particular thing."58 By 1743, however, he lamented, youth had already begun to fall away from the revival spirit, even though it had been "purer" than that of 1735. The fervor of Christian reform was a flickering flame in the rising generation.

Revival preachers were candidly aware that thunderstorms and earthquakes often worked temporarily to frighten people into a sudden respect for God's majesty, but they did not put their trust in these circumstantial conversions. They were impressed instead with the effect of their own preaching. It was not merely the terror that could be produced by dramatizing the fallen creature's damnation, as in Edwards's famous sermon "Sinners in the Hands of an Angry God"; more importantly it was, in Thomas Princes's phrase, "this *searching* Preaching" that was both the suitable and principal *Means* of their Conviction." A preacher, such as Gilbert Tennent, searched out his hearer's hearts by "laying open their many vain and secret Shrifts and Refuges, counterfeit Resemblances of Grace, *delusive* and *damning Hopes*, their utter *Impotence*, and impending Danger of Destruction: whereby they found all their Hopes and refuges of Lies to fail them, and themselves exposed to eternal Ruin, unable to help themselves, and in a lost Condition."59 Thus did preachers exhibit the Spirit's power in Boston until it withdrew its awakening influence by November, 1742, in "a gradual and awful Manner." Divinity worked through the preacher's subtlety in exposing the creature's defenses.

The Awakening was precipitated by the extraordinary, charismatic preaching of George Whitefield, Gilbert Tennent, and Jona-

than Edwards, and the dynamics of the revival were connected with
a public rhetoric designed to exploit subconscious feelings of
guilt and dependency that were weakly defended against by a
hedonistic indifference in the young, or that were easily re-
activated in older personalities that had externally committed
themselves to the evangelical framework already but had grown
conventional in their piety. Formal collective "owning of the
Covenant" on a wide popular basis, rather than scrutinized individual testimony to one's "saving faith," had become a New
England custom after 1700. This practice meant that when a
search for purity and sincerity challenged such a conventional-
ized system, it would still seek a communal form that was not as
elitist as the orthodox Puritan sifting of souls had been in
deciding who could exercise the privileges of the Lord's Supper
and the citizen's vote. Mass revivalism brought together the
themes of popular participation and characterological purity.
Rather than pointing to social control through a theocracy, it
emphasized the duties of families. The preachers characteristically scolded the worldly ways of the young and stressed the need
for restoration of "family government." The revial paradoxically
transcended the family, however, in a public context of high
excitement in which the young person's soul was considered to be
of momentous value and it was linked in hope to a collective
reformation that was identified with the emerging meaning of
history in a coming millennium on earth.[60] Twice-born saints
could expect to enjoy imminent glory, even before the intervention
of the Second Coming.

Enthusiastic religion mingled themes of shame and doubt with
a new self-esteem, of inner guilt with a new sense of initiative,
of a traditional moral code with a new feeling of freedom, of
individual spiritual distinction through the election of saints
with an egalitarian mass participation in communal revivals,
creating a new body of passionate fellow-believers. These
paradoxes of the emotional life made pietism potent for restless
adolescents struggling with their own ambivalent feelings about

family authority within the traditional Puritan legacy of "family government." Peter Thatcher, minister at Middleborough, Massachusetts, whose church won some 174 new communicants in the revival, underscored the power of ambivalency when he noted: "Scores, *this Day*, told me of their Hatred of me above any one." Yet soon afterwards he heard "the *Young People* crying and wringing their Hands, and bewailing their Frolicking and Dancing, their deriding public reproofs thereof..."[61] Confession eased the guilt of hostility to the condemning minister while the aggression itself was redirected to the Old Light critics of the revivals.

The new technique of open-field preaching, initiated by George Whitefield in England and developed further in America in response to his own ostracism from established English pulpits, provided a new locus for confession beyond the family pew, literally and figuratively representing a breath of fresh air in an emotionally confining world. There a new group identity could be formed in view of one's peers. Edwards noted that in 1741 the acts of conversion were more vividly "visible" than before, "more frequently in the Presence of others, at religious Meetings, where the Appearances of what was wrought on the Heart fell under publick Observation."[62] Young people, as Erikson has observed, are often "mortally compulsive and conservative even where and when they seem most anarchic and radical," because they need to bind together "irrational self-hate and irrational repudiation" in the search for an ideological comprehension of the world. His comments had contemporary youth in mind, as illustration of a general theme regarding the life-cycle, but they point as well to the pietists when he adds that fanatic ideologists, psychopathic leaders, and young people are often led together towards "that social frontier where the struggle between conservatism and radicalism is most active." But there also, as he reminds us, "true leaders create significant solidarities,"[63] and the result for the inner life of group identity, according to this version of ego-psychology, is some "tentative combination of dynamic polarities," a mixture of opposing tendencies.[64] These observations strongly resonate with the characteristics of the Awakening as a psycho-social movement. Psychoanalysis is usually regarded as individualistic in theory and application, making it problematical how it can be applied to social movements or group identities. But psychoanalysis has always generated (as Freud and Erikson prove) a deep interest in family and religious life. Where these come together, as in the Awakening, it is no accident that ideas derived from the psychoanalytic tradition should prove to be highly pertinent.

The Awakening shattered the standing order of churches in schisms and withdrawals, and the new methods of itineracy and lay exhorting challenged existing conventions. In this light the movement represented a liberating force. But it also reinstituted community control and conformity as part of its moral intensity, the repressive side of the story has been largely omitted from the accounts which are eager to draw a straight line from the Awakening to the Revolution. No doubt, there were sublimated erotic and hedonistic feelings in the street singing led by James Davenport or in the ecstatic communal joy known to the gracious saints. But it was not freedom from law or society so much as conformity to the censorious pressure of the brethren that followed conversion: "Every church member considered himself his brother's keeper. The most trivial derelictions from duty were noted and reported, and espionage and tale-bearing encouraged as if they were cardinal virtues...Every man was at the mercy of the 'inward actings' of his neighbor's soul."[65] The brethren, as Nathaniel Whitaker (Heimert's Revolutionary Calvinist hero) pointed out, were bound to treat every member as a brother and "to govern him agreeable to the laws of Christ; and if he refuses to submit, they are bound to reject him as an enemy to the laws and Kingdom of Christ."[66]

The precariously seated clergy made an ally out of youth by evoking, interpreting, and legitimating its inner guilt, its public shame, and its ardent hopes for historical meaning and direction. Christian charity and communal commitment in joyous grace to the expectation of millennial progress, before the

Second Coming, guided many lives, but in the mass conditions of conversion saints must inevitably have been vulnerable to an inner sense of possible fraudulence. In any event the growth in the number of churches in the next decade did not keep up with the growth of the population, except in areas where immigration from Germany and Ireland had enlarged the rolls of certain sects.[67] For some leaders the conversion process *was* decisive for long-term character-formation. The experience of being cleansed by the Holy Spirit came to Issac Backus, for example, in 1741 while he was plowing alone in the fields: "My heavy burden was gone, tormenting fears were fled, and my joy was unspeakable."[68] The rhetoric is conventional but Backus, perhaps because he was not converted in a crowd, later became a persistent asserter of the rights of Baptists and of innovative and influential principles of separation between church and state. His father had died the year before his conversion, and his mother, left with eleven children, had sunk into a deep depression from which the Awakening aroused her. The revivalists had come to Norwich to burn over the territory and his mother had found assurance of salvation. No doubt, this example had helped to stimulate the ardors of piety in her seventeen-year-old son, who now had to make up for a missing father, but perhaps historians, or psychoanalysts, can never explain adequately why this decisive experience should have been enduring in Backus or transient in others.

For all his stoic rationalism, forbidding him the consolations of religion, Freud was very much interested in religions. He admired the Puritan poet Milton and named one of his own sons after Oliver Cromwell. By contemporary "counter-culture" standards he was himself deeply Puritan in his devotion to work and his contempt for frivolous self-indulgence. He even believed that religious groups were "the most powerful protection" against mental illness and provided "crooked cures of all kinds of neuroses," which always impeded the formation of groups.[69] For him religion could be a cure, however, in the sense that a phobia can prevent hysteria, and he seriously proposed a comparison between obsessive acts and religious practices. The analogy is well worth exposition and application if we make it without the burden of his polemical supposition that religion is a phobia.

In the neurotic person unconscious guilt is revived by temptation, connected with a repressed impulse, and it gives rise to a dread of misfortune or punishment. Protective measures are thus mobilized, particularly "a special type of conscientiousness directed towards opposing the aim of the impulse."[70] Ritualistic acts function as part of these defenses, which in their weakness also need the support of explicit prohibitions. Because neurotic symptoms are always a compromise, the rituals often license the forbidden impulse under certain conditions, reproducing "something of the identical pleasure they were designed to prevent." As the disease develops, the defensive rituals become increasingly like "the proscribed actions in which the impulse was able to find an outlet in childhood."[71] In neurosis the forbidden impulses are sexual; in religion they are more importantly connected with "egoistic, antisocial instincts." But religion too has its temptations, its guilt, its fear of punishment, its backslidings, its penances. In neurosis there is often a displacement of anxious concern to what appear to be relatively trivial or formalistic matters; religions in a similar fashion, he maintained, are "subject to retroactive reforms which aim at the re-establishment of the original relative values."[72] The compromise element is harder to find in religion, Freud admitted, but it tends to appear in the fact that forbidden acts are often committed in the very name of the religion that forbids them.

Like so many Freudian ideas, what begins as a provocative and illuminating metaphor is ultimately intended to be taken literally, the figurative language resolving into the supposedly scientific theory of libidinal energy. We may well think, on the contrary, that the shift is really from metaphors of intentions to metaphors of mechanics, and we may rightfully resist the reductive strategy involved in saying that an analogy is really an identity.73 Even so, the analogy may still be useful for altering us to certain ironies at work in dynamic processes.

The ironies implicit in Freud's metaphor of the analogy between obsessive acts and religious practices can prepare us, at least, for making a more guarded analysis of the political consequences of the Awakening than historians have generally done, though their stories often belie their opinions. In political terms Heimert concedes that "even in the 1760's the reigning public issue, so far as Calvinists were concerned, was that which also first introduced a 'party spirit' into the politics of Virginia: the rights of evangelical dissenters to religious liberty."74 In this limited but important sense the evangelicals played an instrumental role in liberalizing American political society, though the main credit must go to the Calvinist Baptists and their secular allies, Jefferson and Madison. (Presbyterians and Congregationalists were not averse to conniving with legal establishment if they could be established.) Yet the moral perspective of the revivalists was far from libertarian; it was designed to remedy the decay of "family government" by which heads of families were responsible for indoctrinating children, servants, boarders, and slaves. Already in 1715 a common clerical complaint was "the great deficiency in domestical or family government," and, as Bushman has observed, "the father was the model for all authority--magistrates were called the fathers of their people--and the Biblical commandment to honor parents was expanded to include all rulers." Edwards's disciple Joseph Bellamy also envisaged the state as a happy family.75 The Awakening, as Perry Miller would have it, meant that the leader "could no longer stand before the people giving them mathematically or logically impregnable postulates of the eternally good, just, and honest," but instead "had to get down amongst them, and bring them by actual participation into an experience that was no longer private and privileged, but social and communal."76 Nevertheless, that process was begun in a traditional effort to reassert the controls of "family government" over the young.

Freud's analogy comes into play at this point. Calvinist fear of punishment in being "Sinners in the Hands of an Angry God" is obvious enough. So are the temptations which an unsettled and more secular society offered to the Puritan conscience. The New Light insistent emphasis on the ethic of "disinterested benevolence" illustrates Freud's point about the development of "a special type of conscientiousness directed towards opposing the aim of the impulse." In the ecstatic paroxysms or exuberant singing of the saints in lay preaching and itinerancy, and in the preacher's emphasis on the significance of the individual's inner and outer life there are compromise satisfactions of individualistic and hedonistic impulses which the communal ethic worked to control. Furthermore, in the later attempts which Edwards and others made to return to an earlier form of confessional testimony before the church there is evidence of "displacement" of the Awakening concern for purity, a displacement which, in religion, occurs as "retroactive reforms which aim at the re-establishment of the original relative values."77 Finally, New Lights, some thirty years later, were able to give aggression its license by preaching war against Britain as a holy cause because, as Joseph Bellamy put it, "when natures are in perfect contrariety, the one sinful, and the other holy, the more they are known to each other, the more is mutual hatred stirred up, and their entire aversion to each other becomes sensible."78 Nathaniel Whitaker urged policies of legal confiscation and disenfranchisement against Tories, as well as "holy abhorrence" for "over prudent men," such as Old Light Whig moderates, because God "hates sin with a perfect hatred from the essential holiness of his nature."79 John Cleaveland, who served as chaplain in Washington's headquarters, could sanction aggression against General Gage in the name of religion by branding him "not only a wicked robber, a murderer, and usurper, but a wicked Rebel: A wicked rebel against the authority of truth, law, equity...and humanity itself."80 Thus could rebels brand their enemies rebels in the name of authority.

The influence of the Awakening's Puritanical tone on American politics was evidenced in the recommendation of the Second Continental Congress when it urged the states to encourage "true religion and good morals" by suppressing "theatrical entertainments, horse racing, and such other diversions as are productive of idleness, dissipation, and general depravity of principles and manners."81 Even the principled Separationists, like the Baptists, viewed the Revolution "primarily as a providential act to clear the way for the overthrow of the established system,"82 a political means to a religious end of sectarian freedom. Yet the pietistic Calvinists, as Heimert fully shows, were indeed often at the forefront of radical Whig propaganda and action against conservative colonists. They had acquired in the Awakening the nerve to confront the repressive measures of the established order on religious issues, and their rationalist opponents in the Awakening later did play, on the whole, a more cautious and legally oriented role in opposing British measures. Furthermore, the intensity of pietist concern for authenticity in the churches was easily transferred to political suspicion of half-hearted Whigs.83

Conformity of one's righteous soul to the righteous souls of others within a Puritan ethic was at the heart of the psychology involved in the revivals, but the new self was made in circumstances challenging established clerical authority. In so far as the Pietist clergy could later preach the Revolution as a revival, it was also another means of urging community conformity of souls but in the context of an enthusiasm for spiritual and civil freedom directed against the Satanic British. The Awakening worked through confession in and identification with a group of the chosen, who kept close watch on each other's consciences. It was not the first or the last time that revolutionary sentiment would be tactically allied with men animated by inner feelings of guilt and righteousness, with a passion for collective conformity to puritanical morality and the true faith, with ultimate hopes of a millennium, and with common participation in the cult of communal joy and conformity. The New Lights gave a Puritan cast to a Revolution that others made liberal in largely secular terms. Their spirit found its true heirs in the crusade for temperance after the Revolution and in Isaac Backus's insistence on strict enforcement of Puritan blue laws and Sabbatarianism.[84] When the Baptists produced a devout Jeffersonian in John Leland it was in a preacher who, having moved from Massachusetts to Virginia in 1776 at the age of twenty-two, was not a child of the Awakening, but a young man of the Revolution itself. As the disease develops, Freud observes of obsessional neurosis, its defensive rituals look more and more "like the proscribed actions in which the impulse was able to find an outlet in childhood."[85] The historical process is not a disease, but analogically the history of impulse may sometimes point to fruitful congruences with the history of religious ideas. The self-assertions of people young in the Awakening would later become normalized in a world which, as saints, they did not envisage, a place where Jefferson could speak of "life, liberty, and the pursuit of happiness" as secular goals and enjoyments.

Pietists were not alone--as Keimert implies--in linking a corporate ethic of affective benevolence, a millennial hope, and Whiggism. Even Pietists could use liberal-rationalist contractual language; radical deists preached "benevolence"; and some rationalist Old Light Calvinists opposed religious taxes and were millennially oriented to the Revolution.[86] What distinguished Pietists was their reanimation of Puritan values in the Enlightenment's more egalitarian context: deep mistrust of the natural man and of worldly individualism, brooding concern with personal and collective guilt and sin, a saving-remnant, eschatological sense of history, and anxious surveillance of the consciences of the brethren. The Pietists, in this light, were promise that Franklin, Jefferson, and Madison would not wholly capture the American mind, so long as children of the Awakening were alive, and the revival of revivalism became a recurring American story.

FOOTNOTES

1. See for example Dankwart A. Rustow, ed., *Philosophers and Kings: Studies in Leadership* (New York, 1970).
2. For a contemporary example regarding student revolt see Howard M. Feinstein, "April 1969: A Celebration of the Mass," in Cushing Strout and David L. Grossvogel, eds., *Divided We Stand: Reflections on the Crisis at Cornell* (New York, 1970), pp. 90-127.
3. Cf. Perry Miller, "Jonathan Edwards and the Great Awakening" in Daniel Aaron, ed., *America in Crisis: Fourteen Crucial Episodes in American History* (New York, 1952), p. 6; Edwin Scott Gaustad, *The Great Awakening in New England* (New York, 1957), p. 43.
4. Charles H. Maxson, *The Great Awakening in the Middle Colonies*, unpub. diss. (Chicago, 1920), pp. 149-50.
5. Wesley M. Gewher, *The Great Awakening in Virginia, 1740-1790*, (Gloucester, Mass., 1965), p. 187.
6. *Ibid.*, p. 198.
7. *Ibid.*, p. 112.
8. Martin Ellsworth Lodge, *The Great Awakening in the Middle Colonies*, unpub. diss. (California, 1964), p. 282.
9. C.C. Goen, *Revivalism and Separatism in New England, 1740-1800*, (New Haven, 1962), p. 191.
10. Alan Heimert, *Religion and the American Mind: From the Great Awakening to the Revolution* (Cambridge, Mass., 1966), p. 10.
11. *Ibid.*, pp. 12, 18.
12. *Ibid.*, p. 9.
13. *Ibid.*, pp. 13, 21.
14. *Ibid.*, pp. 21, 494.
15. *Ibid.*, p. 17.
16. *Ibid.*, p. 20.
17. *Ibid.*, pp. 13, 458.
18. *From Puritan to Yankee: Character and the Social Order in Connecticut, 1690-1765* (Cambridge, Mass., 1967), p. 185.
19. *Ibid.*, p. 281.
20. *Ibid.*, p. 282.
21. *Ibid.*, pp. 256-58.

22. *Ibid.*, p. 286.
23. *Ibid.*, p. 266.
24. *Ibid.*, p. 282.
25. *Ibid.*, p. 267.
26. *Ibid.*, pp. 182, 187.
27. *Ibid.*, p. 161.
28. *Ibid.*, p. 265.
29. *Ibid.*, p. 260.
30. *Ibid.*, p. 259.
31. *Ibid.*, pp. 286-87.
32. Julian Marias, *Generations: A Historical Method*, trans. Harold C. Raley (University, Alabama, 1970), pp. 183-4.
33. *Ibid.*, pp. 96, 144.
34. Goen, *Revivalism and Separatism*, p. 34.
35. *Christian History* (1743-44), I, p. 210.
36. Goen, *Revivalism and Separatism*, pp. 115-48.
37. Marias, *Generations*, p. 96.
38. See Lodge, *The Great Awakening*, pp. 261-76.
39. *Christian History*, I, pp. 237-9.
40. See Cushing Strout, "The Pluralistic Identity of William James: A Psychohistorical Reading of *The Varieties of Religious Experience*," American Quarterly, XXIII (1971), pp. 135-52; James, *Varieties of Religious Experience* (New York, 1902), pp. 25, 234-5, 483-4.
41. "A Faithful Narrative of the Surprising Work of God in the Conversion of Many Hundred Souls in Northampton and the Neighboring Towns and Villages," in Vergilius Ferm, ed., *Puritan Sage: Collected Writings of Jonathan Edwards* (New York, 1953), p. 204.
42. *Varieties of Religious Experience*, p. 25.
43. *Ibid.*, pp. 199-200. Edwards, as James notes, also saw how, in conversions, people shape their experience to fit familiar paradigms.
44. Erik H. Erikson, *Young Man Luther* (New York, 1958), p. 41.

45. "A Faithful Narrative," p. 165.
46. *Ibid.*, pp. 167-8.
47. *Ibid.*, p. 190.
48. *Ibid.*, p. 172.
49. "Jonathan Edwards and the Puritan Consciousness," *Journal for the Scientific Study of Religion, 5* (1966), 395. During a brief respite from a psycho-historical conference at Cape Cod in May, 1973, I had the pleasure of visiting a second-hand book store with Professor Bushman and the serendipity of stumbling on a novel about the Great Awakening, Frank Samuel Child's *A Puritan Wooing* (New York, 1898). It tells the story of a young woman in conflict with her Old Light father over a young man. She assuages her guilt in a conversion induced by hearing Edwards, is inspired by Whitefield to become an exhorter, and joins the radical pietist group led by James Davenport, trying to supress her feelings for her suitor in a religious intensity that "disturbed her balance of mind." This much of the tale is congruent with the themes of this essay. (In the conclusion the heroine improbably is restored to health by the splendor of music in Dublin and London.)
50. See *Christian History* (1743-44), I, 183, 191, 196, 198, 200, 252-53, 261, 371, 395, 399-400, 411; II, 14, 108, 150, 253, 340, 347, 375, 378.
51. J.M. Bumsted, "Religion, Finance, and Democracy in Massachusetts: The Town of Norton as a Case Study," *Journal of American History, 57* (March, 1971), 820, 828.
52. *Ibid.*, p. 830.
53. Philip J. Greven, Jr., "Youth, Maturity, and Religious Conversion: A Note on the Ages of Converts in Andover, Massachusetts, 1711-1749," *Essex Institute Historical Collections, 108* (April, 1972), 132.
54. Kevin M. Sweeney, "Unruly Saints: Religion and Society in the River Towns of Massachusetts, 1700-1750," Honors Thesis, History, Williams College (May, 1972), p. 136. Copy shown to me courtesy of library at Historic Deerfield, Massachusetts.
55. *Christian History*, I, 411.
56. *Ibid.*, II, 14.

57. *Ibid.*, I, 371.
58. *Ibid.*, I, 377, 379.
59. *Ibid.*, II, 390.
60. For Edwards's importance in developing a post-millennial optimism, despite his preaching of the terrors of hell, see intro., Alan Heimert and Perry Miller, eds., *The Great Awakening: Documents Illustrating the Crisis and its Consequences* (New York, 1967), xxiii.
61. *Christian History*, II, 90.
62. *Ibid.*, I, 372.
63. "The Problem of Ego Identity," *Psychological Issues*, I (No. 1, 1959), 157-58.
64. *Childhood and Society* (New York, 1950), p. 245.
65. Quoted by Goen, *Revivalism and Separatism*, p. 167. Canterbury suspended or expelled a third of its saints in three years.
66. *A Confutation of Two Tracts* (Boston, 1774), p. 13.
67. For statistics see Gaustad, *Historical Atlas of Religion* (New York, 1962), pp. 4, 167, 162, as well as *Historical Statistics of the United States* (Washington, 1952), p. 25, B12. The calculations are mine.
68. Quoted by William G. McLoughlin, *Issac Backus and the American Pietistic Tradition* (Boston, 1967), p. 14.
69. Sigmund Freud, *Group Psychology and the Analysis of the Ego*, tr. James Strachey (Bantam Edition, 1965), p. 95. (Original edition, 1921).
70. "Obsessive Acts and Religious Practices," in Philip Rieff, ed., *Character and Culture* (New York, 1963), p. 22. (The original essay was published in 1907).
71. *Ibid.*, p. 24.
72. *Ibid.*, p. 25.
73. "Like many of Freud's statements," as A.R. Louch observes, "the theory of infantile sexuality is an eye-opener to the similarities of adult to childish behaviour. But it is an eye-closer to the differences between them, especially once one moves to the theory of personality development which the extended definition generates." *Explanation and Human Action* (Oxford, 1966),

p. 218. Louch defends in principle the sort of piecemeal explaining historians do.
74. Heimert, *op. cit.*, p. 13.
75. Bushman, *op. cit.*, pp. 14, 74.
76. Miller, *op. cit.*, p. 14.
77. "Obsessive Acts and Religious Practices," p. 25.
78. Quoted by Heimert, *op. cit.*, p. 481.
79. *Antidote against Toryism* in Frank Moore, ed., *The Patriot Preachers of the American Revolution* (New York, 1860), pp. 188, 214-15.
80. Heimert, p. 473.
81. Quoted by Edward Frank Humphrey, *Nationalism and Religion in America 1774-1789* (Boston, 1924), p. 423.
82. McLoughlin, *op. cit.*, p. 137.
83. Heimert recognizes this displacement in a footnote, *op. cit.*, p. 505.
84. McLoughlin, *op. cit.*, p. 212.
85. "Obsessive Acts and Religious Practices," *op. cit.*, p. 24.
86. Heimert says pietistic Calvinists rejected legal and social contract theories (*op. cit.*, pp. 304-517), but one of his examples, Levi Hart, specifically originates society in "mutual compact between husband and wife" and compares society to a trading company. *Liberty Described* (Hartford, 1775), pp. 10-11. Also, influential non-Calvinist publicists, like the English Whigs, John Trechard and Thomas Gordon, preached an ethic of "beneficent Affections" and "affectionate Actions," which Heimert mistakenly restricts to pietists. See "Cato's Letters," in David L. Jacobson, *The English Libertarian Heritage* (Indianapolis, 1965), p. 162.

JONATHAN EDWARDS AS GREAT MAN:
Identity, Conversion, and Leadership in the Great Awakening

Richard L. Bushman

Erik Erikson's *Young Man Luther* has raised again the question of the great man's part in history.[1] The early nineteenth-century fascination with heroes who bent the course of events through sheer determination and personal force later faded as new conceptual tools enabled historians to calculate more precisely the impact of social forces. The times, it was then believed, thrust forward the great men, and rather than shaping events to their wills, heroes were as much determined by their environments as the mass. Erikson's biography of Luther does not restore the hero to his former eminence nor discount the weight of social conditions, but it does assert that the relationship of a man and his times is an exchange that goes both ways. A single individual can bring to his age powers that enable him to mobilize forces latent in the mass of men. Not just any power, however imposing, will do. The great man's capacities must be congruent with the needs of his age; when he speaks the age must respond. But his presence does make a difference. The force of one man's will, as Erikson shows in the case of Luther, can shape history.

Through Luther, Erikson examines the nature of the great man's power and shows that his compelling qualities may grow out of his anxieties as much as his strengths. His virtue lies in his unrelenting determination to settle psychological controversies which others experience but face less decisively. While most men conceal their anxieties and compromise rather than reconcile internal conflicts, an unusual integrity in the great man compels him to harmonize the warring elements. From his anguished quest for peace comes a new personal identity and with it a magnificient release of energy and determination. The combination of a compelling new identity and individual magnetism galvanizes others, and the great man, often without calculation, finds himself at the head of a movement.

All this is extrapolation from the one biography Erikson has

Reprinted from SOUNDINGS, *An Interdisciplinary Journal*, Vol. LII, No. 1, Spring 1969.

published, but the notions are so intriguing and *Young Man Luther* so rewarding that similar works on other men seem in order. Only when applied to a number of figures can the merit of Erikson's implicit hypotheses be measured. While of lesser magnitude than Luther and Protestantism, Jonathan Edwards and the Great Awakening of 1740 in New England were similarly related. The revivals of 1735 which foreshadowed the greater outburst in 1740 began in Edward's parish, and for many years he was called to preach wherever ministers wished their congregations to join the movement. No one compelled sinners to face their doom more relentlessly, and no one told better the sweet raptures of grace or explained more precisely where to place one's trust. He was by common consent the most powerful spokesman for the reborn men of his generation.

To understand the sources of this influence, Erikson's model of leadership calls for a reconstruction of the leader's identity and of the emotional needs of his age, for the great man has access to the hearts of other men at the point where the spiritual needs of leader and people converge. In Erikson's scheme, identity is the shape that an individual gives to his life to satisfy himself and his society. It is constituted both by personal likes, dislikes, habits, attitudes, fears, hopes, and capacitites, and by the way he manages all these internal resources withing the limitations of his social environment. As Erikson puts it, identity in the maturing person is "the accrued experience of the ego's ability to integrate all identifications with the vicissitudes of the libido, with the aptitudes developed out of endowment, and with the opportunities offered in social roles."[2] To work with this model in Edwards' case we must delineate the emerging patterns of his thought and feeling and the roles he assumed in his father's parsonage as he grew up. We must also look for strains among these components, for it was the resolution of tensions in conversion which both shaped his personal identity and prepared him for leadership in the Great Awakening.

Erikson draws heavily on psychoanalysis for his insights into Luther, and among psychological systems psychoanalysis is unusually helpful in enlarging the historian's understanding of human character. But more important than the system employed is the ability to enter into the consciousness of another person and to respond to his feelings. Psychoanalysis is particularly useful in the interpretation of early childhood, where an adult imagination is most likely to fail; but so little information on that period remains in most cases, and virtually none for Edwards, that the beginnings perforce must be neglected. Psychoanalytic insights can also help to discover patterns in the materials on later life, and in the analysis that follows I have relied more than once on Erikson's reformulation of Freud to interpret the data.[3] But sensitivity of the sort exhibited by novelists or the best literary critics is the skill most evident in Erikson's work and the one required of historians who would follow him. Effective application of his model of leadership depends mostly upon the exercise of historical imagination in translating the raw facts of a biography into a coherent and believable human experience.

I

Jonathan Edwards was born in 1703 in East Windsor, Connecticut, in the household of the Reverend Timothy Edwards.[4] East Windsor had separated from Windsor in 1694, and in the first year of its independence the parish settled Timothy Edwards as its minister. Fresh from Harvard, he soon married and moved into the house which his father, a prosperous Hartford merchant, built for him in the center of the village. Jonathan was his fifth child and first son, the only son, as it turned out, among eleven children.

The most evident import of Jonathan's genealogy is that he would be expected to attain to eminence. Differing circumstances on the ancestral lines of both mother and father pointed in the same direction: Jonathan would have to be powerful and successful, especially intellectually, to fulfill his family's hopes. Jonathan's mother, Esther, was the daughter of Solomon Stoddard and Esther Warham Mather Stoddard, a very imposing pair of parents.

Solomon Stoddard was the dominant ecclesiastical figure in the Connecticut Valley and a powerful man throughout New England. His voice could disturb the Mathers in their Boston stronghold and was regarded respectfully everywhere. Most noted for successfully challenging the "New England Way" of admitting only visible saints to communion, Stoddard believed that true saints could not be discovered and that upright and orthodox people should be accepted into the Church in the hope that communion would help convert them, a view that many churches in the Connecticut Valley adopted. Solomon was also renowned for the fervency of his preaching and for the recurrent revivals in his Northampton congregation, a tradition Jonathan was to inherit and culminate.

When Solomon accepted the pulpit at Northampton, he met and soon married his predecessor's widow. The daughter of a famed Connecticut minister, and a powerful person in her own right, Esther Stoddard was widely known for her vigorous mind, strength of will, and considerable learning, traits which, along with her name, she gave to Jonathan's mother.

Esther Edwards was remembered by her friends as "tall, dignified and commanding in her appearance," yet "affable and gentle in her manners." Solomon sent her to Boston for her education, and she became especially well acquainted with the Scriptures and with theological writers. After Timothy's death she would ask in the neighborhood ladies to listen to her comments on theology. Some of the listeners thought Esther Edwards surpassed her husband in "Native vigor of understanding."[5]

Knowing this much, it seems safe to say that Esther wanted Jonathan to embody the qualities notable in her father, her mother, herself, and the man she chose to marry. To please his mother fully Jonathan would have to be a man of unusual force and intellect. Values so thoroughly inbred and virtually unchallenged through at least two generations could exert an intense pressure, all the greater because Jonathan was the only son among eleven children. The hopes which only a man child could fulfill necessarily focused on a boy who arrived after four daughters, and the hopes grew more intense as six daughters followed.

A rivalry with the other Stoddard daughters may have heightened Esther's ambition for her son. A hint of this competition infuses all the family relationships. Perhaps the goal was to produce a worthy successor to Solomon; if so, Esther triumphed, for Jonathan was chosen to take the Northampton pulpit. But he paid dearly for his success. His cousins harried him whenever he was in trouble. During the dismissal proceedings at Northampton, one cousin, Joseph Hawley, was the leading spokesman for the opposition. Another, Solomon Williams, wrote the refutation of Edwards' plea for a church of visible saints, pointedly rebuking him for attacking his honored grandfather. Still another cousin, Israel Williams, a powerful figure in civil and commercial affairs in Northampton, had a long record of opposing Edwards' ministry on various counts. As early as the college years, Elisha Mix, a roommate and a cousin on Esther's side, fell out with Jonathan and wanted to move. Jonathan's father complained to Elisha's mother of his bad conduct and reproved her for speaking ill of Jonathan before strangers.[6] This collective animus may measure the determination of the Stoddard daughters to have their sons achieve the stature of Solomon and the disappointment of Esther's sisters at seeing one who was not their own excel.

Timothy's predilections reinforced Esther's high expectations for Jonathan. Timothy was the first in his family to attend college in three generations. His great-grandfather, Richard Edwards, was an ordained minister, a university graduate, and the teacher in the Cooper's Company school in London. He died young, and his widow married a cooper. With him and William, her only son by Richard, she migrated to Connecticut. William would have gone to college had his own father lived, but in America he took up his stepfather's trade. Whatever educational values may have been transmitted across the generations were twice focused on only sons, for William's wife bore him a single son who was named Richard in memory of a father and perhaps of a way of life not wholly forgotten. Timothy remembered of this Richard that, beside the Bible, "Other Good books were in the Season thereof Much Read in his house," providing some evidence of values surviving.[7]

William could not afford college for his son, but in the cooper's shop Richard prospered. He also built up a mercantile business that eventually outgrew one warehouse and required another. Meanwhile he rose through town offices into colonial politics, holding positions as selectman, as deputy to the General Court, and in his later years as Queen's Attorney. When it came time to choose a career for his eldest son, Richard sent Timothy to Harvard to study for the ministry, and perhaps to recover the honor and refinement of the first Richard's station. Timothy's aspirations for Jonathan were at least tinged with the frustrated desires of two generations finally promised fulfillment in a brilliant scion.

After settling in East Windsor, Timothy became well known for his great skill in preparing boys for Harvard and Yale. He simply assumed that Jonathan would be a scholar too and assimilate his father's learning in Latin, Greek, and Hebrew. All the the Edwards' children studied the classical languages under Timothy, and even the girls went on for more schooling. The desks lining the parlor were constant reminders of family expectations. Jonathan quite naturally began Latin at age six when his precocity was fast becoming evident. In the family of Esther and Timothy, the early discovery of Jonathan's great abilities only heightened the parents' hopes and intensified the pressure for achievement.

More remains than the meager information about Esther and Jonathan to tell us about the probable effects of Timothy's character on his son. Timothy was a compulsively exact and exacting man. He schooled his students so well because he tolerated no errors in their recitations, just as he allowed none to himself. He memorized every word of his sermons and delivered them letter-perfect. Measuring corn for barter or in lieu of money payment on his salary, he "made the negro sweep it up very clean" and then measured the sweepings.[8] He delighted in classifying thoughts, arranging them in numbered lists. His tribute to his father "ends with a list of seventeen mercies attending the manner of his death, separates his dying words into thirty-five items, works out six ways in which he glorified God at his death, and proceeds to supply numbered particulars under each."⁹

Timothy displayed all the classic compulsive traits, order, thrift, and obstinacy. When inflation depreciated the value of his salary, he prepared lengthy comparisons of purchasing power at the time he was settled and afterwards to prove he was being cheated. He was never one to yield in disputes with his congregation, either. In the 1730's a young man in town married a local girl without her parents' permission. Timothy wished to censor the boy, but the congregation refused to concur. Considering the case a matter of conscience, Timothy denied communion to the entire town for over three years while the controversy dragged on.

Jonathan's mind, though far more sweeping, poetic, and profound than his father's, bore the marks of its training under Timothy. Jonathan too refused to give an inch when challenged. In the dismissal controversy at Northampton he would not compromise with his parishioners, nor would he yield a point in the debate with Solomon Williams on admission to communion. In all intellectual disputes Edwards stubbornly beat down his opponents, demolishing even the slightest contradictions. He had to prove himself right in every detail. Even in non-combative writings, his arguments were exhaustive. What often appears as repetition was part of a massive effort to block every conceivable loophole. The careful definitions, the close reasoning, the piling up of proofs and illustrations were the natural ways of his thorough and fastidious mind. The truth had to be expressed immaculately and in perfect order, leaving no gaps for error to invade.

His father's parsimony shaped not only Jonathan's attitude toward money-he too argued with his parish over salary-but toward ideas. Ideas were poetry and power for Edwards; with them he negotiated his peace with the universe. But they were also things to be possessed. His delight in discovering Locke was greater "than the most greedly miser finds, when gathering up handsful of silver and gold, from some newly discovered treasure."¹⁰ He pinned papers to his coat while riding as reminders of his thoughts so that none would be lost. All of his ideas, along with many he read, were written down and carefully preserved in notebooks that came to contain many thousands of pages. The productions of mind were hoarded and treasured as valued possessions in a vast miser's store of thoughts.

Timothy's exactions were moral as well as intellectual. He required perfect obedience as well as perfect accuracy. The detailed instructions contained in letters to his family were presumably no less thorough when he was at home. Jonathan's behavior for the most part appears to have satisfied his parents. In one letter, when Jonathan was eight, Timothy said, "I hope thou wilt take Special care of Jonathan that he dont Learn to be rude and naught etc., of which thee and I have Lately Discoursed."[11] But the tenor of the comment was that naughtiness was exceptional. Not until late adolescence did the strains which Timothy's high standards imposed come out. Jonathan gratefully acknowledged that his parents' "counsel and education" had been his "making," but confessed that "in the time of it, it seemed to do me so little good."[12] The entire diary testified to the "good" of that sort of upbringing. Timothy's education implanted a conscience as meticulous and demanding as his standards of scholarship. The comment "it seemed to do me so little good" speaks of long struggles in which part of the self was hopelessly resistant to the pressures of conscience. By the time of the diary, Jonathan had conquered all obvious forms of sin and was struggling with the fine points, like wanting to stop to eat when mealtime came and an occasional listlessness in his studies. But his conscience kept asking for perfection, and he obediently renewed the daily examinations of his soul. He thought once that he must live as if he were to be the only true Christian on the earth in his generation. Timothy's education placed that much of a burden on his boy. Throughout his life, Jonathan continued to abhor himself as a "miserable wretch," "base and vile," and unworthy of God.[13]

There is some evidence that a peculiar combination of fear and love enforced Timothy's exactions. He displayed an extraordinary anxiety for his children's physical safety. An excerpt from a letter to Esther illustrates the point.

> I hope God will help thee to be very careful that no
> harm happen to the little Children by Scalding wort, whey,
> water, or by Standing too nigh to Tim when he is cutting
> wood; and prithee take what care thou canst about Mary's
> neck, which was too much neglected when I was at home...
> And Let Esther and Betty Take their powders as Soon as
> the Dog Days are Over, and if they dont help Esther, talk
> further with the Doctor about her for I wouldnt have her
> be neglected... If any of the children should at any time
> Go over the River to meeting I would have them be exceeding
> carefull, how they Sit or Stand in the boat Least they
> should fall into the River.[14]

That passage may be read as the loving concern of an oversolicitous father, but, as Ola Winslow commented, "instead of quieting childish fears he raised them, as though parental guidance consisted in advance notice of potential disaster."[15] If the attitude was typical, Timothy's anxieties would have reinforced in the Edwards children the ordinary apprehensions of violent destruction. Perhaps on an unconscious level they sensed that under Timothy's apparent strength was a lively sense of the precariousness of existence. At the very least they imbibed a sense of their vulnerability. Small wonder that thunder terrified Jonathan and raised apprehensions of divine wrath.

Timothy's own vulnerability made resistance still more hazardous. Fears for his own destruction arose with anxieties about the children. The myth of his boyhood, based perhaps on fact, perhaps on his own febrile imagination, had him narrowly escaping calamities ranging from drownings and freezings to swallowing peach stones. His letters home from the military expedition which he accompanied as chaplain admonish Esther not to be "discouraged or over anxious concerning me," and follow with such quavering reassurances as, "I have still strong hopes of seeing thee and our dear children once again." His life, like the letters, was suffused with the conditional, "if I Live to come home." Or again: "Tell the children, that I would have them, if they desire to see their father again, to pray daily for me in secret."[16] The conventional sentiment may have had deeper significance in the Edwards household where the children were made to feel some of the responsibility for preserving his rather frail being, making resistance fraught with danger.

Timothy's fragility and perfectionism were slight defects, and the burdens he imposed on his children surprisingly light, considering the emotional hardships of his own childhood. Richard Edwards was one of the few men in seventeenth-century New England to seek and obtain a divorce. After three appeals and a special investigation, his complaints finally moved the magistracy. Timothy's mother, Elizabeth Tuttle, confessed pregnancy by another man three months after her marriage and was unfaithful periodically throughout the twenty-four years of her life with Richard. He never forgave her infidelity and besides bore other perversities "too grievous to forgitt and too mutch here to Relate."[17] Elizabeth's trouble was not mere weakness but a violent malice, bordering on or perhaps symptomatic of insanity. Her brother Benjamin killed their sister with an axe. Another sister killed her own son. Elizabeth threatened Richard with physical violence. Timothy grew up in the presence of distrust and hatred, dependent almost wholly on his father for steady affection and exposed to visible and explosive hostility in his mother. The insistence on rigid control and the precautions Timothy urged on the patient Esther out of fear for his own and his children's safety were modest demands from such a man.

The fear of destruction was always wrapped and muffled in love. Timothy Edwards was indeed an oversolicitous parent, moved by genuine affection and concern. Another letter asks Esther to "remember my love to each of the children, to Esther, Elizabeth, Anne, Mary, Jonathan, Eunice and Abigail," in his usual thorough way naming each individually in order of birth, and then adding, "the Lord have mercy on and eternally save them all, with our dear little Jerusha," the most recent. The next sentence tells much about the warmth of his household: "The Lord bind up their souls with thine and mine in the bundle of life."[18]

Any contemplated disobedience faced this love as well as the implicit danger of destruction. Overt rebellion struck at the loving and loved parent. Jonathan's doctrine that sin was all the more heinous for offending a God who loved the sinner with infinite compassion expressed the anguish felt by rebels in the Edwards household. Unjustifiable resistance wholly deserved its punishment, even if it were complete destruction. All of the Edwards' children remained loyal to their parents and their parents' values. The resentments arising from discipline were necessarily turned inward or diverted to other objects.

A chance event in the family history may have accentuated the apprehensions which Timothy aroused. When Jonathan was seven he passed through a rare naughty spell, resisting for a moment his father's strict control. Immediately afterwards Timothy left with the military expedition for Canada and soon wrote home his quavering hopes for a safe return and the admonitions to pray for his safety. Jonathan's wish to overthrow his father's government seemed to enjoy remarkable success. Suddenly his father was gone and Jonathan was the only male in the house, a situation perfectly designed to revive the furtive romance with the mother characteristic of boyhood a few years earlier. With his conscious mind, Jonathan knew well enough where his father was and that he intended to return, but the direct fulfillment of secret wishes heightened fantasies with immense appeal to the unconscious. When word came back that Timothy had fallen ill and nearly died, the rational faculty would have to struggle desperately to convince itself that those deep wishes had not come precariously close to fulfillment. The brief release of passionate hopes compelled the internal restraining forces to grow all the stronger. All this was stored away in the expanding armory of Jonathan's exceedingly aggressive conscience.

Recreating what we can, then, from the meager facts of Jonathan's childhood, a few themes begin to emerge:

1) Both father and mother had unusually high hopes for Jonathan's intellectual prowess and for the possibility of his becoming eminent.

2) Timothy exacted extraordinarily precise moral and intellectual behavior from his son.

3) Timothy's feelings for his children were an ambivalent mixture of high demands, intense love, and fear of destruction, both theirs and his own.

II

Three essays written by Jonathan, probably between his eleventh and thirteenth years, open a window on his character as it took shape amid the high expectations of the Edwards household. One was an unfinished set of observations on the rainbow, foreshadowing the later notes on natural science. The second was the famous essay on spiders, and the third a facetious rebuttal to the notion of a material soul. The hand of Timothy encouraging and guiding Jonathan's development is seen behind the spider essay, "Of Insects." Like many other New England ministers, Timothy cultivated English correspondents, offering them, in return for their interest, notes on natural phenomena in the New World. More ambitious for his son than himself, Timothy urged Jonathan to write up his observations and send them to England where conceivably they might impress "the Learned world."[19]

"Of Insects" demonstrates how precocious Jonathan was both intellectually and socially. In the letter accompanying the essay, he self-consciously presented himself in a stylized guise suitable for his tender age and also in accord with the conventional proprieties of authorship.

> Forgive me, sir, that I Do not Conceal my name, and Communicate this to you by a mediator. If you think the Observations Childish, and besides the Rules of Decorum,-with Greatness and Goodness overlook it in a Child and Conceal Sir, Although these things appear very Certain to me, yet Sir, I sumbit it all to your better Judgment and Deeper insight....[20]

Particularly the sentence, "Forgive me, sir, that I Do not Conceal my name, and Communicate this to you by a mediator," was an affectation entirely appropriate for his century, but one that had to be learned. Somehow from the books or the guests in the East Windsor parsonage Jonathan had picked up the mannerism and made it his own.

Obviously as Jonathan wrote this essay he did not think of himself as a young future pastor, as might be expected from his upbringing and later life. He accepted that role too; a contemporaneous letter to his sister triumphantly recounted the conversions during a revival time in East Windsor.[21] But in the essay on spiders he appeared as a natural philosopher, and the essay on the soul was weighted heavily with the gestures of an eighteenth-century man of letters.

> I am informed that you have advanced an Notion that the soul is materiall and attends the body till the resurrection as I am a profest Lover of novelty you must immagin I am very much entertained by this discovery (which however [old] in some parts of the world is new to us) but suffer my Curiosity a Littel further I would know the manner of the kingdom before I swear alegance.[22]

The casual, satirical tone, so redolent of fashionable prose postures, stands in marked contrast to the earnest, straightforward style of Edwards' maturity and comes as something of a relief in an anthology of his writing. The two pages on "The Soul" suggest that he toyed with more sprightly life-styles and was for a moment light-hearted before settling down to the life and death issues.

The parenthetical comment, "which however [old] in some parts of the world is new to us," indicates that imitating English manners was more than an amusing posture. Jonathan was a provincial, painfully aware that there were brilliant centers of culture and learning where ideas had grown old before the provinces even heard them. He wanted access to those centers and recognitions from them. The roles of man of letters or natural philosopher were acceptable in the capitals of the English community, and, with Timothy's help, Jonathan cultivated the parts. If Timothy's expertise was limited to ancient languages, he knew of larger fields for the mind and aspired to see his son enter them.

Jonathan's strategy is reminiscent of Benjamin Franklin's, to name but one of Edward's contemporaries with a similar youthful outlook. Franklin too was industriously perfecting his style, using Addison and Steele as his masters, with the intent of winning the attention of great ones. Success in the *New England Courant* fostered high hopes which led first to Philadelphia and then to London, where he introduced himself to polite society with a philosophical essay and a natural curiosity, a piece of asbestos. Defeated for the most part in this first assault, Franklin returned to Philadelphia and built a solid provincial base before trying again and succeeding magnificently as a natural philosopher. His scientific experiments won the recognition of the learned world and helped to establish him as the most cosmopolitan of provincials. In social terms, scientific speculation and experimentation can be interpreted as providing entry to the intellectual life beyond the provinces. Far from being unique, Edwards and Franklin simply took more seriously activities in which many educated Americans dabbled. Science and letters were avenues which talented young men could follow into the great world.

In Edwards' case, the social opportunity must also be related to his personal situation. Ascent into the great world was the fulfillment of his parents' high expectations, or, more accurately, a natural sequel to the rewards his intelligence had won at home. As his parents' ambitions for him became his own ambitions for himself, success in meeting their expectations encouraged him to aspire to success in broader spheres.

The spheres he hoped to conquer grew ever larger after he entered Yale at age thirteen and learned about the marvels of Lock and Newton. Sometime during his college years he began the notes on mind and on natural science which reveal how seriously Edwards took the work of these two intellects. The natural science notes show Edwards exploring every physical phenomenon he observed and in his usual thorough and rational way explaining the facts of physics, biology, and astronomy. "The Mind" contained observations on psychology and metaphysics after the manner of Locke's *An Essay Concerning Human Understanding*. In it Jonathan laid the groundwork of his philosophical idealism.

Both sets of notes were meant to be more than a record of observations. Edwards planned two massive treatises for publication. At the head of the notes on "The Mind" is a formal title: "The Natural History of the Mental World, or of the Internal World: being a Particular Enquiry into the Nature of the Human Mind." The relationship of this work to the notes on natural science was to be explained in the introduction: "Concerning the two worlds-the External and the Internal: the External, the subject of Natural Philosophy; the Internal, our own Minds."[23] With his two volumes

Edwards planned to encompass the whole of existence, the internal and external worlds. He aimed to enlarge upon and perhaps advance beyond Locke and Newton, grounding all in theological metaphysics. Edwards was well aware that his undertaking was presumptuous and cautioned himself "not to insert any disputable thing, or that will likely to be disputed by learned men, for I may depend upon it, they will receive nothing, but what is undeniable, from me."[24] And yet confidence in his own powers and mastery of every intellectual task Connecticut had presented encouraged him to go ahead with his *Summa*. This young provincial aimed high.

The picture of Edwards thus far is relatively conflict-free. Past performance promised future fulfillment of his parents' hopes. His natural gifts and temperament suited perfectly the life they foreway for him. Even the legacy of compulsive thoroughness and logic were put to the service of his identity as scholar and philosopher. In the family, at Yale, and hopefully in the greater English community, society confirmed his belief that the works of his mind were worthy and important and would assure him a place of high respect.

But the promise was not fulfilled exactly as forecast. The two treatises were never published. Although Edwards steadily added to his scientific and philosophical notes, they remained notes. He never publicly assumed the role of natural philosopher, and he dropped the fashionable style of a man of letters in favor of a more somber voice as preacher. His career as pastor and divine absorbed his entire life. The early work was put aside except when it served religion.

The main turning came during the conversion years, but the earliest writings reflect the tensions conversion had to resolve. More was at stake, of course, than boyish dreams of fame. The essay on spiders particularly points to the pitfalls which the high-strung Edwards conscience created even for a boy as obedient at Jonathan and which compelled him to change his life. "Of Insects" is most useful to a biographer if it is read as an unconscious allegory of human existence. Such an interpretation is not far-fetched considering that later Edwards consciously made a spider the emblem of man's plight. Aside from purely scientific curiosity, something held Edwards' attention on spiders hour after hour. During his observations he continually drew parallels with people, and at the end he discussed the ways of God with small creatures in the universal moral order.

The quality which first intrigued him was the "truly very Pretty and Pleasing" ability of spiders to swim through the air from tree to tree and float high in the sky toward the sun. By careful experimentation, he discovered that spiders emitted a fine web which the air bore upwards and which, when it grew long enough, carried away the spider. He hypothesized that it spun the web from "a certain liquor with which that Great bottle tail of theirs is filled," and which dried and rarefied when exposed. He saw the spiders on these webs "mount away into the air" and thought it afforded them "a Great Deal of their sort of Pleasure." Their delight disclosed "the exuberant Goodness of the Creator" who provided for the necessities and also "the Pleasure and Recreation of all sorts of Creatures."[25]

The pleasures of ascent, however, were short-lived, for as the spiders mounted toward the sun in the fair summer weather, they were caught in the prevailing westerly winds and carried to the sea with a great stream of other insects to be "buried in the Ocean, and Leave Nothing behind them but their Eggs." "The End of Nature in Giving Spiders this way Of flying Which though we have found in the Corollary to be their Pleasure and Recreation, yet we think a Greater end is at last their Destruction."[26] The "Greater end" of the pleasing rise was eventual destruction.

The spider's nature made him worthy of this fate. At first appearance "no one is more wonderful than the Spider especially with Respect to their sagacity and admirable way of working." Its maneuvers were "truly very Pretty." The the inner nature of the spider warranted a violent burial at sea, for in essence it was "the Corrupting Nauseousness of our Air." Were spiders in any number to die inland in winter, the spring sun would revive "those nauseous vapours of which they are made up."[27] To prevent them from smelling up the country they were taught to rise and then destroyed.

Edwards here dwelt somewhat pathetically on two themes which sound again more stridently through the "Diary": a pleasurable ascent ends in destruction, and nauseousness lies beneath the pretty appearances. In the "Diary" Jonathan firmly renounced the pleasures of rising as he saw that pride led to destruction. His schemes to achieve eminence in the world had to be abandoned in favor of a life devoted wholly to religion. A loathing of his own vileness also came to obsess him. Later he spoke of sensuality as pollution. "How sensual you have been!" he told one audience. "Are there not some here that have debased themselves below the dignity of human nature by wallowing in sensual filthiness, as swine in the mire, or as filthy vermin feeding with delight on rotten carrion?"[28] "Of Insects" suggests that Jonathan's conscience was already disturbing his complacency in prideful achievement and that the underside of the compulsive perfectionism Timothy implanted was a fear of concealed filth.

Another portentous theme appeared in the early writings. Comparing spiders to humans, Edwards said, "the soul in the brain immediately Percieves when any of those little nervous strings that Proceed from it are in the Least Jarrd by External things." In the essay on the material soul, he asked facetiously if the soul is "a number of Long fine strings reaching from the head to the foot." The image of strings suggests how delicately responsive was his nervous system and how easily jarred. When the spiders were jarred in the course of the experiments, they spun a web and drifted off. The material soul was less mobile, and the main point of the essay concerned the discomforts it suffered "when the Coffin Gives way" and "the earth will fall in and Crush it." Or more excruciating, when other souls were buried in the same grave, they "Quarril for the highest place." "I would know whether I must Quit my dear head if a Superior Soul Comes in the way." When twenty or thirty souls occupied the spot, "the undergoing so much hard Ship and being deprived of the body at Last will make them ill temper'd."[29]

The satirical portrayal of a discontented, nervous soul,

growing ill-tempered as it struggled for a place in the narrow confines of the grave, suggests some of the contrasting pleasures of Edwards' famous booth in the woods. The large family of girls, the guests, the students, and the watchful, demanding eyes of Timothy left little room in the house for peaceful worship. With his boyhood friends, Jonathan built a "booth in a swamp, in a very retired spot, for a place of prayer. And besides, I had particular secret places of my own in the woods, where I used to retire myself."[30] Personal relations all too easily jarred "the little nervous strings" proceeding from his brain, and Edwards struggled hard for mastery of his responses. His diary discloses that he suffered particularly from a "disposition to chide and fret." His own overweening conscience inclined him to snap at others' weaknesses and "to manifest my own dislike and scorn."[31] He eventually decided he could permit himself no evil speaking, not even that which he once thought to be righteous reproof. The dangers of slander or undue vehemence were all too apparent. Even public worship tried him, until by concerted effort he learned to overcome his impatience.[32] Throughout his life he often walked in the fields or rode in the woods, where alone under the sky he more easily composed his soul and made peace with God.

In sum, these early writings confirm to some extent and elaborate the previous speculations on the emotional import of Edwards' early life:

1) For a time anyway, Jonathan aspired to fulfill family expectations through his philosophic writings.

2) The pleasure and excitement of rising was counter-balanced by a fear of destruction because of unworthiness or inward filthiness.

3) The tendency to chide and fret made close personal relations uncomfortable.

III

Edwards' conversion, which drew on all of these themes, occurred over a period of years in his early manhood. Near the end of his college, a case of pleurisy brought him "nigh to the grave" and shook him "over the pit of hell." After that he grew steadily more uneasy about religion, going through "great and violent inward struggles" until he finally broke off "all ways of known outward sin." The "inward struggles and conflicts, and selfreflections" continued, and he made "seeking my salvation the main business of my life" but still did not consider himself converted.[33] Meanwhile he was studying theology in New Haven and preparing to take a temporary pulpit in New York City.

Sometime in his eighteenth or nineteenth year began a series of experiences which he later believed to be gracious. Two slightly differing accounts survive. Edwards wrote the *Personal Narrative* nearly twenty years later, after the first revivals in Northampton. What remains of the "Diary" begins in December of 1722 when he was in New York City and when he had reason to believe grace had already touched him. It records his struggles with sin and his further experiences with grace.

In the "Diary" Edwards charted his cycles of spiritual decay and recovery, the movement from spiritual dullness to the exhilarating moments of rededication. On Saturday, January 12, 1723, in the morning, he enjoyed one of the seasons of grace, and the comment he wrote directly afterwards indicates the nature of the experience. The paramount issue was renunciation of self and complete surrender to God.

> I have this day, solemnly renewed my baptismal covenant and self-dedication, which I renewed, when I was taken into the communion of the church. I have been before God, and have given myself, all that I am, and I have, to God; so that I am not, in any respect, my own. I can challenge no right in this understanding, this will, these affections, which are in me. Neither have I any right to this body, or any of its members--no right to this tongue, these hands, these feet; no right to these senses, these eyes, these ears, this smell, or this taste. I have given myself clear away, and have not

> retained any thing, as my own. I gave them to God, in
> my baptism, and I have been this morning to him, and
> told him, that I gave myself *wholly* to him. I have given
> every power to him; so that for the future, I'll challenge
> no right in myself, in no respect whatever.[34]

Edwards felt compelled to offer more than perfect obedience to God. He searched his soul to be sure nothing was left for himself; everything was given to God, his body and all its senses, all his powers, all enjoyments, the credit for all his efforts, the right to complain or rest, the right to seek anything for himself. He could not permit himself to be "in any way proud." At issue in conversion was the willingness to obliterate selfishness and give up all to God. During the controversy over admission to communion in Northampton, he summarized in a public profession what was expected of saints and put this surrender and the accompanying obedience at the heart. The profession read in the whole:

> I hope, I truly find in my heart a willingness to comply
> with all the commandments of God, which require me to
> give up myself wholly to Him, and to serve Him with my
> body and my spirit; and do accordingly now promise to
> walk in a way of obedience to all the commandments of
> God, as long as I live.[35]

The *Personal Narrative* shifted the stress somewhat to emphasize Edwards' reconciliation with the doctrine of "God's sovereignty, in choosing whom he would to eternal life, and rejectin whom he pleased, leaving them iternally to perish, and be everlasting tormented in Hell." Edwards did not consciously experience the intense fear of divine wrath which usually preceded conversion. He thought his "great and violent inward struggles" were not properly called terror, but as these comments reveal, the fear of punishment was there, probably buried too deep to be felt. The doctrine of election "used to appear like a horrible doctrine," and filled his mind with objections from his childhood up.[36]

For no discernible reason, Edwards suddenly became convinced of God's justice in election. Objections ceased and he rested easy in assurance of divine justice. In connection with this alteration, he tells of his first experience with "that sort of inward, sweet delight in God and divine things" that he later called grace. It came as he read the passage in Scripture saying, "Now unto the King eternal, immortal, and invisible, the only wise God, be honor and glory for ever and ever, Amen." As he read these words, there diffused through his soul "a sense of the glory of the Divine Being; a new sense, quite different from any thing I ever experienced before."[37] As far as Edwards could tell that was the moment of his conversion, and reconciliation with divine power was the critical issue. After that, the thunder that had once terrified aroused sweet contemplations of God's glory.

The two accounts of the experience with grace are easily reconciled, for they have in common a submission to God. The "Diary" stresses the surrender of self and renunciation of pride. The *Personal Narrative* emphasizes the discovery of beauty in God's sovereign right to punish. Both forms of submission can be seen as aspects of a single experience, especially if one remembers how some common vicissitudes of childhood could prepare the way for this very combination. While engaged in passionate rivalry with his father for the love of his mother, a boy imagines himself rising in pride and power to displace his father, thereby evoking paternal wrath. Peace negotiations require both the renunciation of pride and acceptance of the father's superior power, a double surrender morally symmetrical with the two issues in Edwards' conversion.[38]

Edwards' pride could easily have awakened these old memories and their attached apprehensions because his ambition was tied so closely to intellectual achievement, which was also his father's source of pride and a form of accomplishment his mother prized. In seeking to excel as a scholar he inevitably outdid his father and won the favor of his mother. The audacity of the act, though wholly symbolic and unconscious, released the fears which Timothy's compulsive demands and the implicit threats of destruction had formed in Jonathan's conscience. The "torments of hell" included the terror the Edwards children felt toward the imminent possibility of hurting and being hurt by their loving, profoundly fragile, and threatening father. In yielding all to God, Jonathan disclaimed the old rivalry, again symbolically and unconsciously, and placated his archaic fears. The danger of rising to destruction was averted.

Edwards wanted God to sanctify every level of his being, down to the deepest, and the glory of conversion was the comprehensive transformation it wrought. Its power lay in the affinity between theological notions and intimate personal tensions. In conversion Jonathan reconciled himself to God and universal being but the religious symbols also formed bonds with long forgotten memories and with buried conflicts too explosive for consciousness to touch. Conversion resolved tensions along the full range of experience. Until that moment God was the sovereign who judged and punished, shaking men over the pit until they obeyed. The relationship was one of king to subject. As the new "sense of the glory of the Divine Being" came over Edwards upon reading the first epistle to Timothy, he felt a happy yearning to enjoy God, to "be rapt up to him in heaven" and to be "swallowed up in him forever." He prayed "In a manner quite different" from before and "with a new sort of affection." The beauty and loveliness of Christ instead of the fierce power of God impressed his mind. All of Canticles occupied him and especially the verse, "I am the Rose of Sharon, and the Lily of the valleys." These symbols and the whole perception of the divine was softer, warmer, more sensuous.[39] The new relationship was one of lovers. At times the tone was frankly sexual. Some passages in the *Personal Narrative* overflow with a lover's passion.

> The inward ardor of my soul, seemed to be hindered and pent up, and could not freely flame out as it would. I used often to think, how in heaven this principle should freely and fully vent and express itself. Heaven appeared exceedingly delightful, as a world of love; and that all happiness consisted in living in pure, humble, heavenly, divine love.[40]

Or in a different mode: "My heart panted after this, to lie low before God, as in the dust; that I might be nothing, and that God might be ALL, that I might become as a little child."[41] One of the rewards of conversion was that feelings otherwise tightly suppressed flowed freely toward God.

The venting of emotion was possible because vileness was changed to sweetness. The nauseousness of the spider was banished. Whereas sensuality had been and under that name was still described as filth and defilement, the new "delights" were of a "pure, soul-animating and refreshing nature." The happiness of heaven where the inward ardor could "freely flame out" consisted "in pure, humbly, heavenly, divine love." The "ravishingly lovely" beauty of holiness was "far purer than any thing here upon earth"; everything else was "mire and defilement" in comparison.[42] In grace emotions were sweet and calm and flowed freely without polluting. Sensuality was purely joyous.

One final issue came to resolution during conversion. Edwards overcame, partially at least, his uneasiness among people. His disposition to chide and fret had disturbed his personal relations, and he had found peace most easily in solitude. In conversion, he still envisioned himself "alone in the mountains, or some solitary wilderness, far from all mankind, sweetly conversing with Christ, and wrapt and swallowed up in God." But loving and even ardent relations with other Christians were possible. Another of his poetic visions pictured the soul of a true Christian as "a little white flower" standing "peacefully and lovingly, in the midst of other flowers round about." In New York he drew very close to the two saintly people with whom he lived and delighted in long intimate discussions about heaven and holiness.[43]

Edwards' social discomforts did not disappear, for his "heart was knit in affection" only "to those, in whom were appearances of true piety." Indeed he "could bear the thoughts of no other companions, but such as were holy, and the disciples of the blessed Jesus." He disliked visiting among his parishioners where small talk of the world was a necessity. Instead he invited them to his study where he could keep the discussion on religion. The woman he married, Sarah Pierrepont, had been widely reputed for her piety, and even before he met her Edwards wrote a tribute to her "wonderful sweetness" and "singular purity."[44] He could enjoy the intimacies of marriage and friendship only with those whom grace had sanctified, but at least conversion afforded that measure of untroubled intercourse.

IV

The happy visitations of grace continued during his stay in New York and into the following summer spent at his father's house. By the fall of 1723 he had agreed to settle in Bolton, a new town not far from East Windsor, but before his installation, a tutorship opened at Yale, and Edwards persuaded Bolton to release him. From June of 1724, after a winter of private study, until September of 1726, he was the senior tutor and acting Rector, with responsibility to discipline the students as well as to instruct them. After one week on the job, "despondencies, fears, perplexities, multitudes of cares, and distractions of mind" weighed him down and convinced him "of the troublesomeness and vexation of the world." For the three years of his tutorship he was in a "low, sunk estate and condition, miserably senseless" about "spiritual things."[45] The only respite came in the fall of 1725 when he fell ill at North Haven on his way home and his mother came to nurse him.

For many reasons Edwards welcomed the offer which came in 1725 to assist aging Grandfather Stoddard in Northampton. The new position took him away from Yale and it made him heir-apparent to Solomon Stoddard's immense power. Nothing could have thrilled his mother more. The summer following his ordination, Edwards married Sarah Pierrepont, whose piety he had admired from afar and whose life in Northampton parsonage bore out the promise of her early godliness and aristocratic upbringing. She was deeply devoted to her husband--one of her deepest sorrows was to displease "Mr. Edwards"--and her saintliness fully matched his own.[46] A daughter, the first of eleven children, was born in 1728.

Solomon Stoddard died in 1729 and Edwards became chief pastor. He seems never to have regretted the subordination of his youthful ambitions to be a natural philosopher. A ministerial career was perfectly suited to the religious identity formed in conversion. In the pulpit the lonely quest for salvation entered onto a broad stage. His office permitted him to talk freely of God's wrath, or human defilement, and of the exquisite joys of grace. Speaking objectively as pastor, Edwards exposed his soul publicly as he could never do privately. The secret yearnings and dread so long stored in the recesses of his heart became the bread and wine of an open communion with the world. Even the dispositon to chide and rebuke was dignified to a duty. When he admonished, he spoke for God, expressing the righteous wrath of a Holy Father, commanding rather than being commanded, pure instead of vile, terrifying rather than being terrified. And the whole was sanctified and purged of pride because done for God and not for self.

The congregation responded to his quiet, intense preaching. From time to time under Stoddard, revivals had brought unusually large numbers into the Church. Five years after Edwards became pastor, the town experienced a livelier concern with religion than any known before. Two sudden deaths contributed to "the solemnizing of the spirits" of the young, and a controversy over Arminianism set many to asking the true way of salvation. Before lone "among old and young, and from highest to the Lowest; all seemed to be seized with a deep concern about their Eternal salvation."[47] The concern spread from town to town to town until churches all up and down the Connecticut Valley were reporting revivals. The suicide of Edwards' Uncle Hawley in a fit of melancholy over his state slowed the work, but five years later in 1740, when Whitefield visited New England, Northampton and other towns were ripe. The concern spread more widely than ever, engaging thousands of souls this time, and Edwards was in great demand as a preacher and counselor.

Edwards identified these conversions as being of the same species as his own. People felt the same "utter helplessness, and Insufficiency for themselves, and their Exceeding wickedness and Guiltiness in the sight of God," each one considering himself worse than all others just as he had. They were eventually brought to "a Lively sense of the Excellency of Jesus Christ" and "to have their Hearts filled with Love to God and Christ, and a disposition to Lie in the dust before him." In the process of conversion people were also "brought off from their Inordinate Engagedness after the world," though obviously in different ways from Edwards' renunciation of achievement as a philosopher. The same love for others and concern for their souls, the same heightened sense of personal wickedness, the same variations in intensity of devotion all linked the common experience to Edwards' conversion.[48]

His personal influence, of course, does not begin to explain the prevalence of the revivals. All over New England people underwent rebirth in the period of a few years. They followed Edwards, or others like him, because they were ready, not because he personally overpowered them. Something common to all, some prevailing strain on their institutions, some pressure in the culture prepared people for the new life he urged upon them. They listened because the truth of his experience was also the truth of theirs.

I have treated the consciousness of this period at lengh elsewhere, but even in outline the parallels with Edwards can be seen.[49] In Edwards' psyche the most serious conflict leading to conversion was the tension between prideful ambition and the fear of suffering God's wrath for indulging in pride. Conditions in New England in the early eighteenth century put large segments of the population in a similar predicament. The paramount fact of the common life after 1700 was rapid expansion--in population, in numbers of new settlements, in commercial opportunities and involvements, and in the economic horizons of the ordinary man. In Connecticut, for example, population grew nearly five times as fast in the thirty years after 1700 as in the thirty years before; the number of new towns settled doubled; the number of debt cases per capita--a measure of increasing prosperity and commercial growth--increased five times.

The most important and obvious effect on most lives was to

broaden economic opportunities. The new towns offered a host of tantalizing possibilities for incipient merchants. The growing markets outside New England, in Newfoundland and Halifax, in the West Indies, and in Europe, along with the expanding needs of the prospering fishing fleet provided growing outlets for farmers, and the rapid growth of population made speculation in new land very enticing. These developments permitted young men to dream dreams utterly unfeasible earlier. New England had visited a few men with prosperity from the beginning, but very few ordinary men could hope for more than a decent living. William Edwards, for example, had carried on his trade without making great advances. Richard had fared better, building on his father's business, but in the seventeenth century he was exceptionally fortunate. Not everyone could elevate himself in the eighteenth century either, but new opportunities increased the incidence of success. Examples multiplied of small storekeepers who became wealthy merchants and of thrifty farmers who doubled their estates through speculation. By later standards the stakes were small, but the prospects dazzled the first generation of the new century.

Expansion stimulated the desire to rise in the world and yet implicitly threatened destruction, the very ambivalence prominent in Edwards' life. Commercial and agricultural expansion depended heavily on risk-laden speculations: natural disasters, debt foreclosures, and unforeseen calamities of various kinds could wipe out farmers and traders. The psychic hazards were as great as the economic ones. Puritan preachers urged men to follow their callings industriously and to rise through their enterprise. But they condemned men for setting their hearts on wealth and making it their god. The increasing luxury of the eighteenth century and its "Cursed Hunger of Riches" evoked the most bitter indictments. A man never knew exactly where he stood. At one moment he rested in the assurance of his virtuous diligence and of the prosperity heaven had bestowed. At the next a warning from the pulpit started fears that the lust for gold had hopelessly corrupted his soul. Men found themselves in a dilemma comparable to the plight of Robert Keayne, a Boston merchant of the seventeenth century. Keayne prospered in Boston and maintained a respectable reputation until he was accused of unfair dealing and reprimanded in the courts. The confrontation with his guilt put him in fear for his salvation. In hopes of recovering his peace of mind, Keayne wrote an interminable testament justifying his conduct.[50] In the seventeenth century distress like his hung over the few who prospered; in the eighteenth century economic expansion exposed the entire population to these unsettling apprehensions.

Conflicts with authority magnified the guilt and fears of the ambitious. Aspiring men fought with established authority at every level of government, in the town, in the church, and in the colonial government. With innumerable variations, involving large and small enterprises, the pattern repeated itself; ambitious men in pursuit of wealth broke through conventional restrictions and clashed with authorities bent on preserving order. The conflicts were psychically debilitating because the magistracy and ministry were thought to rule by virtue of divine investiture. Authority had a counterpart in individual consciences, and when men resisted they fought against themselves Opposition, however well justified, partook of sinful rebellion.

Another theme in Edwards' life, his prickly relations with associates, appears in the social record also. New Englanders were notoriously litigious, quick to criticize, to sue, or to ask the church to censure. Economic expansion increased the occasions for misunderstandings and ill feeling. The competition for land and trade and for every conceivable economic advantage made enemies of former friends. Every debt case, for example, represented a dispute. A creditor always preferred to settle privately to avoid court costs. Only when prolonged appeals failed did he sue. The storekeeper or wealthy farmer grew exasperated at the delays in payment; the debtor for his part felt the terms unjust, the request for payment over-hasty, or the creditor unsympathetic. The fivefold increase in debt cases per capita in Connecticut between 1700 and 1730 represented at least as large an increase in personal quarrels arising for economic reasons.

The whole society suffered from a painful confusion of identity. People were taught to work at their earthly callings and to seek wealth; but one's business had to remain subservient to religion and to function withing the bounds of seventeenth-century institutions. The opportunities constantly tempted people to overstep both boundaries, thereby evoking the wrath of the powerful men who ruled society. Even relations with neighbors deteriorated as expansion multiplied the occasions for hard feelings. At some indeterminate point social values and institutions stopped supporting the man who placed his confidence in worldly success and instead obstructed and condemned his actions. The pleasurable rise which prosperity afforded carried one at last to destruction.

A widespread uneasiness put people "upon Enquiring, with concern and Engagedness of mind, what was the way of salvation, and what were the Terms of our acceptance with God."[51] The revival preachers confronted their audience with the darkest possible view of their sins and hopeless future. They had fought against God, were filled with pride and vileness, and were worthy of unending torment in the pit of hell. This frank exposure of their dark inward side gave people the courage to bring their sins and insecurity to the surface. The man in the pulpit assuring them that he understood their guilt and the presence of others publicly manifesting their anguish provided communal support for the agonizing confrontation.

The preachers required total humiliation and submission before promising peace. The only hope for reconciliation with God was to confess to utter helplessness and to depend wholly on his grace. For those who heard, moral rectitude and a measure of prosperity suddenly furnished neither peace in this world nor a promise of God's favor in the world to come. Men stood naked under the heavens, helplessly exposed to divine wrath. Edwards noticed people passing from despair to passivity as they recognized the impossibility of earning salvation and gave themselves up to be damned or saved at God's pleasure. Then almost surprisingly hope revived. The good news of the Gospel was heard as if for the first time. The gift of grace seemed sufficient to redeem, and the convert rejoiced in new confidence, founded now on God's loving mercy. They were brought to a "Lively sense of the Excellency of Jesus Christ," and "of the Truth of the Gospel." The sense of sin continued and increased, but now contrition was combined with love and joy.[52] Men felt that they were saved.

With a new identity founded in God's gracious love, converted men renounced their former sources of confidence. The world's wealth no longer appeared so enticing. Edwards noted that in Northampton "People are brought off from Inordinate Engagedness after the World, and have been Ready to Run into the other Extreme of Too much neglecting their worldly Business and to mind nothing but Religion." People seemed to "dread their former Extravagances" and wanted to strip themselves of worldly luxury."[53] After the frenetic itinerant James Davenport urged a New London audience to discard their wigs, fine clothing, and worldly books, the people piled their possessions in a public place and burned them.

Conversion also relieved tensions with neighbors and with authority. The infusion of God's love sweetened all personal relations. "Persons are soon brought to have done with their old Quarrels: Contention and Intermeddling with other mens matters seems to be dead amongst us," Edwards wrote. He cited a number of parishes where old contentions vanished and the congregation was "universally united in hearty affection to their minister." In 1735 his own people "Generally seem to be united in dear Love, and affection one to another," and he "never saw the Christian spirit in Love to Enemies so Exemplified, in all my live." Indeed Northampton "never was so full of love, nor so full of distress as it has Lately been."[54] He composed a covenant to which his congregation subscribed in 1742, pledging themselves not to "overreach or defraud" their neighbors, or "wilfully or negligently" to default on their honest debts. They promised not to "feed a spirit of bitterness, ill will, or secret grudge," and in the management of public affairs not to let private interest and worldly gain lead them into "unchristian inveighings, reproachings, bitter reflectings, judging and ridiculing," but do everything with "christian humility, gentleness, quietness and love.[55]

The results of the revival deeply gratified Edwards. A barely suppressed elation runs throughout *A Faithful Narrative of the Surprising Work of God*, the essay in which he described the love of God and men which came over Northampton in 1735. The Spirit of God appeared to be creating an entire society of saintly men, submissive to God and exquisitely sensitive to religion, a society which confirmed and supported the identity Edwards had assumed in his own conversion. The resonance between Edwards and his people did not continue as perfect harmony. Eventually he demanded more saintliness than they could muster, and his congregation voted 200 to 23 to dismiss him. But for more than a decade, while his words shaped the innermost lives of the reborn, his heart and theirs were as one.

V

Edwards' influence arose from the emotional congruities of his life and his people's: both felt a tension between the yearning to rise in the world and the fear of being destroyed for their pride. In a time of newly opened possibilities for success, heightened aspirations ineluctably entangled men in conflicts with established institutions and values. Widespread contention filled people with guilt, just as the stresses in Edwards' life brought him to an obsession with his unworthiness. The conflict might have been resolved by rationalizing self-interest or by justifying the right to resist authority, and many Americans followed that very course. Edwards, however admitted his utter sinfulness, submitted all to God, and was rewarded with love, joy, and peace. The conversion of thousands during the Awakening signified the general applicability of Edwards' personal solution to the common problem and the implicit acceptance of his leadership.

The sources of pride and guilt doubtlessly varied. Edwards'

intellectual ambitions and the peculiar combination of enveloping love, moral precision, and fear in his father were unique. Strictly personal circumstances could have generated pride and guilt in other lives as well. But the susceptibility to revival preaching in a large proportion of the population, more than chance can account for, is a puzzling fact. Apart from Providence, which can never be ruled out, general social conditions offer the most plausible explanation. The widening economic opportunities of the early eighteenth century, pressing men against rulers, against established institutions like town and church, and against the moral restrictions on covetousness, seem to be the most likely sources of the prevailing distress. Circumstances converged to generate tensions whose psychological structure happened to coincide with that which life in the Edwards' household formed in Jonathan.

Insofar as this analysis is convincing, it confirms Erikson's conception of leadership as the application of the leader's personal identity resolution to the needs of his age. Anyone approaching the problem of leadership, of course, must proceed with humility. Because the influence of one person on another works along subterranean psychological channels, the difficulties in arriving at uncontestable conclusions are immense. The explanation for the power of Joseph McCarthy in the fifties remains conjectural, even when responses from actual participants are still available. But if we are not to abandon all efforts in despair, Erikson's model merits attention. Without claiming scientific certainty for its conclusions, it provides a frame within which to draw together the remaining evidence and to reconstruct lives as imaginatively and as completely as possible.

One virtue of Erikson's work is the incorporation of the personal emotional struggles of which our lives are composed into a coherent system of historical analysis. Attempts to make history "human," to "breathe life" into it, so often lead only to anecdotes or colorful quotations. Erikson's vigorous and well-articulated treatment of human feeling in the framework of his model of leadership makes the moral vicissitudes of life a central component of fundamental historical processes. He helps the historian to describe the bearing of emotions and will as coherently as the impact of the impersonal economic and social forces which once threatened to eliminate personality from historical writing altogether. This entrenchment in an analytical structure is the best assurance possible that personality will be given its due.

It should be apparent that Erikson's model does not apply to every kind of leadership. Most authorities operate within conventions which assure a measure of obedience apart from any personal qualities, and for the most part social forms contain people's anxieties without any extraordinary direction from a gifted man. But at those critical junctures where old values fail and a new order is coming, the way is open for a leader of greater charisma. Then the man of unusual courage and integrity, who successfully contends with the sufferings, self-doubts, and hopes of his time, may, more than we have imagined, exert and influence on the course of events.

FOOTNOTES

1. Erik H. Erikson, *Young Man Luther: A Study in Psychoanalysis and History*, Austen Riggs Monograph No. 4 (New York, 1958).
2. Erik H. Erikson, *Childhood and Soceity*, 2nd. ed. (New York, 1968), p. 261. Erikson also discusses identity in "Identity and the Life Cycle: Selected Papers by Erik H. Erikson," *Psychological Issues*, I (1959), and in Richard I. Evans, *Dialogue with Erik Erikson* (New York, 1967).
3. I give an example of how psychoanalysis can illuminate incidents from adult life in "On the Uses of Psychology: Conflict and Conciliation in Benjamin Franklin," *History and Theory*, V (1966), 225-240.
4. Three biographies of Edwards' life are useful for different purposes. Ola Elizabeth Winslow, *Jonathan Edwards, 1703-1758: A Biography* (New York, 1940), places Edwards in his social setting. Perry Miller, *Jonathan Edwards* (New York, 1949), is a brilliant interpretation of Edwards' thought with suggestive comments on the social structure in the Connecticut Valley. S. E. Dwight, *The Life of President Edwards* (New York, 1830), reprints much of the source material.
5. Dwight, *Edwards*, pp. 16, 18.
6. Jonathan Edwards to Timothy Edwards, Nov. 1, 1720· fragment of a letter from Timothy Edwards to Mrs. Mix. Both are in the Andover collection now on deposit at the Edwin J. Beinecke Library at Yale. I am grateful to Andover-Newton Theological Seminary fro permission to refer to this letter and also to Miss Marjorie Wynne of the Beinecke Library for giving me access to it.
7. Quoted in Winslow, *Edwards*, p. 16.
8. Quoted in Winslow, *Edwards*, p. 21.
9. Quoted in Winslow, *Edwards*, p. 22.
10. Quoted in Miller, *Edwards*, p. 52.
11. Winslow, *Edwards*, p. 41.
12. From the "Diary," in Dwight, *Edwards*, p. 86.
13. *Ibid.*, pp. 81-83.

14. Winslow, *Edwards*, pp. 41, 42.
15. *Ibid.*, p. 43.
16. Dwight, *Edwards*, p. 14; Winslow, *Edwards*, p. 41.
17. Quoted in Winslow, *Edwards*, p. 18.
18. Dwight, *Edwards*, p. 14.
19. Winslow, *Edwards*, p. 36.
20. *Ibid.*
21. Dwight, *Edwards*, p. 21.
22. *Jonathan Edwards: Representative Selections with Introduction, Bibliography, and Notes*, ed. Clarence H. Faust and Thomas H. Johnson, rev. ed. (New York, 1962), p. 11.
23. The intended title page is reprinted in Dwight, *Edwards*, p. 664.
24. From the "Notes on Natural Science," reprinted in Dwight, *Edwards*, p. 702.
25. *Representative Selections*, pp. 3, 6, 7.
26. *Ibid.*, pp. 10, 8.
27. *Ibid.*, pp. 3, 10.
28. *The Works of President Edwards, in Four Volumes* (New York, n.d.), IV, 234.
29. *Representative Selections*, pp. 5, 11, 12.
30. *Ibid*, p. 57.
31. Dwight, *Edwards*, pp. 84-85.
32. *Ibid.*, pp. 85, 88, 89, 90, 94.
33. *Representative Selections*, pp. 57, 58.
34. Dwight, *Edwards*, pp. 78-79.
35. *Works*, I, 202.
36. *Representative Selections*, p. 58.
37. *Ibid.*, p. 59.
38. A more elaborate explication of Edwards' conversion and the psychoanalytic elements involved may be found in Richard L. Bushman, "Jonathan Edwards and Puritan Consciousness," *Journal for the Scientific Study of Religion*, V (1966), 383-396.
39. *Representative Selections*, pp. 59, 60.
40. *Ibid.*, p. 63.
41. *Ibid.*, pp. 63-64.

42. *Ibid.*, pp. 62, 63.
43. *Ibid.*, pp. 60, 63, 64, 65.
44. *Ibid.*, pp. 64, 65.
45. Dwight, *Edwards*, pp. 106, 103.
46. *Ibid.*, pp. 171-172.
47. *Representative Selections*, pp. 74, 75.
48. *Ibid.*, pp. 77, 78.
49. Richard L. Bushman, *From Puritan to Yankee: Character and the Social Order in Connecticut, 1690-1765* (Cambridge, 1967).
50. Bernard Bailyn, "The Apologia of Robert Keayne," *William and Mary Quarterly*, VII (1950), 568-587.
51. *Representative Selections*, p. 74.
52. *Ibid.*, pp. 77, 78.
53. *Ibid.*, pp. 76, 77.
54. *Ibid.*, pp. 76-78.
55. Dwight, *Edwards*, pp. 165-167.

THE MYTH OF FATHER ABRAHAM: PSYCHOSOCIAL INFLUENCES
IN THE FORMATION OF LINCOLN BIOGRAPHY

Donald Capps

The relationship of the historical personality to the myths which attach to him has been of longstanding interest to historians of religion. The study of this relationship contributes to our general understanding of the complex interaction of history and myth in the evolution of religious traditions. Religious traditions are rooted in historical actuality and religious leaders are therefore compelling insofar as they communicate their historical presence to other men. On the other hand, the presence or charismatic power of such leaders is seldom adequately expressed by simply attenting to the fact that they once lived and dwelt among the people. Myths are required to locate the fact of their existence within a rich, inspiring context of meaning.

Oftentimes, myths successfully locate the "life" within the context of a preexisting model or paradigm.[1] Jesus is perceived as the new Adam, the new Moses, the new Abraham. Whether or not Jesus himself considered his life to be the mirroring of these well-established paradigms, his followers and supporters believed it necessary to interpret his life in terms of these primitive mythical models. His own life, in turn, may itself become an exemplary model, worthy of emulation because it has demonstrated its affinity with traditional models. Mircea Eliade captures the dual thrust of this relation of individual lives to exemplary models when he observes: "One of the chief characteristics of the myth...is the creation of exemplary models for a whole society. In this, moreover, we recognize a very general human tendency; namely, to hold up one life-history as a paradigm and turn a historical personage into an archetype.... As Gide has rightly observed, Goethe was

highly conscious of a mission to lead a life that would be
exemplary for the rest of humanity. In all that he did he
was trying to *create an example*. In his own life he, in his
turn, was imitating, if not the lives of the gods and mythical heroes, at least their behavior. As Paul Valery wrote
in 1932: "He represents for us, *gentlemen of the human
race*, one of your best attempts to render ourselves like
gods."[2]

Now, obviously, the relation between the actual life of
the historical personage and the mythical exemplar or biographical myth never admits a perfect fit. Yet followers of
the historical personage have a vital stake in their belief
that he truly fits the exemplary model. And since the exemplary model has already achieved widespread currency within the given religious tradition, it is more likely that the
life of the historical personage will be adjusted to coincide with the model than that the model will be revised to
fit the life.[3] There is nothing in these adjustments to
imply deliberate deception or conscious distortion. It simply means that the model provides the basis for the selective evaluation of the life. Usually, therefore, the highly
idiosyncratic aspects of the leader's life and personality
are muted or entirely eliminated, and those aspects which
coincide with the exemplary model are retained and even highlighted. Again, as Eliade tells us: "To repeat, the historical character of the persons...is not in question. But
their historicity does not long resist the corrosive action
of mythicization. The historical event in itself, however
important, does not remain in the popular memory, nor does
its recollection kindle the poetic imagination save insofar
as the particular historical event closely approaches a mythical model."[4] Eliade then observes that sometimes, though
very rarely, an investigator has opportunity to observe the
actual transformation of the historical event into myth.

This "reduction" of the life to its exemplary model is probably the most typical way in which historical personages come to be related to the myths which attach to them. However, there is an extremely important variation on this typical pattern, one which allows for greater ingenuity and synthesizing skills on the part of those responsible for interpreting the life in terms of longstanding traditions. This variation occurs when the historical personage is believed to have fused in his own life two or more exemplary patterns. This fusion is especially remarkable when it involves two patterns previously considered incompatible. For example, the two patterns may have originated in an earlier split in the religious tradition which the historical personage is now understood to have reconciled; or the two patterns may represent types of religious authority (e.g. prophetic vs. priestly roles) which the historical personage is now understood to have synthesized in his own religious leadership. But, whatever the precise nature of this fusion of two or more exemplary models, the historical personage is understood to be, in some sense, the very embodiment of these exemplary patterns. Hence, his life exemplifies a new image of man in which two or more seemingly incompatible life-models are shown to be reconcilable, perhaps even complementary.[5]

The life-history of Abraham Lincoln constitutes for the historian of religion an extremely fertile ground for investigation of these issues. Like Goethe, Lincoln has come to be understood both as the embodiment of traditional exemplary models and as an exemplar which gentlemen of the human race may profitably emulate. In addition, Lincoln has been understood by his "followers" to have fused two previously exemplary models, these models having been considered irrconcilable by their respective constituencies. And, finally, we are fortunate to be able to observe in Lincoln's martyrdom the transformation of the event into myth. Indeed, the argument which I want to develop in this discussion of Lincoln's paradigmatic death is that the event of his martyrdom was the catalyst for the fusion of two exemplary models previously believed irreconcilable. Thus, while prior to his martyrdom Lincoln was considered by some to be the very embodiment of one exemplary model and by others of the opposing exemplary model, his martyrdom achieved the reconciliation of these two mythological patterns. Thus, the martyrdom was that critical event which was transformed into myth, namely, the myth of his reconciliation of two exemplary models.

Representative Man and Folk Hero: Two Exemplary Models

One of the most prominent uses of exemplary models in popular responses to Lincoln is to be found in Lincoln biography. I shall center attention on this biographical tradition, recognizing that there have been similar efforts to locate Lincoln within the context of these exemplary models in poetry, drama, historical novels and religious sermons.

A limited number of biographies of Lincoln predate his death. The first were published shortly after his nomination for the Presidency in 1860; but these, being essentially campaign biographies, were sketchy and evidenced limited investigation into the details of Lincoln's life. Thus, with the exception of these campaign biographies and William M. Thayer's widely read *The Pioneer Boy*, published in 1863, Lincoln biography consists entirely of works written after his death. After his death, however, biography of Lincoln flourished and continued unabated until the turn of the century. During this 35 year period, there appeared such major biographies as J.G. Holland's *Life of Abraham Lincoln* (1865); Ward H. Lamon's *Life of Abraham Lincoln* (1872); William H.

Herndon and Jesse W. Weik's *Herndon's Lincoln* (1888); John
G. Nocolay and John Hay's *Abraham Lincoln: A History* (1890);
John T. Morse, Jr.'s *Abraham Lincoln* (1893); Ida M. Tarbell's
The Life of Abraham Lincoln (1895); and Norman Hapgood's
Abraham Lincoln: The Man of the People (1899).[6]

After this initial flowering, Lincoln biography was
again revived with the publication of another spate of biographies beginning in 1917. In this second group of biographies were such major works as Lord Charnwood's *Abraham Lincoln* (1917); Nathaniel Wright Stephenson's *Lincoln* (1922); William E. Braton's *The Life of Abraham Lincoln* (1925); Carl Sandburg's *Abraham Lincoln: The Prairie Years* (1926); Albert J. Beveridge's *Abraham Lincoln* (1928); L. Pierce Clark's *Lincoln: A Psycho-Biography* (1933); and Carl Sandburg's *Abraham Lincoln: The War Years* (1939). This second wave of Lincoln biography was accompanied by two major studies of earlier Lincoln myths, including the mythical assumptions of the first period of Lincoln biography. These two studies, Lloyd Lewis' *Myths After Lincoln* (1929) and Roy P. Basler's *The Lincoln Legend: A Study in Changing Conceptions* (1935), were not entirely unique in recognizing that the earlier biographies were shaped according to then prevailing mythical patterns, for the earlier biographers leveled the charge of mythicization at the door of other biographers. But these two studies constituted the first effort in Lincoln scholarship to recognize that all earlier biographies of Lincoln were shaped by myth. Thus, William Herndon's self-congratulatory observation to his collaborator, "Why, Lamon, if you and I had not told the exact truth about Lincoln, he would have been a myth in a hundred years after 1865," does not persuade Lewis and Basler that certain biographers in the early period succeeded in providing a "realistic" portrait of Lincoln. Rather, to these Lincoln scholars, all early biography of Lincoln was profoundly mythical; the pro-

blem, then, was not to distinguish realistic from mythical biographies but to identify the mythical patterns which shaped the various life-histories. Similarly, the biographers writing in this second period evidence less preoccupation with the necessity of avoiding myth.

Before we discuss these mythical patterns, however, we should note that the event of Lincoln's martyrdom was the major contributing factor in the mythicizing of his life-history. As the Lincoln scholar, Richard N. Current, observes: "If Booth *had* missed, our knowledge of Lincoln undoubtedly would be much clearer than it is, much less clouded by mystery and myth. The awful fact of the assassination falls between us and the man.... Lincoln's whole life tends to become obscured by the circumstances of his death."[7] Historians acknowledge that, given his role as President in a time of civil war, some degree of mythicization was perhaps inevitable. Yet, they also point out that the nation's spontaneous grief-reaction to Lincoln's death was so overwhelming that the mythic imagination generated by this emotional outpouring would not be denied. David Donald, Civil War historian, captures the emotional tenor of these troubled times: "The times and events of the Civil War had made a great popular leader necessary. There had been the emotional strain of war, the taut peril of defeat, the thrill of battles won, the release of peace. Then had come the calamitous, disastrous assassination. The people's grief was immediate and it was immense.... Mourning intensified grief. The trappings of death—the black-draped catafalque, the silent train that moved by a circuitous route over the land, the white-robed choirs that wailed a dirge, the crepe-veiled women, the stone-faced men—made Lincoln's passing seem even more calamitous. Over a million persons took a last sad look at the face in the casket and went away treasuring an unforgettable memory."[8]

The first wave of biographies was not unaffected by this emotional response to Lincoln's death. Indeed, as I now want to show, their mythicizing endeavors bore a remarkable similarity to the mourning ritual itself. For, if the funeral train as it circled its way westward united a grieving populace, the biographies began to effect a similar unification on the mythic level. More precisely, they began to unite two seemingly incompatible exemplary patterns--the "representative man" of the East and the "Frontier hero" of the West. Lincoln, through his tragic death, came to be recognized as the embodiment of both exemplary models. Without the tragic, untimely death, there would have been efforts to identify him with one or the other exemplary pattern. Indeed, such efforts were underway prior to his death. But, in the wake of the assassination, biographers sensed theirs to be a more profound responsibility, namely, to demonstrate that the life of Lincoln exemplified a new image of man. Lincoln was larger-than-life because he, alone, had embodied the two exemplary patterns which other men had, at best, embodied singly. In short, the event of Lincoln's martyrdom inspired more than effusive adulation; in addition, this spontaneous outpouring of grief also gave rise to an enduring moral purpose, the mythmaker's task of depicting Lincoln's embodiment of the two exemplary patterns which had most shaped the nation's sense of its heroic dimensions: the Western folk hero and the Eastern representative man.

David Donald points out that Lincoln biography of the early period (1865-1900) has manifested two opposing schools of tradition. One is the Eastern perspective based on the literary tradition of the representative man (following George Washington and Christ) and the other is the Western folk tradition based on the biographical pattern of the folk hero.[9] Now, Donald does not explore the historiographical bases for the myth of the representative man, but it is evident that the foundations for this view were laid by major New England historians of the early 19th Century. As another historian, David Levin, points out, the major historians of that period (Bancroft, Prescott, Motley and Parkman) were romantics who shared a special interest in heroes, especially in men and women who exemplified Emerson's "representative man."[10]

Levin isolates two dominant heroic characteristics in these historians' view of the representative man--naturalness and loftiness. As a *natural* man, he has an underlying simplicity, a moderate amount of passion which expresses itself in warm emotions, a quick sympathy, a delicately balanced sensibility and a natural eloquence which enables him to establish a deep rapport with the people. On the other hand, he has a *loftiness* of spirit, a sense of detachment, of responding to "a necessary law of his being" which informs actions which might otherwise be taken to be prompted by mere personal ambition. Above all, he is a man whose loftiness expresses itself in visible suffering for the whole nation. With sublime patience and constancy, he endures the depths of personal despair and even the misunderstandings of his people in order to accomplish the common good.

Significantly, Emerson himself recognized Lincoln to be an exemplar of his "representative man." In the wake of Lincoln's death, Emerson described Lincoln as "the true history of the American people in his time. Step by step he walked before them; slow with their slowness, quickening his march by theirs, the true representative of this continent; an entirely public man; father of his country."[11] As a representative man, Lincoln met the requirement that he participate deeply in human affairs, in the lives of the people. As Emerson himself put it, "The constituency determines the role of the representative. He is not only representative, but participant.... Man, made of the dust of the world, does not forget his origin...." On the other hand, Lincoln was more than participant in human affairs, the natural man. He was also lofty. Or, as Emerson expressed it, "I count him a great man who inhabits a higher sphere of thought, into which other men rise with labor and difficulty; he has but to open his eyes to see things in a true light and in large relations, whilst they must make painful corrections and keep a vigilant eye on many sources of error."12 In short, Lincoln was that rare man who combined in one being both simplicity and loftiness. He was a man who had not lost touch with his natural origins but who, at the same time, inhabited a higher sphere of thought than other men.

Probably the most concise literary effort to capture Lincoln's embodiment of the representative man image--his naturalness and loftiness--is a sonnet by George W. Bell entitled "The Nation's Seer." Published in 1913, the poem views the naturalness and loftiness of Lincoln as counterpoints: his loftiness is the more remarkable in a man of profound simplicity:

> The tall and stately pine-tree rears aloft
> Its needle-pointed vestments bears its sway,
> As prophet o'er a wilderness, and oft
> Tells to the ear attuned, of storms that play.
> So rose Lincoln to his lonely view
> Above the hill tops springing from the plain;
> Then saw he far beyond, and through and through,
> As earth contact thrilled messages of pain.
>
> A man, our very own, to earth so near,
> So simple in his heartfelt tenderness,
> Yet with a vision, piercing heights, a seer,
> Tracing the storm clouds and the war's duress.
> Seems human life a vain and worthless thing
> Attuned by Lincoln to love's deathless spring?13

This sonnet reads almost as a paraphrase of Emerson's description of the representative man. Lincoln is a man who is close to us, simple in his heartfelt tenderness. At the same time, he is a man who rises to the hilltops and, from this heightened vantage point, sees far beyond what normal men can see.

But poets were not the only literary scholars to view Lincoln as representative man. At the turn of the century, a new kind of scholar had arrived on the scene. These were not Lincoln scholars *per se*, but were, instead, scholars interested in discerning the common characteristics of great men throughout the centuries. Their books usually consisted of essays, each of which attempted to isolate the "greatness" of such heroic figures as Christ, Buddha, Goethe, Napoleon, Cromwell, Bismarck and Washington. Some considered Thomas Carlyle's lectures on "Hero-Worship" their spiritual heritage, and it is interesting to note that Emerson wrote *Representative Men* (which also consists of a collection of essays on great men, including Plato, Montaigne, Shakespeare, Napoleon and Goethe) as a consequence of his correspondence with Carlyle regarding the lectures on "Hero-Worship." In any case, one such essayist who offered a portrait of Lincoln, J.N. Larned, depicted him in representative man terms. In stressing the loftiness of Lincoln's character, Larned describes him as one who stood "like a firm, strong pillar in the midst of the swaying tempest of that uncertain time, for a tottering nation and a shaken cause to hold themselves fast by...." But Larned is convinced that Lincoln's loftiness was the effect of his deep simplicity: "And, yet, from what simplicity of nature that influential strength of the man had come! Here, in truth, was the final secret of it. He had kept his nature as it was given him. He was so little a world-made man,--so very much a God-made man. The child had grown into the man,--not the man out of the child. That rare kind of growth must preserve the best fibre and elasticity of being. It must have helped to produce the quaint, homely humor which some people mistook strangely for clowniness and levity."14

The literary writings of Bell, Larned and others in the early 20th Century clearly indicate that Lincoln as "representative man" was by then firmly established. Through the Eastern biographical tradition, Lincoln could now take his rightful place in the pantheon of great moral and spiritual leaders--not only other political leaders like Napoleon, Bismarck, Cromwell and Washington, but also such paradigmatic spiritual personages as Plato, Buddha and even Christ himself. One suspects perhaps that Lincoln would have found his inclusion in this formidable company somewhat amusing. And yet, as Basler points out, Lincoln was not adverse to comparing himself to the prophet Moses, who would not live to see the promised land, and Christ, who suffered his agonies in the garden of Gethsemene before his final triumph. Thus, Lincoln himself was evidently conscious of his "loftiness" as expressed in visible suffering for the whole nation. And, as we shall note shortly, it was precisely this aspect of the exemplary pattern of the representative man which articulated with his untimely death.

As we turn to the second biographical tradition, we enter the world of "clowniness and levity" which Larned especially deplored. According to David Donald's description, the frontier hero for these biographers was the story teller, the shrewd bargainer, the chaste wooer, the henpecked husband, the man of great physical prowess and the anti-cleric. Thus, Lincoln was portrayed as a great spinner of yarns; as the country lawyer who eschewed fine legal reasoning in favor of shrewd common-sense; as the chaste and honorable wooer of Ann Rutledge, forbearing to plead his own cause until it seemed certain her fiance would not return to claim her; as the wrestling champion of New Salem

and the indefatigable splitter of rails; and as the deeply
religious man who preferred to avoid the formalities of
church-going. Lincoln as "frontier hero" originated in the West
and was more truly folkloristic than the Eastern tradition of
the representative man. As Donald points out: "The grotesque
hero--the Gargantua or the Till Eulenspiegel--is one of the
oldest and most familiar patterns in folk literature. In
America the type had been already exemplified by such favorites
as Davy Crockett, Mike Fink, and Paul Bunyan. Of a like cut was
the myth of Lincoln as frontier hero.... He was Old Abe, a
Westerner, and his long flapping arms were not the wings of an
angel."[15]

Significantly, this Western tradition in Lincoln biography
emerged as a reaction against the Eastern representative man
model. William Herndon, Lincoln's law partner in Illinois and
lifelong friend, was fearful that Lincoln's life would be
entirely enveloped in myth if the Easterners had their way. So
he determined to present a "realistic" Lincoln which his former
neighbors in southern Illinois would recognize. He interviewed
these Illinoisians for his biography, and while most of those
who knew Lincoln firsthand were dead, their descendents were
only too willing to repeat what they knew on hearsay. Nor was
Herndon unusually discriminating in sifting his materials. It
was Herndon who first publicized the story of Ann Rutledge, a
large measure of fancy mixed with a small kernel of fact, and
who depicted Mary Todd as the shrewish wife whom Lincoln ought
never to have married. Herndon also portrayed Lincoln as an in-
fidel.

Professor Donald credits Herndon with having singlehandedly
established the Western tradition of Lincoln biography: "The
folklore Lincoln is essentially Herndonian." To be sure,

> He did not originate the pattern. The saga of "the
> Pioneer Boy, and how be became President" was popularized
> in a series of campaign biographies during Lincoln's
> lifetime. And of course the acceptance and diffusion
> of the legend was conditioned by the excitement of the
> times--by the emotional impact of devastating war, hard-
> won victory, and calamitous assassination. But from the

> very beginning Herndon conceived his biography of
> Lincoln as a study in Western character; he consciously
> planned it to illustrate the "original western and
> south-western pioneer--the type of...open, candid,
> sincere, energetic, spontaneous, trusting, tolerant,
> brave and generous man."16

In spite of Herndon's positive intentions, however, his work was roundly castigated. Leaders of the Republican party thought it demeaned their leader.17 The general reading public wondered what was to be gained from painting Lincoln's origins in such earthly light. Herndon's argument, that he wanted to show how one man rose from "putrid, stagnant" origins to the "topmost round of the ladder," was not compelling. As the daughter of his collaborator, Dorothy Lamon Teillard, complained of this general reaction: "It was thought his fame would suffer if all the ugly facts were known. But it was prompted in part also by the timid and the conventional cowardly notion that opinions of the time about social standing, about education, and about religion would somehow suffer if all his experiences and opinions were frankly told...."18 This general reaction to Herndon's work does not obviate the fact that the frontier hero tradition made its mark. The story of Ann Rutledge was hardly demeaning to Lincoln. Indeed, it captured the imagination of a nation ambivalent about Lincoln's widow. Also, the frontier emphasis on Loncoln's physical prowess, especially as it centered around his rail-splitting activities (and not his wrestling matches), was symbolic of the continuing strength which he had infused into the Republican party.

Yet, in spite of these obvious survivals of the frontier hero tradition, students of the Lincoln myth have argued that this tradition did not fare nearly as well as the Eastern tradition as the movement toward the fusion of these two traditions took hold. The subordination of the Western tradition was evident, they argue, in efforts to render that tradition more gent-el. As Basler describes this fusion of the two traditions:

> Thus the wilderness hero has remained somewhat a local
> legend confined to the Lincoln country. The drinking,
> cock-fighting, rough-and-tumble hero, 'the big buck of
> the lick' who dared anyone to 'come on and whet his horns,'

>the lover of braod humor--such a hero was worthy idolatry on the frontier, perhaps, but not in New England. Hence New England made its own Lincoln which it was able to a certain extent to foist upon the Loncoln country. And as the spiritual picture grew, the reminiscences became more and more in keeping with it. What there is of the frontier hero in the great Lincoln of poetry and fiction, is spiritualized and hallowed by the simple process of omission, emphasis, and invention, *which has so largely biased even the biographical accounts.*19

Here, Basler recognizes the fusion of the two traditions, but believes that the frontier hero tradition was necessarily shortchanged as the spiritualizing process ran its course. David Donald makes a similar point when he describes the fusion of the two traditions, though he makes a greater case for a reciprocal give-and-take. Thus, he notices that "By the centennial year of Lincoln's birth the frontier stories that had been considered gamy and rough by an earlier generation had been accepted as typical Lincolnisms; and on the other side, the harshness of the Herndonian outlines was smoothed by the acceptance of many traits from the idealized Lincoln. The result was a 'composite American ideal,' whose 'appeal is stronger than that of other heroes because on him converge so many dear tradtions.'"20

The Transformation of the Frontier Hero Model

Here, then, we come to the very crux of the issue. There is no question that the Eastern tradition of the representative man influenced Lincoln biography from the beginning. Uncertainty arises, however, when Lincoln scholars attempt to assess the role of the Western frontier tradition as the two tradtions were merged. Was the Western tradition so thoroughly spiritualized that its unique contribution to the Lincoln myth was effectively lost? Did the Eastern tradition so dominate the mythicization of Lincoln that it admitted only those aspects of the frontier hero model that were already consistent with the model of the representative man? Basler and Donald attempt to answer this question by identifying those aspects of the frontier hero model which were "spiritualized" in the fusion of the two traditions. In following this procedure, however, the Western model would necessarily appear to have fared badly in the fusion process, if only because it had far more to lose as the life-history of Lincoln became "spiritualized." The real question, then is whether the biographical tradition of the frontier hero was the mere victim of this spiritualization process, or whether it may actually have played a major role in this very process? We can begin to shed light on this question by considering the transformative effect on Lincoln's assassination on the frontier hero model. Can we realistically expect that, after Lincoln's tragic death, the frontier hero could nay longer be considered a merely comic figure ala Crockett, Fink and Bunyan? In my judgment, the frontier hero myth underwent considerable transformation in the years following Lincoln's death, a transformation which is evident in biographers' efforts to come to terms with his frontier years. His assassination forced them to consider what there was about his frontier beginnings which enabled Lincoln to rise far above the essentially ludicrous folk hero; especially was there some profoundly tragic element in frontier life which prepared Lincoln for the tragedies to come? In this view, it was not simply a matter of the frontier hero pattern being incorporated into the Eastern myth of the representative man and thereby spiritualized. Rather, the frontier hero pattern was itself undergoing transformation as a consequence of Lincoln's tragic death, and it was this transformed frontier hero which came to be fused with the Eastern model. We might say, therefore, that aspects of Herndon's portrayal of Lincoln were rejected from the composite heroic image not merely because they were inconsistent with the Eastern model, but because they had become incompatible with the frontier hero pattern as Lincoln's martyrdom had begun to transform it. Or perhaps behind his earthy realism, Herndon was struggling to articulate the tragic dimension of frontier society; there are elements of this tragic sense in his account of the death of Ann Rutledge.

How did Lincoln's death transform the frontier hero myth in the direction of the tragic? The answer is really quite simple, but its implications are most profound. Consider the characteristics of the frontier hero as Professor Donald enumerates them. Each of these characteristics represents a social role: Concerning sociality at the community level, the frontier hero is a spinner of yarns, the shrewd bargainer, the combatant, the eschewer of institutional religion; and at the domestic level, he is the chaste wooer and henpecked husband. Among adult domestic roles, the father image is notoriously absent. What the frontier hero model lacks in its comic version is the frontier hero as father. And yet, as Basler points out, Lincoln's image as "Father Abraham" was a great source of consolation to the nation as it mourned his death:

> Lincoln as he walks at midnight is the symbol of all ideals of democratic humanity, but he is also the tender memory in apparition of the beloved personal ssint, the folk Father Abraham....The conventional picture given by the builders of the gentle legend is that of Father Abraham, a kindly, pleasant old man with a humorous smile which often fades into a look of sadness. He is forever enshrined in popular memory dressed in black, with tall hat and black shawl. The touch of earthiness is never in the picture drawn with loving fancy. He is never thought of as having any personal interest or ambition. It is only as the guardian angel of his children that he overlooks the vast arena of war and sadly smiles as the blood sinks into the thirsty sand. He bears his own burden uncomplainingly and gladly seeks to lighten the burden of others. His sad, plain features are simply glorious in their reflection of benignity, devotion, and a wisdom passing that of earth.21

Here, in the image of Father Abraham, we find the sense of tragedy which was lacking in Donald's description of the frontier hero. Perhaps under normal conditions it was possible for Lincoln's contemporaries to identify as frontier heroes those who symbolized resentment of the domestic roles of husband and father. But the tragic implications of this omission of the father ideal were probably always just below the surface. In times of severe social stress, the need became great for a hero capable of embodying a father ideal. In spiritualized accounts of the life of Lincoln, therefore, concerted efforts were made to play down Lincoln's own resentment of the dometic roles of husband and father, and to emphasize his role as the faithful and longsuffering father of a tragically divided national household.

Of course, this tragic transformation of the frontier hero model through recognition of Lincoln's father role did not introduce an entirely new element into frontier mythology. Basler notes that intimations of the Father Abraham image were evident in Lincoln's earlier frontier experiences, including his alleged gentleness toward animals as a child and his kindness toward widows and orphans as a circuit-riding lawyer. Yet, as John William Ward points out, these very attributes were earlier accorded Andrew "Stonewell" Jackson, also noted for his protection of small children and helpless women.[22] Thus, elements of the Father Abraham image predated Lincoln. Nonetheless, it was not until the event of Lincoln's assassination that the image of Father Abraham irrevocably transformed the comic model of the frontier hero into as essentially tragic one. And, if a tendency toward fatalism was already part of the frontier hero model, Lincoln's sudden and violent death gave the model a previously inconceivable tragic depth.

It should be acknowledged that Eastern biographers were not unaware of the tragic dimensions of Lincoln's assassination, noting its parallels to the life of Christ: Both went to their deaths on Good Friday, Lincoln having chosen Ford's Theatre because the play being presented there, unlike the other available fare in town, satirized the Northerner. Was this not itself a final acto of suffering servanthood? However, without discounting the mythic importance of these Christological parallels, it should be noted that they play largely on the element of coincidence and generally fail to penetrate the deeper levels of the tragedy of Lincoln's death. As the Lincoln funeral train circled its way westward after the assassination, the grieving populace saw less the Godforsaken son of man and more the immobile face of their dead Father Abraham. And, when poets like Vachel Lindsay proclaim, "He cannot sleep upon his hillside now. He is among us--as in times before," their words conjure up in our own minds less the image of the resurrected savior and more the presence of Father

Abraham standing watch over his lost children of Israel.[23] In short, the image of Father Abraham is central to the myth of the living Lincoln and, as such, is distinguished for its restorative quality: "He bears his own burdens uncomplainingly and gladly seeks to lighten the burden of others." Hence, this image is perhaps most exemplary of the Lincoln myth itself, for it was that very myth which followed the divisive acts of war with words of fatherly consolation.[24]

Diffusion of the Father Ideal

Exemplary patterns such as those of the representative man and the frontier hero are not easily transformed. As we noted earlier, the great tendency is toward the omission of those characteristics of the historical personage which do not fit the exemplary patterns. Obviously, aspects of his life were played down and various adjustments in the life-history were made as biographers began to fuse Eastern and Western exemplary models. However, the image of Father Abraham is a striking addition to the exemplary model and there must therefore have been an intense need in frontier America for a mythic element of this nature.

A thorough investigation into the spontaneous emergence of the Father Abraham image is well beyond the scope of our present discussion. Nonetheless, in the work of Erik Erikson, we have a conceptual framework which is capable of at least identifying the psychosocial factors in frontier society which gave rise to this transformation of the myth of the frontier hero. Erikson's life cycle theory provides this conceptual framework through its motif of intimacy vs. isolation. In my judgment, the emergence of the Father Abraham image was an attempt by frontier society to come to terms with the psychosocial conflict of intimacy vs. isolation, especially as this conflict was reflected in what Erikson has called the "diffusion of the father ideal."[25] Father Abraham, as a strong father image, symbolizes the nation's longing for the restoration of its former sense of family unity.[26]

In elaborating the social and cultural concomitants of the individual life cycle, Erikson suggests that the crises encountered in various life stages have their counterparts in the social order; in the case of the intimacy-isolation conflict, the corresponding social dimension is that of social patterns of cooperation and competition. We can point to a number of emerging social institutions in frontier America and especially in Lincoln's southern Illinois, which reflect its preoccupation with patterns of cooperation and competition. Consider, for example, Lincoln's own chosen occupation as lawyer. It has frequently been noted that the moral leadership of frontier communities in the mid-nineteenth century was passing from the clergy to the lawyer who, in liason with the businessman, developed norms and procedures for regulating cooperation and lawful competition. The court house challenged the church as the moral, social and even geographical center of the new town, and the courtroom itself became the scene of both conviviality and combat. In consonance with this general trend, Lincoln without much seeming conflict decided on a legal career, thereby participating in the shaping of new forms of social commitment.

On the other hand, these new forms of social commitment created new tensions in the domestic sphere. The "new town" concept, vigorously supported by young Lincoln (first as a surveyor for new town developers and then as a lawyer sympathetic to new town business interests), challenged the subtle balance of intimacy-isolation which the rural family enjoyed. Lincoln's biographers cite at least two occasions when Lincoln and his wife, living in Springfield at the time, burst out of their home onto the street in heated argument. On one of these occasions, Lincoln is said to have chased Mary from the house, shouting, "You make the house intolerable, damn you, get out of it." On the other occasion, Sunday morning churchgoers were startled to see Mary threatening her husband with a kitchen knife, and he attempting to push her back into the house with remonstrances about their making an awful scene in front of their church-bound neighbors.[27] The very fact that neighbors recalled these incidents, when they would have remained private in a more rural setting, indicates the degree to which family intimacy was being relinquished to communal forms of intimacy--patterns of cooperation, competition and friendship appropriate to the more densely populated frontier town.

Undoubtedly, Lincoln's biographers have seriously distorted a complex interpersonal relationship in claiming that Mary Lincoln's allegedly shrewish ways drove her husband out of the house and into politics. Nonetheless, they are quite right in noticing the tension between those two social institutions, the familial and the political, a tension attributable in large measure to the emergence of the new town. And underlying this tension was a basic intimacy question which all of Lincoln's frontier contemporaries faced. As the psychoanalyst L. Pierce Clark points out, Lincoln had a larger vision of his political task than the achievement of domestic tranquality, and that is the "high task of binding other human beings in a great and enduring friendship." Given this task he "fully recognized that [his] love for his fellow man must be severely taxed in that it leads diametrically away from the exclusive inbinding of love of man for woman."[28] The new town and its cooperative ventures initiated the valuation of friendship above the more private intimacies of family life. And, it is perhaps not insignificant that the most influential biography in the Western tradition was written by a lifelong friend who used his biography as a vehicle to accuse Lincoln's wife of attempting to subvert his husband's career.

In another paper, I have described Lincoln's difficult relations with women during his courtship period, and especially his problems in making a marital commitment, and have shown how they reflect his own deeply personal concern with conflicts of intimacy and isolation. I have further suggested that Lincoln's response to the secession of the southern States during his Presidency was informed by his handling of intimacy and isolation conflicts in his own marriage.[29] I shall not repeat that discussion here, but rather pursue the other major dimension of the intimacy-isolation conflict, one which bears more directly on the theme of this paper, i.e. Lincoln's attitudes toward the father-son relationship.

We may address this dimension of the intimacy-isolation conflict by noting that the diffusion of the father ideal in frontier America made possible the high valuation placed on friendship as opposed to family ties. As Erikson points out, in frontier America "The boy's male ideal is rarely attached to his father, as lived with in daily life. It is usually an uncle *or friend of the family*, if not his grandfather, as presented to him (often unconsciously) by his mother."30 Whatever the reasons for this diffusion of the father ideal through the son's disinclination to identify with his father (Erikson himself suspects the mother's unconscious but persistent belittling of her husband's safe but sedentary ways), the fact is that Lincoln himself seemed to have no significant emotional attachment to his father. He left his father's farm for the town as soon as he reached age 21 and was legally free to go, and his subsequent visits home were infrequent and apparently prefunctory. The incident which reveals most about their relationship, however, took place in 1851 near the time of his father's death. As Richard N. Current points out:

> Yet there must have been a real estrangement between him and his father. He did not take the trouble to see the old man during the latter's last illness, though it was a trip of only seventy-odd miles from his own home in Springfield to his father's residence in Coles County. Again and again Thomas' stepson appealed to Abraham, saying in one letter: "I hast to inform you that father is yet a Live & that is all & he Craves to See you all the time & he wants you to Come if you ar able to git hure...." Abraham did not even bother to answer all the letters. He finally wrtoe (1851) to explain that both his own business and his wife's sickness prevented him from visiting his father. "Say to him," he advised his stepbrother, "if we could meet now, it is doubtful whether it would not be more painful than pleasant; but that if it be his lot to go now, he will soon have a joyous meeting with many loved ones gone before; and where the rest of us, through the help of God, hope ere long to join them." He did not attend the funeral.31

Even allowing for Lincoln's characteristic irony, his attitude about his father's impending death support's Current's contention that there must have been a "real estrangement" between son and father.

Interestingly enough, however, the most unlikely of Lincoln

biographers doubts their relationship ended on this note of estrangement. L. Pierce Clark, redoubtable psychoanalyst-turned-biographer, believes that eventually Lincoln was spiritually reconciled to his father, much in a manner reminiscent of what Freud identified as the child's "defferred obedience" toward a deceased parent. The occasion was the unexpected death in 1862 of Lincoln's favorite son, William. When William died, Lincoln experienced the profound burden of fatherhood and, in Clark's view, the result was that Lincoln became as entirely different man. But first, Clark's description of the experience itself:

> At the boy's sickbed he walked the floor, saying sadly, "This is the hardest trial of my life." One would have expected from the nature of Lincoln's personality that thr essence of his love brought forward from his attachments to his mother and Anne Rutledge would have been so concentrated in his attachment for his son that a depression of considerable intensity would have occured; this, indeed, did happen. Instead of a long period of depression, however, in which there was inability to work, insomnia, thought of suicide, etc., as had been present at the death of Anne and at his failure to make the marriage bond with Mary Todd, the depression was very short. The whole period of sorrow, embraced in an incipient phase of sadness, was entirely removed in the short period of three days.32

We shall not pause to explore the implications of Clark's suggestion of a psychological link between Lincoln's attachments to women and his father role. Rather, of more direct relevance is his explanation for Lincoln's ability to recover from his grievous loss in a relatively short period of time:

> It is interesting to observe by what mechanism this condition seemed to have been curtailed. Lincoln shut himself in his room alone, and saw little of his wife or other son, and in the depths of his despair he turned to religion. That which he had known purely as a form of speech or argumentative rhetoric, and embracing more deeply much which we have seen in an expression of antagonism to the concept of authority as proceeding from God, etc., was now transformed. At this religious experience following his son's death he made a full reconciliation with God and accepted him as his personal God, and from that time on it was seen that a calm and peace entered into his attitude toward life that he had never before known.33

Clark identifies this experience as a religious conversion, but one which effected greater inner peace than is customary. The reason for this greater sense of peace, in his judgment, is that Lincoln through this episode "reconciled himself to the earthly as well as to the Heavenly father, and that at last antagonism toward the earthly father had been removed and he was at peace with the conflict within his own soul.[34]

I know of no other Lincoln scholar who attributes a religious conversion to Lincoln, and it is especially surprising that the suggestion of a relatively positive religious experience would be advanced by an orthodox Freudian. While the death of Lincoln's favorite son was unquestionably an event emotionally compelling enough to precipitate a conversion, there is no solid evidence to support the view that this was in fact what happened. Nonetheless, the event clearly establishes Lincoln's own sense of the burden of fatherhood and, whether or not it led to a spiritual reconciliation (or even psychological identification) with his earthly father, it leaves no doubt that Lincoln himself knew the pain and heartache of a father's love for his lost child.

It would be convenient but historically irresponsible to suggest a causal link between the death of his son and Lincoln's emergence as the nation's Father Abraham. But it is not far-fetched to suggest that his own spontaneous irruption of emotion at the unexpected death of his favorite son kindled in Lincoln a profound sympathy for the reciprocal feelings of the nation's own favorite sons as they marched to their deaths proclaiming their allegiance to "Father Abraham." As Lloyd Lewis points out: "Toward the common soldiers Lincoln was instinctively a father.... It was the natural way of his heart."[35] Thus, as the bereaved father, Father Abraham bears his own burden uncomplainingly (as evidenced in the brevity of his period of mourning) and gladly seeks to lighten the burden of others. The war demanded this deeper form of cooperation, one more intimately painful than that of friendship, especially friendship established on the recognition of a common enemy. It would appear, then, that with the emergence of the myth of Father Abraham, the diffusion of the father ideal was temporarily arrested as the ideal became reinvested in Father Abraham.

It is said, of course, that national leaders trend on extremely dangerous ground when they approach their leadership responsibilities in terms of family relations. Psychohistorians have been among those who fear this influence of "irrational" motives and attitudes on the decision-making process. And the spontaneous emergence of the myth of Father Abraham indicates that, in times of national crisis, the populace will impute these irrational motives to its leader whether justified or not. On the other hand, Lincoln's own sensitivity to this mythic impluse enabled him to appreciate the fact that the myth of Father Abraham strikes a deeper chord than the ideal of friendship, and this appreciation in turn inspired him to infuse the myth with the force of historical truth.

FOOTNOTES

1. For an interesting discussion based on Karl Jaspers notion of the "paradigmatic individual," see Antonio S. Cua's "Morality and the Paradigmatic Individuals," *American Philosophical Quarterly*, vol. 6, no. 4 (October, 1969), pp. 324-29.
2. Mircea Eliade, *Myths, Dreams, and Mysteries*, trans. Philip Mairet, (New York: Harper Torchbooks, 1967), pp. 32-33. My italics.
3. For an extremely interesting example of such an adjustment, see Kenelm O.L. Burridge, *New Heaven, New Earth: A Study of Millenarian Activities* (New York: Schocken Books, 1969).
4. Mircea Eliade, *Cosmos and History*, trans. Willard R. Trask, (New York: Harper Torchbooks, 1959), p. 42.
5. Arthur F. Wright addressed this problem in his essay "Sui Yand-Ti: Personality and Stereotype," in Arthur F. Wright, ed., *Confucianism and Chinese Civilization* (New York: Atheneum, 1965). Wright points out: "It would be too much to say that the elite and popular images of Yang-ti fused into a single myth, but it is certain that the two images, influencing each other, have drawn closer together during the thriteen centuries since the death of Yang-ti." p. 186.
6. A useful summary of the major Lincoln biographies written prior to 1935 may be found in Roy P. Basler's *The Lincoln Legend: A Study in Changing Conceptions* (New York: Octagon Books, 1969), pp. 8-34.
7. Richard N. Current, *The Lincoln Nobody Knows* (New York: Hill and Wang, 1958), pp. 272-73.
8. David Donald, *Lincoln Reconsidered: Essays on the Civil War Era*, 2nd rev. ed., (New York: Vintage Books, 1961), pp. 145-46.
9. *Ibid.*, p. 148.
10. David Levin, *History as Romantic Art* (Stanford: Stanford University Press, 1959), p. ix.
11. Ralph Waldo Emerson, quoted in Carl Sandburg, *Abraham Lincoln: The War Years* (New York: Dell Publishing Company, 1959), pp. 882-83.

12. Ralph Waldo Emerson, "The Uses of Great Men," in *Representative Men: Seven Lectures* (New York: AMS Press, 1968), pp. 3-35.
13. See Roy P. Basler, p. 198.
14. J.N. Larned, *A Study of Greatness in Men* (Boston: Houghton, Mifflin Company, 1911), pp. 300-301. Another famous essayist in this tradition, Gamaliel Bradford, chose not to write an essay on Lincoln. However, his reasons for not doing so are suggestive. As Roy P. Basler points out: "Bradford, who splendidly interpreted in his 'psychographies' so many American heroes, never attempted a portrait of Lincoln." I have checked his numerous comments on Lincoln scattered through several volumes. Together with this work (*The Haunted Biographer*, which consists of "dialogues of the dead" between the spirit of Lincoln and those of Shakespeare, Lamb, Twain, Moody and John Wilkes Booth) they indicate an interest that is profound, and at the same time, an amount of uncertainty that is not common to Bradford's work as a whole. It is interesting to speculate that for the great 'psychographer' as for so many Lincoln biographers, Lincoln was too complex a soul. To quote Bradford's own phrase, "He still smiles and remains impentrable." pp. 50-51.
15. David Donald, p. 154.
16. David Donald *Herndon's Lincoln* (New York: Alfred A. Knopf, 1948), p. 371.
17. There is a parallel here with Arthur F. Wright's study of Sui Yang-ti. Wright points out that popular anecdotes and tales were drawn upon by the political leaders insofar as these were consistent with an accepted historical version of a given event in the life of Sui Yang-ti. *Op. Cit.*
18. Quoted by Roy P. Basler, p. 10.
19. *Ibid.*, p. 147. My italics.
20. David Donald, pp. 162-63.
21. *Ibid.*, pp. 200, 125-26.
22. John William Ward, *Andrew Jackson: Symbol for an Age* (New York: Oxford University Press, 1953), pp. 197-98.
23. This is not to deny another significant link between Lincoln and Christ, i.e. the fact that scholars recognize similar histori-

ographical problems in reconstructing the lives of Jesus and Lincoln. Van Harvey's observation is typical: "If historians are unable to decipher the mystery of Abraham Lincoln, even though they possess volumes of authentic sayings, untimate letters, and the accounts of eyewitnesses, are we to believe that we can encounter the real Jesus of Nazareth on the basis of a handful of sayings preserved in no chronological order by a community that was especially anxious to prove that he was the Messiah?" *The Historian and the Believer* (New York: Macmillan, 1966), p. 193.

24. The power of this image of "Father Abraham" to unify as well as console the nation is attested by the fact that the Lincoln myth appealed to southerners' sense of obligation to the legacy of their own fathers. As Michael Davis points out: "The Lincoln legend...acted as a kind of force attracting Southerners back into the Union of their fathers.... The conscious conciliators of the New South found in Lincoln a most usuable symb-l of reunion; in praising Lincoln they announced to the North their willingness to share in those very national virtues for which the North had canonized Lincoln as its martyr-hero." *The Image of Lincoln in the South* (Knoxville: The University of Tennessee Press, 1971), p. 170.

25. Erik H. Erikson, *Childhood and Society*, 2nd revised edition, (New York: W.W. Norton and Company, 1963), pp. 312-13.

26. At the risk of indulging in Spenglerian fancies, we may note that the evolution of the American myth bears remarkable affinities to Erikson's life cycle. The 1970s and the Revolutionary War marked the period of the nations's concern with identity vs. identity diffusion. The 1960s and the Vietnam War ushered in the period of generativity vs. stagnation. And, almost equidistant between the two, the 1860s and the Civil War epitomized the intimacy-isolation conflict.

27. There is a parallel to these episodes in the famous "chamber pot" episode in Gandhi's autobiography. See Erik H. Erikson, *Gandhi's Truth* (New York: W.W. Norton and Company, 1969), pp. 232-33.

28. L. Pierce Clark, *Lincoln: A Psychobiography*, (New York:

Charles Scribners' Sons, 1933), p. 505. Another form of this argument for the transfer of emotion from family to state appears in A. Bronson Feldman, "Abe Lincoln: The Psychology of a Cult," *Psychological Studies of Famous Americans: The Civil War Era*, edited by Norman Kiell (New York: Twayne Publishers, 1964), pp. 116-34.
29. Donald Capps, "Intimacy Vs. Isolation: A Psychological Motif in the Life and Myth of Abraham Lincoln." Unpublished paper presented at the annual meeting of the Society for the Scientific Study of Religion, 1973.
30. *Childhood and Society*, p. 312. My italics.
31. *The Lincoln Nobody Knows*, p. 30.
32. L. Pierce Clark, "Unconscious Motives Underlying the Personalities of Great Statemen and Their Relation to Epoch-making Events (I. A Psychologic Study of Abraham Lincoln)," *The Psychoanalytic Review*, vol. 8, no. 1, 1921, p. 15.
33. *Loc. cit.*
34. *Loc. cit.*
35. Lloyd Lewis, *Myths After Lincoln*, (New York: Readers Club Press, 1941), p. 305.

IDENTITY AND CONVERSION
Reflections on Nineteenth Century American Religious Experience and Identity

Robert Michaelsen

How did man's need for individual identity evolve? Before Darwin, the answer was clear: because God created Adam in His own image, as a counter-player of His identity, and thus bequeathed to all man the glory and despair of individuation and faith. I admit to not having come up with any better explanation.1

Erik Erikson defines identity as "a *subjective sense* of an *invigorating sameness* and *continuity*," and he appeals to William James's description of those occasions when one feels himself to be "most deeply and intensely active and alive. At such moments," James continues, "there is a voice inside which speaks and says: '*This* is the real me!'"2 Erikson "locates" this sense both "*in the core of the individual*" and "*in the core of his communal culture*."3 It is also a sense which, one might say in non-technical language, has both an emotional and an ideological aspect. From the integration of these various elements--individual and communal, psycho-somatic and social, emotional and ideological--a firm sense of identity emerges. Again, in non-technical language, the self or "the real me" "gets it all together", or, if that is too voluntaristic in its connotations, is gotten all together. Finally, in Erikson's view, adolescence is the critical stage or time for this process.

The religious experience of conversion is usually understood also as a process of integration. In the language of William James, it is a "process of unification" through which "the divided self" is put together; it is a process in which a sense of "firmness, stability, and equilibrium" succeeds "a period of storm and stress and inconsistency."[4] This process is both emotional and ideological, personal and communal. Emotionally, the convert feels a sense of release ("spontaneous awakening"[5]), oneness in himself and with others and perhaps the world of nature, and a renewed or new sense of strength. "The 'ego'," writes E.D. Starbuck, a younger contemporary of James and also a psychologist, "is lifted up into new significance."[6] Ideologically, the convert comes to be, perhaps for the first time, completely at home in the religious and theological system in the context of which his conversion experience is elicited and understood. Finally, while conversion might occur at any age, typically adolescence is regarded as the most critical and propitious age for the experience.

It is significant that William James, while focussing primarily on religious conversion, pointed out that "religion is only one of many ways of reaching unity." Indeed, James continued in a statement which anticipates Erikson, "the process of remedying inner incompleteness and reducing inner discord is a general psychological process, which may take place with any sort of mental materials...."[7] Identity crises may be resolved in various ways; the traditional religious form was but one. James also pointed out that the typical religious conversion might be seen primarily as one form of identity crisis or crisis of maturation. In his preface to Starbuck's *Psychology of Religion* James observed that the conversion experience

> may in countless cases be a perfectly normal psychologic crisis, marking the transition from the child's world to the wider world of youth, or from that of youth to that of maturity....[8]

The American Puritans and their descendants, however, saw the conversion experience (or the experience of "saving grace") as the *only* accessible means of unification, and they understood that means in the context of the classical Augustinian world-view. Without conversion life was hell;

one remained forever an incomplete and divided self. With it one could live as he was meant to live. Divine power was his, by grace, and he could now practice "true virtue"-- i.e., play all his roles like the God-created being he was meant to be. The conversion experience was crucial for identity in this system; individuals who lived under the system had to come to terms with that experience in one way or another. Every person, and especially every young person, was expected to have the experience. Its importance was as great to the Puritans and their descendants as was the vision quest among American plains Indians.

While conversion was understood to be a process of decisive significance, these early American descendants of St. Augustine rarely permitted themselves to live happily ever after. Life was a process, a continuing struggle, a pilgrimage. Once lifted from the pit of despair it might go on as a series of advances from plateau to plateau, with occasional precipitous falls in between. One would continue to be threatened by guilt, stagnation (the word "dullness" was often used), and despair.

I do not intend to identify Erikson's idea of identity with the traditional notion of conversion; I see similarities, but there are also clear differences. Nor do I intend to engage in a systematic discussion of the literature and concept of conversion as it might relate to Erikson's concept of identity. I do find it interesting that such pre-Freudian American psychologists as James and Starbuck discussed to a considerable extent the problem of the unification of the self, not only as a religious problem but as a preeminently *human* problem. And I see certain parallels between their ideas and Erikson's. But there are also real differences, most notably the absence in James and Starbuck of the Freudian framework and of Erikson's keen sense of the importance of communal factors. My chief intention, however, is to examine the conversion experience as a significant phenomenon in the process of identity. I do so in the context of early and mid-nineteenth century America and specifically in two families: the Beecher family and the James family. I note its central importance in the former and the reduced importance of its traditional ideological garb in the latter. I note also in and through the lives of the members of these families some trends in American identity in this century. In these lives one can see the signs of a crucial change whereby the traditional religious conversion experience lost its central significance and was replaced, on the one hand, by stress on continuity which tended to short-circuit the process of unification, or on the other hand, by an attempted direct look at "raw" experience without benefit of exclusivistic or monistic ideology. In the former instance, "the real me" developed smoothly from infancy on. ("The child is to grow up a Christian and never know himself as being otherwise," wrote Horace Bushnell, opponent of conversion and apostle of "Christian nurture".[9]) In the latter, "the real me" ebbed and flowed like the tides of consciousness.[10]

The Primal Paradigm[11]

It was God who called the true self forth, who created man in His own image and, after man's fall from grace, restored that image. But how was that miracle of restoration or transformation effected in one's life? Through a sacramental system, said the Catholic tradition. Through saving faith, said Puritan Protestantism, and, by virtue of this, consigned sensitive men and women to lifelong soul searching. One sought to know and to obey the truth. But, above all, one wanted to feel it, to experience it, to be sensibly assured of God's saving power in one's own life.[12] Given the magnitude of man's sin and of the consequent gulf between him and God, this was no easy matter. Just any experience would not do; even "peak" experiences could be the result of false exuberances or enthusiasms. A miracle was required, a miracle as great as the incarnation; indeed, saving faith was the miracle of the incarnation reenacted in the individual soul. Hence the experience of saving faith was a special experience, a discreet experience, which had its own unique quality. Jonathan Edwards compared it with the taste of honey; it was that real--and that ineffable.

This Puritan stress on a distinctive inward experience made a deep impact on American spirituality. A controlled inward intensity was sought. Treatises were written and sermons preached to help men to discern the signs within themselves. Then a whole system--the revival system--was built to elicit the coveted experience of conversion.

The Beecher Family: Romantic Union and Moral Zeal

I turn first to the Lyman Beecher family to illustrate the personal and secondarily, the communal results of this kind of Puritan spirituality at a critical and relatively late stage in its development. This family graphically illustrates the dialectical dance that went on between thought or belief (ideology) and experience. What one believed colored his experience, and one's experience affected his belief. As a result of their own experience Lyman's children could not support or endure his thought system. That experience forced a closing of the gap between God and man and a blurring of the focus on the distinctiveness of the experience of saving faith. It precipitated a lifelong struggle on the part of most of the Beecher offspring to affirm publicly the friendliness of God and the universe.

In so doing, the Beechers projected upon American society
the effects of their own inward and pathetic struggles.
That was half of Lyman's legacy to his family; the other
half was a moral dedication which all shared with him.

Lyman Beecher, who was born on the eve of the American
Revolution and died during the Civil War, called his revised Calvinism "clinical theology." Under the tutelage
of his Yale mentor, Timothy Dwight, followed by more than
thirty years in the pastoral ministry, Lyman became an
accomplished minister to sick souls. His home was his
primary clinic. He sired thirteen children by two wives,
and he labored mightily for the salvation of every one of
the eleven who survived infancy.

Henry Ward, Lyman's most famous son, labelled Lyman's
system "*alleviated* Calvinism" The "alleviation" was such,
however, as to put even greater pressure on the individual
than had unrelieved Calvinism. Lyman lifted the will out
of the endless chain of cause and effect into which Calvin
and his consistent followers seemed to have bound it. By
doing so he gave greater weight to individual effort in the
salvation process. At the same time, however, he did not
abandon original sin, total depravity, eternal punishment,
and the mysterious ways of a righteous but inscrutable
deity. The conversion experience was crucial. That determined whether one was bound for heaven or for hell. It
was an experience in which one repented for his sin and
gave up his own will for God's will. But the experience
could not be achieved by will alone. It also required
divine action. At the same time, the individual was under
indictment if the experience was not achieved.[13] Professor
Henry F. May correctly points out that Harriet Beecher
Stowe and her generation

> had to confront not neo-orthodoxy, but orthodoxy.
> Hell was not a metaphysical necessity or an ab-

> sence from God, but a real place full of real fire.... In this place oneself and most of the people one loved were probably destined to spend an eternity of torture.14

By 1819 Lyman was the father of eight children by Roxanna Foote, who had died three years earlier. The five oldest ranged in age from eight to nineteen. These were the critical years, as Lyman himself recognized in a letter to his oldest son, William, who was then seventeen: "You occupy that period of life in which there is more hope than in any other."15 There began about that time a series of written exchanges between father and children, letters which are filled with urgency, poignancy, longing, and turmoil; letters which illustrate the trials of this intelligent, articulate and relatively strong-minded quintet of young people in their efforts to fit with integrity into their father's scheme. This correspondence, together with Lyman's letters to younger children, exchanges among the children themselves, and other types of personal and semi-personal Beecher documents, constitute a rich source from which to document a marked change in American spirituality.16

The Beecher home was not all morbidity or dullness. As a conscientious evangelical Christian and ministerial father, Lyman did agonize over the state of his children's souls. But he was also an indulgent father who loved to take his children hunting and fishing, who could turn routine household work into a game, and who, on occasion, even danced an old routine for his children's delight. From 1810 to 1826 the family was located in Litchfield, Connecticut, a community of extraordinary cultural depth considering its location. There the Beechers were very active participants in community life. The romantic poets and the novels of Scott were read in their home. Outside the home the old order was changing. The Congregational Church was disestablished in Connecticut in 1817, a move which Lyman fought but later came even to value. Unitarianism was on the rise in the state to the north. Lyman was a sworn enemy of that development and moved into the heart of Unitarian territory in 1826 to do battle with it. Good strategist that he was, he set out to learn all he could about his adversaries. In the process, his children also learned. Lyman was also a vigorous and vocal moral reformer. The Beecher home was very much alive to the moving issues and ideas of the day.

The very vitality of the Beecher home no doubt increased the burden of concern with the soul experienced by the children. Exposure to the ideological storms and stresses of the time increased psychological pressures within them. It is perhaps remarkable, then, that so many of the Beechers not only survived, but went on to achieve some distinction in their own right and to live remarkably long lives.[17]

"I have no child prepared to die," wrote Lyman to William in 1819. "My son, do not delay the work of preparation. Awake to the care of your soul. Time flies; sin hardens; procrastination deceives.... Do not put off the subject...." Then he summarized the state of the other accountables in his family:

> I talked and prayed with Edward before he left home (for Yale), and shall attend to Catharine, and Mary, and George, and Harriet, with the hope that God will bless them with salvation. A family so numerous as ours is a broad mark for the arrows of Death. I feel afraid that one or more of you may die suddenly, and I be called to mourn over you without hope.... But, oh my son, save me from such an hour on your account. Let me not, if you should be prematurely cut down, be called to stand in despair by your dying bed, to weep without hope over your untimely grave. Awake, I beseech you, my dear son, and fly to Christ. So your affectionate father prays with weeping.[18]

Poor William never quite made it. "I am completely down in the dumps," he wrote his oldest sister Catharine five years later. "I was an imaginative boy, somewhat romantic with a sprinkling of minor notes--a sort of sad longing--a feeling I never should be anything--a sort of black sheep feeling...." He complains that he did not know how to study and hence could not keep up with his younger brother, Edward, who went on to success at Yale and Andover. William was in and out of a dozen or more jobs. When not regularly employed, he often returned home where, he reports, "the great question was, 'What shall we do with William?'" Finally he was converted while working in a hardware store in Boston. Then, surprisingly dissuaded by his father, he decided to become a minister. And there followed a life of itinerancy from one poor and dissatisfied congregation to another.[19]

The experience of Edward, the second son, contrasted sharply with that of William. He too had his soul troubles, especially after he went to Yale in 1818. But during his senior year he attained the coveted experience, the first of the Beecher children to do so. While that experience, as we shall see, did not quite fit the Lyman Beecher system, Edward's description of it was sufficiently persuasive that Lyman triumphantly welcomed him to the firm.[20] And with that there began a correspondence between Edward and his brothers and sisters in which the second son occupied a surrogate fatherly role.

The one who looms largest in this early correspondence is Catherine, the oldest of the brood. Hers is an especially poignant story, and yet she emerges in the end as perhaps the strongest of the lot, especially in her resolve to "do good." When Lyman's first wife, Roxanna, died, much of the care of the seven younger children fell to the sixteen year old Catharine. She was a strong and capable young woman who managed superbly to rise to the occasion.

Catharine put the crucial religious question in an early letter to Edward: "How can I make myself feel?"[21] How can I have the right feeling, the requisite sense experience? Shortly after she put this question her situation was immeasurably complicated by the accidental drowning of her "affianced lover" Alexander M. Fisher of Yale. Fisher apparently also had not received the desired religious experience. Hence, his ultimate destiny was much in doubt. The anguished Catharine asked her brother: "Oh, Edward, where is he now? Are the noble faculties of such a mind doomed to everlasting woe...? Could I but be assured that he was now forever safe, I would not repine. I ought not to repine now," she continues in self-condemnation, "for the Judge of the whole earth cannot but do right."[22] But there was the difficulty. "Right," according to the received Calvinist view, would be condemnation to eternal hellfire if the young man had not had that experience which certified his chosen status.

Catharine was plunged into a period of deep religious questioning and despair: She is greatly afflicted. She knows not where to turn for comfort. She longs for God to "take possession of the heart that He has made desolate," but most of the requisite signs are not to be found within her: "I feel no realizing sense of my sinfulness, no love to the Redeemer, nothing but that I am unhappy and need religion; but where or how to find it I know not." Her case, she concludes, "is almost a desperate one."

For more than a year Catharine opened her troubled heart to both her father and her brother, but to no avail. "When I began to write to you on the subject which now occupies my thoughts," she complained to Edward, "it was with a secret feeling that you could do something to re-

move my difficulties. But this feeling is all gone now."
To her father she confessed that she was

> like a helpless being placed in a frail bark, with only a slender reed to guide its way on the surface of a swift current that no mortal power could ever stem, which is ever bearing to a tremendous precipice, where is inevitable destruction and despair.
> If I attempt to turn the swift course of my skiff, it is only to feel how powerful is the stream that bears it along. If I dip my frail oar in the wave, it is only to see it bend to its resistless force.
> There is One standing upon the shore who can relieve my distress, who is all powerful to save; but He regards me not. I struggle only to learn my own weakness, and supplicate only to perceive how unavailing are my cries, and to complain that He is unmindful of my distress.

Lyman assured his daughter that help was aviable. At the same time, like a good consulting clinician, he observed to Edward that Catharine's case was "awfully interesting," that "there is more *movement* than...ever before...and she is now...handling edge tools with powerful grasp...." The prognosis was positive.

For nearly two years following Fisher's death, Catharine lived with his parents in Franklin, Massachusetts where she taught his two sisters, studied mathematics with his brother, and listened to the "fearless and pitiless preaching" of Nathaniel Emmons, one of the most unyielding of the proponents of "consistent Calvinism." (Emmons' preaching was significantly influential in driving Horace Mann from orthodoxy to Unitarianism.) During that time Emmons preached a memorial sermon on Professor Fisher in which he lauded Fisher's worldy accomplishments but left Fisher's ultimate state very much in doubt. "I felt," Catharine wrote to her father after hearing this sermon,

> that I *could not* bend the knee, nor open my lips to pray to a Being whose character, to my blinded eyes, was so veiled in darkness and gloom. And

for a time, with mournful desperation, I thought I would seek religion no more....²³

Catharine did not have the coveted conversion experience during this desperate period, and apparently never in her lifetime. She climbed slowly out of the pit of despair through a resolve "to do good," to pursue a course that would lead "to a more extended usefulness." With the help of Edward and her sister Mary she opened, in Hartford, "a school intended exclusively for those who wish to pursue the higher branches of female education."²⁴ She quickly developed a theory of education which was based on the assumptions that "all intelligent beings are formed with a supreme desire for happiness, and are continually regulated by this principle..." and that God has so made men and women that they can promote their own happiness by "*doing right*." Pupils should be taught, by appeal to their reason and their affections, that rectitude will lead to their happiness. "No other motives can operate so powerfully..." in producing a good life. It is clear that this is a theory which is a far cry from even "alleviated Calvinism."²⁵

In the meantime, Edward was having his difficulties. Seemingly a successful minister-scholar, he too continued to be deeply troubled by a view which seemed to make God a wrathful tyrant who punishes man for not doing the good which man is incapable of doing. This seemed to be the father's view, but it was not congenial to Edward's mind or to his heart. All through his childhood, according to Catharine's account of what Edward related to her, "as far back as memory could reach he never had a feeling of conscious alienation from God, or of hostility or revolt." At the time of his conversion he sought to know God "face to face, as a man talked with his friend...." Seeking such a friend, he turned to the New Testament and found there a God who suffers with man and thus reveals human qualities.

Edward was still troubled, however, by the Calvinist notions of original sin, total depravity, and eternal punishment. How could these be squared with the suffering God--the face-to-face-friend--that he had found in the New Testament? Finally, Edward hit upon the truth of the *pre-existence of souls*--hardly a Calvinist notion! Man in this life suffers and atones for sins committed in his own *previous* lives, not for the sin of Adam. This truth came to him, Edward reported to his younger brother Charles, as "a virtual revelation." Revelation indeed; Edward's experience was such that he could only compare it with that of the Apostle Paul who "was caught up to the third heaven" where he "heard things which it was not lawful to utter," or like "Moses descending from the mount--his face transfigured--must he needs draw a veil over his countenance." How else could he confront Lyman who "had no place in his system for this new revelation"?

Edward's "revelation" signals the beginnings of a profound break with the past. God was not, in this view, so much the counter-player as a friendly ally in the struggle with the effects of one's former lives. Having vindicated God's innocence the next step was to join the romantics in discovering and vindicating man's innocence. Edward did not take that step. But his view was conducive to a blurring of the sharpness of identity presupposed in the Calvinist understanding.

Edward's "secret revelation" was not to be disclosed for another twenty-five years, but it was known and relished in the intimate circle of his siblings. Charles reports that at the age of fourteen he "instantly as by a kind of intuition" accepted Edward's new doctrine. Sixty years later he wrote that he had "never doubted it since." The "secret revelation" was also of keen importance to the spiritual development of Edward's younger sister Harriet.26

As child number six, Harriet stood near the middle of the Beecher brood. The relative anonymity of this location was aggravated by the death of her mother when Harriet was four and the remarriage of her father a year and a half later. (She clearly felt a "generation gap" between herself on the one side and her father and his second wife on the other. This is evident in the autobiographical treatment of the character of Dolly in *Poganuc People*.) Harriet was a bright youngster with a great range of imagination. She developed early in life habits of careful observation of her fellows and of herself. She understood her introspection, quite naturally, in the language of religious search. At the age of twelve she wrote a surprisingly adult compostion on the subject "Can Immortality of the Soul be Proved by the Light of Nature?" Two years later, while hearing her father preach a communion sermon on the Johannine text, "Behold, I call you no longer servants, but friends," she experienced what she took to be a genuine conversion. The preacher's theme, Harriet wrote later, "was Jesus as a soul friend offered to every buman being," as a person "patient with our errors, compassionate with our weaknesses, and sympathetic for our sorrows.... Oh! how much I need such a friend...." But before she could freely receive Jesus as a friend, according to the clinical formula, she had to come to terms with her own "conviction of sin" or rather her lack thereof. She concluded, quite logically, however, that if Jesus was the right kind of friend he could even take care of that apparent lack. Hence she trusted "Him for the whole," with the result that her "whole soul was illumined with joy..." and "it seemed as if Nature herself were hushing her breath to hear the music of heaven." As soon as she could get Lyman's attention she rushed into his arms and eagerly announced that she had given herself to Jesus, "and He has taken me." "I never shall forget the expression on (my father's) face...it was so sweet, so gentle, and like sunlight breaking out upon a landscape. 'Is it so?' he said, holding me silently to his heart, as I felt the hot tears fall on my head. 'Then has a new flower blossomed in the kingdom this day.'"[27]

But was the conversion genuine? That question came back to haunt Harriet. The business about the "conviction of sin" seemed, on reflection, to be a suspicious short-cut, a subterfuge. The scarred older sister, Catharine, had her doubts. She "was afraid that there might be something wrong in the case of a lamb that had come into the fold without being first chased all over the lot by the shepherd...."[28]

Harriet's doubts surfaced repeatedly in her late teens and early twenties. "My whole life is one continued struggle," she wrote to Edward, her newly accepted father confessor, when she was sixteen.

> I do nothing right.... My deepest feelings are very evanescent.... I don't know as I am fit for anything, and I have thought that I could wish to die young.... You don't know how perfectly wretched I often feel: so useless, so weak, so destitute of all energy.... I wrote rules; made out a regular system for dividing my time; but my feelings vary so much that it is almost impossible for me to be regular....

It costs her great effort "to express feelings of any kind" to her fellows. Yet "the desire to be loved forms...the great motive" for all her actions. She wishes that "the Savior were visibly present in this world, that I might go to Him for a solution of my difficulties...." But she wonders if God "really loves sinners before they come to Him?" Edward assures her that God *is* her friend, that in Christ he grieves and suffers with her. But she responds that the book of Job, which she has just been reading, does not contain the views which Edward presents to her. Her case, like Job's, seems hopeless. It is

> exactly as if I had been brought into the world with such a thirst for ardent spirits that there was just a possibility, though no hope, that I should resist, and then my eternal happiness made dependent on my being temperate.29

In the Summer when she became eighteen (1829), Harriet thought she had reached a distinct turning point. While she began that summer "in more suffering" than she had felt "ever before," she later reached the high point where she could say that she had "never been so happy," she reported to Edward, with whom she shared her euphoria. She knew, she confessed, that he could *feel* as she did because the two of them, like few others, knew Christ as "their best friend."30

But her "long course of wandering" did not cease. Two remarkable passages emerge from letters written three years later. In these passages she appears as a kind of burned-out case, and she very perceptively understands her soul struggles in their American religious context. First, she announces a firm resolve to think positively:

> (T)his inner world of mine has become worn out and untenable, I have at last concluded to come out of it and live in the external one...to give up the pernicious habit of meditation to the first Methodist minister that would take it, and try to mix in society somewhat as another person would....
> I have come to a firm resolution to count no hours but unclouded ones, and to let all others slip out of my memory and reckoning as quickly as possible..
> ..31

Some months later, after having moved with the family from Boston to Cincinnati where Lyman took up the job of establishing Lane Theological Seminary, Harriet observed that in America, vehement and absorbing feelings become

> deep, morbid, and impassioned by the constant habits of self-government which the rigid forms of our society demand. They are repressed, and they burn inward till they burn the very soul, leaving only

dust and ashes. It seems to me the intensity with which my mind has thought and felt...has had this effect. It has withered and exhausted it, and though young I have no sympathy with the feelings of youth. All that is enthusiastic, all that is impassioned in admiration of nature, of writing, of character, in devotional thought and emotion, or in the emotions of affection, I have felt with vehement and absorbing intensity,--felt till my mind is exhausted, and seems to be sinking into deadness. Half of my time I am glad to remain in a listless vacancy, to busy myself with trifles, since thought is pain, and emotion is pain.32

How could a daughter of Lyman Beecher live only externally and "count only the sunny hours"? (Harriet's rendering of *Horas non numero nisi serenas*, an inscription on a sun-dial in Venice.) And, most significantly, how could she do so without assurance of salvation? Surely the "pernicious habit of meditation" must continue until that assurance was achieved. And just as surely there were still live coals in the ashes of that soul, coals which would be fanned into flame again and again as Harriet endeavored to express the intensity of her emotions in a thousand different ways. And repeatedly she would experience what she later called "the burning *inward* of a deep, unsaid dissatisfaction."33

Harriet spent the next eighteen years in Cincinnati. During that time she married Calvin Stowe and gave birth to six children. In that bustling border city she was exposed at first hand to some of the harsher realities of slavery. Like most of the Beecher family, she agonized over what the Christian could say to that evil. For twenty years after writing the above, her soul was pitched back and forth between despair and hope. Then, out of the depths of these inner struggles, she spoke her word against the evil of slavery.

In 1843 Harriet's brother, George, regarded by some as the most promising of Lyman's sons, killed himself.34 This event, Harriet wrote, "shook my whole soul like an earthquake...." She saw in it a threat to all--"father, brothers, husband," and--not least--herself. Now at the age of thirty-two, she experienced deeper anguish than she had ever known before. She was not prepared for this threat to her world. She felt "haunted," "pursued," "harassed," "anxious," and "alone." She had not fully submitted herself to God. She must endeavor to do so with even greater resolve. She was rewarded within a year by another high: "*All* changed," she wrote to her half-brother Thomas in June of 1845.

> Whereas once my heart ran with a strong current to the world, now it runs with a current the other way.... The will of Christ seems to me the steady pulse of my being.... I seem to see the full blaze of the Shekinah everywhere....[35]

But again the relief was temporary. The effort was great and the circumstances difficult. Calvin was away much of the time. The children were young. Cincinnati weather and atmosphere depressed her. "I am sick of the smell of sour milk, and sour meat, and sour everything," she wrote her husband with some complaint. The "clothes *will* not dry, and no wet thing does, and everything smells mouldy; and altogether I feel as if I never wanted to eat again." While she found Calvin's letter to be "a very agreeable contrast to all these things...," she confessed that her own health was "bad enough and daily growing worse.... Upon reflection," she concluded, "I perceive that it pleases my Father to keep me in the fire, for my whole situation is excessively harassing and painful...."[36] Things grew worse until she reached a state of near collapse. Then the family rallied to her aid and enabled her to spend nearly a year seeking rest and "a cure" in Brattleboro, Vermont. Temporary relief was found again. But six months after her return to Cincinnati, her eyesight began to fail and she found herself in a "strange state." Then cholera ravished Cincinnati and, while Calvin was in Europe, the dread disease claimed her youngest son, Charley. That experience was the final burst of flame which tempered the steel of her soul to its point of remarkable productivity. It was at Charley's "dying bed and his grave," she wrote later,

> that I learned what a poor slave mother may feel when her child is torn away from her. In those depths of sorrow which seemed to me immeasureable, it was my only prayer to God that such anguish might not be suffered in vain. There were circumstances about his death of such peculiar bitterness, of what seemed almost cruel suffering, that I felt I could never be consoled for it, unless this crushing of my own heart might enable me to work out some great good to others....37

Within two years of Charley's death the family moved to Maine, Harriet gave birth to her seventh child, and she began to write *Uncle Tom's Cabin*. She often said later of that work, which made her famous, that it was not she but God who wrote it. Whatever the case, it is clear that the book represented a kind of culmination of her own inner struggles. It was Harriet's theodicy. As a daughter of Lyman she was appalled at human slavery. As a sister and a mother who had experienced the death of her loved ones, she identified with the sufferings of slaves. As a tormented soul who must know God as a friend, she declared him as such even to those who knew the depths of human misery. "This story," she wrote of *Uncle Tom's Cabin or Life Among the Lowly*, "is to show how Jesus Christ...has...a mother's love for the poor and lowly, and that no man can sink so low but that Jesus Christ will stoop to take his hand...."38

Harriet was forty when she began writing *Uncle Tom*. For the next thirty years she turned out an average of nearly a book a year. Many of these, as Charles H. Foster has shown in *The Rungless Ladder*, were started under the impact of her own inner experience. Religiously, that experience led her in various directions. When her oldest son Henry was accidentally drowned at the age of nineteen, Harriet was plunged into a state of spiritual and emotional turmoil similar to that which Catharine had experienced many years earlier at the drowning of Professor Fisher.[39] Shortly after Henry's death, two unusual "phenomena" occured which led both Calvin and Harriet to speculate that Henry's spirit might be endeavoring to communicate with them. But Harriet could not be sure. Her good friend Oliver Wendell Holmes wrote to her that it was understandable that she might find comfort in spiritualism, which modified "the sharp angles of Calvinistic belief, as a fog does those of a landscape."[40] Her Italian experience led Harriet to identify briefly in her imagination with Roman Catholicism. (*Agnes of Sorrento*.) Finally, she joined the Episcopal Church where she hoped, in Foster's words, to find "a stray against religious and moral confusion."[41] Toward the end of her life her contact with reality steadily diminished and for the last decade she needed to be almost constantly attended by another person.

Calvinist orthodoxy precipitated psychological and ideological crises which it was unable to resolve. The Beecher family illustrates this in mircrocosm. While the father, in his efforts to preserve and advance what he regraded as the essential elements in the Calvinistic understanding of the human predicament, stressed sharp discontinuity between God and man and between the old self and the new self, the children came to assert continuity. The father belonged to an elite corps of Calvinist evangelicals which sought to bring the populace up to the stern demands of a distant and rigorous ruler-God. The children tended to ally themselves increasingly with popular sentiment for a humanized God and a divinized man. Catharine settled early on moral resolve and assumed moral ability. She and Harriet both later found some solace in the dignified formalism of the Protestant Episcopal liturgy. Edward, Harriet, and Henry stressed the love, even the mother-love, of Christ as contrasted with the stern justice of the Father-God. Nearly all of the Beecher offspring found comfort and inspiration in a benevolent deity's presence in the seemingly friendly world of nature. Several flirted with spiritualism and one, Isabella, the youngest daughter, actually became a Spiritualist. She also declared that she was to be the new messiah, an equal partner with Jesus Christ. George, the third son, developed a fatal romance with perfectionism. He completely exhausted himself in his efforts to live at that high level of spiritual and emotional transport which had been exhibited on occasion by Sarah Edwards (Jonathan's wife), and at the age of thirty-four, while serving as minister of a New School Presbyterian Church in Chillicothe, Ohio, he took his own life.[42] There is a considerable range of spirituality and its effects in this microcosm. But all exhibited the same tendency to narrow the gap between God and man and to blur the Edwardian focus on discreet religious affections.

None exhibited the above tendency more clearly than the most popular and most influential of the Beecher sons, Henry Ward. Henry was the seventh child and the fourth son. His mother died when he was three and, as noted, Lyman remarried a year and a half later. Henry seems to have suffered considerably under these circumstances. He, more than any of his brothers and sisters, complained of a lack of mother-love, on the one hand, and the seeming distance of the father, on the other. Henry was slow of speech and, although he was not the youngest of the first wife's children, he was often treated as the baby. Even so, his older sisters were not entirely adequate mother surrogates and his stepmother seemed cold and distant. All of his life he was to contrast the warmth of his real mother with the coolness of his stepmother. Of the latter he wrote:

> Although I was longing to love somebody she did not call forth my affection and my father was too

> busy to be loved. I think it would have been
> easier to lay my hand on a block, and have it
> struck off, than to open my thought to her....
> I was afraid of her. I revered her, but I was
> not attracted to her. I felt that she was ready
> to die, and that I was not.43

She impressed him as saintly but distant. He needed someone close and loving. That is the image he had of his real mother, and that is the image he projected upon the whole world in his exuberant and compulsive efforts to solve publicly his own inner crisis.

Henry's sense of bieng low man on the sibling ladder is perhaps implied in his first known letter, written at the age of five in reference to his stepmother: "Dear Sister, We are al wel. Ma haz a baby. The old sow has six pigs." Of his soul troubles as a youngster he wrote later:

> (A)t intervals for days and weeks I cried and
> prayed. There was scarecely a retired place in
> the garden, in the woodhouse, in the carriage
> house, or in the barn that was not the scene of
> my crying and praying. It was piteous that I
> should be in such a state of mind and that there
> should be nobody to help me and lead me out into
> the light...I wanted to be a Christian. I went
> about longing for God as a lamb bleating longs
> for its mother's udder.44

From such longing developed an idealization and idolization of his real mother which was to shape his own understanding of religion. At the age of fourteen or fifteen, he reports, he "began to be distinctly conscious that there was a silent, secret, and, if you please to call it so, romantic influence which was affecting me...." This was his mother with whom he came to "have more communion...than with any living being...." No "devout Catholic éver saw so much in the Virgin Mary as I have seen in my mother...."[45] In Henry's religious novel, *Norwood*, the young hero, Barton Cathcart, "desires the (religious) truth as an unweaned child yearns for its mother's breasts."[46]

At the age of sixteen Henry experienced a conversion when "there arose over the horizon a vision of the Lord Jesus Christ as a living Friend...." Young Beecher had "an intoxicating sense of God as one who loves 'from the fulness of His great heart....'" After describing a similar experience, Barton Cathcart was asked if that experience had left any lasting effect. "In truth it did," he replied: "It awakened all my mother in me."[47]

Henry never split openly with his father. As a lad he attempted to escape the intolerable psychological pressures of the Beecher home by running away to sea. But old Lyman--who wanted every Beecher boy in the ministry--outsmarted him. He talked Henry into going instead to preparatory school. It was while he was there that Henry found Jesus as a friend. He hinted this to his father and that seasoned shepherd quickly took measures to drive this would-be rebel into the fold. Under Lyman's ministrations, Henry joined his father's Boston church and entered Amherst College to prepare for the ministry.

While at Amherst, Henry found other friends outside the family circle. There began a pattern of dependency on such close associates which was to continue throughout his lifetime. Henry required warmth, affection, and even adulation in those close to him. Under such circumstances he became remarkably adept at playing upon the more tender notes of human emotion.

Over a long ministry, which spanned the middle years of the nineteenth century, Henry moved farther and farther out of Lyman's orbit. In the process he came as close as any nineteenth century minister to being the national chaplain of his time. His sermons were often front page news. His writings were widely read. He was the object of much adulation. Henry did not speak as clear and distinct a word as Lyman had. In fact, his published work often seems bland

and confused in comparison with Lyman's. But in that, too, he spoke to his age. It was a time to make the rough edges smooth, to take the harshness out of religion, and to put a smile on the deity's countenance. It was a time to exalt even the humblest sentiment and to give play to even the commonest emotion.

No son or daughter of Lyman Beecher openly rebelled against him, but, in one way or another, they all appropriated views which clearly differed from his. Still, most of them shared their father's zest for life, his moral zeal, and his Protestant patriotism. There was an enormously human quality about the man, and despite all of his advertisements of eternity he thoroughly relished this life. At his last public appearance, when he was well past his allotted three score and ten, he said that if God gave him an option either to enter heaven immediately or to begin his life over again and work once more he *"would enlist again in a minute."*[48] Any true Beecher would have chosen to enlist. That much of the energizing force of consistent Calvinism came through loud and clear. Without that the second generation modifications of Lyman's views might simply have thinned out into sheer sentimentalism. But a combination of romantic union and moral zeal was suited to the Beechers and their age.

THE JAMES FAMILY

The "idealists lose individuality in the absolute mind...the naturalists lose it in 'streams of consciousness'..."[49]

The elder Henry James was a contemporary of the Beecher children. (He was born June 3, 1811, just eleven days before Harriet was born.) He also had in common with them a prodigious, Calvinistic father and a need to affirm himself over against the harsher psychological and theological aspects of his father's religion. And he too came to affirm romantic union and to express moral zeal. But there were also real differences between the families and the reactions of the children. Henry's father seems to have epitomized the self-made man of the Protestant ethic in a clearly more urban entrepreneurial environment than the Beecher parsonage in Litchfield. Henry broke with his father in a more decisive and dramatic manner than any Beecher youngster did with Lyman. He also went further into romantic union than any Beecher did--so far, in fact, that, in his own philosophical views, the self became lost, and in his own life, his identity seems to have remained in an almost perpetual state of diffusion. Finally, a lifelong income from his father's estate enabled Henry to rebel and to live in more comfortable circumstances.

The Father, William of Albany

Late in the year 1832 there was probated in Albany, New York a will of extraordinary interest and content. It was the will of a man who was reputed to have accumulated a fortune second in size in New York only to that of John Jacob Astor. The will was also carefully drawn so as to exert a minimum continuing control over the heirs. In order to counteract "the lamentable consequences which so frequently result to young persons brought up in affluence from coming at once into the possession of property," the will provided that the estate was not to be settled until the youngest grandchild reached the age of twenty-one! Furthermore, the carefully picked trustees were given "extensive and extraordinary power" to "discourage prodigality," "furnish an incentive to economy and usefulness," punish "idleness and vice," and reward "virtue...." Any heir who led "a grossly immoral, idle or dishonorable life" was to be deprived of his share of the wealth. The author of the will was aware that the exercise of this weighty discretionary responsibility might be "painful," yet, he concluded, "it is my full intention and earnest wish that it shall be carried into execution with rigid impartiality, sternness and inflexibility."50

The first American William James had migrated from Cavan County, Ireland around 1789. Since he does not appear to have sprung from a family of wealth, it is evident that he became a man of great business acumen and enterprise. The will attests to his thorough dedication to the Protestant ethic. Other than money-making, one commentator says, "it is perfectly clear that...religious discipline was (his) one consuming passion."51 He was a pillar in an Albany Presbyterian Church and appears to have enforced a rather rigid family regimen of prayers, Bible reading, and church attendance. Available evidence throws little light on his own religious experience, however. Indeed, according to one family legend, he is even supposed to have left his Ireland home to escape his father's pressure upon him to enter the ministry. In any case, he emerges in the early nineteenth century as a firm believer and loyal practitioner within an Americanized Calvinist tradition. Providence required an ordered life and smiled upon the elect, including the United States of America. The few items that survive him, in addition to the will, give further evidence on this score. As one of the prime movers in the building of the Erie Canal, and as a prominent Albany citizen, William was invited to speak at the opening of that Canal in 1823. He described the Canal as "a work which sheds additional lustre on the United States, bearing the stamp of the enterprising spirit and resolution" of this nation. And, he concluded on an even higher note, that

> nothing but the torpid stupidity of atheism can
> prevent the reflecting mind from perceiving the
> special intervention of providence in protecting
> and advancing our national honor and greatness.52

In his family, as in his business life, William was a man of large and dedicated energies. He outlived two wives, and by them and the one who survived him, be begat fourteen children. We see his family life chiefly through the eyes of Henry, his fourth child by his third wife. Henry's brief fictionalized account is both autobiographical and ideological in nature. Hence, the picture that emerges seems to be more programmatic than analytical. In any case, what we see is more an institution than an intimate family circle. The household was large, including various relatives and servants in addition to the numerous children. Certain predetermined regularities were followed. The head, who was much preoccupied with the habits of industry, did put in regular appearances at meals and prayers. Henry characterized the religion of the household as "a higher prudence" in which conventional virtue was extolled and God was pictured as a distant and perennial enforcer of a rigid moral code. It was evidently the kind of religion--or religious style of life--which could lead a man to draw a detailed and stringent will.

The conventional picture of the stern and distant Calvinist disciplinarian father is dramatically relieved at just one point when William suddenly appears as a deeply solicitous father. Henry was involved at the age of thirteen in a serious accident which so severely burned his right leg that he was confined to his bed for nearly two years, and two thigh amputations had to be performed--without benefit of anaesthesia. He recalled vividly, in his mind or his imagination, that his father's sympathy with his suffering "was so excessive that my mother had the greatest possible difficulty in imposing due prudence upon his expression of it."⁵³

One final bit of surviving evidence concerning William's relations with his son Henry is an irrate letter in which William bitterly complains to a lawyer friend that young Henry, then eighteen years of age and away from home (presumably at college), had wantonly drawn or overdrawn upon his father's credit for books, "Taylors," "segars and oysters," incurring a debt on the last two items of some "50 to 60 drs." The profligate youth had "so debased himself as to leave his parents house in the character of a swindler." As supporting evidence, the father offered drafts which disclosed the son's "progress in arts of low vileness--and unblushing falsehood...." The creditors were in hot pursuit and the sadly indignant father proclaimed that such behavior would surely land the culprit "in a prison of some kind directly...."⁵⁴ Three years later the old man died, cutting of the son, if that is proper language, with a mere annuity of $2,500 per year and strongly hinting that to get more, the boy's course must be stringently righted and steadied.

The will was far too complex and unmanageable to survive contesting in a court of law. Thus Henry, who was twenty-one when his father died, found himself the happy recipient of his full share of the father's millions. This share was sufficient to support him handsomely for the rest of his life. There was no need to cultivate the acquisitive self. Henry had a golden opportunity, all but unparalleled in the America of his day, to pursue concerns of the spirit. This he did with relish, with keen determination, and not entirely without fear and trembling.

The Transcendental Self: The Elder Henry James

"We are all without real selfhood, without the selfhood which comes from God alone. We have only a showy and fallacious one...."

"My being lies utterly outside *myself*...lies, in fact, *in honestly identifying myself with others*" by becoming ever more like the Divine "who is without selfhood..."55

In 1844, after having engaged in spiritual pursuits for some dozen years, Henry found himself launched dramatically and wholly unexpectedly on a seemingly endless slough of despond:

> One day...towards the close of May, having eaten a comfortable dinner, I remained sitting at the table after the family had dispersed, idly gazing at the embers in the grate, thinking of nothing, and feeling only the exhilaration incident to a good digestion, when suddenly--in a lightning-flash as it were--'fear come upon me, and trembling, which made all my bones to shake.' To all appearance it was a perfectly insane and abject terror, without ostensible cause, and only to be accounted for, to my perplexed imagination, by some damned shape squatting invisible to me within the precincts of the room, and raying out from his fetid personality influences fatal to life. The thing had not lasted ten seconds before I felt myself a wreck; that is, reduced from a state of firm, vigorous, joyful manhood to one of almost helpless infancy. The only self-control I was capable of exerting was to keep my seat. I felt the greatest desire to run incontinently to the foot of the stairs and shout for help to my wife,--to run to the roadside even, and appeal to the public to protect me; but by an immense effort I controlled these frenzied impulses, and determined not to budge from my chair till I had recovered my lost self-possession. This purpose I held to for a good long hour, as I reckoned time, beat upon meanwhile by an ever-growing tempest of doubt, anxiety, and despair, with absolutely no relief from any truth I had ever encountered save a most pale and distant glimmer of the divine existence, when I resolved to abandon the vain struggle, and communicate without more ado what seemed my sudden burden of inmost, implacable unrest to my wife.
>
> Now, to make a long story short, this ghastly condition of mind continued with me, with gradually lengthening intervals of relief, for two years, and even longer.56

Physicians were of no help to Henry, but while at "a famous water cure" he experienced some balm in the English countryside and in the ensuing sense of the innocence of the animal world. "How sweet it would be to find oneself no longer man," he thought, "but one of those innocent and ignorant sheep pasturing upon that placid hillside...."[57] Henry felt now his "first immortal longing 'to bathe myself in innocency.'"[58] Perhaps a return to infancy was not all bad. At any rate, Henry began a process of recapitulation or rebirth in which restored innocence was the initial step. This is not surprising in Henry's case. His fictionalized autobiography throbs with a sense of violated innocence, of the cruel injustice perpetrated upon his young spirit. The "offence" of his early religious training, he charges, was "that it prematurely *forced* my manhood...."[59] A stereotyped identity was developed in a hot house atmosphere. Now it must be destroyed before a true identity could emerge. The first step in restructuring was the return to innocence.

Erik Erikson, in his discussion of the life cycle and the epigenesis of identity, stresses the centrality of trust which issues in the capacity for faith.[60] The problem of how one could trust God loomed large in the Calvinist psyche. That problem broke out in epidemic proportions in the early nineteenth century. Henry James found himself in a vice-like grip between the demands of his father's inner-worldly asceticism and his own desire for spontaneous expression. Two painful and entirely misleading things were forced upon his "credulous mind" at an early age, Henry charged. One was the sense of an early arrived at individuality, a "prematurely vitalized" selfhood seen as capable of "commerce with the most High." The other was "the fiction of a natural estrangement" between that self and God. Hence, he must wrestle like Job but without even the limited advantage of Job's seasoned sinews. The results were awesome and heartrending.

> I doubt whether any lad had ever just so thorough and pervading a belief in God's existence as an outside and contrarious force to humanity, as I had.... And I am sure no childish sinews were ever more strained than mine were in wrestling with the subtle terror of his name.

The only thing that prevented his manhood from being "wilted in the cradle," that kept him from becoming "a thoughtful, anxious, and weary little slave" before he had entered his teens, was "Nature's indomitable uprightness.... Nature itself came to my aid when all outward resources proved treacherous...."[61]

The forced individuality and adulthood of Henry's childhood was followed by a long moratorium. For a time he sought to follow his father's desires by studying law. Then, still within the father's ideological orbit, he attended Princeton Theological Seminary for about a year and a half. That involved, however, more of orthodoxy than he could take. At twenty-nine he married and settled into a life of independent study, reflection, and writing. Three years later he sought Emerson's advice about the proper pattern for his life:

> Here I am...ignorant in all outward science, but having patient habits of meditation which never know disgust or weariness, and feeling a force of impulsive love toward all humanity which will not let me rest wholly mute, a force which grows against all resistance.... What shall I do? Shall I get me a little nook in the country and communicate with my *living* kind--not my talking kind--by life only...? Or shall I follow some commoner method-- learn science and bring myself into man's respect, that I may thus better speak to him?[62]

But then, just what was that truth he was to communicate?

The experience which "bathed him in innocency" also cleansed him of the encumbrances of misunderstood selfhood. He denied all of his previous work. That work was but a show, a sham in the pursuit of truth, a groping about in an effort to discover true selfhood. But truth was not to be achieved that way. It "must reveal itself..." Innocence opened one to that revelation.

While still suffering under the effects of his *angst* experience, Henry was introduced to the thought of Immanuel Swedenborg. That Swedish mystic helped Henry discover a satisfying intellectual framework for explaining his experience and finding a way out of it. A follower of Swedenborg gave James's experience a label: It was "a *vastation*." As a consequence of viewing reality incorrectly, James was in a precarious position. If he persisted in his incorrect views he would inevitably sink further into "hell" ("consumation" in Swedenborg's *Dictionary of Correspondence*). But his condition was not without hope. If his views were amended, he could realize new selfhood, new spiritual fulfillment, he could enter "heaven."[63]

James learned, with the aid of Swedenborg, that the individual self of Calvinism is a falsehood. True selfhood is realized only in identification with humanity, with universal selfhood. What he called "the divine natural humanity" is that state of "most triumphant harmony" intended and effected by the Creator.

Swedenborg's fundamental exegetical principle also confirmed a conviction James indicates he had reached just prior to his *Angst* experience: The "book of Genesis was not intended to throw direct light upon our natural or race history, but was an altogether mystical or symbolic record of the laws of God's *spiritual* creation and providence."[64] Such a method proved of inestimable value in interpreting not only the Bible but all of existence. Here was the way out of Plato's cave.

The Swedenborgian intellectual framework and the symbolically restored innocence prepared the way for a high kind of spiritual or mystical experience which was to go far toward sustaining the elder Henry James for a lifetime. One sees evidences of this kind of experience only occasionally in James's writings and through the eyes of his associates and his two famous sons. In an undated letter to a frequent correspondent he described one such experience as follows:

> The other day I had a *living* experience of the truth.... The conditions were simple.... I was obliged to go out some two miles into the New York harbour, to see a prisoner confined there on one of the islands. The steamboat which goes early in the morning had left to my regret, and I was obliged to take a small row-boat, rowed by an old man. The day was stormy, the wind blew a piercing blast, the waves ran high, and I said to myself as my nerves began to quiver, it looks as if we should never get safe across. The thought of wife and child and friend no more to be seen on earth, gave me a shudder of disgust, and very soon my bosom was a scene of most uncomfortable disorder and perturbation. I made a desperate inward effort to save myself from childishness by seizing vigorously upon the truth, when a soft voice--angelically sweet and potent though inaudible--reduced

> my rising chaos to instant order and peace, by telling
> me that all this appearance of things, this conflict of
> good and evil, of safety and danger, and so forth, was
> a *mere* appearance Divinely permitted in the interest of
> our eventual spiritual freedom, while the sole reality
> or truth was God, in whom all was infinite serenity,
> success and safety for all his creatures, without the
> slightest justification consequently, even for a moment,
> of any of our perturbations or anxieties. O how deli-
> cious a calm thereupon came over the uplifted waves of
> my breast! My poor old oarsman, who seemed a moment
> before an inauspicious Charon ferrying me over to death
> and its shades, grew into a laughing vigorous youth
> sporting forever on summer seas, and we chatted lovingly
> and freely as if our boat were bearing us away from tur-
> moil and insanity to enchanted isles of innocence and
> bliss. I could only adore the Divine greatness in si-
> lence, and lament that I could hope to keep up the savour
> of His presence only so feebly after I should come back
> to Broadway and falsity.[65]

How could one sustain that level of experience? Swedenborg had been granted entry into the new Jerusalem. He had spent the last half of his life describing its wonders. James seems to have remained poised at the gates, troubled by the recurrent rise of the old self and by the exceedingly great difficulty of communicating his newly discovered truths to others. "Henry James said to me," noted Emerson, that "he wished sometimes the lightning would strike his wife and children out of existence, and he should suffer no more for loving them." James regarded all such selfish anxiety as a sin against which he must constantly struggle. "My besetting sin is anxiety," he wrote in 1869, "and no sooner does any occasion for it arise...than the whole 'clanging rookery' of hell comes darkening the air, and settling down in my devoted bosom as if it were their undisputed nest...."[66] He must "universalize" his "sympathies." The end must be "the reconciliation of the individual and the universal interest in humanity...."[67]

Henry's communication problem was succinctly put by William Dean Howells, who is reported to have said about James's book, *The Secret of Swedenborg*: "He kept it."[68] His oldest son, William, observed somewhat sadly that "probably few authors have so devoted their entire lives to the monotonous elaboration of one single bundle of truths...." The "true relation...between mankind and its

Creator..." was "the burden of his whole life, and its only burden ...."[69] Within the James family the father's preoccupation had become something of "a gentle joke." With the publication of *Substance and Shadow* in 1863, another "attempt to say exactly what he meant," William drew a picture to be put on the title page of the new book. It showed a man beating a dead horse.[70]

William hints that the elder Henry's intellectual problem stemmed from the fact that he had "no properly psychological doctrine" of the self.[71] Generally, Henry used the words "proprium" and "selfhood" to designate selfishness or selflove. Sometimes, however, his usage appears so broad as to encompass self-consciousness. This confusion means that one is not always certain whether selfishness alone or self-consciousness as such is considered the barrier to fulfillment.

In either case, the elder Henry regarded the human predicament as being problematic. Conventional morality and religion tended to confirm self-centeredness. Furthermore, "the natural inheritance" of that self-consciousness which distinguishes man from animal and makes him capable of "spiritual life" is nothing more, on its own, than "an unsubdued forest where the wolf howls and every obscene bird of night chatters."[72] Escape from such a predicament was much to be desired. It necessitated a dramatic change. Henry fully expected that change.

Annie Fields is reported to have said that the elder Henry James was "anointed with the Isle of Patmos."[73] The New Jerusalem, our "glorified natural humanity," afforded dramatic escape from the egocentric predicament. Expounding a social theory which combined elements of Swedenborg and Fourier, James envisioned a society which

> would guarantee to every man, woman and child, for the whole term of his natural life, food, clothing, shelter, and the opportunities of an education adapted to his tastes; leaving all the *distinction* he might achieve to himself, to his own genius freely influencing the homage of his fellow men.[74]

When man's "spontaneities" are so released, said William in describing his father's position, they will "work harmoniously, will all work innocently, and the Kingdom of Heaven will have come."[75]

Henry Jr. wrote of his father's "remarkable and constant belief... in the imminence of a transformation scene in human affairs...." His "constitutional optimism" was fed very little "by any sense of things as they were or are, but rich in its vision of the facility with which they might become almost at any moment or from one day to the other totally and splendidly different."[76]

It has been suggested by Ralph Barton Perry, that Henry James Sr. turned his father's Calvinism on its head. "For Calvinism, men fall collectively, and are saved individually."[77] From early in life the individual is doomed to that Job-like wrestling that, according to Henry's own accounts, characterized his childhood and youth. From this struggle there emerged, in the Calvinist paradigm, either a clear identity under God or eternal lostness. Henry concluded, however, that such sharpness of focus on the individual is sin and that salvation comes instead through identity with the race.

From this universal selfhood, Henry moved easily into utopianism. And his utopianism sometimes appeared in the form of a highly universalized Americanism. On July 4, 1861, for example, in response to the invitation of his fellow citizens in Newport, Rhode Island, Henry spoke on the universal significance of the Civil War. Since America was above all nations the birthplace of the "New Man" or the Universal Self, the War was seen by Henry as the necessary passage of that new manhood from youth to maturity. This relatively new nation was "no mere civil polity, designed...to lead men out of barbarism into civilization. On the contrary, we find citizens and out of citizens aspire to make them men." This Americans do by affirming "the Divine Incarnation in every form of human nature, the unlimited indwelling of the infinite Godhead in every man... avouching ourselves finally to our own consciousness and the world's willing recognition as a faultless human society...." We proclaim "the gradual but complete subjugation of the selfish instinct...to the service of the social instinct." The one remaining obstacle standing in the way of this grand achievement was slavery. Hence, the time of war against this curse was either "the hour of our endless rise into all beautiful human proportions, into all celestial vigor and beautitude, or of our endless decline into all fernality and uncleaness...." Therefore, "we must not hesitate a moment to fight it manfully out to its smiling blissful end, feeling that it is not our own battle alone..." but that of "universal nature itself."[78]

Here is a vision in which the self, the individual flesh and blood man, seems to disappear or be caught up into a mass of divinized humanity. "In his eagerness to transcend the merely private and to open his embrace to what could be shared with all," wrote F. O. Mathiessen, "James sometimes lost touch with the image of any concrete man."[79]

Henry Jr. said his father's style affected him "as somehow too philosophic for life, and at the same time too living...for thought...."[80] Something similar might be said of the man. He is variously described as selfless and detached and yet passionately human. In his lifelong struggle to embody his ideas in his own life he scrupulously--even religiously--avoided jobs, associations, schools, rituals and forms--in short, anything which might have given formal and symbolic expression to his identity. From this angle, he comes through as an almost disembodied spirit. Yet he seems to have been an intensely warm human being, almost universally loved by his family and associates, widely known for his wit and his charm, and exceedingly interesting as a person--one might even say, as a character. George Bernard Shaw declared to Henry Junior that "the most interesting member of his family was neither himself nor his brother (William) but their father...." This characteristic Shavian remark was apparently received as praise most welcome. "Put beside either son," Mathiessen concluded, "the father displays, in his maturity, a unique spaciousness and serenity."[81]

Henry was more given to contemplation than to action. "I love the fireside rather than the forum," he observed. "I can give ecstatic hours to worship or meditation but moments spent in original deed, such as putting a button upon my coat or cleansing my garden-walk of weeds, weigh heavily upon my shoulders."[82] William described his father, somewhat expansively perhaps, as "a religious prophet and genius," a saint and a mystic. He was, to William's mind, a primary *homo religiosus*, one of those "whose rare privilege it has been by the mere example of their own bosom-experience, to prevent religion from becoming a fossil conventionalism, and to keep it forever alive." But his experience was "very peculiar indeed," said the son. It was more akin to absorption mysticism than to that kind of experience which heightens self-awareness. "He fairly revelled in the emotion of humanity, and lost himself in the sentiment of unity with his kind, like a river in the sea." When depressed, he murmured the Psalms of David to himself by the hour, "apparently without a feeling of personal application." A close friend of Henry's wrote that he sometimes felt "away down at the bottom of the man so sheer a humility and self-abasement as to give me an idea of infinity."[83]

As a person, Henry had greatest impact on his family. In child-rearing he sought to do the very opposite from what had been done to him. Rather than forcing an early maturity he endeavored to prolong the innocency of childhood.[84] He was firmly convinced that "as you inconsiderately shorten this period of infantile innocence and ignorance [of sin] in the child, you weaken his chances of a future manly character."[85] In the education of his children, Henry sought to give maximum attention to fostering their predilections while paying little or not attention to preparing them for particular vocations. He would have none of that forced circumstance of going to college and preparing oneself for a profession which he had found so unbearable in his own life. To a large degree, he succeeded in these goals.

The effects of Henry's pedagogical ideas and practices are most fully and sensitively documented in his second son's recollections. An old daguerreotype of Henry Jr. at ten standing next to his father recalls for the son "in so welcome and so definite a manner my father's cultivation of my company." He remembers those early years as a time of a "general Eden-like consciousness."[86] His father, Henry writes of his own youthful experience,

> had a wonderful way of being essentially right without
> being particularly or, as it were, vulgarly, determinant
> .... What we were to do was just to *be* something, some-
> thing unconnected with specific doing, something free and
> uncommitted, something finer in short than being *that*,
> whatever it was, might consist of.[87]

The son marvels "at the manner in which the door appears to have been held, or at least left open to us for experiment, though with a tendency to close...before any very earnest proposition in particular." And he concludes that "we actually profited more than we lost...by the degree to which we were afloat and disconnected...."[88] Henry was especially appreciative of the total absence of pressure to enter business.

But the second son's recollections are not without some hint of a felt inadequacy with this method of indirection. His seems to be essentially a novelist's complaint about the lack of definiteness of feature, the paucity of detail and form in his father's house. (It is not clear to me to what extent the novelist's complaint is also the man's.) There were the small but important embarassments of childhood stemming from the father's apparent lack of profession and the absence of a clear objective character in the family's religion.[89] It is true that there was much religious instruction "of the most charming and familiar" variety. Above all there was the impact of the father who possessed "the religious spirit" to a greater extent than anyone else in the son's experience. Yet the son wondered that the father could do so without apparent resort to "a single one of the outward or formal, the theological, devotional, ritual, or even implicitly pietistic signs by which we usually know" the religious spirit. Young Henry could loose himself in the beauty of his father's faith and life. Still he

> was troubled all along just by [the] particular crooked-
> ness of our being so extremely religious without having,
> as it were, anything in the least classified or striking
> to show for it.... I would have been thankful for a
> state of faith, a conviction of the Divine, an interpre-
> tation of the universe--anything one might have made bold
> to call it--which would have supplied more features or
> appearances....[90]

That which the son thought of as "humanly most interesting, attaching, inviting..." seemed to be of no importance to the father. "Didn't I discern in this from the first a kind of implied snub to the significance of mine?" The answer is equivocal. The father towers; he lives and breathes. Yet the son wishes that he might have known the father at the time of the father's "vastation." Here would have been "the *real* right thing...the hurrying drama of the original rush...." But it "was all a play I hadn't 'been to,' consciously at least--that was the trouble; the curtain had fallen while I was still tucked in my crib, and I assisted but on a comparatively flat home scene at the echo of a great success...."[91]

Henry Jr. closes this section on the religious atmosphere of his home with a reference to the father's habit of reading to the mother from his own works. Here the mother emerges as the son's more direct access to identity, to the definiteness he so much needed:

> How can I better express what she seemed to do for her second son in especial than by saying that even with her deepest delicacy of attention present I could still feel, while my father read, why it was that I most of all seemed to wish we might have been either much less religious or much more so?

The father's style lacked specificity. He "had terms, evidently strong, but in which I presumed to feel, with a shade of irritation, a certain narrowness of exclusion as to images.... Variety, variety--*that* sweet ideal, *that* straight contradiction of my dialectic, hummed for me...."[92] So also did individuality, the personal, the concrete.

The Willed Self: The Son, William of Cambridge

"My first act of free will shall be to believe in free will.... I will posit life...in the self-governing *resistance* of the ego to the world. Life shall [be] doing and suffering and creating."[93] "The knower is an actor...."[94]

What the younger Henry James described as "that incorrigible vagueness of current in our educational drift"[95] had carried his older brother William, by the age of twenty-eight, to such varied ports as a year of painting with William Hunt in Newport, a year of chemistry under Eliot at Harvard, the Harvard Medical School, and an intense period of biological field experience under Agissiz in Brazil. These periods of concentrated study were interspersed with times of physical and emotional ill-health which in cumulative effect came close to doing him in. Like his father, he went through a long moratorium. He also was subjected, unexpectedly, to the most shattering kind of *angst* experience.

"The worst kind of melancholy," he wrote later in describing that experience, "is that which takes the form of panic fear." Then there follows this illustration from his own experience:

> Whilst in this state of philosophic pessimism and general depression of spirits about my prospects, I went one evening into a dressing-room in the twilight to procure some article that was there; when suddenly there fell upon me without any warning, just as it came out of the darkness, a horrible fear of my own existence. Simultaneously there arose in my mind the image of an epileptic patient whom I had seen in the asylum, a black-haired youth with greenish skin, entirely idiotic, who used to sit all day on one of the benches, or rather shelves against the wall, with his knees drawn up against his chin, and the coarse gray undershirt, which was his only garment, drawn over them inclosing his entire figure. He sat there like a sort of sculptured Egyptian cat or Peruvian mummy, moving nothing but his black eyes and looking absolutely non-human. This image and my fear entered into a species of combination with each other. *That shape am I*, I felt, potentially. Nothing that I possess can defend me against that fate, if the hour for it should strike for me as it struck for him. There was such a horror of him, and such a perception of my own merely momentary discrepancy from him, that it was as if something hitherto solid within my breast gave way entirely, and I became a mass of quivering fear. After this the universe was changed for me altogether. I awoke morning after morning with a horrible dread at the pit of my stomach, and with a sense of the insecurity of life that I never knew before, and that I have never felt since. It was like a revelation; and although the immediate feelings passed away, the experience has made me sympathetic with the morbid feeling of others ever since. It gradually faded, but for months I was unable to go out into the dark alone.
>
> In general I dreaded to be left alone. I remember wondering how other people could live, how I myself had ever lived, so unconscious of that pit of insecurity beneath the surface of life. My mother in particular, a very cheerful person, seemed to me a perfect paradox in her unconsciousness of danger, which you may well believe I was very careful not to disturb by revelations of my own

> state of mind. I have always thought that this experience
> of melancholia of mine had a religious bearing.
> ...[T]he fear was so invasive and powerful that if
> I had not clung to scripture-texts like 'The eternal God
> is my refuge,' etc., 'Come unto me, all ye that labor and
> are heavy-laden,' etc., 'I am the resurrection and the
> life,' etc., I think I should have grown really insane.[96]

This clinical description is followed in *The Varieties of Religious Experience* by a discussion of the manner in which such a "sick soul" is healed, such a "divided self" unified. Through "conversion"

> a self hitherto divided, and consciously wrong inferior
> and unhappy, becomes unified and consciously right su-
> perior and happy, in consequence of its firmer hold upon
> religious realities.[97]

Such a route may have been open to the Albany grandfather, but it was not easily accessible to the grandson. Intellectually, he was a product of that revolution in thought which had thoroughly undermined the religious securities of an earlier age. "Religious realities," to make him whole, had to be verified in *experience*, without the supports of Biblical authority, communal testimony, or theological doctrine. And while he recognized the vitality of religious experience, he was, himself, rarely vivified by it.

William was sustained in his *angst* experience by a kind of religious memory, symbolized in comforting scriptural words. Perhaps what really sustained him was the memory of his father's experience: William's account is followed by a footnoted reference to "another case of fear equally sudden"--that of Henry Sr. Henry had also clung to a memory--"a most pale and distant glimmer of the divine existence...." But he had found his way out of melancholia, his healing, through an experience of the absorption of his individual self in the universal self. William could not take that route. While the memory of his father might provide a final bond against the threatened disintegration of self, it could not bring integrity. The father, who had protracted the son's childhood and protected his innocence, could not now provide access to maturity. He who had known "religious realities" in his own way but had eschewed all symbols of these realities could not provide depth of religious experience for his son.

The critical movement in William's purchase on identity was an act of the will, or rather an affirmation of belief in the will: a willing of the will. "I think that yesterday was a crisis in my life," he noted in a diary entry dated April 30, 1870.

> I finished the first part of Renouvier's second 'Essais' and see no reason why his definition of Free Will--'the sustaining of a thought *because I choose to* when I might have other thoughts'--need be the definition of an illusion. At any rate, I will assume for the present--until next year--that it is no illusion.[98]

This assumption extended well beyond the next year. In fact, it was to sustain James through a lifetime of threatened identity. Action followed upon willing and in action was knowledge, exhilaration, meaning. Believing also followed upon willing, especially when action required it.

It was just eight years after this decisive act of the will that William, only recently married and by now an established professor at Harvard, wrote, in a latter to his bride, about that vivifying and unifying attitude of which, "when it come upon" a man, he could say: "*This* is the real me!" Then he added:

> This characteristic attitude in me always involves an element of active tension, of holding my own, as it were, and trusting outward things to perform their part so as to make it a full harmony, but without any *guaranty* that they will.

Such a guarantee would have a stagnating effect. Excitement, zest, "a sort of deep enthusiastic bliss"--these flow from the risk involved without a guarantee.[99] And yet, so also may anxiety, and despair.

James's act of willing was apparently decisive, then. It was a necessary act for survival, and it enabled him to achieve a firm and necessary hold on identity. The willed self--the here and now, concrete, empirical individual--had to be affirmed over against the amorphous, universal, transcendental self; the purposeful course over against the vague drifting; the son over against the father. From this point on James appeared to have realized a high degree of unification of self. He clearly entered upon a period of extraordinary productivity.[100]

James's act of willing also became paradigmatic. His "will to believe" was a very welcome word to an age in which traditional beliefs were under both direct and oblique attack. The method of the will, and especially the will to believe, assumed preeminence in a significant shift in religious sensibility and thought.[101]

But James's method was also ambiguous in personal, religious and communal effect. The will could not effect "conversion" in any traditional sense; it could not assure "unification of the divided self" by that route, nor could it incarnate or vivify the "religious realities" of the father's world. The act of will secured a precarious beachead on a dark and foreboding island. But counterattack threatened. Reinforcements of will, of act, and of belief--or the will to believe--were required to enlarge the hold and even amidst impressive signs of triumph James continued to live under the threat that, without warning, the beachead might be wiped out.

The offshore batteries of the father's world did provide some help (William enjoyed relative economic, moral, and civic security). But the father's "presence" was ambivalent in its influence. William was too much of an empiricist to find much comfort in his father's peculiar brand of spiritual metaphysic. Nevertheless, he greatly admired and respected his father's experience. But he could not share that experience. Out of need, and perhaps out of envy, he might will the "religious realities" of his father's world, but he could not experience them.

William described his father's experience as a vivid instance of that kind of religious experience which consists in "an acute despair, passing over into an equally acute optimism, through a passion of renunciation of the self and surrender to the higher power."[102] Both clinician and son show through this statement. The father's example aroused and kept alive the son's interest in religious experience. It also engendered a kind of filial nostalgia. William defended religion on his father's account. He also wanted to maintain, in his own life, the spirit of his father's religion without its form, and to pass on something of that spirit to his own children.[103] Yet William's own religious experience was but a shadow, a pale reflection of his father's. What Henry had experienced as vivid reality, William admired or curiously gazed at from a distance. It was an act of faith with William that "the evidence for God lies primarily in inner personal experience"-- such as his father had had. But William testified again and again that he did not have that experience. He recognized "the deeper voice" when he heard about it, but he did not hear that voice directly.[104]

When asked why he believed in God if he had not experienced God's presence, James responded characteristically that he did so because he *needed* that presence and hence it "must" be true.[105] He described the most popular of his lectures, "The Will to Believe," as "something like a sermon on justification by faith."[106] Against a reductionist positivism that lecture affirmed "the right to believe." It was also spoken from the heart of one who must believe in order to live, whose will to believe seemed at times so strong as to spin out of itself the very substance of belief.[107] Yet that will to believe seemed to some observers to be little more that a wish or a longing.[108] From the far side of Jordan James caught a glimpse of the promised land, but he could not cross the river. Indeed, perhaps neither river nor promised land existed.

This is not to suggest that James's "will to believe" and his religious views generally were without what might be called a positive effect. Indeed, his influence was wide and lasting. His *Varieties of Religious Experience* received almost universal acclaim. All save the most conservative religious thinkers and the most obvious skeptics found in it a comfortable and welcome support. It was democratic and non-dogmatic in its documentation of the validity of religiousness. At the same time, however, taken altogether, James's views show a radical shift in religious focus-- from God to man, from transcendental self to empirical self, from an outer world seemingly dominated by theological realities to an inner world of expanding consciousness. This shift was aided by a process which at first blush looks like legerdemain. Beginning with a preference for "*physical* facts and possibilities" in religion over those of "a philosophic character,"[109] James proceeded to deny that he had had any *personal* experience of such "physical facts" of a religious nature, but then he went on freely to encourage the will to believe in such facts and possibilities. It is at this point of prescription, rather than at the point of preference or description, that James seems to some observers to be rather thin. Yet his position can be seen, on the one hand, as a necessary one for personal reasons,[110] and, on the other hand, as a logical extension of his own clinical and catholic interests in human experience.

By exchanging his father's telescope for his own microscope, by shifting from metaphysics to clinical and laboratory observation and analysis, James contributed significantly to an emerging new understanding of human experience which was not critically dependent on supernatural entities or a belief system which seemed no longer viable. At the same time, however, if this understanding was to be straightforward it still must deal with the reality of the divided self and its needed unification. Here again James was both catholic and clinical. Unity could be achieved by various ways, some religious and some not.[111] And perhaps James's most significant contribution to that necessary human process came out of his characteristically clinical interest in and report on his own personal experience.

Returning to "the real me" of William James, we discover a process, a continuing "active tension" involving elements of memory, active will, deliberate risk, conscious experimentation, and openess to a wide range of experience. Throughout his life there continued a potential for both vivid consciousness and threatened diffusion or even destruction. In the last years of his life he knew both.

Twenty years after his initial testimony of dynamic selfhood James experienced perhaps the most heightened sense of being "most deeply and intensely alive."[112] This occurred in the Adirondacks in July of 1898 while he was preparing his Edinburgh lectures on "the varieties of religious experience." One clear night, he wrote to his wife, conditions were just right to get

> into a state of spiritual alertness of the most vital description. The influences of Nature, the wholesomeness of the people around me...the thought of you and the children, dear Harry on the wave, the problem of

> the Edinburgh lectures, all fermented within me till
> it became a regular Walpurgis Nacht. I spent a good
> deal of it in the woods, where the streaming moonlight
> lit up things in a magical checkered play, and it seemed
> as if the Gods of all the nature-mythologies were hold-
> ing an indescribable meeting in my breast with the moral
> Gods of the inner life. The two kinds of Gods have noth-
> ing in common.... The intense significance of some sort,
> of the whole scene, if one could only *tell* the signifi-
> cance; the intense inhuman remoteness of its inner life,
> and yet the intense *appeal* of it; its everlasting fresh-
> ness and its immemorial antiquity and decay; its utter
> Americanism, and every sort of patriotic suggestiveness,
> and you, and my relation to you part and parcel of it
> all, and beaten up with it, so that memory and sensation
> all whirled inexplicably together; it was indeed worth
> coming for, and worth repeating year by year, if repeti-
> tion could only procure what in its nature I suppose
> must be all unplanned and unexpected. It was one of the
> happiest lonesome nights of my existence....[113]

There followed upon this experience a decade of great intellectual productivity, seasoned, as it were, by occasional experiences of sudden "*opening*" to "*distant realities*...."[114] It was also a decade of declining health. The Adirondack experience so stimulated James that he over-extended himself in mountain climbing and suffered damage to his heart. Toward the end of this decade, James was subjected to another kind of experience, similar in being "unplanned and unexpected" but very different in content and effect. This was an experience in 1906 of acute identity confusion--"the most intensely peculiar experience of my whole life."[115] It came in the form of three dreams which were telescoped in such a manner that James was unsure when or by whom they were dreamed. "Decidedly I was losing hold of my 'self'" he reports.

> Most human troubles look towards a terminus. Most fears
> point in a direction, and concentrate toward a climax.
> Most assaults of the evil one may be met by bracing one-
> self against something, one's principles, one's courage,
> one's will, one's pride. But in this experience all was
> diffusion from a centre, and foothold swept away, the
> brace itself disintegrating all the faster as one needed
> its support more direly. Meanwhile vivid perception (or
> remembrance) of the various dreams kept coming over me
> in alternation. Whose? *whose*? WHOSE? Unless I can *at-
> tach* them, I am swept out to sea with no horizon and no
> bond, getting *lost*.

James's account of his emotional involvement in, and reaction to, this series of dream experiences reminds one of Rudolph Otto's description of encounter with the *mysterium tremendum*. The effect is one of both terror and fascination. But the fascination, in James's case, is more in the clinical observer than in the threatened self. The existential person wants out. The experience is clearly not a case of "mystical illumination," says James; it threatens darkness, not light. Yet the clinical observer sees the experience as promising. There was a keen "sense that *reality was being uncovered*" and this sense was "mystical in the highest degree." The experience documented the dynamic and expandable nature of consciousness which James the psychologist had already described in much of his writing. Here was a range of experience which the scientific world had hardly touched but which nevertheless was very promising in terms of "noetic value." Its religious significance was also incalculabe for it might provide access to "the mothersea and fountain-head of all religions"--"the mystical experience of individuals...."[116] Yet the threatened self literally trembled before the experience.

"The genius of being is whimsical rather than consistent," said James. Life, nature, being, self--"it is process all."[117] Hence any description falsifies because it stops the process. The same is true of the effort to see and describe "the real me" who was William James. There is a fluidity and complexity of identity and roles which heightens one's fascination with the subject but also makes efforts at description difficult. There is James the son who must will himself in distinction from his father's selfhood. If the will becomes too directive, however, it stagnates the self. It can also cut one off from the unplanned albeit sometimes threatening irruptions of the "extended subliminal self."[118] There is James the clinician, whose very attitude of scientific scrutiny perhaps tended to foreclose the possibility of full-scale mystical unification. There is James the empirical psychologist who, as John Dewey later pointed out, tended to reduce the subject "to a vanishing point."[119] Hence, the willed self fluctuates--and disintegrates. And, through it all, there is James the mortal self, sensetive to the nihilistic other before which all men, and this man in particular, must fall.[120]

On this last score, as in most human essentials, James was no different from other human beings, including ourselves. What he did was to develop a new or at least different approach to the human problem of "individuation and faith." It is an approach which was keenly cognizant of life as process, and yet of needed points of concentration in that process. If he leaned heavily on the will to believe, perhaps he had no option. (Do we?) His condition differed most sharply from ours, perhaps, in cultural context. Because of a goodly inheritance and because he lived in a time of relative moral and civic certainty, he quite naturally was or at least gave the appearance of being an American individualist and optimist.[121] We, living in a time of more apparent moral and civic dissary, experience a greater need for an identity which is at home both in the intimacy of face-to-face community and on the whole space ship earth.

Concluding Statement:

For centuries Western man sought identity in dialogue with God. The American Puritans continued and even intensified this search as they endeavored to experience God's saving grace. Under the impact of the scientific revolution, however, the terms of the dialogue changed dramatically. The Beecher family experience illustrates the softening of the earlier images of deity and the supernaturally transformed self. The elder Henry James appeared to dissolve individuality in a great sea. Like Emerson, he anticipated a coming Asian drift in American consciousness, a trend toward the immersion of self hood in all mankind, in the universe, in *The All*. The dialogue becomes a chorus or silence. Conversion becomes immersion. William turned from his father's idealism to the specificity of the willed self. But that self is shifting and transitory, a fluctuating consciousness in a pluralistic world. The dialogue gives way to reverie or dream as the deity--the "objective other"--is replaced by a wider consciousness whose mysterious limits are yet to be probed. Could this willed self hold together against life's onslaughts? Could the positive thought put down fears and anxieties as great, if not as identifiable, as those of hell? And could the self survive in a genuinely pluralistic universe?

Beechers and Jameses alike benefitted from an American identity of apparently continuing viability. Like the early Puritans, they seemed still to live in an anchored society. This was of crucial importance to the dynamics of their own personal identity. A later generation must deal, however, with both the discontinuation of the dialogue and the dissolution of societal support. It must grope for a kind of world identity; and it must find vivifying experiences and compelling paradigms analogous to those of conversion and its traditional context.

FOOTNOTES

1. Erik Erikson, *Identity, Youth and Crisis* (New York, 1968), p. 40.
2. *Ibid.*, p. 19, and *The Letters of William James*, edited by Henry James (his son) (Boston, 1920), Vol. I, p. 199.
3. *Identity, Youth and Crisis*, p. 22.
4. William James, *The Varieties of Religious Experience* (New York, 1928), pp. 175-176 and the whole lecture on "The Divided Self, and The Process of Unification." On conversion see also Edwin Diller Starbuck, *The Psychology of Religion; An Empirical Study of the Growth of Religious Consciousness* (London, 1901), with a preface by William James; and Arthur Darby Nock, *Conversion* (London, 1933), which treats the subject in the centuries immediately before and following the beginnings of Christianity.
5. Starbuck, *op. cit.*, p. 92.
6. *Ibid.*, p. 119. This, of course, is pre-Freudian language.
7. *The Varieties of Religious Experience*, p. 175. Cf. Starbuck's discussion of "conversion as a normal human experience" in his *The Psychology of Religion*.
8. *The Psychology of Religion*, p. ix. This preface was written in 1899, before the publication of *The Varieties of Religious Experience*. Cf. Erik Erikson's brief remarks on conversion in *Young Man Luther* (New York, 1962), pp. 41 and 96.
9. Horace Bushnell, *Christian Nurture* (New York, 1890), p. 10. Bushnell first developed this view in print in 1847 under the title *"Views of Christian Nurture."*
10. On this sort of transition see William A. Clebsch, *American Religious Thought: A History* (Chicago, 1973), pp. 112-124.
11. I use "paradigm" in a double sense--as a model or pattern, like a Platonic form, and as particular instance or example. There is a continuing interaction between the two. Individuals are shaped by prevailing models of selfhood, by ideological molds. At the same time, the concrete experience of some individuals may give rise to a change of model or even a shattering of the prevailing molds.
12. Owen C. Watkins, *The Puritan Experience* (London, 1972), p. 5.

13. For Henry Ward's terminology see William G. McLoughlin, Jr., *The Meaning of Henry Ward Beecher: An Essay on the Shifting Values of Mid-Victorian America* (New York, 1970), p. 12; emphasis is added. On the historical context and development of Lyman Beecher's outlook see Vincent Harding, *Lyman Beecher and the Transformation of American Protestantism* (University of Chicago Ph.D. dissertation, 1965).

14. Henry F. May, Introduction to *Old Town Folks* by Harriet Beecher Stowe (Cambridge, 1966), pp. 8-9.

15. *Autobiography and Correspondence of Lyman Beecher*, edited by his son, Charles Beecher (New York, 1864), Vol. I, p. 390.

16. Thomas, one of the younger sons, reports that when he was eleven his father said to him: "This is the most important year of your life, my son; you have come to the turning point of your history;" and thereafter "by many letters and words I was certified four times a year or oftener that I was at an 'important,' 'critical,' 'decisive' turning point..." in a letter to Charles in *The Autobiography and Correspondence of Lyman Beecher*, Vol. II, p. 504. When James, the youngest child, went to Dartmouth at the age of sixteen the father remonstrated with him over his "eternal destiny." (Letter, July 13, 1844, in the Thomas K. Beecher Papers, Cornell University Library.).

17. Seven of the eleven Beecher children who reached maturity were considered important enough to be included in the *Dictionary of American Biography*. Furthermore, the average length of life of the eleven who survived infancy was seventy-seven years. Excluding the one who died before age fifty--that is George, who apparently took his own life--the average length of life rises to over eighty! The dates of father and children are as follows:

    Lyman, 1775-1863.
    Catharine Esther, 1800-1878
    William Henry, 1802-1889
    Edward, 1803-1895
    Mary, 1805-1900
    George, 1809-1843
    Harriet Elizabeth Beecher Stowe, 1811-1896
    Henry Ward, 1813-1887
    Charles, 1815-1900
    Isabella Beecher Hooker, 1822-1907

Thomas, 1824-1900
James, 1828-1886

18. *Autobiography and Correspondence of Lyman Beecher*, Vol. I, pp. 390-391.
19. On William see Lyman Beecher Stowe, *Saints, Sinners and Beechers* Indianapolis, 1934), pp. 138 ff., and a letter from Catharine Beecher to Edward Beecher, March 27, 1825, in the Beecher Family Documents, Mount Holyoke College Library.
20. Robert Merideth, *The Politics of the Universe: Edward Beecher, Abolition, and Orthodoxy* (Nashville, 1968), pp. 26-27; letters from Edward Beecher to Catharine Beecher, August 1822, and Edward to Lyman, March 27, 1822, in Papers of the Beecher and Stowe families, Schlesinger Library, Radcliffe College; and *Autobiography and Correspondence of Lyman Beecher*, Vol. I, pp. 428, 460, and 476.
21. Quoted in a letter from Edward in response to Catharine, March 29, 1822, Radcliffe Collection.
22. In *Autobiography and Correspondence of Lyman Beecher*, Vol. I, pp. 479-480; also the following pages, up to p. 503, which contain excerpts from correspondence relating directly to Catharine's experience.
23. *Ibid.*, Vol. I, pp. 481-497.
24. Charles E. Stowe, *The Life of Harriet Beecher Stowe Compiled from her Letters and Journals* (Boston, 1890), p. 26; *Autobiography and Correspondence of Lyman Beecher*, Vol I, p. 508; and Edward to Catharine, August 23 and 30, 1822, Radcliffe Collection.
25. Catharine Esther Beecher, *Suggestions Respecting Improvements in Education* (Hartford, 1829), pp. 44-45; Catharine to Edward, August 23, 1828, Mount Holyoke Collection. Cf. also two other published works by Catharine: *Elements of Mental and Moral Philosophy* (Hartford, 1831) and *Letters on the Difficulties of Religion* (Hartford, 1836). In the latter she wrote: "God does not require anything of us but what we have *full ability* to perform." Catharine did join her father's church, but apparently without the requisite conversion. Some sort of filial and perhaps personal compromise must have been effected. Mae Elizabeth Harveson, *Catharine Esther Beecher: Pioneer Educator* (Philadelphia, 1932), p. 32, mentions the

church affiliation but does not document it. See also Kathryn Kish Sklar, *Catharine Beecher: A Study in American Domesticity* (New Haven, 1973).

26. For an account of Edward's "revelation" see Merideth, *op. cit.*, pp. 47-49, and Catharine to Edward, August 23, 1828, Radcliffe Collection. Charles developed Edward's doctrine into a kind of Christian spiritualism in his book *Spiritual Manifestations* (Boston, 1879).
27. Charles E. Stowe, *op. cit.*, pp. 33-34.
28. *Ibid.*, p. 35.
29. *Ibid.*, pp. 36-47.
30. *Ibid.*, p. 48.
31. *Ibid.*, p. 50.
32. *Ibid.*, p. 67.
33. Letter to her half-brother Thomas, June 2, 1845, in *Autobiography and Correspondence of Lyman Beecher*, Vol. II, p. 488.
34. A verdict of suicide seems to be a reasonable reading of the evidence despite the finding of coroner's jury that Geory met his untimely death by accident. See Catharine Esther Beecher, *The Biographical Remains of Rev. George Beecher, 1809-1843* (New York, 1844), p. 341, and Barbara Cross, Introduction to the reissued *Autobiography and Correspondence of Lyman Beecher* (Cambridge, 1961), p. xiii.
35. Letter, June 2, 1845, in *Autobiography and Correspondence of Lyman Beecher*, Vol. II, pp. 493 ff.
36. Charles E. Stowe, *op. cit.*, pp. 111-112.
37. As quoted in Charles H. Foster, *The Rungless Ladder; Harriet Beecher Stowe and New England Puritanism* (Durham, N. C., 1954), p.
27. See Foster for a fuller account of the experiences leading up to Harriet's decision to write *Uncle Tom's Cabin*.
38. Charles E. Stowe, *op. cit.*, p. 154.
39. Foster, *op. cit.*, p. 130, and Harriet Beecher Stowe letter about Henry's death in Annie Fields, *Life and Letters of Harriet Beecher Stowe* (Boston, 1898), pp. 280-281.
40. Foster, *op. cit.*, p. 130.
41. *Ibid.*, p. x.

42. On affinities with nature see: William G. McLoughlin, Introduction to *The American Evangelicals, 1800-1900* (New York, 1968), pp. 19-20; and Catharine Esther Beecher, *Letters on the Difficulties of Religion*, p. 189, and *The Biographical Remains of Rev. George Beecher*, pp. 19, 66, 84. On Isabella see her "Confession of Faith," April 14, 1885, in *The Connecticut Magazine*, Vol. IX, (1905), No. 2, and the article on her in the *Dictionary of American Biography*. On George see Catharine Esther Beecher, *The Biographical Remains of Rev. George Beecher*, pp. 71, 78, 83 ff., 180.
43. McLoughlin, *op. cit.*, p. 66; see also Paxton Hibbon, *Henry Ward Beecher* (New York, 1942), p. 19 and William C. Beecher and Samuel Scoville, *A Biography of Henry Ward Beecher* New York, 1888), p. 66.
44. McLoughlin, *op. cit.*, pp. 14-15.
45. Lyman Beecher Stowe, *op. cit.*, p. 241.
46. McLoughlin, *op. cit.*, p. 14.
47. *Ibid.*, pp. 17, 76.
48. *Autobiography and Correspondence of Lyman Beecher*, Vol. II, p. 552.
49. Reinhold Niebuhr, *The Nature and Destiny of Man* (New York, 1943), Vol. I, p. 23.
50. *The Last Will and Testament of William James, Esq., of the City of Albany.* Excerpts from the will can be found in C. Hartley Grattan, *The Threee Jameses* (New York, 1962), pp. 18 ff., along with a summation of most of the available evidence on William of Albany. See also Harold Larrabee, "The Jameses: Financier, Heretic, Philosopher," in *The American Scholar*, Vol. I (1932), pp. 401-413.
51. Grattan, *op. cit.*, p. 14.
52. *Ibid.*, pp. 15-16.
53. *The Literary Remains of the Late Henry James*, edited by William James (Boston, 1884; Upper Saddle River, N. J., 1970), p. 147.
54. Quoted in Austin Warren, *The Elder Henry James* (New York, 1934), pp. 17-18.
55. *The Literary Remains of the Late Henry James*, pp. 16, 75.
56. *Ibid.*, pp. 59-60.
57. *Ibid.*, pp. 61-62, emphasis in original. Note the similarity

to Walt Whitman's desire to emulate the placid cows.
58. *Ibid.*, p. 151.
59. *Ibid.*, p. 184.
60. Erikson, *Identity, Youth and Crisis*, pp. 96 ff.
61. *The Literary Remains...*, pp. 158-191 for the whole story, and 185-186 for the citations.
62. Quoted in Henry James (Jr.), *Notes of a Son and Brother* (New York, 1914), pp. 182-183.
63. For the account of the influence of Swedenborg see *The Literary Remains...*, pp. 63 ff.
64. *Ibid.*, p. 58.
65. Quoted in F. O. Mathiessen, *The James Family* (New York, 1947), pp. 10-11.
66. *Ibid.*
67. Ralph Barton Perry, *The Though and Character of William James* (Boston, 1936), Vol. I, p. 47.
68. Grattan, *op. cit.*, p. 90.
69. In his Introduction to *The Literary Remains...*, pp. 9-10.
70. Grattan, *op. cit.*, p. 86.
71. Introduction to *The Literary Remains...*, p. 43.
72. Henry, as quoted by William, *ibid.*, pp. 49-50.
73. Mathiessen, *op. cit.*, p. 16.
74. *Ibid.*, p. 12.
75. Quoted in Perry, *op. cit.*, Vol. I, p. 35.
76. *Notes of a Son and Brother*, pp. 210, 224.
77. Perry, *op. cit.*, Vol. I, p. 13.
78. Henry James, *The Social Significance of Our Institutions* (Boston, 1861), pp. 28-34.
79. Mathiessen, *op. cit.*, p. 14.
80. *Notes of a Son and Brother*, p. 80.
81. Mathiessen, *op. cit.*, p. 7.
82. Quoted in *ibid.*, p. 5.
83. Introduction to *The Literary Remains...*, pp. 73-76.
84. See Henry, Jr's account of the pattern of "protracted childhood" that prevailed in the James home, in *Notes of a Son and Brother*, pp. 167 ff.

85. Gay Wilson Allen, *William James: A Biography* (New York, 1967), p. 21.
86. Henry James (Jr.), *A Small Boy and Others* (New York, 1914), pp. 69-71.
87. *Notes of a Son and Brother*, pp. 49 ff. The elder Henry James, says Leon Edel, gave to Henry, Jr. "no sense of values save to realize the value of *all* life and *all* experience." *Henry James: The Untried Years, 1843-1870* (Philadelphia, 1953), p. 116.
88. *Notes of a Son and Brother*, pp. 112, 116.
89. *Ibid.*, pp. 69, 167, and *A Small Boy and Others*, pp. 232 ff.
90. *Notes of a Son and Brother*, pp. 167-169. Edel, *op. cit.*, p. 112, points out that, through his father, Henry Jr. "was exposed much more to religious *feeling* than to religion itself."
91. *Notes of a Son and Brother*, p. 174.
92. *Ibid.*, p. 180. "Behind the warm show of tenderness and affection" toward his father, we catch, as Edel points out, Henry Jr's "uncertainty and emotional confusion. Every now and again the father peeps from behind his son's flowing sentences as a rather ineffectual old man; and Henry occasionally slips in an undesigned word of mild contempt." *Op. cit.*, p. 51. Edel thinks Henry Jr. might have been a little too hard on his father.
93. *The Letters of William James*, Vol. I, pp. 147-148.
94. Mathiessen, *op. cit.*, p. 210.
95. *Notes of a Son and Brother*, p. 1.
96. *The Varieties of Religious Experience*, pp. 160-161. James's account gives the impression that this was someone else's experience, but it is generally agreed that the experience was his own.
97. *Ibid.*, p. 189.
98. *Letters*, Vol. I, p. 147.
99. *Ibid.*, Vol. I, pp. 199-200. This is the letter quoted by Erik Erikson and repeated at the beginning of this essay. See footnote #2.
100. See Perry, *op. cit.*, Vol. I, p. 378: "The year 1878 was a turning point in his career, as well as in his personal life."
101. Gratten, *op. cit.*, p. 127: "His principle subject was always himself and in satisfying his own needs, he found himself

satisfying those of thousands."
102. Introduction to *The Literary Remains...*, p. 72.
103. Immediately after his father's death William wrote to his wife: "You must not leave me till I understand a little more of the value and meaning of religion in Father's sense.... It is not the *one* thing needful, as he said. But it is needful with the rest. My friends leave it altogether out. I as his son (if for no other reason) must help it to its rights in their eyes...." Perry, *op. cit.*, Vol. II, p. 323. See also Vol. I, p. 467 on William's "filial piety," and *Letters*, Vol. I, p. 221 on William's desire to pass something of his father's faith to his own children.
104. *Letters*, Vol. II, p. 211. James called this capacity his "mystical germ." When asked in 1904 if he had "ever experienced God's presence" James replied: "*Never.*" *Ibid.*, p. 214, emphasis in original. See also Perry, *op. cit.*, Vol. II, p. 323; James's "A Suggestion About Mysticism," written in 1910 and published in *Collected Essays and Reviews* (New York, 1920); and Hal Bridges, *American Mysticism from William James to Zen* (New York, 1970), pp. 12 ff.
105. *Letters*, Vol. II, p. 213.
106. Gay Wilson Allen, *William James* (Minneapolis, 1970), p. 23.
107. "God himself...*may* draw vital strength and increase of very being from our fidelity...." "Is Life Worth Living?" An address delivered and printed in 1895, p. 47.
108. James, said one of his severest critics, George Santayana, "did not really believe; he merely believed in the right of believing that you might be right if you believed." *Character and Opinion in the United States* (New York, 1934), p. 47. William A. Clebsch argues against this view; he claims that it is based on overly narrow attention to such essays as "The Will to Believe" and not on the full range of James's thought. *Op. cit.*, p. 165.
109. James wrote to Thomas Davidson in 1884: "I confess I rather despair of any popular religion of a philosophic character; and I sometimes find myself wondering whether there can be any popular religion...without the presence of that element which in the past has presided over the origin of all religions, namely, a belief

in new *physical* facts and possibilities." And he asked, "Are the much despised 'Spiritualism' and the 'Society for Psychical Research' to be the chosen instruments for a new era of faith?' *Letters*, Vol. I, pp. 236-237.

110. James's interest in psychical research seems to have been more than a matter merely of scientific curiosity. He is also reported to have patronized, on occasion, Christian Science healers.

111. *The Varieties of Religious Experience*, p. 175.

112. See note #2.

113. *Letters*, Vol. II, pp. 76-77.

114. "A Suggestion about Mysticism," p. 505. The publications of this decade include *The Varieties of Religious Experience, Pragmatism, A Pluralistic Universe*, and *Some Problems of Philosophy*.

115. "A Suggestion about Mysticism," pp. 505 ff. Erik Erikson discusses this experience and reproduces much of James's description in *Identity, Youth and Crisis*, pp. 204-207.

116. *Letters*, Vol. II, p. 149.

117. "A Pluralistic Mystic," in *Memories and Studies* (New York, 1911), pp. 405-406.

118. *Letters*, Vol. II, pp. 149.

119. John Dewey, "The Vanishing Subject in the Psychology of James," in *The Journal of Philosophy*, Vol. 37 (Oct. 24, 1940), pp. 589-599. See also Milic Capek, "The Reappearance of the Self in the Last Philosophy of William James," in the *Philosophical Review*, Vol. 62 (1953), pp. 526-544.

120. James, who said of Emerson that he had "too little understanding of the morbid side of life" (*Letters*, Vol. II, p. 197), endeavored to avert his own eyes from that same reality. Yet an examination of what Grattan calls "his private psychological history" indicates that even though his efforts to avoid that sober reality were persistent and even approached the fatuous, he could not fully exorcise it. Grattan is quite severe with James on this point (*op. cit.*, p. 147).

121. James, said Santayana, represented, in "his way of thinking

and feeling...the true America, and represented in a measure the whole ultra-modern radical world." *In Winds of Doctrine* (1913), pp. 203-204, as quoted in *William James: Philosopher and Man*, Quotations and References, Compiled by Charles Herrick Compton (New York, 1957), p. 176.

SECTION III

Methodological Studies

We have deliberately chosen not to locate papers on methodological issues in the opening section of the volume. The reason for this decision is itself of methodological importance. When methodological essays are located at the beginning of a collection of psychohistorical essays, this immediately telegraphs the editor's assumption that methodological considerations are a necessary prologomenon to the psychohistorical studies themselves. We wanted to make a different statement concerning the relation of methodology to more specific psychohistorical studies. By placing methodological studies in the final section of the volume, we are dramatizing our conviction that methodology is the end result of psychohistorical study, especially as these methodological considerations address the potential role of psychohistory in opening up of new areas of inquiry in religious studies.

This procedure reverses the usual relationship between studies and method in psychohistory. The issue is not primarily that of refining our methods as we essay the task of developing biographical studies of religious figures. Rather, the basic methodological issue is "What is the nature and scope of psychohistory's contribution to the study of religion?" Thus, the fundamental methodological problem as we conceive it, and as the closing session of the symposium itself bore out, is not primarily the matter of the use of psychology in historiography. Rather, for those in religious studies and allied disciplines (and, daresay, for Erikson himself) the basic methodological problem concerns the use of psychohistory in elucidating man's religious sensitivities.

This formulation of the issue invites and has engendered a variety of responses. Some have suggested that we need to expand the method to include the psychohistory of leading religious families. Others have proposed that we move into collective biography, the study of two or more religious figures who, for any of a number of possible reasons, merit reciprocal study. Still others have recommended a considerably expanded psychohsitorical method, one which would require the psychohistorican to train his eye on persistent cultural themes rather than biographical subjects. The two former proposals assume that psychohistory will continue to maintain its biographical cast as it continues to address religious themes, suggesting only that the definition and scope of biography be expanded. The latter recommendation proposes that psychohistory design itself in such a way that it takes *culture* as its object of inquiry, stressing those cultural or cross-cultural themes which are relevant to religion. All three proposals, however, share the common assumption that psychohistory cannot conceive its contribution to religious studies as simply the proliferation of psychohistorical "studies," as if an ever-expanding "who's who" in religious history exhausted its potential.

Judging by the papers in the volume as a whole, it would appear that psychohistory will retain its biographical cast as it continues to address religious studies, especially if this biographical thrust does not result in the neglect of the larger problems of cultural process. Put more positively, they indicate that biography, in the context of religious studies, has traditionally proven a potent means of addressing these larger issues. But, beyond this general agreement, it is difficult to ascertain the precise direction of these ventures into larger cultural issues. For some, the problem of the relation of myth and history has much to recommend it. For others, there is great promise in the problem of the genesis and transmission of paradigms of the self. For still others, the basic problem will be the innovative role of charismatic individuals in the shaping of religious institutions and systems of belief. One would hope that such diversity will be sustained. And, certainly, these do not exhaust the list of fundamental problems which a biographical approach to the study of religion may address.

Unfortunately, these responses to the fundamental methodological consideration of the potential contribution of psychohistory to religious studies are essentially *ad hoc*. Being issue and problem centered, they do not provide anything approximating a wholistic view of the relation of psychohistory to religious studies. Various papers collected in this volume make specific suggestions concerning this very problem, and the proposals indicated above (family history, collective biography, cultural themes) have broader implications which merit further alteration. Nonetheless, it is fair to say that the relation of psychohistory to religious studies remains rather embryonic in this collection of papers. To a large extent, this is due to the fact that most of the papers concern themselves with the problematic nature of psychohistory, but generally fail to address the elusive quality of religion itself. Questions concerning the nature of "religion" or "the religious" are rarely asked in these papers. And, thus, the potential use of psychohistory in elucidating "the religious" is hardly broached. In addition to this, psychohistorians themselves do not seem as conscious as they might of the "hermeneutical" importance of biography. Biography need not simply be viewed as a useful approach to problems involving religion or the religious. It may well be considerably more fundamental than this, and even in some sense foundational for religious studies. For example, in his discussion of biography in his consideration of a need for an "expanded hermeneutics," Jürgen Habermas observes: "It was no accident that Dilthey took biography as the starting point of his analysis of understanding. The reconstruction of the structure of a life history that can be remembered is the model for the interpretation of symbolic structures in general. Dilthey chose biography as a model because life history seemed to ahve the merit of transperancy."[1] Thus, if religious studies is fundamentally concerned with the interpretation of symbolic structures (and following Clifford Geertz, Robert Bellah and others, there is much sentiment in favor of this view), psychohistory need make no apology for its biographical focus. Indeed, it may be

---

[1] Jürgen Habermas, *Knowledge and Human Interests*, Jeremy J. Shapiro, trans. (London: Heinemann, 1972), p. 215.

appropriate to resist tendencies within psychohistory to replace biography with cultural themes.

Of course, none of the foregoing comments actually explains why psychohistory as practiced by students of religion should have developed this biographical focus. However, it would appear that the subjective involvement of these psychohistorians in their psychohistorical researches has dictated this biographical focus. Since this suggestion bears directly on the argument developed by James Dittes, we shall not labor the point here. However, it is interesting to note that William James has suggested that those aspects of our world which are important to us, even awaken our devotion, are more likely to lend themselves to the idiographic mode of inquiry. As he puts it: "The first thing the intellect does with an object is to class it along with something else. But any object that is infinitely important to us and awakens our devotion feels to us also as if it must be *sui generis* and unique. Probably a crab would be filled with a case of personal outrage if it would hear us class it without ado or apology as a crustacean, and thus dispose of it. 'I am not such thing,' it would say; 'I am myself, myself alone.'" Hence, the issue between the idiographic and nomothetic modes of inquiry comes down to importance; if the focal object of our research is important to us, even awakens our devotion, then we are liable to carry out our examinations in the idiographic mode. It is safe to say that the participants in the symposium shared a common devotion to the religious individual. Perhaps some have become engaged in psychohistory in order to do something meaningful with their nostalgia of the Kierkegaardian era, for that period in religious studies when we took with great seriousness the category of the individual. In any case, psychohistory in the context of religious studies represents the recovery of the idiographic mode and, more importantly, of the devotion which evokes its use.

THE INVESTIGATOR AS AN INSTRUMENT OF INVESTIGATION:
SOME EXPLORATORY OBSERVATIONS ON THE COMPLEAT RESEARCHER

James E. Dittes

First, some psycho-historical context:

    Calvinism--founding colonies and colleges with the same determined commitment--endowed American academe with a dual heritage: complete trust in the ordained regularities of the universe in which we live, and complete mistrust of the unruly inner passions by which we live. Divine whim and human "subjectivity" were suppressed together, especially, in the colleges that were founded to be intellectual fortresses for the New England outposts of God's chosen people. Law and order became norm for university as much as for universe, and the waywardness of human emotions its greatest threat (even, or maybe especially, when the emotions were enlisted in God's service, as in the Witch Trials and the Great Awakening). If God must be banished from any recognizably personal involvement in the now safely mechanized affairs of the universe, of course the intellectual academic (a redundancy in our Calvinized lexicon), is forbidden any affective intrusion into the safely mechanized scrutiny of that universe. If the universe is so strictly regulated, so must be the search to know those regularities.

    America's great Calvinist--whose career was yoked to all the Big Three, Yale, Harvard, and Princeton--would have been heartily reassured--and so, I judge, are most readers--by the much-quoted opening line of Perry Miller's biography "The real life of Jonathan Edwards was the life of his mind."[1] This becomes a charter for inquiry that safely exiles the passions, people, and events of Edwards' life to an incidental "external biography," where Edwards would have wanted them. First in natural science (the arena in which American Calvinism was especially to flourish) then in theology, Edwards subjected to strict regimentation all that we might recognize as personal life. Diet and sleep, family life and friendships, and study habits above all, were put under the control of Edwards' constant scrutiny and "Resolutions" and his fiercely determined will. But whether in theology or science, whether in Edwards, Miller, or other Calvinists, Miller is right in ascribing this "particular kind of objectivity" *not* to insensitivity to "the passions, the feuds, and the anxieties" of the day, but to "an effort to protect himself against their clutch." Such effort, as every suppressor of passions and every guardian of law and order--in psyche, in society, in science--well knows, is very strenuous.

American academics have traditionally sought this strenuous refuge in the formal intellectual discipline of their classroom, in the highly formal bureaucratic structures by which they govern their universities, and especially in the strict rules they have imposed on their research. "Control" is the pass word; "contamination," "uncontrolled," "subjectivity" are some of the main fail words, as often as not--the main point here--used interchangeably. The hero and the model is the white-frocked scientist in his lab sterilized to exclude all living organisms, for what is living threatens control. It is not just the research materials that must be sterilized against stray living contaminants--test tubes, Jonathan Edwards, human "subjects" in psychological research who must be purged of the "response sets" and the "predispositions" they bring into the laboratory with them. Even more critically, the investigator must be sterilized; for his own individual feelings, intuitions, attitudes, his emotional investments loom as the most feared contaminant of all. By the Calvinistic canons of both the sciences and the humanities, the "subjectivity" of the investigator is the greatest threat to the "objectivity" of the investigation. In the academic lexicon, "subjective bias" becomes a redundancy, "unobtrusive" the new name for the old virtue of self-denial, "independent findings" a phrase that salutes similarity not uniqueness of results, and "reproduction" important only when it occurs without benefit of interpersonal intercourse. The canons and canon-makers have insisted that the risk of losing whatever richness might derive from a researcher's full and complete response to his material was a small price to pay for the control and reliability that derives from restricting him to what is most verbalizable and most common with other researchers.

No wonder when Norman Mailer confronted close-up one of the supreme products of this most Calvinistic, WASPish endeavor--the moon landings[2]--he found himself recoiling from this polished and sterilized achievement by porbing deeper in himself as a living reference point and reflection. The objective event had been sterilized so lifeless and painted so drab a grey that to write this history in living color he had to convert his account into his own type of psycho-history. He told us what was happening to himself--Aquarius--and in this flowing barely controlled aquatic image, gave us a depth perception, even though refracted, of the event.

And now, not only Norman Mailer, but large segments of our society wrench to free themselves from the strangling bondage of depersonalized technocracy, by celebrating "human encounter" and "whole personhood" wherever it can be found--and maybe even elsewhere--so, too, even among academics, sometimes in extreme measure. Some classrooms become dedicated to human encounter, above all. In governing the university, some departments and committees have been liberated into free-for-alls. And as for research and scholarship, anonymity and impersonality is no longer fashionable in some quarters, replaced by TV interviews, active public roles and personal, bold prefaces, that often parade details of personal history, and health, social prejudice and musical tastes somewhat beyond the bounds of scholarly relevance. As the Puritans discovered periodically all too well, in such places as Salem and the Connecticut valley, bound passions once unleashed burst out in excesses that only seem to prove the wisdom of the binding.

But in less extreme form, it also seems increasingly fashionable in some quarters for the author to appear prominently in his research report. His personal history, his motives for the research, his emotional reactions to his materials, what he really did and thought during the study (as contrasted with the expurgated and stylized account of procedures that is conventionally reported), his inner history as the research proceeded,--at the very least, the rediscovery of "I" on his typewriter--the once-banned personal is now sometimes welcomed as an adornment of the research. Probably among no group of scholars is this more the case than among those who claim or accept the label "psycho-historaian," for they are already committed to the crucial relevance of the personal in activities and events from which the relevance has often been denied. Why should not this include, first of all, their own activity as an investigator? Erik Erikson has demonstrated particularly successfully how to use one' own reactions as a useful organ of discernment in his research. One-fourth of his last book[3] tells us as much about Erikson as it tells us about Gandhi, but it tells us more about Gandhi by telling us about Erikson. In the symposium that gave rise to his volume it quickly became the norm for each participant to preface his formal presentation with an autobiographical account of how he related himself to his topic. This refinement will probably be excised by the intimidations and impersonality of publication; what may seem natural and useful and not threatening to get out of control around a table in Southern California in the spring may seem too risky at a typewriter in the fall. (This is the point to acknowledge the advantage I have in revising my informal symposium remarks while in the city of Rome, among a people as vibrantly immune to Calvinistic fearfulness as they are repugnant to it, a people who have learned how to make feelings a natural and indispensable part of the way they do all business.) Not surprisingly, among the psychohistorians those who have claimed special alliance with Erikson have been particularly vigorous about including accounts of their personal histories and reactions in the course of their own writings. Indeed, this roster is large and varied enough that illustration for most points I want to discuss can be drawn from this group.

One cannot consider this roster without being made aware of another matter that highlights my ascription of scholarship's depersonalization to its Calvinistic heritage. For the correction to that depersonalization appears to be coming, not surprisingly, from another tradition. The Jewish tradition has always stood firmly for the wholeness of human life--finding identity, as does Erikson, in getting the parts put together, the parts of the whole person, and the individual as part of his group. (The question has been asked before: Could anyone but a Jew have rediscovered the oneness of personality, the continuities between infancy and adulthood, between unconsciousness and conscious, between indivdual and family and culture that Freud showed us?) So, being alerted by Mailer to see his own Jewishness as the necessary antidote to the WASPish depersonalized success and successful depersonalization of Apollo, we realize that other pioneers in the rescue of the human from Calvinistic restriction have also been Jewish. (And maybe we even get a further clue as to why a Methodist minister's son, and especially one with the Scottish-sounding name of McGovern, was not the one called to lead Calvinistic America out of its bondage to narrow concerns for law and order.)

Putting the personal to work

But the canons of scholarship have their rational foundations, as well as their ideological and psychological roots, and these need to be respected and honored. If more personal responses of the investigator have been exaggeratedly excluded from authorized research, it is hardly any improvement for the essential rationality of scholarship to be obscured by an unduly rebellious and egocentric protest against that exclusion.

After a certain amount of acted-out and written-out protest against the depersonalizing taboos, and after assertions *that* the person of the investigator should not be excluded from his study, it must be approaching the time (in this particular identity-crisis) in which we need to pay more constructive attention to *how* the investigator can be a part of his investigation in a way that makes its results both more meaningful and more reliable. This essay makes--I make--a small venture in that direction.

First, it tries--I try-- to sort out some of the different ways that the person of the researcher can become involved. Fighting for or against the Calvinistic restrictions, we take extremes and argue that the investigator's personal affect should be all out of or all in his research. But leaving this emotional battle behind, it may be possible to see some middle ground, to see different and limited ways in which the researcher's personal affect may be a part of his research.

Second, the essay takes--I take-- one of these intermediate positions and tries to specify some of the procedures and rules by which the investigator can carefully use his personal involvements and reactions, not simply to repudiate or flount conventional scientific canons, but in the service of them. I seriously propose to try to "get it all together," to move beyond excessive restrictions and beyond protest against excessive restrictions, to accept the essential validity of conventional scholarly canons and procedures, but also to accept the *whole* involvement of the investigator (as enforcers of these canons have not always done). Are there not methods, describably methods, with enforceable criteria--so that we can say whether the methods have been used reliably or not, whether the results are enhanced or not--by which investigators can, and for that matter, do make controlled, disciplined, yet free use of their own personal reactions, as one more tool of discerning investigation?

Different modes of investigator's involvement

Let me venture to distinguish, and to label, four different modes by which the personal reactions of the investigator--dare we invoke the symbol "I"?--do and do not become part of his investigation. It is, of course, a rough typology and rougher labeling, no sooner done than needing refinement. But some such distinctions may be a necessary and useful start.

1. *Incongruent*: I's personal involvement, reactions are suppressed.
2. *Introductory*: I's personal involvements lead to the investigation.

3. *Instrumental*: I's personal involvement is intrinsic part of the investigation.
4. *Inflated*: I's personal involvement dominates investigation.

These form a continuum of mounting involvement by I. The first category simply refers to the conventional Calvinistic view that the person of I is irrelevant or damaging to his study and needs to be carefully suppressed. This doesn't need much more discussion here. But there is some point to pressing the distinction among the last three, since, at the present crude state of affairs, they are often confused, and probably ought not to be any longer.

The modes labeled "Introductory" and "Inflated" both tell us much about I, but not in a way that proves particularly illuminating of the subject of the investigation. In "Inflated" I goes so far (in excessive reaction to "Incongruent"?) as to let his own feelings dominate; he abandons the distinction between himself and his subject; he gives us his inner history, but we can no longer tell how to let it point beyond I to his subject. He repudiates conventional canons of research. In "Introductory" I doesn't go quite far enough to let himself enlighten his subject. He tells us the motives and background and influences by which he arrived at his subject; but from then on, after the autobiographical preface, it's business as usual. The third mode "Instrumental" represents the admission of I into the investigation, not to lead to it, and not to dominate it, but to contribute to it. (Eventually, there must be sub-types and diversities recognized within this type, but for now it seems useful enough to distinguish this general strategy from the others.) If "Incongruent" sends personal feelings scurrying away from the lab or libe or other site of investigation, "Introductory" keeps them waiting at the gate, "Inflated" lets them in, to take over, and the third position lets them in as instrumental enrichment, but they must still follow the rules of the house. In what follows, it will be convenient and I hope accurate to take the work of Robert Coles and Robert Lifton as examples of #2, "Introductory," some writings of Robert Bellah as a spokesman for #4, "Inflated," and Erik Erikson as illustration of #3, "Instrumental."

But even better than citing such examples, it may be useful to have a single instance immediately at hand, a subject that invites study, and can permit study in any of the types/strategies. I choose an actual instance from my own experience. If it is an instance of more interest to social scientists than to historians, well, that's what my own experience yields, and concreteness always trades off depth for breadth.

<u>Mr.M.</u>

Mr. M., a middle-aged man, wrote to me, telling of several mystical experiences and asking if I was interested in hearing more about them. I sensed in this letter a blend of several different requests: He wanted to share with me, as a man of religion, his insights, so that I might better understand the spiritual truths he had discovered in these experiences. But he had also chosen to write to me knowing that I was a psychologist, and he seemed to want to share his experiences, also, so that both he and I might better understand the experiences. These mixed purposes matched purposes of mine: I have found helpful spiritual insight in unexpected places before; I have what might be called "pastoral"--or more coldly, "clinical"-- concerns for persons who feel dilemmas in their lives and seek counsel; and, of course, I do have research interests in exploring religious experience. I telephoned Mr. M. We discovered we had rapport, and we arranged a personal conversation, then, later, another. Together, our talks lasted several hours. In the talks, I sensed more explicitly several reactions in myself that had been latent in my reactions to his letter and are implied in the sentences above. For our purposes here, let me try to hold these up and make them very explicit. Then we can look at the alternative ways that these reactions of mine might have fed into my (and his?) research purposes. (I have written elsewhere of the possibilities of using personal reactions[4] in the service of pastoral or clinical response to persons.)

First, I felt *protective* towards Mr. M. When he told of how others had brushed off his inquiries, I bristled with indignation and fantasied writing scathing letters to these narrow-minded and hard-hearted people. When he described the behavior of family and friends towards him, I often felt he was submitting too meekly to being pushed around, and I felt like taking him by the arm and helping him stand up to these people. When he expressed some anxiety about being overwhelmed by his experiences, or when he expressed despair over ever understanding them, I quickly offered reassurance. When colleagues, whom Mr. M. and I invited into one conversation, later dismissed him as a crank, I mounted a defense of his sanity.

Second, related to my protectiveness, I felt *ambivalent* over how much authority to credit his religious revelations. (This is, of course, related to the mixture of purposes he and I both had in the conversations.) Was he my (research) "subject" which would presumably make me--does not this monarchical usage still linger prominently in our use of the term "subject"?--his sovereign? Or was I his attentive pupil, and he my religious tutor? In more exaggerated form than I actually felt it: Was he prophet or patient, inspired or insane? In appraising historical figures, we often find it convenient to say that one can be both. But this is a hard synthesis to sustain in face-to-face encounter, when one feels a need to get relative roles clear. I am accustomed to treating a person's report of his mystical experiences, respectfully, as an item of behavior to be fit into larger patterns of his experience. His account is to be interpreted ("reduced," critics would say, but I would not) by linking it, through chains provided by psychological and sociological categories, to other elements of his life, past, current, and future. In such analysis is where my craft, my discipline, my expertise, my authority lies, an authority "over" his experiences that I would claim and Mr. M. recognized. On the other hand, I also felt inclined to credit (and Mr. M. claimed) a certain *sui generis* validity to his experiences, transcending my psycho-social analysis. *Logically,* validity and analysis are by no means incompatible. The most striking revelations vouchsafed to men--at least in frames of reference provided by Western historical religions--are totally embedded in their on-going experiences. But *psychologically*, I repeat, the synthesis is hard to maintain; we want to relate the question to one of hierarchy and status and to decide who is over whom. So the tension persisted in our relationship: Did I have something to tell him, or did he have something to tell me?

Protectiveness and ambivalence over relative authority--these, then, were two feelings I noted in myself. They hardly overwhelmed me, or dominated our conversations, as they do in this particular account. Nor did they interfere with my relationship--relationships, I should say--with Mr. M. By usual criteria, I think I learned, and analyzed, and counseled well. But the feelings were present, and the question here is whether and how these feelings could have been managed and used in a way that enhanced the analysis. (How they can enhance the learning and the counseling seems more obvious, and, as I have said, is a matter for discussion elsewhere.)

First of all, these are *my* reactions, and, most obviously, they tell something about me--as I am sure the reader has been saying to himself in the above paragraphs. These reactions follow from and are therefore clues to motives and history of mine. In particular, and most obviously, they seem to point to some uncertainties, some mixture, perhaps simply confusion, in my own vocational and ideological commitments.[5] The reader may have noticed the language--"chains," "craft," "lies"--with which my statement about scientific expertise (and, apparently, also my ambivalence about it) got expressed. Two of the positions, those I have labeled "Incongruent" and "Introductory," are based on the fact that these reactions reflect important personal characteristics of myself. Though they evaluate that fact differently, both would separate these personal reactions from the analysis itself. The fourth position--"Inflated"--tends to ignore this fact that these reactions reflect *my* personal history and outlook. The third, the one I propose to encourage, recognized this fact, but suggests, boldly enough, that the reactions may *also* point to more than just my own characteristics; my reactions may also reflect some of Mr. M's input into our relationship as well, and in ways that are useful to the analysis.

Incongruent: Separation of person and work

What is the relevance of these personal reactions to my psychological analysis of Mr. M.? None! thunders the conventional puritan scientific view, except as impediment and distortion, and the more these can be suppressed neutralized, or otherwise purged from the situation, the better the analysis. Whether I feel protective toward Mr. M. or hostile or suspicious, whether I feel arrogantly in possession of superior powers because of my scientific skills, humbly self-effacing before his superior religious powers, or ambivalent--all these feelings should make no difference when it comes to practicing my professional competence with Mr. M, exploring with my technical skills the nature and implications of his mystical experiences. My analysis should come to the same conclusions as that of an equally skilled and schooled colleague who has quite different feelings from those I have. The hypotheses I propose, and the evidence I marshall to evaluate them stand or fall on the objective data in Mr. M's account, and can only suffer distortion by the intrusion of my own personal reactions.

The more risk that the situation has mobilized my personal reactions, the more I must take precautions to be sure that they have been controlled and not allowed to affect the investigation; the more the reader suspects such reactions may be present, the more he will demand evidence of these precautions. If I follow this approach in reporting on my analysis of Mr. M., I will be sure to demonstrate that my judgments were made "blind" or were confirmed by another person who *was* "blind," or are based on quantified data which have been manipulated without human contamination, or that my personal reactions were neutralized by the conscious recognition and strong ego made possible by prior thorough psycho-analysis.

Such is the conventional view, and I have labeled it "puritan" because it reflects, in my judgment, an exaggerated and irrational fear of human emotions quite as much as it reflects a rational philosophy of science. The fact that my reactions to Mr. M. reflect personality characteristics and personal history of mine is (irrationally, and fearfully) escalated into the only fact worthy of attention. It is as if death, destruction, and pollution is all one thought of in connection with automobiles and therefore automatically would ban automobiles as unmitigated threat.

Unclean test tube" is the image that automatically comes to mind to express the effects of human involvement in the laboratory[6] "contaminated by...needs, anxieties, self-deceptions and intentions." Perhaps the reader only has to ponder the degree of uneasiness he has felt over the intrusion into the discussion of my own candid, though quite limited self-disclosure. Though what I have reported about myself is hardly alarmingly pathological and is not even very unusual, and though it is a reasonable illustration for the discussion at hand, it may still trigger a few pangs of distress for breaking the established barrier between the personality of the investigator and his work. (And perhaps this present effort to break the barriers between the personal reactions of the reader and his reading is even more distressing.)

How can human reactions be best managed so as to enhance analysis? By sternly suppressing them, says this view, and ideally by eliminating them altogether from any effect on the investigation.

Introductory: Personal history as occasion for research

But this is too sterile and anonymous for the taste of some, especially, perhaps, psychiatrists, and especially, perhaps, psycho-historians. The investigator is very much present in his interviews, especially perhaps in his own mind as he writes the report. The study plays an important role in his life, perhaps *the* most important role at the time, and it may seem quite artificial to a writer, and perhaps to a reader, to separate the rest of the personal history of the author from this emportant element in that history. So we have become accustomed in recent publications to learn much about the author, his background, his motives for the study, his relationship with his subjects, whether living or dead, and his reactions to his material. This is the kind of material that occupies TV interviews with authors, also. This has been increasingly true of Erikson's writings, as will be noted in more detail below. Robert Coles has given us much personal narrative in his recent volumes on children.[7] He tells us the considerations and events that led to his study, his feelings about his interviewees as he approached thme and as he heard them out. He tells us how he evaluates the facts he relates. Robert Bellah introduced his recent collection of essays[8] with an autobiographical statement. So did Robert Lifton[9] who also prefaces each essay with an account of how it fit into his career. Though Lifton's reports tend to be limited to more external circumstances, he includes one intriguing paragraph (on page 5) proposing the ideal of actually using the investigator as an instrument. He says that he approaches this strategy in his essay on the Hiroshima bomb survivors, that he lets his own horror at atomic destruction guide his understanding of the survivors' reactions. But this is by no means explicit in the chapter. In fact, I would judge that the recording and categorizing of survivors' reactions is a fairly impersonal process that would not have been done differently by one who reported himself immune to atomic horrors.

The important point about these examples and about this approach is that the personal narrative leads us *to*, but *not into* the investigation. It tells us how the researcher was drawn to his subject, or to his subjects, and they to him, how rapport was established, and frequently something of how the investigator felt afterwards. We discover the personal context of the research, but it is left as context. The research itself is essentially business as usual, the investigator's reactions do not become part of his data and do not seem to feed his thinking; it is not evident how data or interpretations would be different if the researcher had not made himself so evident, or if a researcher of quite different personal involvement had been at work. Hearing I talk about himself, we cannot particularly predict what he will say about his subject. It is more interesting to read a book after having met the author, via one medium or another, and perhaps a reader who knows the author understands more accurately or more fully the author's interpretations. So the personalization may facilitate communication as it facilitates the research in the first place. But this needs to be distinguished from more systematically letting one's own reactions enter into the research and become an incremental part of the data and of the process of interpreting the data.

I might report on my interviews with Mr. M. as I did above, indicating my immediate reactions, and going still further to point out the personal characteristics represented by these reactions. I might point out how this protectiveness and readiness to respect his views is characteristic of a kind of concern for the underdog, and attracts me to respond to and to hear out people like Mr. M. I might even point out how these personal characteristics aided our rapport. So, too, with what could be described as my still incompleted religious and ideological pilgrimage made evident by some of my reactions to Mr. M. If I used these reactions in this way to indicate how I got into the interviews with Mr. M., to demonstrate how we established the rapport that got him into the interviews, and also to interest the reader enough to get *him* more involved in the report, then I would be doing essentially what I judge Coles, for example, to be doing. (If I would limit myself more to external circumstances, concerning the letter, the telephone call, the business of scheduling our meetings, then I would be coming closer, I think, to Lifton's mode.) But what I actually observed and concluded and reported about Mr. M. would not be substantially different from what it would be if I did not have, or did not report, my personal reactions.

Inflated: Personal involvement replacing investigation

    This is not the occasion for reviewing or evaluating the many reactions against positivism and analysis that have enlisted social scientists and historians uder such banners as "phenomenology," "existentialism," "historicism," "ethnomethodology," "client-centered," "sui generis," or "symbolic realism."[10] But I do want to locate this cluster of perspectives and to distinguish this kind of view from others which also want to attenuate analysis in abstract categories and to give more authority and more attention to the raw experience.

    The most powerful and persuasive attacks on the superrationalism and puritanic narrowness of conventional scholarly analysis has been generated by these various schools of thought. (Grouped here in category #4, though this attack and the general appeal to the importance of full personal experience, including the involvement of the investigator with his material could be shared by the viewpoints I have wanted to separate as "Introductory" and "Instrumental.") Most people who would be making the kind of attack I have modestly ventured above against the Calvinism of conventional science would be doing so on behalf of one of these schools; and most readers of my earlier attack would automatically suppose that I speak for one of these schools. But in reacting against conventional scholarship and conventional analysis, these schools tend to take more extreme positions than their attack on puritanism and positivism requires. They tend to ask the investigator to *substitute* the immediate experience for the conventional analysis rather than to *supplement* the one with the other. In particular, they tend to obscure two distinctions I would want to preserve, first, the distinction between the experience of the investigator and the experience of his subject, and, second, the more crucial distinction between the role of the investigator and the role of his subject. The investigator is asked, in one way or another, to experience--and report--what his subject experiences, and to relinquish a separate, autonomous analytic perspective. And, as often as not, he is asked to substitute active participation and partisanship for detached investigation. Thus, my interest in setting apart, under categories I have numbered 2 and 3, approaches that share with this mode the concern for immediate experience and the suspicion of abstractly mediated analysis, but which want to retain the integrity of the investigator as one with skills and vocabulary and a role that separates him from his subject. The "Introductory" and "Instrumental" modes need to be separated from the "Inflated" mode to emphasize the possibility of acknowledging personal involvement of the investigator with the experience of his subject without making it sovereign to the investigation. These other categories represent two different ways of trying to preserve the integrity of the investigator without challenging either his or his subject's integrity as persons.

If Mr. M. describes spirals of wind and light and a voice calling out a name, I would not, following this perspective, yield to my curiosity or to my habits of speculation or to my training at analysis in order to explore the symbolism that spirals or wind or light may have in his individual experience. I would not explore the memories they may call forth and speak to, except as he volunteered these associations, for that would be to impose my craft on his experience. Nor would I speculate about what function these spirals and voices might have served for him, what effect they may have had on him, in ways that he may be unaware of; for that would be to posit elements from my training, not from his experience. And that would be to yield to an arrogance that some of my feelings in this situation found repugnant. So I would yield to these feelings, and listen to Mr. M. to learn about these new dimensions of experience that have been made available to Mr. M. and which transcend my own experience of psychological theories and analysis. Something like this seems to be what is recommended by Bellah, for example, in the paper referred to above.

Investigator as instrument of his investigation

In the essay in which he seems to be recommending the position just described--the investigator as "inflated" in his investigation--Robert Bellah urges this view: "....reality is seen to reside not just in the object [i.e., the investigator] but in the subject and *particularly in the relation between subject and object*."[11] I have italicized the phrase that I would take more seriously than I think Bellah does. The "*relation* between subject and object" between the investigator and his subject (or subjects) is precisely the place to look, I think, for clues as to how the personal reactions and involvements of the investigator can become an additional, incremental instrument for his research.

The personal reactions of the investigator *are* products of his own personal history, in ways that may have little or nothing to do with his research subject, as has been acknowledged above. But they are also triggered by, and a product of, his relationship with his subject (or his subjects). The investigator's feelings are mobilized *in* him and are therefore more or less distinctive to and more or less revealing of him. But they are mobilized *by* his relationship with a particular subject, and may therefore be more or less distinctive to and more or less revealing of that subject as well. *This* is the basis for supposing that his personal reactions can become trustworthy, reliable--"controllable" if you wish--guidelines to enhanced understanding of the subject. The investigator "perceives" his subject, interprets his subject in many more modes and with far more organs of perception than are admitted in conventional research. The irrational elements of the researcher's response to his subject can augment his more rational responses and become an incremental "sensor." The irrational elements of the researcher's response to his subject can be brought under the control of and put into the service of his rational investigation.

It is for this possibility that I want to plead here for serious and systematic exploration. At this point, obviously, it is only a possibility to be explored. The investigator has been used so little as this kind of instrument--and even then, in ways often disguised in research reports--that we have very little experience to guide us to see the potential utility, nor, even more important, to guide us to formulate the rules necessary for responsible use, and control, of this instrument.

This possibility represents a far more conservation methodological proposal than that advanced by existentialists and others classified above under the label "inflated." But I suspect that it may offer as much as is really wanted by many who react against narrow positivism and puritanism, and who over-react even to the point of "inflation." This may be a way of correcting the puritan super-rational bias and of admitting more of the investigator's legitimate personal involvement into the explicit work of his investigation, without repudiating the conventional canons of "objective" research. If so, it may appeal to some in both groups who now find themselves polarized as defenders of scientific rigor in the "incongrous" camp and champions of personal involvement in the "Inflated" camp.

Erik Erikson devoted the first 100 pages of his book on Gandhi to telling us much about himself and his involvement with the study of Gandhi. I think this is an important methodological discussion which, in some respects, might be regarded as a postscript to the book on Luther and perhaps as a rejoinder to some of the methodological critics of that book. It is as though Erikson had countered, "All right, if you think the facts on a historical figure like Luther become too elusive and too garbled for psychological accuracy, I will take a more contemporary figure and consult the archives and interview eye-witnesses. But notice how the archives tell us more about the whims of the archivists and eye-witnesses tell us more about themselves than either can tell us about our subject. And notice especially how the personal involvement of the investigator becomes apparent in the proceedings, the closer they are looked at."

Insight into Gandhi is often forthcoming, in fact, when Erikson is most candidly reporting his own feelings. For example, when mill-owner Ambalal proved to be a stubborn and shrewd interviewee, this could have proved an annoyance and frustration for a more determined objective pursuer-of-facts; Ambalal's tactics threw up impediments in the search for accurate information, an impediment some historians would say would only be compounded if they admitted their own feelings of annoyance. Instead Erikson tuned into these feelings and thereby discovered more about Gandhi's experience than could have been garnered from inducing Ambalal to yield a few more facts: He discovered what a stubborn and shrewd antagonist Gandhi had been coping with, and therefore, presumably also, something about the stubbornness and shrewdness Gandhi must have had to bring to the encounter.

The most compelling example, however, is the 25-page "Dear Mahatma" letter that erupts mid-way in the book. In this scathing, affectionate outburst, Erikson lets his own feelings toward Gandhi explode. They are complex feelings, full of admiration, especially for Gandhi's high principles, and full of despair and scolding, especially for Gandhi's sabotage of these principles in his personal life. Erikson seems to represent this letter as a catharsis, getting these feelings out of the way of subsequent study of Gandhi. But I ask any reader to test for himself whether he does not know Gandhi more fully and more accurately through this 25-page emotional outburst by the author than he does from the other hundreds of pages of cooler analysis. Neither, I think, would Erikson have left the passage at the heart of the book, however cathartic it may have been, if he thought it did not also yield unique insight of a significant order.

How could my own reactions to Mr. M., described above, become clues that can be tracked back to tell us something about Mr. M.? If I feel protective toward Mr. M., is this a clue as to how he presents himself to me, and presumably to others? Since I have already conceded, indeed emphasized, how my reactions can be clues to *my* history, it may be necessary first to say a few words about the *relationship* between investigator and subject which produces these data.

One might think of the relationship as "additive." If I feel protective towards Mr. M., some portion of this protectiveness can be attributed to my own predisposition to feel protective, and this portion of these feelings can be used as evidence of this trait of mine. If we had some way of assessing the strength of this trait, then we would have a kind of baseline, representing what *I* brought to the relationship. If my feelings of protectiveness towards Mr. M. appeared stronger than what could be attributed to this constant baseline, then that excess feeling could be regarded as my reaction to what *he* brought to the relationship. It would be something like establishing normal body temperature on a thermometer. The average normal temperature is 98.6°F and any incremental body heat can be attributed to the body's reaction to--its "relationship" to--some other organism. Certain patterns of increment may suggest the body's "relationship" to one kind of organism, other patterns suggest the presence of other organisms. To be more precise, "normal" body temperature varies from individual to individual, and for any one individual, from time to time; so the physician can make a more precise judgment about any incremental heat by knowing what the "normal" baseline temperature is for that individual for that time of day, for that season (and for any other situational effects he wants to control).

This is a way of thinking that is sometimes introduced into discussions of therapists' use of "counter-transference" as an instrument for making inferences about the patient, inferences based on feelings which he mobilizes in the therapist. The therapist is supposed to have his own predispositional feelings under control so that either they are reduced to a baseline of zero, or else are very well known, an identifiable baseline.

This way of thinking and the analogy with body temperature is helpful so far as it goes. However, mobilization of feelings is not additive, but multiplicative. I do not really have constant feelings of protectiveness, as I have constant body heat, and I do not impose these on all people, in all situations; that would be pathological, if I did. I am just as capable of feeling defensive, aggressive, manipulative, or bored toward a research "subject" as protective. My trait of protectiveness is latent until triggered into manifestation by some characteristics of Mr. M. in the relationship with me. My feelings are--even in the mathematical sense, as well--a "product" of both Mr. M and me.

In this case, my feelings of protectiveness, once I become

aware of them, made me sensitive, in turn, to some of the mannerisms in Mr. M. which seemed to be eliciting my reactions. It was not so much that he was openly apologetic and self deprecatory--*that* would not have required my own feelings to detect. He presented himself, though simply and not belligerently, as a person of polish and confidence, intelligence and education. When he made some conventional deferential remarks about visiting a professor in a great university, these came through as signals of social grace, not of personal apologia. But there were ways that he seemed to be sabotaging this self-presentation: His tone was too mild; his speech and dress were careless; he backed away from topics just when he was going well. I began to want him--for my sake and his--to come through more, to come up to his potential, and I found myself coaxing and coaching and reassuring in subtle ways. I found myself lessening my demands on him and taking extra care not to make remarks that might seem threatening or offensive. I was protective.

In abstracting and emphasizing this aspect of our relationship, I must also emphasize that it was relatively minor and subtle. Our relationship had many facets and our conversation many topics which thoroughly engaged us. Indeed, it was precisely because it was essentially a "normal" and satisfactory relationship that I became more aware of these feelings of protectiveness that were also present. They surprised me; and, so far, I can propose no better "base-line"--or more precisely, indication that a "base-line" is being exceeded--than just such surprise. Ordinarily a straightforward interviewer and candid conversationalist, I was pulling my punches; I was trying to help him hold up his part of the conversation rather than working on my part.

Sensing the feelings led me to detect what it was in his manner that they were reciprocating. He was pulling his punches, too. Toward me--and, therefore, I had to suppose, towards many/most others--he seemed to be adopting a strategy of putting himself down before others could, of underachieving and moderating his claims for himself, presumably to forestall the risks of accountability and counter-claims, of surrendering without a fight so as to avoid a fight. I was reminded of the peace-making signals that Erikson found appropriate to discuss in relation to Gandhi, the animal, for example, that bares its neck to trigger an enemy's mercy.

If an investigator distinguishes the process of formulating hypotheses from the process of testing them, then the clues from the investigator's personal reactions probably belong more in the hypothesis-forming stage than in hypothesis-testing. Personal reactions are so multiply determined as hardly to lend themselves to the kind of control that is implied when we begin to speak of "testing" hypotheses. In the case of Mr. M., my surprising feelins of protectiveness led me to posit some hypothesis, which I tried to test with other data. If this need to pull his own punches was so strong as to disrupt the otherwise natural tone of the relationship between us, perhaps this need was also strong enough at least to be one of the factors present in the mystical experiences which disrupted an otherwise smooth pattern of life for Mr. M.

Were the experiences related, then, to times in which Mr. M. felt the risk of making exaggerated claims for himself? Well, yes, one occurred the very day he received an unexpected promotion to a position of authority--a matter he had neglected to mention to me previously. Another experience was closely related in time and in his associations to his marriage, and the third, in his associations though not in time, to the period of leaving home.

Did the experiences have a content that could reasonably be interpreted as dealing with this kind of ambivalence? Well, they were full of powerful forces, natural and spiritual, which rekindled Mr. M.'s comfortable feelings of humility but which also, in one way or another, acknowledged and approved his new autonomy and responsibility. One voice specifically instructed him to marry; the visual symbolism of another episode suggested to him the path away from his parents' home; the verbal and visual elements of the promotion-day experience were loaded with sensations of power and of approval.

Was there more direct evidence in Mr. M.'s account of any of the ambivalence and vacillation I posited? Decidedly so. Did the experiences have any effect on this? Well, he had proceeded with the marriage and had carried out the responsibilities of his new authority with a flair and manifest success.

Without strain, the pieces fit together into a pattern of understanding the role of the experiences in his life. It's hardly a surprising or unusual interpretation--at least Mr. M. found it not threatening. But it is not a pattern that would have suggested itself to me amidst the tangled web of Mr. M.'s account, and perhaps not to others, aside from tracking back the thread of clues beginning with the mild surprise I felt at my own protective reaction to Mr. M.

Related to all this, of course, was the set of feelings I have labeled as ambivalence over his authority and the kinds of inferences I found myself tracking back from this feeling. In short, the mixed reaction I had--was he competent or incompetent, prophet or patient, someone to be heeded or someone to be helped?-- seemed to derive from the mixed signals he was giving off as to how he regarded himself. Some of these I have described in the immediately preceding paragraphs. Furthermore, I was led by my own reactions to recognize that if I was treating him ambivalently, so, probably, did most people. The question that pervaded, and to some extent vexed, our relationship--our relative status-- was, more likely than not, a persistent question that pervaded and vexed most of his relationships and most of his life. So, in the complex interactions in which others' attitudes toward us influence how we feel about ourselves, and vice versa, it was reasonable to suppose that, in his relationship with me, we had a fair sample of an unresolved tension that pervaded his emotional life. This could be tested and readily confirmed with conversation about his work life and family life and social life. And, in turn, this perception gave considerably more leverage in understanding the intensity and the quality of his religious life.

Perhaps this was such a prominent theme that it could have been readily discerned through other avenues. Or perhaps, it came into focus more sharply and more promptly by accepting one obvious fact; though our roles as research "subject" and investigator were rather specialized and isolated roles, unlike other social relationships, they also were just another form of social relationship; therefore, though the dilemmas and tensions seemed to arise out of the unique situation of the investigation, they were in fact representative and characteristic of many situations. This obvious fact is, in practice, denied by many investigators. It is not uncommon for a researcher to take the following attitude towards such a situation: If our interview is for the purposes of gathering data, and if the interview does not go smoothly, then data cannot be adequately gathered; the interview must be repaired for the sake of the investigation. In contrast, I am simply urging to take the possibility more seriously that the breakdowns in the interview *are* important data.

To propose that the scientist exploits these affective impediments (which is how puritanized science regards any affect in the investigator) is hardly more or less than to recommend the practice already demonstrated by the most alert scientists, who have always been ready to be open and curious about the unwelcome artifacts intruding into their laboratories. Pavlov's initial studies of salivation were considerably inconvenienced, for example, by the bad habit the dogs got into, of salivating prematurely, as soon as the experimenter appeared and before he produced the meat. So Pavlov decided to study this inconvenient and intrusive bad habit.

Examples at Santa Barbara

The principle example has been of the investigation of a single individual, and has relied much on the model of how a psychotherapist might adopt such strategies in conducting individual therapy. But I see no reason that the principle of using personal reactions as guides into the material does not apply equally well for more remote and more general investigations.

When the two historical papers on Gandhi, for example, were first presented to the symposium that generated this volume, there was noticeable affective reaction by the audience, including myself, at several points. Perhaps the reader--if he can force himself out of the habit of covering and eliding over any affective response while engaged in reading scholarly papers--can identify any point at which he felt mild, but definite feelings, perhaps feelings that surprised him a bit.

The most notable affective reaction to Stephen Hay's conference paper (which is not the essay included in this volume) was the delighted laughter that greeted his account of Kasturba's stubborn non-violent resistance to some of Gandhi's demands. This simple, illiterate woman stood up to her husband, the would-be Mahatma, and he backed down, and we enjoy the account. Why laughter? Perhaps this is a kind of "base-line" response having little or nothing to do with Gandhi: perhaps it reflects our nervousness about contemporary male-female relations in our culture; perhaps it is such a standard comic episode--Punch and Judy, Blondie and Dagwood--that we are conditioned to laugh, regardless of who plays the roles, at the victimized partner having the last word. But having said even that much, have we not already said much about how we perceive Gandhi, and therefore perhaps something of how he represents himself to us. Do we delight in seeing every saint put down, every healer getting a taste of his own medicine? Or does our laughter suggest that Gandhi is a particular kind of hero and saint for us, one who arouses more openly ambivalent attitudes than others, one perhaps whose own humility seems not quite sufficient or genuine enough so that we welcome his humiliation by one still more humble. Or perhaps Gandhi's saintliness is so complete as to threaten us and we accordingly find welcome comfort in discovering that he is only one more subdued husband. Whatever it is, there *is* something about Gandhi that our non-rational selves perceive, and laugh at, something that is worth exposing and exploring to supplement and to guide our rational appraisal.

Probably the most notable affective reaction to David Newhall's paper was the author's. He was clearly angry, angry at the exploiting British, as he readily conceded in discussion after his presentation. Unseemly as this may be for a philosopher and historian--and it is carefully not made explicit at any point in the paper, and may not be apparent in the written version at all--this passion pervades the presentation and gives it its point. Without experiencing David Newhall's passion, one cannot experience as well *Gandhi's* dilemma nor understand so well *his* passion.

Conclusion:

This discussion recommends more careful attention to the possibility of the controlled use of the investigator's own experience, to such a discussion, the most appropriate conclusion is: Try it.

FOOTNOTES

1. Perry Miller, *Jonathon Edwards* (rpt. 1959; New York, 1949).
2. Norman Mailer, *Of a Fire on the Moon* (New York, 1970).
3. Erik H. Erikson, *Gandhi's Truth: On the Origins of Militant Nonviolence* (New York, 1971).
4. E.g. "Who Calls as Healer," *The Christian Ministry*, 4 (July) 1972, pp. 6-14. *The Church in the Way* (New York, 1967).
5. I have written about this in several more or less autobiographical and confessional statements. See my chapter in the forthcoming *Psychologist Christian*, edited by Newton Maloney and to be published by Baker Book House; the last chapter in my *Minister on the Spot* (United Church Press, 1970); my reply to Robert BEllah in the January 1973 *Bulletin of the Council on the Study of Religion*, "Purging the soul with the sins, or the risk of Uncle Thomism among the humanists."
6. I. Silverman and A. D. Shulman, "A Conceptual Model of Artifact in Attitude Change Studies," *Sociometry*, 33 (1970), 97-107.
7. Robert Coles, *Children of Crisis: A Study of Courage and Fear* (New York, 1967); *Children of Crisis: The South Moves North* (New York, 1970).
8. *Beyond Belief* (New York, 1970).
9. *History and Human Survival* (New York, 1970).
10. The last is the useful term recommended by Robert Bellah in his important "Christianity and Symbolic Realism," *Journal for the Scientific Study of Religion*, 9 (1970), 89-96. Reprinted in *Beyond Belief* (New York, 1970).
11. Bellah, *ibid.*, p. 93.

PSYCHO-BIOGRAPHY AND THE HISTORIAN OF RELIGIONS:
SOME METHODOLOGICAL SUGGESTIONS

Frank Reynolds

The history of religions (Religionswissenschaft) has traditionally been one of those humanistic disciplines which has maintained a rather high degree of self-consciousness concerning its relationship to the other sciences of man. The leading historians of religion who have attempted to give definition and structure of their own field of study have clearly recognized the necessity of utilizing contributions from other areas of scholarly specialization such as philology, history, anthropology, sociology, and psychology. For example, Joachim Wach, in his classic articulations of the form and scope of the discipline, provided an important position not only for each of these approaches, but for the philosophy of religion and theology as well.[1] Moreover, those who have undertaken the task of recounting the development of the history of religions have given great prominence to the work of scholars who have focused their studies in other disciplines. To cite just one case in point, Mircea Eliade, in his article "History of Religions in Retrospect: 1912-1960," devotes a great deal of attention to the contributions of men such as Max Weber, Emile Durkheim, Lucien Levy-Bruhl, and Sigmund Freud.[2] However in spite of the recognition which their predecessors have given to the role and contribution of other forms of humanistic and social scientific scholarship, contemporary historians of religion have become increasingly aware that changes within their own style of interpretation, and within other fields of study clearly call for a new approach to the problems and possibilities of interdisciplinary encounter. In this paper I will attempt to make some contribution to what Charles Long has called a more "relational" understanding by examining a few recent trends in the history of religions, in the psychoanalytic interpretation of religion, and in the various correspondences between the two.[3] With this background established, I will then turn to a more direct consideration of two particular areas in which historians of religion could profitably utilize some of the methods and insights which have been developed within the psychoanalytic tradition, and specifically within the work of Erik Erikson.

In the development of both the history of religions and the psychoanalytic tradition, the second decade of the 20th century constituted a time of crucial innovation. Though the origins of the "scientific study of religion" have often and correctly been traced to the writings of Max Mueller in the latter half of the 19th century, the publication of Rudolph Otto's *Idea of the Holy* in 1916 marked a shift in paradigms which gave the discipline a new direction and new life. And it was during the same decade that Sigmund Freud published his *Interpretation of Dreams* which was the first in the series of great works through which he established psychoanalysis both as a therapeutic technique and as a tool for the interpretation of culture and religion. Like a number of other important studies which were written at about the same time (for example, Karl Barth's *Commentary on the Epistle of the Romans* in the theological field and Emile Durkheim's *Elementary Forms of Religion* in the sociology of religion), the works of both Otto and Freud marked a strong reaction against the kind of increasingly arid rationalism which had become dominant in the West during the late 19th and early 20th centuries; however, viewed in terms of their positive contributions, Otto and Freud presented very different and in many respects antithetical interpretations of religious experience and life.

As even the most cursory reading of the two authors makes clear, Rudolph Otto understood religion in terms of transcendence, whereas Freud interpreted it in the context of fantasy and projection. Clearly Otto's great contribution is to be found in his phenomenological analysis of the Holy as it was manifest in religious experiences of the classical type. For Otto the Holy was a *sui generis* category which differentiated religion from all other forms of human experience, and could be described only by generating a distinctive vocabulary which included such terms as "ganz andere," "mysterium tremendum," "majestas," and "mysterium fascinosum."[4] By way of contrast Freud's discussions of religion were generally carried on in terms of infantile processes and conflicts which, in his view, produced the fantasies and projections which constituted the religious world. Although Freud left the way open for the kind of "higher reading" of his position which has been proposed by Peter Homans in his recent book, *Theology After Freud*, he himself tended to associate religious fantasies with illusion, and to utilize his concept of projection to bring into question any specifically religious or ontological reference of religious experience and beliefs.[5] Thus a dichotomy was established which has persistently characterized the relationship between the religio-historical and Freudian styles of interpretation. Among historians of religion who have followed Otto in emphasizing transcendence and the sacred, psychoanalytic interpretations have generally been deprecated as an inadequate and even dangerous form of reductionism. And on the other side, among those who have adopted psychoanalytic perspective and have continued to emphasize the dimensions of fantasy and projection, the work of historians of religion has been quite consistently ignored.

Although subsequent historians of religion and psychoanalytic interpreters have remained true to the basic orientations which were established by Otto and Freud, significant advances have been made in both fields. Basically these developments can be characterized in terms of an increasing concern on the part of both historians of religion and psychoanalytic interpreters to deal with questions of cosmological and social order, and, in so doing, to give more serious attention to the phenomena of myth and symbol, of ritual and ethics, and of culture and social organization. Each tradition of interpretation has come at these questions from its own distinctive starting point, but by confronting similar issues and materials, scholars in the two fields have opened up new possibilities for dialogue, real encounter, and mutual stimulation. In the history of religions the drive to move beyond the range of problems which Otto treated as central has been particularly evident in the work of Mircea Eliade and Joachim Wach, while in the psychoanalytic tradition new ground has been broken by Carl Jung and Erik Erikson.

In the work of Eliade and Jung the new concerns are expressed primarily in cosmological terms, and are closely associated with the study of classical forms of mythology and symbolism. In his introduction to *The Sacred and the Profane* Eliade specifically pays his respects to the work of Otto, but goes on to affirm that, in contrast to his German predecessor, he is setting out to discuss not simply the irrational dimensions of the transcendent, or even the relationship between its rational and irrational components, but rather "the sacred in its entirety."[6] And this sets the stage for his study of religion in terms of hierophanies and archetypes, and his various discussions of specific myths and symbols through which the cosmos "speaks" to men, and through which men, in turn, discover the structure and tonality of the world in which they live. On the other hand Jung, starting from a psychoanalytic perspective, develops an interpretation in which fantasy comes to be tested by reality and is gradually transformed into myths and symbols which have a genuine "objective" validity. Thus Jung goes beyond the Freudian view of religion as pure fantasy and projection and affirms a movement from fantasy to the discovery of archetypes, and a closely correlated progression from a developmental mythology to a mythology which has a truly cosmological reference.[7] To be sure the direction from which the two scholars have approached their study of archetypes, myths, and symbols establish crucial differences which prevent any easy assimilation of the two modes of interpretation. However, in contrast to Otto and Freud (who are concerned with religion as transcendence on the one hand, and religion as fantasy or projection on the other) Eliade and Jung share many common interests (clustering around their concerns with an objective or cosmological order, archetype, myth, and symbol) and, as a result, have established an arena within which real dialogue is possible.8

The trend which has led historians of religion and psychoanalytic interpreters into a consideration of similar kinds of issues can also be discerned by considering the works of Joachim Wach and Erik Erikson. Like Eliade, Wach began with the historian of religion's characteristic recognition of the primacy of transcendence in the religious life, and like Eliade he sought to broaden the scope of interpretation by focusing attention on the cosmological dimension of religion as this had been expressed in mythic and symbolic (and, in his case, dogmatic and doctrinal) forms. However, Wach went still further by emphasizing the importance of supplementing the study of theoretical expressions of religion such as myth and doctrine with an equally serious study of practical (i.e., cultic, meditational, and ethical) expressions, and also with a careful study of the communal and sociological forms in which religion has become institutionalized. Following a different path Erikson began with the psychoanalyst's characteristic focus on infancy and childhood, and on the primacy of fantasy and play, but soon went beyond this kind of concern and began the task of interpreting developed mythic and symbolic conceptions of the world, the role which ritual and ethics play in individual and social life, and the way in which myths, symbols, and rites interact with the on-going experience of particular peoples. Again, as in the case of Eliade and Jung, Wach and Erikson remained faithful to the religio-historical and psychoanalytic traditions in which they were nurtured, but at the same time they extended those traditions in such a manner that common problems were posed, and an even broader and potentially more fruitful arena of discussion was established.

In very recent years further developments in the two areas of study have led to an increasingly comprehensive correspondence between the kinds of materials and problems being considered. More specifically, historians of religion have begun to examine the religious aspects of popular culture much more seriously than they had done in the past, and to give much more attention to the elements of spontaneity, popular imagination and fantasy, while psychoanalytically oriented interpreters have begun to deal more directly and sympathetically with classical religious expressions, and to take much greater account of the religious dimensions of transcendence. Within the history of religions Mircea Eliade, in a number of different essays, has dealt with the religious element which he finds embedded in various literary and artistic expressions of contemporary imagination and fantasy. And beyond this, a number of younger historians of religions are beginning to study, *as fully religious forms*, the more popular, spontaneous aspects of primitive and ancient traditions, the vast storehouse of folklore and popular stories in which imagination and fantasy play an important role, and a variety of liminal, iconoclastic, and even libidinal religious figures such as the trickster.[9] On the psychoanalytic side the trend toward a more sympathetic treatment of the great classical forms, and the new openness to the dimensions of transcendence and soteriology in religion, are perhaps most vividly evident in the work of Erik Erikson. In his discussion of the various "developmental tasks" which punctuate the human life cycle, Erikson gives great importance to a final stage which he associates with the achievement of personal integrity, and he describes the stage of integrity in language which is meaningful in a religio-historical context (for Erikson a *homo religiosus*, in the full sense. is one who actualizes the goal of integrity at a comparatively early period in his life). And in his last two major works, *Young Man Luther* and *Gandhi's Truth*, Erikson carries through studies of great religious leaders in which their experiences with realities which they considered to be ultimate or transcendent are treated with both seriousness and empathy. Moreover, Peter Homans has gone well beyond the limits of Erikson's position by highlighting certain strands within the psychoanalytic tradition (beginning with some suggestive references in the works of Freud himself) in which projection and fantasy are presented in such a way that they can be explicitly and positively correlated with the experience of transcendence.[10]

Assuming that our way of reconstructing the development of the two traditions has merit, it should be clear that the customary charges of reductionism leveled by historians of religion against the psychoanalytic approach, and the equally traditional neglect of religio-historical work by psychoanalytic interpreters, are rapidly losing the grounds which, at an earlier period, gave them support. There remain, of course, basic differences in starting points and perspective, and these differences will certainly persist for many years to come. Within the history of religions attention continues to be focused primarily on culturally significant religious discoveries, and on the founding, structuring and development of religious traditions. And this makes it necessary and proper that a certain primacy continue to be given to the dimension of transcendence and hierophany, that the ordering which is manifest in myth and doctrine, in cult and ethics, and in the patterning of religious communities be viewed within that context, and that spontaneity and fantasy be recognized as a further dimension of the religious life which is closely associated with the phenomena of renewal and creativity. Within the psychoanalytic tradition, on the other hand, primacy continues to be given to the processes of personal development, thus making it quite natural and proper for psychoanalytic interpreters to take as their starting point a consideration of the spontaneity, play and projection which are especially characteristic of infancy and childhood, and to build on the insights gained in that context to interpret the more established ordering of the world in which a man or society lives, and to explore, beyond this, the way in which transcendence comes to be more fully actualized in the "higher" experiences of integration and salvation. However what is important to note is that when the differences between the two styles of interpretation are viewed in this way, the relationship between them becomes one in which a creative tension can be discerned, and therefore one in which real dialogue and mutual enrichment are possible.

There are clearly a variety of ways in which both religio-historical and psychoanalytic interpreters could benefit from a self-conscious grappling with the methods and insights which have been developed in the other area. It should be quite obvious from what has already been said that both groups could quite profitably explore the very different ways in which those who have worked within the other field have dealt with the religious dimensions of transcendence and soteriology, of order as it is expressed in myth, symbol, et.al., and of spontaneity and fantasy.[11] But in order to carry on the discussion at a more specific level I will speak directly as a historian of religions, and will suggest two closely related areas of research in which a creative assimilation of some of the concerns and methods developed within the psychoanalytic tradition could be extremely helpful in developing a more adequate style of religio-historical interpretation. I have chosen to focus on the study of myth and symbol on the one hand, and the study of sacred biography on the other, both because these are topics which are of great importance and interest to historians of religion and also because they constitute areas in which the work of Erik Erikson has a special relevance and significance.

Historians of religion have long been engaged in the study of myths and symbols, and the way in which those myths and symbols have provided a basic grounding for the life of traditional cultures; and in the process they have acquired a whole battery of very useful methodological tools. However, by taking more seriously into account certain key aspects of the approach which Erik Erikson has developed, particularly in his *Childhood and Society*, at least two important new dimensions could be incorporated into the established patterns of religio-historical research. In the first place, by giving much more careful and sophisticated attention to the various points at which a given mythic complex is correlated with particular phases and details of the life cycle of the people who remember and accept it, historians of religion could develop significant new insights into its religious and psycho-social structure and functions. Though this approach can be fully applied only in situations where it is possible to gather

extensive information concerning both the mythic traditions of
a given group and the details of the particular patterning of
the life cycle of the people within it, a number of such cases
do exist and they should be exploited to the full.[12] And
secondly, Erikson's insights into the process of interaction
through which a new generation simultaneously assimilates and adapts
the mythic, symbolic, and ritual tradition which it receives from
the preceding generation could greatly aid historians of religion
as they strive to develop more effective methods for dealing
with the very vexing problems of religious change. Some important suggestions for exploring the ways in which changes in mythic
and ritual patterns occur in traditional societies have been made
from an anthropological perspective by W.E.H. Stanner in his
classic study of the Murumbutu tribe in Australia, but Erikson's
psychoanalytically oriented work opens up still other possibilities which deserve to be considered with equal seriousness.[13]

Though historians of religion have given a definite preeminence to the study of myths and symbols, they have also dealt
extensively with sacred biographies (i.e., the idealized accounts
of the lives or acts of founders, saints, martyrs, cultural and
national heroes, etc.) and have worked through a variety of ways
of interpreting their development and of understanding their
meaning.[14] But in this area, too, a serious encounter with the
work being done within the psychoanalytic tradition, and particularly the psycho-historical studies carried through by Erik
Erikson, could lead to deeper insights, and to a more dynamic
style of religio-historical interpretation. It is of course
true that a dearth of appropriate data makes any meaningful
psycho-historical study of most of the personages who were the
subjects of the great classical sacred biographies (e.g. Lao
Tse, Sakyamuni, and Jesus, as well as less clearly historical
figures such as Rama and Krishna) simply impossible. However,
beginning with the acceptance of this rather obvious fact, it
would be both possible and fruitful for historians of religion
to explore, through a more developed kind of psycho-historical
method, the way in which various classical models have operated,

along with other psychological, sociological and religious factors, to inform and mold the lives of subsequent religious personalities.15 And it would be both possible and fruitful to go beyond this to explore the ways in which the life experiences of these later figures, their own self-interpretations, and the ways in which they came to be idealized by their followers conformed to the earlier paradigms, adapted them, and, in some very rare cases, established new models which were truly original and distinctive.16 Actually, so far as I am aware, no religio-historical studies which attempt to analyze these kinds of processes have yet been published; however there is a growing interest in the subject, and several significant projects are presently nearing completion.17

These two rather specific examples of areas in which the emerging correspondences between the history of religions and psychoanalytic modes of interpretation might be profitably exploited are intended to be only illustrative and suggestive. Nevertheless, by moving beyond a purely theoretical and historical disucssion and by pointing to areas in which particular research programs and projects could be developed, I have intended to suggest that it is primarily through such research (rather than prolonged interdisciplinary "dialogue") that further progress can actually be achieved.

FOOTNOTES

1. For a full presentation of Wach's position see his *Religionswissenschaft: Prolegomena zu ihrer wissenschafts theoritschen Grundlegung*, Veröffentlichungen des Forschungsinstits für vergleichende Religionsgeschichte an der Universität Leipzig, no. 10 (Leipzig: J.C. Hinrichs, 1924).
2. *Quest* (Chicago and London: University of Chicago, 1969) pp. 12-36.
3. Charles Long, "The Meaning of Religion in the Contemporary Study of the History of Religions." *Criterion* II, 2 (Spring, 1963) pp. 23-26.
4. Otto attempted to relate man's religious experience to his rational capacities through his discussion of what he called "schematization"; however even his strongest admirers have recognized that his efforts at this point did not meet with great success.
5. Peter Homans, *Theology after Freud* (Indianapolis and New York: Bobbs Merrill, 1970).
6. Mircea Eliade, *The Sacred and the Profane*, (New York, Harcourt, Brace & Co., 1957), p. 10.
7. This interpretation of Jung's position is developed by Peter Homans in a paper entitled "Nostalgia and Distance: Comments on Eliade's Contribution to Contemporary Self-Understanding" to be published in a forthcoming issue of the *Journal of Religion*.
8. In this connection it is interesting to point to Eliade's quite regular participation in the yearly Eranos meetings in Switzerland which have been attended mainly by scholars in the Jungian tradition. See, for example, his several contributions in the *Eranos Jahrbuch*.
9. The increasing interest in studies of this kind is reflected in comments made by Jonathan Z. Smith, "The Wobbling Pivot" *Journal of Religion*, iii, 2 (April, 1972) pp. 134-149.
10. Peter Homans, "The Problem of Projection: Clue to Rethinking the Psychoanalytic Approach to Religion" to appear in a forth-

coming volume entitled *Psychoanalysis and Catholicism*, ed. Benjamin Wolman (New York: Internation University Press, 1972). As Homans points out in his article, Erikson, though he was obviously concerned to deal sympathetically with the so-called "higher" forms of religious experience, left the dominant Freudian imagery of fantasy and projection basically unchallenged.

11. To cite just one example of the kind of work which is presently being done in this latter area, Ed Piper, a doctoral candidate at the Divinity School of the University of Chicago, is now in the process of writing a dissertation in which religio-historical and psychological (including psychoanalytic) methods are being used to carry through a study of the North American Indian trickster figure; and what is particularly important, the study aims both at enhancing our present understanding of the trickster as a mythological, folkloric figure and, at the same time, seeks to advance our understanding of play and spontaneity as a psychological and psycho-social phenomena.

12. An interesting attempt to pursue this line of investigation in the context of West African religion has been made by Robert Pelton in an unpublished seminar paper on the Dogon trickster. An equally interesting effort to apply some of Erikson's insights to the interpretation of a mythic-symbolic complex coming from a society about which we have practically no empirical sociological data (and to do so with appropriate methodological restraint) has been made by Lucy Bregman in another unpublished paper entitled: "The Figure of Tiamat."

13. *On Aboriginal Religion*, Ocenaia Monograph No. 11 (Sydney: University of Sydney, N.d.).

14. For instance, see the recent study of a Japanese Buddhist example by Joseph Kitagawa entitled "Master and Savior" which appears in *Studies of Esoteric Buddhism and Tantrism* (Koyasan, Japan: Koyasan University, 1965).

15. Though he works within a very narrow historical frame of reference it is worth noting that Harold Kahn, in his recent *Monarchy Through the Emperor's Eyes* (Cambridge, Mass. Howard

University, 1971) provides a very interesting and suggestive analysis of the way in which the traditional models of Chinese sacral kingship are implicated in the development of the personal and public life style of an individual Chinese ruler.

16. Writing from the point of view of an anthropologist Kenelm Burridge touches upon many of these issues in his brilliant study of a series of prophetic leaders of a cargo-cult movement in Melanasia. See *Mambu* (Harper Torchbook; New York and Evanston: Harper and Row, 1970).

17. In his University of Chicago dissertation on Cardinal John Henry Newman, Donald Capps gives considerable attention to the role which was played in Newman's religious and psychological development by the martyrdom tradition in Christianity, and more specifically by the sacred biography of his personally chosen patron, Saint Philip Neri. Other directly relevant dissertations which are still in process include one by Joanne Punzo Waghorne on C. Rojagopalacari entitled "Images of Dharma: The Indian Personality in Change," and a second by Timothy Jensen entitled "Sri Ramakrishra and the Quest for Spiritual Vocation."

ACEDIA: THE DECLINE OF DESIRE AS THE ULTIMATE LIFE CRISIS

Bert Kaplan

Acedia, the fourth of the cardinal sins (also Sloth), emerges into Western consciousness in the writings of the desert fathers of the fourth century. It is described as a state resulting from the isolation and loneliness of the hermitage in the desert, a fatigue attributable to the conditions of withdrawal and fasting of the Christian retreat. The word itself comes from the Greek term translated as "not-caring state." In its earlier usage it seemed to be reserved for the special malaise of monks who in the midst of their monastic life fell into lassitude, laxness and apathy. Acedia is both a failure to find the world and its activities interesting, and a religious hopelessness which points in the direction of the collapse of the optimistic transcendental structures of Christian life.

Chaucer in "The Parson's Tale" gives a conventional account of Acedia in the Parson's sermonizing on the Seven Sins. Acedia ...takes from a man the love of all goodness.

> ...it does everything sadly and with peevishness, slackness, and false excusing, and with slovenliness and unwillingness; for which the Book says: 'Accursed be he that serveth God negligently.'
>
> Now certainly this foul sin of acedia is also a great enemy to the livelihood of the body; for it makes no provision for temporal necessity; for it wastes, and it allows things to spoil, and it destroys all worldly wealth by its carelessness.
>
> Then arises the dread of beginning to do any good deeds; for certainly, he that is inclined toward sin, he thinks it is so great an enterprise to start any works of goodness. He tells himself in his heart that the circumstances having to do with goodness are so wearisome and burdensome to endure, that he dare not undertake any such works, as says Saint Gregory.
>
> Now enters despair, which is despair of the mercy of God, and comes sometimes of too extravagant sorrows and sometimes of too great fear: for the victim imagines that he has done so much sin that it will avail him not.

to repent and forego sin; because of which fear he abandons his heart ot every kind of sin, as Saint Augustine says.

I am calling your attention to Acedia because it is a good starting place for a discussion of the category Desire, the relation of Desire to its objects, its precarious situation in the world, the circumstances of its decline and finally the possibilities of its restoration.

In Plato's *Symposium* the participants at the banquet make speeches in praise of love, setting out the importance of love in human affairs, the necessity of being careful to love the right objects in the right way, the function of love in inspiring good behavior and in bringing all men and all things together. Socrates in his usual fashion undercuts all of the previous talk by proposing to discuss the truth about what love is rather than praising it or its effects. His idea is that he who loves something must necessarily be "in want" of that thing, that love is therefore to be properly understood as lack. This definition becomes pivotal for the general comprehension of man in philosophical anthropology, in economics and sociology and in theology. It proposes that man exists in a condition of material, social, intellectual, and spiritual privation; in Sartres' phrase, that he is an "homme de besoin."

Modern psychologists speak frequently of needs but treat need as something, like a certain quantity of energy to be got rid of, rather than the absence of something. Sartre says that "Desire is the presence of an absence." This lapse of historical memory, is the cause of endless confusion when the method of empirical observation is brought to bear on "something" that is an absence. Taking the Platonic understanding of man as Desire as my starting point I have undertaken what might be described as a brief meditation on Desire. In the present paper I shall focus on the problems or difficulties that Desire has and particularly on the conditions of the decline of Desire and its confrontation with its own non-Being.

I shall not apologize for the poetic "language" of desire that is being used here. There is a considerable tradition in

Western philosophy and literature which treats Desire as the fundamental human category not only as it defines the human reality, but also as the constituting force of the organic world. It appears that all living things have in common the condition that they can exist only by transactions with their environments in which they acquire nutriments and convert that which is other into themselves. Any relief from the general rule of organic insufficiency seems to be only temporary since life uses up whatever it manages to acquire.

Kierkegaard's aesthetic anti-hero speaks of the world as "desire's twin." The world belongs to desire in the sense that it consists of objects of interest to desire. It may be that the "known" or "experienced" world of the Kantian transcendental ego might more easily be regarded as the desired world with a consequent change of emphasis from cognitive to conative categories. However, the question of the relative claims to primacy of these two and of which includes the other is not our concern here. There is substantial philosophic support coming most notably from such figures as Spinoza, Leibniz, Schopenhauer, and Nietzsche in favor of the primacy of Desire.

It is a temptation to suggest a grand simplification; namely that the person be understood as desire, and the experienced world as desire's objects. This is a radicalization of the ontological difference between self and world but at the same time suggests the nature of the unity of these separate poles and their mutual dependence and coherence. The self is a ghostly self consisting of absences. It is the self of the non-being of things that Sartre speaks of, something like the modern physicist's realm of anti-matter. The world is its mirror image and consists materially of those things that are absent in the self.

For Desire that question of good "object relations" is crucial. Almost the sole criterion for psychological health is whether or not our objects are good. If we like them, want them, find them interesting, love them, our success in acquiring them or possessing them is secondary. Desire's relationship to its objects is so close that not to welcome them as good is sickness and is the sign of a mixed up psyche. The confusion that what seems "so lovely fair that my senses ache at thee" is in fact corrupt and foul is such a basic crack in the world that it can be understood as psychosis. Melanie Klein speaks of the "paranoid position" and the "depressive position" to indicate the seriousness of the disturbance that it creates.

The idea of "the reality principle" represents a completely different understanding of the world, which while it may be understood to contain satisfying or potentially satisfying objects, is in its main lines indifferent or hostile to desire. Rather than being desire's twin, it is the hard rock that stands between desire and its satisfying objects--it is often a terrain from which satisfying objects are absent or lost. Psychoanalytic theory suggests that this world comes as a surprise to desire.

The world that feeds and provides care and shelter for the babe in the womb and at its mother's breast unfortunately turns into a hostile one to the weaned child. In varying degrees its good objects are at least partially withdrawn and provided only on a conditional basis. While many children, sadly, do meet great severity, privation, and harshness early in life, I believe the full seriousness of weaning is ordinarily encountered, in this country and in this period, by the young adult who has recently left his or her family, that most womb-like of human institutions and has "come into the world." Students report that the sense of being weaned from family care develps slowly over a period of years and that it is experienced partly as a function of their own desire for independence and freedom. Nevertheless, the full force of the fact of being alone in an indifferent world is a good deal more than they have bargained for. The crisis of this period of life may be regarded as a re-experiencing of the anxieties of the earlier period of weaning, but this time without the support of the family.

We may compare this view of the period of the so-called "identity crisis" with that of Erik Erikson. The comparison bears on the question of whether the structure of privation that

I am delineating is omnipresent. Is it the dominant aspect of every moment of life? Or, as in Freudian theory, do one set of problems give way to a subsequent set? Are the problems of the oral stage replaced replaced twenty years later, for example, through the achievement of genital sexuality?

Erikson's position seems to be half way between. He says that the "late adolescent crisis...can hark back to the very earliest crisis of life--trust or mistrust toward existence as such." He sees the young man as one who "faces as permanent the trust problem." However, in its essentials the identity crisis is simply that of the problem of the establishment of a firm identity with all of the Freudian connotations of potency, force, activity, productivity, and generativity. It seems as though the doubts of the earlier period have been overcome or left behind with the question becoming "to do it if you can, and if you can, to do it." The mastery of the problems of the identity crisis is in a new-found strength and maturity. Erikson divides the Freudian achievement of genital potency among several of his developmental stages, treating separately the achievements of intimacy and generativity, but the Freudian understanding underlies what he says. The important thing is whether the young adult reaches a point in which his actions are the expression of the potency and strength of his maturity rather than of the weakness and insufficiency of his life up to that point. It corresponds to the Nietzschean sense that life should be lived out of the plenitude of its being and as an overflowing of its powers.

The viewpoint of this paper is that there is no end to insufficiency and longing and that the sense of power reached by the young man on the basis of his initially successful sexual and social experiences are not images adequate to the problems of human existence. Genital sexuality even when it is expanded by Erikson to include the capacity for intimacy and generativity is still only another partial solution. The mature ripening of the human spirit must surely come in another form than that of the arrival of the full physical powers of the individual. The problems of the oral phase and of the relationship of desire to the world are not to be settled in this manner.

In the world of the weaned person the objects of desire are lost, absent, difficult to reach, or in the possession of someone else. It is the world of Labor that follows the expulsion from the Garden of Eden. It is the time of the search or hunt, or of waiting and hoping. It is the Marxian world of scarcity which leads to universal competition because even those who "have" must protect what they have won from those who have not. One might call it the world of the lean and hungry, where desire is intense and the hunt is urgent. Despite the suffering and frustration and the empty landscape, it is a moment when desire and the world are both strong and are firmly planted in the natural order. In this world there is no doubt about the goodness of the object sought, the problem desire faces is its absence. Even if the objects at hand become bad, the absent good object continues to be believed in.

Let us suppose that the child who has known the goodness of his mother's love is orphaned. He has an understanding of that goodness that he will never lose. But goodness itself may be lost, perhaps forever. The child grieves his loss, but hopes for its restoration. Hope becomes the medium or form in which desire is kept intact. The absence is suffered but in a basic way the individual's relation to the world is intact and perhaps even strengthened. The good object is also intact and believed in, even though it is nowhere in view. The child usually graduates from the mode of hoping to that of actively seeking. Hunting in one of its many forms seems to describe this activity. If his hunting is unsuccessful he may try to construct the good object out of his need much as one might build a house to keep one sheltered. Or he may give up the active search and live by cherishing in memory the goodness he once knew.

. There are may important words in our language and presumably in others that indicate the various forms taken by desire. They range from remembering to expecting, from waiting to chasing, from looking, to listening to touching, from thinking and imagining to creating and constructing. A considerable part of the answer to the question of what a person is doing can be given in terms of the form of his desire rather than of its object. We can look forward to an inquiry which provides a picture of the diverse forms of desire and consider them in relation to the nature of desire's terrain. The kind of "waiting" that Beckett's characters do, for example, has as *its* twin the bleak landscape in which nothing of significance happens or can happen. The waiting is for a miracle and in *Waiting for Godot*, desire has been educated by long experience not to believe in, or hope for miracles.

The Beckett characters and Beckett world seem to exist at the farthest reach of desire's tether. Suffering and hope have both disappeared but there is still a "waiting without hope" hidden within which is the keenest "hunger" and desire for Godot, just as Beckett's painting of the "disconsolate" landscape has as its twin the sharpest need. It does seem, however, that in these plays the terminus of desire is contemplated, described, considered, and perhaps anticipated. In a word, there is a confrontation with desire's decline and disappearance.

Before this happens, the career of desire may take that intensified form we call suffering. This phenomenon is filled with ambiguities and even mysteries. Taken most simply it can be understood as the absence of desire's objects when desire is at its strongest and most needful. It can be taken as a sign that life is strong and intense. However, a new and surprising element sometimes appears to complicate the simple picture being painted here. Suffering sometimes and perhaps always comes to have a positive aspect and itself becomes the desired object. The Graham Greene novels, for example, provide the image of the person who can no longer suffer; who suffers the absence of suffering because there is no longer anything he desires. But in a more mundane way there are the familiar patients at the psychiatrist's office who appear to make a career of their suffering and if not to enjoy it at least to have all of their interest centered in it.

In this respect suffering may be said to have become the object of their desire.

Freudian theory understands the desire for suffering as the desire of a "guilty creature" for punishment. Caught between a murderous id and a punishing conscience, ego turns to self-torment. The phenomenon points in the direction of the Freudian formulation of the death instinct which also it is proposed takes the form of hatred toward desired objects.

I am not sure that such a complicated notion as the desire for suffering is credible or even intelligible. There is not time here to do much more than to raise this question. The form of intelligibility that seems most immediately acceptable in the context of the present discussion is that the desire for suffering, taken as the desire for desire, is credible as arising only in the situation in which desire is endangered or lost; a distinction being made between suffering and the desire for suffering. Thus when the Graham Greene character says to his confessor "Father, help me. I cannot suffer," his cry comes as desire's last cry before acedia.

The crisis of Desire is clear enough. There appear to be several aspects to this crisis. One is that Desire's situation is a situation of Scarcity. What is needed is simply not there, or not there in the quantity wanted. In Norman O. Brown's phrase, "There is only one story--that somebody was starved." This phrase suggests a certain desperation to the situation of desire. Desire exists but is not fed adequately. A question arises as to whether starvation endangers it. It is obvious that the absence of "food" simply makes desire more intense. It is less clear how starvation might lead to the decline of desire since considered abstractly, human life belongs to the realm of organic life and cannot exist except in the terms of the organic, that is, by ingestion of food. Without food there is no viability even of desire. At what moment does the increase of privation lead to the decay of desire? It is unclear what the principle is that produces the change. It may be that is is a question of the kind of food that is available so that it is bad food that leads to loss of appetitie. The Lestrygonians section of Joyce's *Ulysses* makes marvelous capital of the bad egg, the spoiled fish, the diet of "marge and potatoes" that undermines the constitution, the vegetarian's unsatisfying nut steak, poisonous though attractive berries, and the unsanitary Burton restaurant the grossness of which leads Bloom to think "Couldn't eat a morsel here.... Get out of this." Bloom contrasts the food of the gods, "quaffing nectar, golden dishes, all ambrosial" with the "tanner lunch we have--boiled mutton, carrots and turnips, bottle of Allsop." Bloom suggests that it is essential to know the difference between good and bad food and that the eater must be discriminating and careful about what he puts into his mouth instead of gorging himself on whatever is at hand.

The "bad egg" and the "spoiled fish" are potent symbols of the puzzling and contradictory nature of the bad object. If it is an object for us at all it should be on the basis of our desire for it and its goodness. But if it turns out to be an "apple of Sodom" what is lost is not simply the object but the appetite itself. Why are the bad egg and the unpalatable nourishment so destructive to desire? The ordinary understanding is that the desired object is appropriated and converted into the self; if, however, the self turns into what it has eaten, the goodness or badness of its food is crucial to it.

The decline of desire is not only the response to privation with the feeling of loss, disappointment or discouragement. There is the more radical possibility of a terminus in which not the object but Desire itself is endangered. One opposite of Desire is Fulfillment; another, however, is Indifference. I suggest that the true crisis of life is the confrontation with the prospect of Indifference.

The crisis of desire and its confrontation with the possibility of its non-being is the subject of a very strong analysis by Soren Kierkegaard. He called this coming face to face with the self's terminus, despair. It is a sickness unto death in the way that falling can be understood as the process of dying. Kierkegaard's great idea was that this kind of dying was not an event which occurs and is then finished but is a form of existing which continues to that each moment is a moment of dying or of contracting the sickness.

For Kierkegaard's aesthetic man, the form of dying was not dying because of the lack of what one desired, but rather being tired and bored with what one has--plus the realization that all mundane objects were very much like each other so that nothing could be achieved by changing them. It is not that earthly food is harmful or poisonous but that from the point of view of spirit its nourishment is limited. The aesthetic crisis is that which begins in the desire for the interesting, ends in boredom, ennui and lassitude. The danger to Desire is described here as fulfillment. The diagnosis of the sickness is the Christian one that a vast sin of omission has been committed--the sin of not loving the Divine.

The transition from the most intense and acute suffering to the "not caring state" of Acedia is one of the two most radical transformations possible in life. If, following Kierkegaard we think of the transition from the non-being to the being of the self as a New Birth, the transition from the self's being (as Desire) to non-being, is a Death. This Death is not the despair at not yet being born but rather a loss of whatever being it had managed to acquire. In the Platonic and Christian traditions Being itself is eternal and therefore not subject to loss or gain. Man, however, can acquire being, as in Kierkegaard's analysis, and I would like to add here, can lose it as in the fall into the indifference, carelessness, thoughtlessness, negligence, and lassitude of the not-caring condition of acedia.

A few concluding speculative remarks may be attempted to suggest the historical movement relating to acedia and the decline of desire. However, I will continue to assume that the basic structures discussed here are primordial and to date at least have not been historically altered in any fundamental way. If acedia emerges into Western consciousness in the context of monasticism it has its roots in antiquity. On the one hand, we find the other-worldliness of Neo-Platonism and Christianity as a reaction to the physical grossness and world-weariness of Rome (as pictured in the *Satyricon*, both of Petronius and Fellini). On the other, there is the Aristotelean realism and adhesion to the world of substance and particularities. Monasticism, in its early medieval form, can be connected with the mysticism and asceticism of Neo-Platonism. But monasticism was not without its critics and its withdrawal from the world into prayer and contemplation seemed to many to lead away from reality. There is an ample Christian literature dealing with the dangers of monastic isolation. It is perhaps too large a step to link this literature to the opposition to monasticism. It did seem to many, however, that the withdrawal into contemplation and meditation could lead to the condition of loss of interest in the world, to melancholy and despair. Cassian, for example, speaks of "penal despair," "dejection, listlessness and wearyness of heart," that can appear in the monastery. Ultimately the tension within Christianity was resolved in favor of Aristotelian nominalism and the monastic orders themselves became worldy and active along with the rest of the church. At the historical moment of Erikson's *Luther*, this worldliness of the church is understood as Gluttony and Luther's sense of "horror at his own avariciousness and sadistic orality" is regarded as the condition for melancholia. The consequence is a kind of *anorexia nervosa*--a loss of appetite. This is a more sophisticated view of acedia than the one I have inclined toward which emphasizes the predicaments of the "oral" stage and proposes that we never get over them. I personally find the simpler view more convincing, but I am happy to be instructed by Dr. Erikson on this point.

The return of the good appetitie is one image of the restoration of health. Eating with gusto and enjoyment and valuing what one is eating is the symbol that the patient is well again, as is his feeling hungry and wanting to eat. It means simultaneously that both Desire and its objects are accepted. Such a restoration, if it is more than temporary, must mean that a change has occurred. Psychoanalytic thinking seems to link this change to what has been called the education of desire. Through its repeated experiences of loss and recovery Desire learns to limit its greed and to become more reasonable, and to develop a certain limited optimism that lost objects will sometimes return. It also learns that its own activities can influence that situation and that it can actually create out of its own efforts objects of value.

This Freudian understanding seems however, to be a mild, almost feeble climax to the career of Desire. Christian thought especially as it is influenced by Platonism provides a much more exuberant and potent image of restoration, namely the elevation of desire. The problem about loving objects is that they are only objects and the nourishment they provide is both insufficient and temporary. While we may endow these objects with the attributes of divinity as Proust's heroes do, sooner or later their mundanity is revealed. If Desire is to be recovered it must be on the basis of the discovery of that which is worthy to be desired without reservation. Desire must find its destination in the Divine. This does not mean the abandonment of all mundane objects although in Christian monasticism and asceticism it took this form. It does involve loving these objects in a different way. It involves a loosening of ties to particular loved objects and the emergence of a relationship to the world taken as a whole and to the reality of the creation of that world.

ERIKSON'S ORIENTATION AS PROCESS PHILOSOPHY

Walter H. Capps

> "*Mutual activation* is the crux of the matter; for human ego strength, while employing all means of testing reality, depends from stage to stage upon a network of mutual influences within which the person actuates others even as he is actuated, and within which the person is 'inspired with active properties,' even as he so inspired others. This is *ego actuality*."
>
> — Erik Erikson, from
> *Insight and Responsibility*

This paper consists of a series of related suggestions, all designed to identify some of the conceptual and structural features of Erik Erikson's psychology (and philosophy) of religion. The starting point is the observation that when Erikson directs personality theory toward an understanding of religion, he treats the *ego* (rather than id or superego) as the crucial linking term. This focus wasn't dictated by Erikson's Freudian legacy, nor is it very common in post-Freudian inquiry, particularly, in neo-Freudian analyses of religion. Erikson's preoccupation with ego as mediator between two dynamic realities gives his orientation a "process" cast. This characteristic is apparent in Erikson's fascination with cycles (as in *Identity and the Life Cycle*), developmental stages, instances of growth, motion, transition, movement, etc. Like process thinkers before him, Erikson is interested in the way in which processes are formed. In all process philosophy, a logos principle is called upon to regulate flux. Erikson looks to the ego to perform this regulative role, then applies his findings in both individual and corporate terms. Finally, the science of psycho-history becomes a product of the combination of interests we have identified, for psycho-history implies that a process is influenced and regulated by individual ego mediation.

Freud, Lifton, and Brown

This ego-centric bias constitutes a departure from Freud's attitude toward religion. Certainly, like Erikson, Freud sought balance and harmony between the three components of the personality. Healthy personal development required that psychological tension be successfully controlled. This implied that ego, id, and superego be harmonized with one another. But when addressing himself to the subject of religion, Freud's prime intention was not to harmonize the personality, but, rather, to provide a psycho-genetic account of man's belief in God. He saw in religion the postulation of warrants, sanctions, and authority for personal attitude and behavior. Thus, in his portrayals of religion, Freud concentrated on the constitution of the superego (defining superego as "the moral factor which dominates the ego"). His contention was that religion is a product of deception and illusion, stimulated by the constructive capacities of the superego. When analyzing religion, Freud was strikingly superego-centric. Erikson, as we shall note, is disposed another way.

Before developing Erikson's position, we should look at other contemporary psychologists and psychoanalysts whose attitudes toward religion have been formed within the Freudian school. Robert Jay Lifton's recent work on "protean man," for example, provides an intriguing contrast. Whereas Freud forcused on superego while giving a psycho-genetic account of religion, Lifton concentrates on what happens to the self (as well as to ideological stances) when the superego is no longer functioning effectively. For Lifton's "protean man," the shifting boundaries in the conceptions of the relationships of life to death make it difficult, if not impossible, to sustain a sustained pattern of overarching meaning. In Freud's approach, religious meaning was certainly accessible and attainable, but its authenticity could not be confirmed objectively. For Lifton's "protean man," the overarching system of warrants, sanctions, and justification is absent. Lifton is concerned to trance the consequences in individual and corporate behavior. Protean man is a modern personality type whose identity is flexible, tentative, and impermanent, and who lacks location and direction.

Though he doesn't work out the implications for religion in detail, Lifton's attitude is a variation on the original Freudian theme: religion is given place precisely at the point at which the individual seeks warrants or sanctions for his attitude and behavior. Appropriately, Freud associated religion with conscience. And, when the conceptual eleborations occur, the links between religion and the absence of an effective ideology are made explicit. All such associations rest on two assumptions: (1) that religious matters can be translated, more or less, into psychological terms, and (2) that the translation can be effected through a concentration of the constitution of the superego. There are hints in Lifton's writings that "protean man" could become "post-protean" if he could only find a way to renew his bond with the "underlying symbolic matrix" of human meaning, In Lifton's view, "protean man" has become id-oriented because his superego-orientational capacities have been diminished and foreshortened.

Norman O. Brown, on the other hand, offers a portrayal of the religious personality wherein an id-orientation is both deliberate and celebrated. In Brown's view, religion pertains to the discovery, facilitation, and channeling of deep-seated libidinal energy, or raw motivational human power. Religion's chief associations are with sexuality, not with ideology, for the ideological dimension serves as a threat to full, vibrant, and healthy religious life.

In working out this schema, Brown returns to the fundamental Freudian dilemma of the conflict between basic subjective instincts and constructive objective compulsions, and locates that conflict intra-subjectively. Following Geza Roheim, Brown is impressed by the case for "man's neotenic retardation and biologically delayed maturity" and is compelled by the prospect that culture functions to keep infantile urges repressed. In Roheim's view, culture is a defense mechanism, since culture and neuroses are products of the same psychological syndrome. It follows, therefore, that the movement toward maturity consists in regaining the "paradise lost" of infancy? Maturation implies this since the child within each person is frustrated by the substitutuinary adult. Put in another way, the desire for happiness is in conflict with reality. The compulsions of the pleasure principle are opposed to the dictates of the reality principle. Consequently, in Brown's translation of Roheim's insights, the essence of man's being is repressed. The true essence of man, for Brown, lies in "infantile sexuality." "Only in the unconscious does the pleasure principle reign supreme." "The eternal child in us is frustrated by the tyranny of genital organization." Thus, in the clash between pleasure and reality principles, libidinal resources must be tapped so that the pleasure principle will be adhered to. The only remedy is the enunciation --rather than the renunciation--of bodily desires. Only in this way can one experience a rebirth, indeed, a new birth. Religion, like creativity, is conceived predominantly through the rediscovery of the id.

The subtle differences between these several approaches can be detected in the personality types which each holds up for examination and, sometimes, for emulation. Lifton's examples are contrast persons, those whose relationships with other persons are subject to dramatic role diffusions: students, who have suddenly become mentors; sons, not yet fathers, who undertake to edify and embellish fathers; subjects of authority who, sometimes unwittingly, undertake to rewrite the canons of authority; survivors of Hiroshima, living as though they were dead; the listless American soldiers in the Vietnam War, fighting for principles they neither understand nor appreciate. Lifton applies Jean-Paul Sartre's description:

> I left behind me a young man who did not have time to be my father, and who could now be my son. Was it a good thing or a bad? I don't know. But I readily subscribe to the verdict of an eminent psychoanalyst, I have no superego.

All such superego-less persons are protean--protean because the lack of a compelling overarching meaning structure prompts them toward programmatic tentativeness and flexibility. Accordingly,

Lifton's research is directed toward characterizing the ideological breakdowns which prompt or allow the development of the protean character. He has ambivalent feelings toward protean man, at once applauding his intentions and yet prophesying that his goals will not be accomplished. His conviction is that no one can finally endure the absence of a sustaining superego. Eventually, protean man will make up for the lack by devising or making up his own symbolic system.

Whereas Lifton's examples are petulant sons who exercise a symbolic form of fatherlessness, Brown's examples are orphaned children who triumphantly resist fatherhood. Brown's heroes—William Black, St. Francis of Assisi, Rousseau, Rilke—are all children. All of them exhibit a childlike simplicity, a primeval (or primordial) innocence, a libidinal playfulness in their apprehension of the world. It may not be accurate to call them "free spirits," for their distinguishing characteristic derives from an awareness of the body rather than spirit. Yet in both body and spirit, they are certainly libidinally free. All of them recognize the immediacy of their libidinal selves, and they strive to be true to its dictates.

Erikson's examples, by contrast, are young persons wiser than their years and/or older persons who maintain a youthful outlook. It would be difficult to conceive of any of them as "old men." When he refers to them as religious geniuses, Erikson acknowledges that their peculiar religious sensitivities have been extraordinarily developed. But this does not mean that they are persons who have extraordinary beliefs, or who hold views regarding the nature of the supernatural which are either radical or uncommon. Erikson's examples are not persons who are known for their abilities to throw off the shackles of constricted libidinal experience. They are not ones who have success stories to tell in their quests to become liberated. They are not necessarily libidinally free spirits, not re-naturalized persons who have learned to resist or fend off the intrusions of institutionally sanctionable, stratified social and cultural systems. His examples are neither Dionysian or Apollonian, in these respects. And when he identifies examples of religious genius, he doesn't single out the most apparent practitioners of the devotional life, the saints, the recluses, the hermits, those who confess that this world cannot be home. Nor do such figures easily qualify as gurus, not even Gandhi. Instead, Erikson's persons are distinctly public figures. They are known almost as much for their social, political and cultural achievements as they are for any special expertise they may bring to the religious life. Luther was a genius in Erikson's view, not because of his mastery of devotional exercises, but because he found a constructive way to balance ego and ethos. He was an ideological innovator not because his theology was systematic and comprehensive, but because it was catalytic. He was a "cultural worker" because his own striving for a sanctionable sense of identity and integrity was instrumental in effecting an important, widespread socio-cultural transition. Luther's religious task was cultural work. Similarly, Gandhi's path to holiness lay in innovative revolutionary action. And so it goes. Erikson's persons are those for whom there are clear correlations of ego and ethos. Martin Luther King would undoubtedly qualify. The same would be true of Black Elk, Cesar Chavez, and Chief Joseph. Like Erikson himself, his persons conform to the model of the wiseman or the sage: the one who perceives how the forms of the world are laid out, and who, sensing that, is in touch or counsel with the rhythms that lead to balance, harmony, and a vigorous reconciliation of the relevant psychological polar forces. Thus, Erikson's examples are ceaselessly involved in the setting of boundaries. They are concerned about parameters, point s or orientation, and relative position. Accordingly, may of Erikson's instincts and tools derive from psychology of art--from the techniques of visual portrayal. And they are directed toward identifying man's place with respect to the reservior of appropriate human resources.

The Role of Ideology

Understandably, then, ideology is given a functional role. It is used. It is employed. It is made serviceable. It is never approached as though it possessed an incontestable, permanent, intractable, status. Neither is ideology regarded as a self-contained body of truths to be prized and sustained for its own sake. Instead it is motivated toward long and short term goals. It is always susceptible to interpretation, and it is amenable to modification depending upon the ethos-and-ego circumstances with which it interacts. In providing direction and sanction, it serves the causes of identity and integrity. And it is always conceived in reciprocal relationship with the other components of cultural organization. Thus, it is part of the vocation of *homo religiosus* to find ways to fashion, refine, refurbish, apply, extend and modify conceptual ideology both for himself and those whom he representatively champions. Always ideology is conceived under the interests of human integrity, within a context which finds ego and ethos to be intermeshing.

In some respects, Erikson's theory of interpretation is similar to Max Weber's functional approach to ideology, Emile Durkheim's work on the "*collective conscience*," and to subsequent work on these subjects which has been done by Weber's and Durkheim's successors, followers, and critics. In all three instances, there is a clear attempt to treat ideology as being affected, influenced, and regulated by the dynamics of social organization. However, what Durkheim and Weber worked out sociologically, Erikson conceived in psycho-social and psycho-historical terms. His interest lies in detailing the interdependence of ideological structure and personal identity, where each is mirrored in the other. While Durkheim and Weber focused on social matrixes, Erikson concentrates on the lives and careers of significant persons. But in both situations, the relationship between theory and action is reciprocal.

When Weber directed his own sociological analyses to an examination of individual persons, he did so via the instrumentation of "ideal types." Erikson's examination of individuals is less comprehensive and typological. Instead, he works with selected historical individuals, and, on that basis, comes to suggest some characteristics of *homo religiosus*, whom he identifies as being engaged in cultural work. Weber, on the other hand, distinguished various sorts of cultural work and, correspondingly, various sorts of cultural workers. That is, working from "ideal type" to example, he perceived that the figure of *homo religiosus* could conceivably be refracted into any one of several cultural vocations.

The dynamism of Erikson's perspective is due to his tendency to employ an organic conceptual model to trace the growth of selected human lives, nations, and cultures. Whatever he touches-- young people, older people, specific historical personages, America, etc.--is conceived according to the categories of organic development. Such development, wherever it occurs, is marked by the stages of the life cycle. Thus, America, as well as Luther, Gandhi, and Jefferson, manifests an infancy and adolescence. Nations and cultures, as well as individuals, suffer identity conflicts and become enmeshed in crises of confidence.

The perspective becomes complex by virtue of the fact that these several forms of organic development are occurring simultaneously. As nations and cultures develop, so too do individuals within such nations and cultures. Sometimes Erikson is content to trace and interpret one such instance of organic development (as, for example, when he deals with youth). But, frequently, he treats compound instances, or examples in which at least two instances of organic development are interlaced (as, for example, when he deals with religious figures). Religious persons are those for whom there is clear reciprocity between ego and ethos. Thus, to talk about the reciprocity between ego and ethos is to point to a situation in which the human life cycle and the larger cultural life cycle are co-present.

But the interdependencies of life cycles is compounded even further through the insertion of Erikson's own personal chronicle. No interpreter works in a vacuum; but Erikson interprets within the context of his own personal developmental history. Thus, for him, interpretive work pertains to the interpreter's quest for self-knowledge. The various stations of the personal chronicle mark stages of progressive insight. In short, the selection of topics to be analyzed is suggested, in part, by the plot in Erikson's own life story. Interpretation of organic life cycles is employed for purposes of self-knowledge. As a consequence, the "hermeneutics" which is cultivated in this fashion is highly idiosyncratic. Definite hermeneutical principles are followed, to be sure, but they hardly form a systematic and comprehensive hermeneutical position or system.

These tendencies help explain why the interest in combining general history with a particular life history is never used to develop a more general philosophy of history. Erikson never claims that psycho-history is a new way of doing--or re-doing--history. Instead, it is a method and it embodies a constellation of selected interests. But it is not designed to supplant other ways of reading history. When he employs the life cycle better to understand American history, for example, his intention is simply that. He does not cite American history to assure the worth of the paradigm. In other words, this is neither Toynbee nor Spengler; nor are these Hegelian-like pretentions. Erikson does think in terms of national and cultural histories but not of universal history.

And yet, while ther is no general philosophy of history there are clear signs of an implicit *weltanschauung* in his work. For example, in the very suggestion that ideologies must be conceived functionally, there is recognition that ideologies are subject to change. By itself, this would not be enought to make reality *process*, but the supplementary supports for this inference are many and impressive. We cite the disposition toward cycles, the use of the organic model, the tendency to see all things in terms of growth and development, etc.

In addition, there is a kind of mysticism surrounding the entire attitude. Erikson seems to suggest that ideologies are subject to change because they are finite and fragile. If ideologies were not subject to change, they could be taken too seriously, uncautiously, inflexibly, and, to add a religious dimension, too idolatrously.

Young Man Luther

The self-consistency of Erikson's egocentric orientation is

the major sore point, perhaps, in interpretations of *Young Man Luther*. For Erikson, Martin Luther was a case study, used to describe how a prominent historical figure forged an identity, both individually and corporately, in relation to an overarching meaning schema dominated by belief in God. To approach Luther in Erikson's way is to view theocentricity in egocentric terms. In this perspective, Luther's theocentricism is regarded as a more or less effective way of stipulating the reciprocity between ideology and self-identity. Luther's theocentric proclivities are perceived to serve a specifiable function. And Erikson can go on to stipulate an exact matching of belief in God with personal psychological need. Since it had not been customary to view Luther's career in this way, it is understandable that Erikson's critics have supposed his interpretation to be a genetic account. Accordingly, many of them have resisted the assumption that a theocentric religious stance can be depicted in egocentric terms. They believe this to be "reductionistic" to his critics, Erikson's theses amount to saying that religion cannot be accounted for psycho-genetically: theocentricity can only be approached in theocentric terms. Thus, the charges against Erikson's interpretive--not Luther's--anal fixations. Theocentrically, it might seem to matter little that Luther suffered from constipation. Theocentrically, issues about Luther's parents--their relationship with each other, their attitude to their son Martin, etc.--may appear to be of peripheral concern only. The same line of theocentric interpretation would find all suspicions regarding Luther's toilet training to be nontranslatable into questions about his personal spirituality.

What Erikson's critics sometimes fail to realize, however, is that *Young Man Luther* offers description and interpretation rather than explanation. Erikson was not concerned to account for religion or to explain it away. Rather, he was simply opening up such areas of inquiry to new lines of interpretation, and more as a lesson to psychologists than to theologicans and church historians.

He expressed himself this way during the Santa Barbara symposium, during the course of which he was asked about his intentions in writing *Young Man Luther*. A portion of his response was phrased as follows:

> The Luther study is called "a study in psychoanalysis and history." But you ought to consider how impossible it would be for anyone in one lifetime to combine enough clinical experience with sufficient expertise in the sociology and history of religion. I wrote it because I was so attracted by "young man Luther" that I had to do it. My own childhood probably had a lot to do with it. Also, I never knew at the time how much I was impressed by him. I certainly was enormously impressed by Gandhi, during the time when people were impressed by Lenin and Wilson.
>
> At any rate, one important goal was to make psychoanalysts aware of the historical dimension, and not just to teach historians about psychoanalysis. Let me say that I hope "psycho-history", as a word, will gradually disappear. History has always been psychological, but the psychological factor has been largely implicit. What we have now is a step which cannot be avoided; that is, a certain psychological self-consciousness or consciousness in history, but certainly also a historical consciousness within psychoanalysis. The Luther book had to serve simply as a statement of that kind.

Certainly, it was not normative explanation Erikson sought in *Young Man Luther*, but augmentation and refinement via the testing of an added frame of reference. Yet, in doing this, Erikson did indeed come to arrange hallowed materials, theologically speaking, around an "alien" point of orientation.

We call it "alien" simply in recognition of the fact that an egocentric bias does not mesh well with fundamental religious aspirations. Normally, in both eastern and western religious traditions, egocentricity is regarded with large suspicion. And often it has been repudiated because it is understood to run contrary to authentic religious currents.

One need only cite St. Augustine's vivid attempts to place the ego under proper controls, his penchant for sacrificing the ego to the superego, as well as the numerous examples of mistrust of ego-initiative which cover the pages of Christian history. In matters of personal piety, it is *humilitas* that is prized, and, by contrast, ego-initiative has been classified as *superbia*. The ego has hardly ever been held up for glorification under Christian auspices unless certain qualifying and refining precautions and safeguards are honored first. Frequently the only way to sustain ego-initiative is by affirming and denying it simultaneously through complicated dialectical interplay.

Under the assumption that it is "they will, not mine, be done," ego-initiative has gone begging for religious sponsorship and sanction. And active cultural work has been viewed as being perilous whenever it comes close to the suggestion that man's salvation is the consequence of human agency. In religious circles, when human agency poses this threat, it has been cancelled out. It cannot be allowed to place the priority of divine initiative in peril. In the east, too, loss of ego is often required so that raw, unsanctified individuality will not frustrate the achievement of personal salvation.

Erikson does not challenge this pattern. Rather, he seeks to trace and describe it. Yet, in associating wholeness with ego-integrity, he disallows the possibility that personal salvation can be acquired by nullifying the operation of either superego, ego, or id, or by sacrificing any of these to any of the others.

The real crunch in Luther's case is that Erikson's egocentric bias cannot sustain the simplicity of Luther's prescribed *sola fide* program. In ego-ethos terms, it can never be *sola* anything, for the components are plural and they exist in reciprocal harmony. And, if it isn't *sola*, it cannot be a choice between faith and works; instead, it is a matter of discerning the fittingness of each to vital and sanctionable ego-ethos intermeshings. That is, it cannbe be *fides* either, if *fides* construed in super-ego terms, connotes unqualified theocentricity. For Erikson, *fides* is always integrally associated with trust (trustworthiness as well as thrustfulness), and both are marks of integrity. Accordingly, when *fides* is regulated by integrity, it refers to organic wholeness rather than to undiminished singleness-of-mind.

But, lest the theologians and church historians become overly anxious, the true point of Erikson's story is that Martin Luther qualifies as *homo religiosus* even in egocentric terms. He had already qualified that way when the matter was viewed from the other perspective. Hence, Erikson's account is corroboration rather than qualification. The traditional assessment of Luther as *homo religiosus par excellence* can be sustained, even according to the new or revised criteria. But there is a significant shift--and, perhaps, a formidable price to pay. As cultural worker, Luther comes to be regarded as a judicious man, not simply as a pious or dutiful man. In Erikson's view, Luther recognized that devotion to God required something more complicated than simple obedience to the compulsions of the superego. Rather, the religious task involved a wise refereeing and a creative reworking of the relationship between a prevailing sense of "we-ness" and a compelling sense of individuality. And within that dynamic interdependency, Luther sought a basis of stability. Perhaps to his own amazement, the basis itself was both integrative and catalytic. *Homo religiosus* in Erikson's terms, is never a zealot on behalf of ideological truth. He is never an ideologue.

But we can reach the same contention by another route.

Current Religious Change

As is well known, the 60's and 70's have been a time of tremendous upheaval for many persons living in the western Christian world. Time after time, they have discovered that their individual and corporate world orders have become radically and often dramatically altered. The transformations are reflected in large and numerous shifts in theological conceptions as well as in changes in social attitudes and psychological awarenesses. Many formally religious persons--nuns and priests, for instance--have been in a state of transition. For a significant number of them, transition was transition out. For others it was transition within. But for all of them, transitions accompanied alterations within self-consciousness. For many of them, the upheavals were so radical that the individual was left convinced that he was a different person than before. Significantly, many of the same persons report that they had understood themselves to be theologically circumspect before; and yet they hadn't perceived who they really were. They confessed to holding to the tenets of the faith without being in touch with their "true selves."

It is altogether conceivable that the pervasive "religious transition" just referred to can be interpreted as a shift from a superego to a libidinal locus of personal religious orientation. This would place the fact that many persons with strong constitutional adherences to religious authority came to realize that they had been sustaining posture of faith without actually being in touch with their own libidinal dispositions. Then, through the stimulation of sensitivity sessions, encounter groups, re-evaluation counseling, or Vatican II theological transformations--which sometimes also functioned as rites of initiation to the counter culture (or a baptism into humanistic psychology)--many of these persons abdicated the superego orientation in favor of one which was prompted by the dictates of the id. It was appropriate for them to become intrigued by Hermann Hesse's novels, or attracted to meditation, or even open to Asian religious currents. Each of these moves is fitting.

In psychological terms, previous superego validation had been achieved at the price of satisfying libidinal experience. When this lack became apparent, the tendency was reversed--witness the case of "protean man"--and libidinal experience came to run far ahead of the superego's tolerance level. Previously, the acceptance of religious authority implied an arrested libidinal self-consciousness. Once the flaw was discovered, a remedy was sought in the expansion of libidinal awareness, by deliberately dissociating it from superego sanctions. Instead of receiving the fundamental orientational cues from an overarching pattern of ideological meaning, the person in transition came to give greater credence to non-superego, inner urgings. For this reason we refer to the religious transition as a shift in psychological orientation too.

But if Erikson is right, neither the older nor the newer religious orientation is good for long if either was achieved at the expense of the other. The dominantly superego orientation cannot survive--as the history of transition shows--unless the other layers of the personality are either bracketed or unacknowledged. And, in the same way, libidinal orientation will disappoint (as Lifton knows) unless there is some way to relate it to superego references. Neither orientation is self-sufficient unless mediated and regulated by a perceptively functioning ego. Neither one can survive unless both are brought reciprocally under the ministrations of the ego. Eventually, of course, the imbalances must be redressed.

Though many of Erikson's multiple achievements are well known, it is not always recognized that his schema lends insight to religious and cultural transition. The psycho-social roots of this are the related contentions (1) that the *telos* is always psychological harmonization (i.e. the reconciliation of superego, ego, and id), (2) that this goal implies personal growth, and (3) that growth is dynamic and requires movement. In other words, in Erikson's scheme the harmonization of the three factors or layers of the personality is temporized. Correlation of the three factors is effected via the components of time. Thus harmonization is a *process*--a process of perpetual adaptation, adjustment, and habituation--rather than a sheer act of unification. All of this is in keeping with Erikson's recurrent contention that human life is to be viewed in terms of an ongoing dynamic cycle.

It is a psycho-historical process, and it can be referred to to interpret multiple socio-cultural transitions. Erikson uses it, for example, to show how ideology becomes transformed under classic individual attempts to achieve identity and integrity. He invokes it too when describing how *homo religiosus* functions in times of significant social and cultural change. The scheme can also be directed more specifically to shifts in patterns of personal and corporate spirituality. The key to this use of the scheme is the insight that, conceivably any one of the three personality factors (superego, ego, and id) can be treated as loci of orientation for the religious life. Because religion is most frequently construed as belief in God (or acceptance of authority), the superego orientation has been most prominent. But religion can also be associated with the workings of the id--witness the definitions of religion which play upon sensitivity, creativity, or deep-seated inner feeling. And, on occasion, religion has been denominated egocentrically; although, as we have pointed out, this alternative has been conspicuously rare.

Any one of the personality factors can be regarded as loci of orientation for the religious life. And, in point of fact, all three of them have functioned in this way. But times of transition occur when the psychological locus of spirituality shifts, as, for example, from superego to id. Yet, in Erikson's scheme, all such shifts must be viewed as events or stages within some more comprehensive process. In Erikson's terms, no single-factor personal orientation is good for long if it is achieved at the expense of the others. Psychological health, as well as religious integrity, demands that the personality be harmonized. It must be brought under the mediation and regulation of the ego. A dominantly superego religious orientation **cannot survive--as the** recent story of "transition" illustrates--unless a layer of man's personality is simply bracketed, unacknowledged, or cancelled out. And, in the same way, even the shift from superego to id can only be sustained through eventual superego representation. In other words, libidinal orientation will disappoint unless there is some way to tap a sustaining "underlying symbolic matrix." Not until the shifts back and forth are regulated by the ego is the personality harmonized and the religious life stablilized. And the process is ongoing. Closure at any one point is subject to reformulation because of other psychological increments. And lack of closure is the price to be paid for the healing of the self's assorted provincialisms.

This must be the reason that the goal is never a material something. The *telos* can never be reified. It is never an objective which can be ascribed with ontological status. The goal is not happiness *per se*, nor pleasure, nor any other hypostasized form of manhood, nor an ideal set of human or humane conditions, and not even the realization of individual or corporate potentialities. Rather, in Erikson's view, the goal is *integrity*. And integrity is integration. It is "proclivity for order and meaning," an "acceptance of one's one and only life as something that has to be," a "willingness to defend that (life) against all threats," and a compelling insight that "the individual life is the accidental coincidence of but one life cycle with but one segment of history." From that stable point, integrity trusts life and faces death. If it must be named, it is wisdom. It is wisdom, because it knows the place of things—from play objects to the components of the engaging cycle—and discerns their loci of orientation.

Erikson: A Process Thinker

One can approach the same thought by observing that Erik Erikson qualifies as a process thinker. The process he enunciates most frequently and clearly is the several-staged human life-cycle as this affects—and is affected by—the quest for self-identity. But at every stage of the life cycle, a fundamental and perpetual give-and-take between the several layers of the personality occurs. Throughout the process, the two dynamisms interact. At every stage, it is not only positive pole seeking harmony with negative pole, but also the ego functioning perceptively to reconcile the id with the superego. When there is a contest between trust and mistrust, the goal is not to isolate trust or mistrust, but to allow trust over mistrust. Thus, it is not trust cancelling mistrust, for example, but trust referring or mistrust. The negative and positive poles are always balanced. At a subsequent stage, the goal is the achievement of a "sense of self control without loss of self-esteem" Further on, the personality seeks a "balance between the expansiveness of generosity and preoccupying self absorption." At each point, the negative and positive poles are harmonized. The goal alway is a psychological balance within which the negative pole is controlled by its positive polar opposite. Thus, the final *telos* is not ego-integrity pure and rarified, but an ego-integrity which recognizes

the presence, force, and recurrence of despair. For Erikson the
tension at all stages of the human life cycle is never equalized,
or averaged. Instead, it is reciprocated in a fashion which
fixes the priority of the positive pole according to a rhythm
which also entails negative placement. Reciprocity occurs
through the effective reconciling work of the ego in stabilizing
the communication and interaction between superego and id.

As process orientation, Erikson's scheme resembles the
patterns of thought of more obvious and celebrated spokesmen for
the position in very striking ways. All of the necessary elementary formal components of process thought are present in his
formulations. For example, though he doesn't use process language when referring to the "realm of possibility," he does find
place for its functional equivalent. Erikson's overarching body
of conceptual material or ideological content offers many of
the same services for instance, as Whitehead's "eternal objects."
And, though he doesn't name the psycho-historical context as an
"actual occasion," the description he gives to precise "situations"
possesses telling formal and structural process capacities.
Furthermore, true to typical process tendencies, Erikson has a
place for a "reconciling agent"--the structural referee--who
blends the "eternal" and "actual" dimensions together, creatively
and perceptively fashioning and weaving ideological content into
specific psycho-historical stiuations. In both Erikson's scheme
and the more typical process structure, the relationship between
these three elemental components--ideological structure, actual
occasion, and mediating referee--is formed reciprocally. Because each of the three is a dynamic reality, each is tempered
by the others. The interrelationships between the three factors
are pliable; they are formed in concert; they are orchestrated.
This is why it must be process. And this is why the formation of
process is ongoing and innovative.

Pictorially and structurally, Erikson is Heraclitus speaking
again, though in more elaborate and sophisticated psychological
terms. All is flux, and the flux possessses it own *logos*. Life
is like a stream; one can never step twice in the same place;

other waters are always rushing on. Even in more than superficial ways, the association of Erikson with Heraclitus is intriguing and instructive. Heraclitus defined harmonization as "the attunement of opposite tensions," thus forecasting Erikson's reconciliation of the positive and negative consciences. Both Erikson and Heraclitus were preoccupied with children. Erikson's persistent interest in the combinations of form children create when they are given toy-blocks to play with can be interpreted as an experimental commentary on Heraclitus' observation that the makeup of reality is "like a child playing draughts." It is Heraclitus' world, but the words are Erikson's:

> And being somewhat of an expert in play I must add that while we remember great men usually as severe creators, they are certainly the ones in whom a divine playfulness is undiminished in its capacity to transcend in new formulae some of the traumatic discrepancies of the times.

Both Erikson and Heraclitus are disposed to visual and optical allusions. Erikson's life-long interest in the visual dimension, the mechanics of visual portrayal, and even in ways of conducting psychoanalytical inquiry by optical and visual means is specific enunciation of Heraclitus' flux-filled suggestion that "the eyes are more exact witnesses than the ears." It is a kinetic vision. And, in kinesis, what one knows depends upon where one stands. What one perceives, in part, is who one is. And one's position shifts, the panorama changes and self-identity is fixed differently. Since motion is perpetual, the constellation of things is altered constantly and perceptibly. The patterns of things are discernible, but discernment is akin to artistic perception (as in studying arrangements between play objects). In Erikson's words, "life is for seeing." And given the intricacies of the human life cycle, the definition of wisdom that may pertain best to Erikson's outlook is Heraclitus' "to know the thought by which all things are steered through all things."

ERIK HOMBURGER ERIKSON
A BIBLIOGRAPHY OF HIS BOOKS AND ARTICLES

1930

"Die Zukunft der Aufklaerung und die Psychoanalyse." *Zeitschrift der Psychoanalytik Paedagogie*, IV (1930), 201-16.

1931

"Bilderbuecher." *Zeitschrift der Psychoanalytik Paedagogie*, V (1931), 13-19.

"Triebschicksale im Schulaufsatz." *Zeitschrift der Psychoanalytik Paedagogie*, V (1931), 417-45.

1935

"Psychoanalysis and the Future of Education." Translation of "Die Zukunft der Aufklaerung und die Psychoanalyse" (1930). *Psychoanalytic Quarterly*, V (1935), 50-68.

1936

Review of *Psychoanalysis for Teachers and Parents*, by Anna Freud. *Psychoanalytic Quarterly*, V (1936), 291-3.

1937

"Configurations in Play: Clinical Notes." *Psychoanalytic Quarterly*, VI (1937), 139-214.

Revised for *Childhood and Society* (1950), chapter VI.

"Traumatische Konfigurationen im Spiel." Shorter version of "Tranumatische Konfigurationen im Spiel: Aufzeichnungen" (1937). *Zeitschrift der Psychoanalytik Paedagogie*, XI (1937), 262-92.

"Traumatische Konfigurationen im Spiel: Aufzeichnungen." Translation of "Configurations in Play: Clinical Notes" (1937). *Imago*, XXIII (1937), 447-516.

1938

"Dramatic Productions Test." In: *Explorations in Personality*. Edited by Henry A. Murray. New York: Oxford University Press, pp. 552-82.

"Section on Play Therapy: A Panel Discussion with Maxwell Gitelson and Others." *American Journal of Orthopsychiatry*, VIII:3 (1938), 449-524, especially, 507-10.

1939

"Observations on Sioux Education." *Journal of Psychology*, VII (1939), 101-56.
Revised for *Childhood and Society* (1950), Chapter III.

1940

"Studies in the Interpretation of Play: I. Clinical Observations of Play Disruption in Young Children." *Genetic Psychology Monographs*, XXII (1940), 557-671.
Revised for *Childhood and Society* (1950), Chapter VI.

"Problems of Infancy and Early Childhood." *Cyclopedia of Medicine, Surgery and Specialities*. Vol. XII. Philadelphia: F.A. Davis, 1940, pp. 714-30. Also in *Outline of Abnormal Psychology*. Edited by G. Murphy and A.J. Bachrach. New York: Modern Library, 1954, pp. 3-36.
Revised for *Childhood and Society* (1950), Part I.

"Concerning the Interrogation of German Prisoners of War." Unpublished paper written for the Committee on National Morale for the Coordination of Information.

"On the Feasibility of Making Psychological Observations in Internment Camps." Unpublished paper written for the Committee on National Morale for the Coordination of Information.

"On Submarine Psychology." Unpublished paper written for the Committee on National Morale for the Coordination of Information.

1941

"Further Explorations in Play Construction: Three Spatial Variables in Their Relation to Sex and Anziety." Abstract. *Psychological Bulletin*, XXXVIII (1941), 748.

1942

"Comments on Hitler's Speech of September 30, 1942." Unpublished paper written for the Council on Inter-Cultural Studies.

"Hitler's Imagery and German Youth." *Psychiatry*, V (1942), 475-93.
Revised for *Personality in Nature, Society and Culture*. Edited by Clyde Kluckhohn and Henry A. Murray. New York: Knopf, 1948, pp. 485-510.
Revised for *Childhood and Society* (1950), Chapter IX.

1943

"Observations on the Yurok: Childhood and World Image." *University of California Publications in American Archaeology and Ethnology*, XXXV:10. Berkeley: University of California Press, 1943, pp. iii-v, 257-301.
Revised for *Childhood and Society* (1950), Chapter IV.

1945

"Plans for the Veteran with Symptoms of Instability." In: *Community Planning for Peacetime Living*. Edited by Louis Wirth. Palo Alto, Calif.: Stanford University Press.

"Childhood and Tradition in Two American Indian Tribes: With Some Reflections on the Contemporary American Scene." In: *The Psychoanalytic Study of the Child*. Vol. I. Edited by Otto Fenichel, *et al*. New York: International Universities Press, pp. 319-50.
Revised for *Personality in Nature, Society and Culture*. Edited by Clyde Kluckhohn and Henry A. Murray. New York: Knopf, 1948, pp. 176-203.
Revised for *Childhood and Society* (1950), Part II.

1946

"Ego Development and Historical Change." In: *The Psychoanalytic Study of the Child*. Vol. II. Edited by Otto Fenichel, *et al*. New York: International Universities Press, pp. 359-96.
Revised for *Childhood and Society* (1950), Part III.
Revised for *Identity: Youth and Crisis* (1968), Chapter II.

1949

"Ruth Benedict." In: *Ruth Fulton Benedict: A Memorial*. Edited by Alfred L. Kroeber. New York: Viking Fund, pp. 14-17.

1950

Childhood and Society. New York: W.W. Norton, 400 pp. Second, enlarged edition, 1963.

"Growth and Crisis of the 'Healthy Personality.'" (With Joan M. Erikson.) In: *Transactions of the Fourth Conference on Infancy and Childhood*, Supplement II. Edited by Milton J.E. Senn. Written for the Fact-Finding Committee of the Midcentury White House Conference. New York: Josiah Macy, Jr., Foundation, pp. 91-146.
Revised for *Childhood and Society* (1963).
Revised for *Identity: Youth and Crisis* (1968), Chapter III.
Revised for *Personality in Nature, Society and Culture*. Edited by Clyde Kluckhohn and Henry A. Murray. New York: Knopf, 1953, pp. 185-225.

1951

"Sex Differences in the Play Configurations of Pre-Adolescents." *American Journal of Orthopsychiatry*, XXI:4 (1951), 667-92.
Revised for *Childhood in Contemporary Culture*. Edited by Margaret Mead and Martha Wolfenstein. Chicago: University of Chicago Press, 1955, pp. 324-41.
Revised for *Childhood and Society* (1963), Chapter II.

"Statement ot the Committee on Priviledge and Tenure of the University of California Concerning the California Loyalty Oath: An Editorial." *Psychiatry*, XIV:3 (1951), 244-5.

1952

Review of *Children Who Hate*, by Fritz Redl and David Wineman. *Basic Book News and Bibliography* (May, 1952), 1-3.

"Cross-Cultural Patterns in the Adjustment and Maladjustment of Children: 1. Deviations from Normal Child Development with Reference to Cross-Cultural Patterns. 2. Etiology of Maladjustment in the Environment of the Child." Abstract. In: *Scandinavian Seminar on Child Psychiatry and Child Guidance*. Geneva: World Health Organization.

"'Remarks' Made at an Interagency Conference at Princeton, New Jersey, Sept. 21-25, 1951." In: *Healthy Personality Development in Children As Related to Programs of the Federal Government*. New York: Josiah Macy, Jr., Foundation, pp. 80-95.

1953

"Uber den Sinn der Inneren Identitaet." In: *Gesundheit und Mitmenschliche Beziehungen*. Edited by M. von Eckhardt and W. Villinger. Munich: Ernst Reinhardt, 1953, pp. 137-52.
Revised for *Identity: Youth and Crisis* (1968), Chapter II.
"On the Sense of Inner Identity." Translation of "Uber den Sinn der Inneren Identitaet." In: *Health and Human Relations*. Report of a Conference Held at Hiddensen, near Detmold, Germany, August 2-7, 1951. New York: The Balkiston Co., pp. 124-46.

"The Power of the Newborn." (With Joan M. Erikson.) *Mademoiselle*, LXII (June, 1953), 100-2.

1954

"Wholeness and Totality: A Psychiatric Contribution." In: *Totalitarianism*. Proceedings of a Conference Held at the American Academy of Arts and Sciences, March, 1953. Edited by Carl J. Friedrich. Cambridge, Mass.: Harvard University Press, pp. 156-71.
Revised for *Identity: Youth and Crisis* (1968), Chapter II.

"The Dream Specimen of Psychoanalysis." *Journal of the American Psychoanalytic Association*, II:1 (1954), 5-56. Also in: *Psychoanalytic Psychiatry and Psychology, Clinical and Theoretical Papers, Austen Riggs Center*. Vol. I. Edited by Robert P. Knight and Cyrus R. Friedman. New York: International Universities Press, pp. 131-70.
Revised for *Identity: Youth and Crisis* (1968), Chapter IV.

"Identity and Totality: Psychoanalytic Observations on the Problems of Youth." *Human Development Bulletin*. Fifth Annual Symposium. Chicago: The Human Development Student Organization, 1954, pp. 50-82.

1955

Review of *The Origins of Psychoanalysis*, by Sigmund Freud. *International Journal of Psychoanalysis*, XXXVI:1 (1955), 1-15.

1956

"The Problem of Ego Identity." *Journal of the American Psychoanalytic Association*, IV:1 (1956), 56-121.
Revised for *Identity: Youth and Crisis* (1968), Chapters IV and V.

"Sigmund Freud's Psychoanalytische Krise. Festvortrag zur Freuds 100 Geburtstag." In: *Freud in der Gegenwart*. Lectures given at the Universities of Frankfurt and Heidelberg. Edited by T.W. Adorno and W. Dirks. Frankfurt: Europaeische Verlagsanstalt, 1957, pp. 10-30.

"The First Psychoanalyst." Translation of "Sigmund Freud's Psychoanalytische Krise." *Yale Review*, XLVI (Autumn, 1956), 40-62. Also in: *Freud and the Twentieth Century*. Edited by Benjamin Nelson. London: George Allen and Unwin, Ltd., 1957.
Revised for *Insight and Responsibility* (1964), pp. 17-46.

"Ego Identity and the Psychosocial Moratorium." In: *New Perspectives for Research in Juvenile Deliquency*. U.S. Children's Bureau Publication No. 356. Edited by H.L. Witmer and R. Kosinsky. Washington, D.C.: U.S. Department of Health, Education and Welfare, pp. 1-23.
Revised for *Identity: Youth and Crisis* (1968), Chapter IV.

1957

"The Confirmation of the Delinquent." (With Kai T. Erikson.) *The Chicago Review*, X (Winter, 1957), 15-23.
Revised for *Identity: Youth and Crisis* (1968), Chapter VI.

"Trieb und Wmwlt in der Kindheit." In: *Freud in der Gegenwart*. Edited by T.W. Adorno and W. Dirks. Frankfurt: Europaeische Verlagsanstalt, 1957, pp. 43-64.

1958

"Identity and the Psychosocial Development of Children." In: *Discussions on Child Development*. Proceedings of the Third Meeting of the Child Study Group, World Health Organization, Vol. III. New York: International Universities Press, pp. 16-18, 91-215.

Young Man Luther: A Study in Psychoanalysis and History. Austen Riggs Center, Monograph No. 4. New York: W.W. Norton.

"On the Nature of Clinical Evidence." *Daedalus*, LXXXVII:4 (Fall, 1958), 65-87. Also in: *Evidence and Inference*. The First Hayden Colloquium. Edited by Daniel Lerner Glencoe. Cambridge, Mass.: M.I.T. Press, 1958. Glencoe, Ill.: The Free Press, 1959.
Revised for *Insight and Responsibility* (1968), pp. 47-80.

1959

"Identity and the Life Cycle: Selected Papers." A reprint of three previously published papers: "Ego Development and Historical Change" (1946), "Growth and Crises of the 'Healthy Personality'" (1950), and "The Problem of Ego Identity" (1956). With an historical introduction by David Rapaport. *Psychological Issues*, Vol. I, No. 1, Monograph 1. New York: International Universities Press, pp. 1-171.
Revised for *Identity: Youth and Crisis* (1968), Chapters II, IV, V.

"Late Adolescence." In: *The Student and Mental Health*. Edited by Daniel H. Funkenstein. New York: The World Federation for Mental Health and the International Association of Universities.

"Identity and Uprootedness in Our Time." In: *Uprooting and Resettlement*. Vienna: Bulletin of the World Federation for Mental Health.
Revised for *Insight and Responsibility* (1964), pp. 81-107.

"Psychosexual Stages in Child Development." In: *Discussions on Child Development*. World Health Organization Study Group. Vol. IV. New York: International Universities Press, 1959, pp. 136-54.

1960

"Youth and the Life Cycle: An Interview." In: *Children*. Vol. VII:2. Washington, D.C.: U.S. Department of Health, Education and Welfare, pp. 43-9.

1961

"The Roots of Virtue." In: *The Humanist Frame*. Edited by Julian Huxley. New York: Harper & Row, pp. 145-66.
Revised for *Insight and Responsibility* (1964), pp. 109-57.

"Childhood and Society." In: *Children of the Caribbean*. San Juan, P.R.: Printing Division, pp. 18-29, 151-4.

"Preface." In: *Emotional Problems of the Student*. Edited by Graham B. Blaine, Jr., and Charles C. McArthur. New York: Appleton-Century-Crofts.
Revised for *Identity: Youth and Crisis* (1968), Chapter IV.

1962

"Youth: Fidelity and Diversity." *Daedalus*, XCI:1 (1962), 5-27.
Revised for *Identity: Youth and Crisis* (1968), Chapter VI.

"Reality and Actuality: An Address." *Journal of the American Psychoanalytic Association*, X:3 (1962), 451-74.
Revised for *Insight and Responsibility* (1964), pp. 159-215.

1963

"The Golden Rule and the Cycle of Life." *Harvard Medical Alumni Bulletin*, XXXVII:2 (Winter, 1963). Also in: *The Study of Lives: Essays on Personality in Honor of Henry A. Murray*. Edited by Robert W. White. New York: Prentice-Hall, pp. 412-28. Revised for *Insight and Responsibility* (1964), pp. 217-43.

Youth: Change and Challenge. Editor. New York: Basic Books, 1963. *The Challenge of Youth*. Paperback edition of *Youth: Change and Challenge*. New York: Doubleday, 1965.

1964

"Inner and Outer Space: Reflections on Womanhood." *Daedalus*, XCII:2 (Spring, 1964), 582-606. Revised for *Identity: Youth and Crisis* (1968), Chapter VII.

Insight and Responsibility: Lectures on the Ethical Implications of Psychoanalytic Insight. New York: W.W. Norton.

"Memorandum on Identity and Negro Youth." *Journal of Social Issues*, XX:4 (1964), 29-42.

1965

"Psychoanalysis and Ongoing History: Problems of Identity, Hatred and Nonviolence." *The American Journal of Psychiatry*, CXXII:3 (1965), 241-53.

"Concluding Remarks." In: *Women and the Scientific Profession*. Edited by J.A. Mattfeld and C.G. Van Aken. Cambridge, Mass.: M.I.T. Press, pp. 232-45.

1966

"Eight Ages of Man." *International Journal of Psychiatry*, II:3 (1966), 281-300. Reprinted from *Childhood and Society*, second edition (1963).

"The Concept of Identity in Race Relations: Notes and Queries." *Daedalus*, XCV:1 (Winter, 1966), 145-70. Revised for *Identity: Youth and Crisis* (1968), Chapter VIII.

"The Ontogeny of Ritualization in Man." *Philosophical Transactions of the Royal Society of London*. Series B, No. 772, Vol. CCLI (1966), 337-49. Revised for *Psychoanalysis--A General Psychology*. Essays in Honor of Heinz Hartmann. Edited by Rudolph M. Loewenstein, *et al*. New York: International Universities Press, 1966, pp. 601-22.

"Concluding Remarks, Discussion on Ritualization of Behavior in Animals and Man." *Philosophical Transactions of the Royal Society of London*, Series B, No. 772, Vol. CCLI (1966), 513-24.

"Words for Paul Tillich." *Harvard Divinity School Bulletin*, XXX, 2 (1966), pp.

"Gandhi's Autobiography: The Leader as a Child." *The American Scholar*, XXXV:4 (Autumn, 1966), 632-46.

1967

Review of *Thomas Woodrow Wilson: Twenty-eighth President of the United States* by Sigmund Freud and William C. Bullitt. *The New York Review of Books*, VIII:2 (1967), 3-6.
Also in *International Journal of Psychoanalysis*, XLVIII:3 (1967), 462-8.

"Memorandum on Youth." *Daedalus*, XCVI:3 (Summer, 1967), 860-70. Revised for *Identity: Youth and Crisis* (1968), Chapter I.

"Memorandum on the Military Draft." In: *The Draft: A Handbook of Facts and Alternatives*. Edited by Sol Tax. Chicago: University of Chicago Press.

1968

"The Human Life Cycle." In: *International Encyclopedia of the Social Sciences*. Vol. IX. New York: Macmillan, pp. 61-5.

Identity: Youth and Crisis. New York: W.W. Norton.

"On the Nature of Psycho-Historical Evidence: In Search of Gandhi." *Daedalus*, XCVII:3 (Summer, 1968), 695-730. Also in: *Philosophers and Kings: Studies in Leadership*. Edited by Dankwart A. Rustow. New York: George Braziller, 1970, pp. 33-68.

"Insight and Freedom." South Africa: University of Capetown.

1969

Gandhi's Truth: On the Origins of Militant Non-violence. New York: W.W. Norton.

"On Student Unrest and Remarks on Receiving the Foneme Prize." Second International Convention. Milano, Italy: Foneme Institute, 1969.

1970

"Reflections on the Dissent of Contemporary Youth." *Daedalus*, XCIX:4 (Summer, 1970), 730-59. Also in: *The Twentieth-century Sciences: Studies in the Biography of Ideas*. Edited by Gerald Holton. New York: W.W. Norton, 1972, pp. 3-32.

1971

"Words at Delos." *Ekistics*, XXXII:191 (October, 1971), 259-60.

"Notes on the Life Cycle." *Ekistics*, XXXII:191 (October, 1971), 260-65.

1972

"On 'Play.'" In: *Play and Development.* Edited by Maria Piers. New York: W.W. Norton, pp. 127-68.

"Environment and Virtues." In: *Arts of the Environment.* Edited by G. Kepes. New York: Braziller, pp. 60-77.

"On Protest and Affirmation." *Harvard Medical Alumni Bulletin* (July-August, 1972), pp.

"By Way of a Memoir." In: *Clinician and Therapist, Selected Papers of Robert P. Knight.* Edited by Stuart C. Miller. New York: Basic Books, pp.

1973

"Thoughts on the City for Human Development." *Ekistics*, XXXV: 209 (April, 1973), 216-21.

"The Wider Identity." In: *In Search of Common Ground: Conversations with Erik H. Erikson and Huey P. Newton.* Edited by Kai T. Erikson. New York: W.W. Norton, pp. 44-96.

1974

Dimensions of a New Identity. The 1973 Jefferson Lectures. New York: W.W. Norton.

"Reminiscences." First Peter Blos Biennial Lecture. *Psychosocial Process*, Vol. III, No. 2, Fall 1974.

1975

Life History and the Historical Moment. New York: W.W. Norton.

All of Erik Erikson's books and a number of his articles have been translated into foreign languages. We have included here only the English editions of his books. Where an article appeared first in German, we have repeated the entry only when the article was translated into English; otherwise we have included only articles in English.

BRARY OF DAVIDSON COLLEGE

cked out for two weeks. Books
be rene